GUIDED READING

GUIDED READING
Good First Teaching for All Children

Irene C. Fountas and Gay Su Pinnell

HEINEMANN
Portsmouth, NH

Heinemann
361 Hanover Street
Portsmouth, NH 03801-3912
Offices and agents throughout the world

The authors and publisher wish to thank those who generously gave permission to reprint borrowed material.

Running Records by Marie Clay. Used by permission of the author and publisher, Heinemann Education, Auckland, New Zealand.

Excerpt from *My Dog Willy* by Catherine Peters. Illustrated by Ashley Wolff. Copyright © 1995 by Houghton Mifflin. Reprinted by permission of the publisher.

Excerpt from *At the Zoo* by Catherine Peters. Illustrated by Sally Noll. Copyright © 1995 by Houghton Mifflin. Reprinted by permission of the publisher.

Excerpt from *Dad*, PM Starters One. U.S. edition © 1996 Rigby, A division of Reed Elsevier Inc. Text © 1996 Beverley Randell, Jenny Giles, Annette Smith. Photographs © 1996 Nelson Price Milburn Ltd. Reprinted by permission of the publisher.

Excerpt from *Wake Up, Dad* by Beverley Randell. Illustrated by Elspeth Lacey. Text © 1994 Beverly Randell. Illustrations ©1994 Nelson Price Milburn Ltd. Reprinted by permission of the publisher, Rigby, A division of Reed Elsevier Inc.

Excerpt from *Greedy Cat Is Hungry* by Joy Cowley. Pictures by Robyn Belton. Text copyright © Joy Cowley 1988. Illustrations © Crown copyright 1988. Published by Learning Media Limited, New Zealand. Reprinted by permission of the author and publisher.

Excerpt from *Mrs. Wishy-Washy* by Joy Cowley. Illustrations by Elizabeth Fuller. © 1980, 1990 Thomas C. Wright, Inc./The Wright Group. Reprinted by permission of the publisher.

Excerpt from *The Hungry Giant* by Joy Cowley. Illustrations by Jenny Cochrane. © 1980, 1990 Thomas Wright, Inc./The Wright Group. Reprinted by permission of the publisher.

Excerpt from *Greedy Cat* by Joy Cowley. Pictures by Robyn Belton. Text copyright © Joy Cowley 1983. Illustrations © Crown copyright 1983. Published by Learning Media Ltd., New Zealand. Reprinted by permission of the author and publisher.

Excerpt from *Rosie at the Zoo* by Joy Cowley. Pictures by Christine Ross. Text copyright © Joy Cowley 1984. Illustrations © Crown copyright 1984. Published by Learning Media Limited, New Zealand. Reprinted by permission of the author and publisher.

Excerpt from *The Princess, the Mud Pies, and the Dragon* adapted by Lily Ernesto. Illustrated by Oki Han. Copyright © 1995 by Houghton Mifflin. Reprinted by permission of the publisher.

Excerpt from *Danny and the Dinosaur* by Syd Hoff. Copyright © 1958 by Syd Hoff. Reprinted by permission of the publisher, HarperCollins Publishers.

Excerpt from *Keep the Lights Burning, Abbie* by Peter and Connie Roop. Pictures by Peter E. Hanson. Copyright © 1985 by Carolrhoda Books, Inc. Reprinted by permission of the publisher.

Excerpt from *Cam Jansen and the Mystery of the Monster Movie* by David A. Adler. Illustrated by Susanna Natti. Text copyright © David A. Adler, 1984. Illustrations copyright © Susanna Natti, 1984. Reprinted by permission of the publisher, Puffin Books.

Excerpt from *Molly's Pilgrim* by Barbara Cohen. Illustrated by Michael J. Deraney. Copyright © 1983 by Barbara Cohen. Illustrations copyright © 1983 by Michael J. Deraney. Reprinted by permission of Lothrop Lee & Shephard Books, Division of William Morrow, Inc.

Excerpt from *The Hungry Kitten* by Beverley Randell. Illustrations by Leanne Fleming. Copyright © 1994. Reprinted by permission of the publisher, Rigby, A division of Reed Elsevier Inc.

Excerpt from *Cookie's Week* by Cindy Ward. Illustrations by Tomie dePaola. Copyright © 1988. Reprinted by permission of the publisher, Sandcastle Books, A Division of Putnam.

Excerpt from "Grouping Students for Literacy Learning: What Works" by the Massachusetts Reading Association Studies and Research Committee. From *Massachusetts Primer* 1991, published by Massachusetts Reading Association. Reprinted by permission of the Editor.

All excerpts from KEEP books by permission of the Literacy Collaborative, The Ohio State University.

Library of Congress Cataloging-in-Publication Data

Fountas, Irene C.
    Guided reading : good first teaching for all children / Irene C. Fountas and Gay Su Pinnell.
        p.   cm.
    Includes bibliographical references and index.
    ISBN 0-435-08863-7 (alk. paper)
    LB1573.F64   1996
    372.4—dc20   96-32481
                                                  CIP

Editor: Toby Gordon
Production: Renée Le Verrier and Melissa L. Inglis
Text Design: Joni Doherty
Cover Design: Darci Mehall
Manufacturing: Louise Richardson

Printed in the United States of America on acid-free paper
08 07 06 05   VP   32 33 34

with much love to

Catherine A. Fountas

and

Elfrieda H. Pinnell,

our very first teachers

Contents

Foreword

by Mary Ellen Giacobbe

Several years ago I was working with a group of teachers, helping them think about their teaching of writing. One first-grade teacher was particularly frustrated because her students had a lot to say but would not write. We discussed possible minilessons that would help show her students how letters and sounds are used to communicate ideas. Later, in her classroom, I modeled a piece of writing, showing the children how to say a word, listen for the sounds, and write letters for the sounds they heard. At the end of the demonstration, one boy threw his arms up in the air: "So that's all there is to it? Why didn't someone tell us this before?"

I had that same why-didn't-someone-tell-us-this-before feeling as I read *Guided Reading: Good First Teaching for All Children*. Though there are some books and journal articles that mention guided reading, none has treated the topic with such depth and breadth within the context of a balanced literacy program. Irene Fountas and Gay Su Pinnell help teachers understand, first, how to assess children through careful observation and then how to go the next step, take the children from where they are to where they need to go.

At a recent conference at Lesley College in Cambridge, Massachusetts, Barbara Watson, a New Zealand literacy educator, reminded attendees of how important it is for teachers to teach. "It's not enough just to create opportunities for children to do things they can already do," she said. "Instead, it's up to us to provide powerful teaching so that children can move, or better yet, leap forward."

In recent years we have come a long way in our thinking about helping beginning readers. Many classrooms are print-rich and have the best reading materials that money can buy—big books, charts, an abundance of quality children's literature. However, although whole-class experiences such as shared reading and literature discussions offer children many important benefits, it's difficult for teachers to observe reading behaviors in individual children in order to help them build an effective independent reading process.

This comprehensive book addresses the questions teachers most often ask about teaching reading. How do I use running records to assess and guide reading? How do I group and regroup children? How do I match books with readers? How do I teach for strategies? What *are* strategies? What about children who don't know any letters and/or sounds? What will all the other children be doing while I'm conducting guided reading groups? How can I organize instruction to meet the needs of all my students? How do I keep records of what everyone is doing? How do I evaluate my teaching of guided reading?

In answering these questions (and many more), the authors draw from their own teaching and from their numerous years of research and experience helping teachers develop literacy programs. As they lay out their guided reading approach, their utmost respect for both teachers and students is ever present: children can learn to read and teachers can play an important role. And, as they continue to encounter diverse student populations, they are constantly reassessing their beliefs and practices.

There have been many debates about teaching practices and how we can reach all our students. Some educators believe the problem is an emphasis on phonics versus no phonics, basal readers versus literature-based instruction, homogeneous grouping versus heterogeneous grouping, early intervention versus wait-and-see, accepting approximations versus expecting correctness, and direct (explicit) instruction versus discovery. As we go back and forth on these issues, one of the most important variables is an individual classroom teacher who understands how children acquire literacy and the role she or he plays helping each child achieve his or her potential. When we help teachers see possibilities in their teaching, we help their students. This book is filled with possibilities for veteran teachers and is a *must* for students in undergraduate and graduate language arts courses.

Many features in this book help teachers continue their learning. Suggestions for professional development at the end of each chapter encourage readers to observe and study their students and to conduct their own classroom-based research. A self-assessment for guided reading lets teachers see where they are on the continuum and where they want to go.

The appendixes are a treasure in and of themselves—alphabet books, icons for managing center activities, record-keeping forms, transcripts of book introductions and running records, and most needed of all, a bibliography of leveled books.

On the first page in Chapter 1, Gay and Irene remind us that "All children possess the fundamental attributes they need to become literate." *Guided Reading: Good First Teaching for All Children* provides the best help available to support classroom teachers as they work toward making literacy a reality for all children.

Acknowledgments

This book is about teaching and learning, both ours and the committed teachers with whom we are privileged to work. It is also about the many children and adults we have taught and from whom we continue to learn.

We could not have written the book without the many wonderful people who joined with us to make it a reality. First, we are deeply indebted to the many teachers who have allowed us to enter their classrooms to observe, interact, have conversation, snap photographs, film videotape, collect samples and learn from their work with children. Classroom teachers have been our valued colleagues and there are too many of them to list here, but we do want to express much appreciation to Ida Patacca, Kate Bartley, Sharon Esswein, Pat Prime, Irma Napoleon, Susan Sullivan, Stephanie Ripley, Florence Metcalf, Amy Davis, Susan Sanchez, Marie Crispen, Becky Eston, and Kim Dell Isola, who have generously shared their classrooms, their children, and their expertise with us.

We wish to express special appreciation to the teachers who participated in Early Literacy Learning Initiative (now called the Literacy Collaborative) study groups from 1989 to the present. Their work has contributed significantly to this volume. The first study group included: Sue Hundley, Connie Compton, Melissa Wilson, Stephanie Hawking, Ann James, Bette Coles, Carole Spahr, Paula Connor, Diane Powell, Synda Slegeski, Julie Wittenberg, Melanie Murnan, Mary Ann Penzone, Jean Westin, Tennie Tyler, and Robin Holland. Members of the kindergarten group were: Ida Patacca, Beth Sherwood, Francee Eldredge, Connie Jones, Elizabeth Sturges, Laura Locke, Hope Perry, Dody Brooks,

Traci Michalek, Grace Wiley, Mary Ann Ewert. We also acknowledge the contributions of Ohio State colleagues Colleen Griffiths, Tina Henry, Andrea McCarrier, and Ann James, as well as Kim Dell Isola, Linda Garbus, and all the teachers at Memorial Spaulding who contributed to the leveling of books for the booklist.

We also acknowledge the leadership of John Hilliard, Director of Federal Programs, and Arleen Stuck who have supported the Early Literacy project and whose work has made a difference in literacy for thousands of Columbus children. We are grateful to OSU graduate students who contributed significantly to the process: Elizabeth Strong, Connie Compton, Nancy Ryan Nussbaum, Andrea McCarrier, Katie Button, Joan Wiley, Cheri Williams, Linda Mudre, Wendy Morton, Nancy Anderson, and Karen Holinga.

We are indebted to our many university colleagues whose knowledge, patience, support, and friendship continue to sustain us in our work. Our special appreciation goes to Andrea McCarrier whose commitment to quality literacy for all children has been a constant source of strength, and to Mary Fried whose brilliant teaching and ongoing consultations have enriched and extended our understanding of teacher-child interactions. Special thanks are also due to Tina Henry, Joan Wiley, Carol Lyons, Diane DeFord, Rose Mary Estice, Sue Hundley, Mary Snow, and Billie Askew, our friends and colleagues who have been generous in their encouragement and dialogue as we have built new understandings of the teaching and learning process. And we especially acknowledge William Wayson for his insightful contributions in helping us understand the context of schools.

We want to express our gratitude to our ever-patient, committed, and energetic staff including Polly Taylor, who typed and corrected the manuscript, and to Heather Kroll, Jennifer Warner, Erika Hession, and Josh Elmes whose teamwork and spirit make good things happen for children and teachers. Our admiration and special appreciation go to Kristen Swanson for her many contributions, including her artistic talents in designing the alphabet chart and letter books.

The entire team at Heinemann deserves our special recognition. For her graceful patience as we missed many deadlines, her spirited encouragement, her understanding and commitment to teachers and children, and her attention to the layers of detail in the construction of the manuscript, we are very much indebted to Toby Gordon, our editor. Melissa Inglis and Renée Le Verrier, production editors, and Alan Huisman, copy editor, have attended to every detail of this book with care and guided this project with a commitment to excellence, and we were most pleased to have them as part of our team.

Our love and thanks go to our families and special friends who fill our lives with caring and support every day of our lives. We send special thanks to Ronald Melhado for his belief in our need to immerse ourselves in work that brings lasting rewards.

We owe many thanks to Martha King who continually reminds us of the importance and power of language and language learning and to Charlotte Huck who has always helped us to sustain the joy of reading for ourselves and our students. We also thank Don Holdaway, a brilliant teacher, who has been our teacher as we studied early literacy learning. And, we acknowledge our large debt to the pioneering work of Moira G. McKenzie, mentor, scholar, and friend.

We are especially grateful to our friend and colleague Mary Ellen Giacobbe who teaches us to stay focused on what matters for children and who generously gave of her time and energy to share her words in our book. Her willingness to join with us in this publication has made this book very special for us.

Finally, we express our deep respect to Marie M. Clay, whose research, writing, and leadership has changed our professional lives. Her insights and commitment to children has created a richly shared learning community that is changing the face of literacy education. We have been privileged to be part of this community, which provided a backdrop against which we could combine our efforts and put our thinking and our practice into words.

Irene C. Fountas
Gay Su Pinnell

Introduction

The last twenty years have brought sweeping changes in literacy education. New information on how children learn language and become literate; the writing process and whole language movements; the negative aspects of ability grouping; and the growing popularity of children's literature captured the attention of committed educators. New ideas were translated into policy and teachers began implementing changes, sometimes with extensive professional development and a rich array of materials but often without those essential support systems. In many places teachers formed their own support groups and pressed on toward change.

And changes took place. Teachers used more and more varied texts to support reading; they used children's literature instead of controlled vocabulary texts; they created communities of learners who were of varying age and experience; and they placed more emphasis on learners' construction of knowledge through their own discoveries.

These changes, while positive, have left teachers with a dilemma: how can I provide young readers with materials and instruction that fit their individual levels of development?

If the teacher's job is to take each child from where he[1] is to where he needs to go in reading, then that teacher must assess individuals. With a class of twenty to thirty-five youngsters, grouping

---

1. **Wherever possible we have used plural pronouns to avoid sexist language. When unable to avoid a generic singular pronoun, we have alternated the masculine and the feminine.**

for instruction makes sense. As teachers, we want to make learning manageable yet avoid the negative aspects of grouping. We want to be sure children are working with materials that help them take the next step in learning to read. The books they read should offer just enough challenge to support problem solving but be easy enough to support fluency and meaning.

But providing appropriate texts is only the beginning. The critical element is the skillful teaching that helps young readers learn the effective strategies they need to become independent. This book addresses the decisions teachers must make regarding all aspects of guided reading: observing reading behavior, gathering evidence of mental processing, grouping and regrouping children, selecting books, introducing stories, supporting reading, and managing learning activities.

The ideas in this book are drawn from many years of classroom research on early literacy. We have worked with comprehensive literacy programs in hundreds of school districts in many parts of the country. Based on our own experience and research, we describe best practice in guided reading for kindergarten through third grade, placing it within the perspective of a thematic integration of reading and writing. We also focus on specific guidelines for forming and re-forming reading groups, selecting and introducing texts, and teaching for strategies. Multicultural texts are emphasized and are included in our descriptions of the classroom book collection. We also provide examples of management tools and suggest ways to help children who need extra support.

Chapter 1 is an overview of the assumptions and procedures of guided reading. Because we wish to emphasize that guided reading is not an isolated process, Chapters 2 and 3 look at literacy learning—the foundation on which the teacher makes instructional decisions about guided reading—and present an overview of a balanced literacy program. Chapters 4 and 5 present practical ideas for organizing the literacy environment and managing the process of guided reading, key elements in making instruction work.

Chapters 6 and 7 return to the important concept of assessing children's learning, presenting techniques for observing reading and writing behavior as a tool for making instructional decisions; the running record, the most powerful tool for fine-tuning guided reading, is described in detail in Chapter 7. Dynamic grouping is described in Chapter 8. Chapter 9 helps teachers create and use a leveled set of books.

Chapters 10 and 11 delve more deeply into the specific procedures of guided reading: selecting and introducing texts and teaching for strategies during and after the children have read the selected book or piece of written material. Chapter 12 specifically describes how teachers can support children's development of effective processing. Chapter 13 focuses on children's learning about letters and words and on how teaching changes over time as children's knowledge grows. Chapter 14 deals specifically with how guided reading changes from its beginnings in kindergarten through third grade. Chapter 15 emphasizes appropriate safety nets for children who are having difficulty in learning to read.

In writing this book we recognize the importance of professional development and collegial support. Continued learning is essential if teachers are to accomplish their goals. Each chapter suggests professional development experiences that will help both experienced and preservice teachers develop an effective guided reading program.

The appendixes are practical tools: a leveled book list, icons to use to manage guided reading, fold-up letter books, an alphabet chart, and record sheets for assessment.

Our book list is always being revised, and new books are added regularly; the best way to test such a list is for teachers to use these books with children and reflect on the result. We invite you to use the form in Appendix K to give us your feedback; we will use your input in future revisions of our list.

Our work is based on the theory that learning is a constructive activity. Ultimately readers discover the principles of literacy and make them their own, but as Marie Clay has said, they do not have to do it alone. The primary classroom is the laboratory in which children discover literacy: but the most essential element in that process is the teacher who provides the raw material—demonstrations, explanations, appropriate materials, feedback, and encouraging and revealing interactions.

This book focuses on helping children begin to read and become strategic users of literacy. Skillful teachers make it easy for the child to make the demanding journey to literacy rapidly, joyously, and in good company. Good first teaching is the foundation of education and the right of every child.

What Is Guided Reading?

Guided reading enables children to practice strategies with the teacher's support, and leads to independent silent reading. NEW ZEALAND DEPARTMENT OF EDUCATION

As teachers we provide the range of experiences and the instruction necessary to help children become good readers early in their school careers. All children possess the fundamental attributes they need to become literate, and some may have developed a great deal of expertise in written language by the time they enter first grade. A few children may actually be reading and know how to learn more about reading. Others may know so much about written language that they can make their own way into literacy simply by encountering good texts and receiving encouragement.

But most children need teaching. Before the end of second grade the great majority of children will have become good readers and writers. There will be a range of rates of learning and, just like everything else, some children will like reading more than others and be more skilled at it. Others may need a safety net such as Reading Recovery. Basic reading, though, is within the reach of every child. The key is good first teaching.

Guided Reading Within a Literacy Program

A balanced literacy program regularly provides several kinds of reading and writing.

By reading aloud, teachers help children experience and contemplate literary work they cannot yet read. In shared reading, children participate in reading, learn critical concepts of how print works, and get the feel of reading. Literature circles enable children to think more deeply about text as they talk with one another and co-construct new understanding. It is through guided reading, however, that teachers can show children how to read and can support children as they read. Guided reading leads to the independent reading that builds the process; it is the heart of a balanced literacy program.

I It gives children the opportunity to develop as individual readers while participating in a socially supported activity.

I It gives teachers the opportunity to observe individuals as they process new texts.

I It gives individual readers the opportunity to develop reading strategies so that they can read increasingly difficult texts independently.

I It gives children enjoyable, successful experiences in reading for meaning.

I It develops the abilities needed for independent reading.

■ It helps children learn how to introduce texts to themselves.

What Is Guided Reading?

Guided reading is a context in which a teacher supports each reader's development of effective strategies for processing novel texts at increasingly challenging levels of difficulty. The teacher works with a small group of children who use similar reading processes and are able to read similar levels of text with support. The teacher introduces a text to this small group, works briefly with individuals in the group as they read it, may select one or two teaching points to present to the group following the reading, and may ask the children to take part in an extension of their reading. The text is one that offers the children a minimum of new things to learn; that is, the children can read it with the strategies they currently have, but it provides opportunity for a small amount of new learning.

The purpose of guided reading is to enable children to use and develop strategies "on the run." They are enjoying the story because they can understand it; it is accessible to them through their own strategies supported by the teacher's introduction. They focus primarily on constructing meaning while using problem-solving strategies to figure out words they don't know, deal with tricky sentence structure, and understand concepts or ideas they have not previously met in print. The idea is for children to take on novel texts, read them at once with a minimum of support, and read many of them again and again for independence and fluency.

The ultimate goal in guided reading is to help children learn how to use independent reading strategies successfully. Teachers, based on their knowledge of children, possible texts, and the processes involved in reading and learning to read, make a series of complex decisions that influence and mediate literacy for the young children in the group. Guided reading also involves ongoing observation and assessment that inform the teacher's interactions with individuals in the group and help the teacher select appropriate texts.

A sample guided reading lesson

Pat is working with five first graders, all of whom can read texts with natural language patterns and two or three lines of print per page. Each child has a body of "known" words that she recognizes quickly. The words each child knows are not identical, of course, but their repertoires overlap. All five children can write their name and many other words; they can hear sounds in words (most of the beginning and ending consonants) and use their letter-sound knowledge to construct words as they write their own messages.

Pat uses her detailed knowledge of the children to select a new book for today, one that will be easy for the children to read, so that accuracy is not an issue. Instead, Pat wants to focus on building the problem-solving abilities or processing power of each child in the group. She has a large selection of books from which to choose, but she has made it easier for herself by organizing them by level of difficulty. For this group, she selects books from level C. About ten titles are available in her collection of guided reading books. This group may read five or six of the titles on this level or may move to the next level more rapidly. Pat will be thinking about this decision as she works with and observes the group.

Today, she pulls out five copies of *Spider, Spider* by Joy Cowley. She calls the group members together, and she gives them a copy of the book. (This time she sits with them on a rug.) First, she introduces the book. For this group, Pat decides to talk about most of the pictures and to use some of the language of the book. This is the group's first book on this level and some of the language patterns and words may be difficult for them. Her introduction is informative but brief. She encourages the children to notice aspects of the book by pointing out features of the pictures and print. Several children notice things in the pictures and either ask questions or make comments. For example, David notices the familiar word *no*. Janna says she doesn't like spiders.

As she introduces the book, Pat asks the children to repeat some of the story language. There is conversation as the children notice and point out things in the pictures. She also asks them to locate an important word, *come*, on several pages. Then she tells the children to get started with their reading. Each child reads the whole book softly while Pat observes. She may interact briefly with some of the children to encourage them to think about the story and use strategies to solve difficulties, but she tries not to interrupt. Today, Pat notices that *Spider, Spider* is very easy for David and may not be offering him enough of a challenge; she thinks David may need to work with another group.

All the children are able to read the book, but Pat notices that several of them have had to do some problem solving on the word *not*. Most were successful. For example, on the line "No, no, Spider, not me," Shana read accurately up to the word *not* and then said, "No, no, what's that word?" showing that she recognized something about it. She went on to the word *me*, but then stopped, went back to the beginning of the line and read it accurately. This behavior provides evidence that Shana was able to check on her own reading (self-monitoring), to search for more information, and to self-correct.

After the reading, Pat takes the children back to page 3 in the story. She writes the word *no* on a white board on the easel that is always nearby. She asks the children to read the word. Then she writes *not*, and says, "Some of you noticed that this new word is like *no*." She asks several children to read the words, pointing out the part that is alike and the different ending. When she asks children to read the word *not*, she empha-

sizes the *t* at the end. Then she asks them to locate *not* in the text. She is trying to help them realize that a good reading strategy is to think of a word like the one you are trying to solve and also to notice word endings and beginnings. Finally, Pat asks the children to read, "No, no, Spider, not me" in unison with fluency and phrasing.

Several children say that they like the book and want to read it again, so Pat adds it to the "browsing box" of previously read texts. Pat dismisses the group without extending the text through another activity. Occasionally, the books read by the group lead to additional activities, but Pat places great value on children's having the opportunity to read many new texts and to reread familiar ones. She thinks that extending every book through art, writing, or drama is impractical and could interfere with time needed to read widely, enjoying and practicing the process.

She asks Janna to stay and takes a running record of Janna's reading of the new book the children read the last time they met. This gives her a chance to observe Janna's independent reading of a text that has been read once before. Pat rotates the children and takes a running record on each of the five about every two weeks.

Pat's interactions with the group will change over time. Children take increasing responsibility for the first reading of a text. Conversation between Pat and the children is woven throughout guided reading, before, during, and after, but the main discussion times either precede or follow reading the story.

Essential components

This example illustrates some of the essential components of the process—observation, powerful examples, and support for young readers. We wish to make our definition of guided reading very clear. While there are many adjustments and variations related to the age and level of children, in guided reading:

∎ A teacher works with a small group.

∎ Children in the group are similar in their development of a reading process and are able to read about the same level of text.

∎ Teachers introduce the stories and assist children's reading in ways that help to develop independent reading strategies.

∎ Each child reads the whole text.

∎ The goal is for children to read independently and silently.

∎ The emphasis is on reading increasingly challenging books over time.

∎ Children are grouped and regrouped in a dynamic process that involves ongoing observation and assessment.

The overall purpose of guided reading is to enable children to read for meaning at all times. The instruction may involve brief detours to focus children's attention on detail, but the construction of meaning overrides.

The place of guided reading in the child's developing knowledge

Children learn to read by reading, and reading begins long before a teacher uses guided reading in school. Early literacy learning begins almost from the moment children are born. They encounter the symbols of literacy in their world—signs for stores and restaurants, for example—and begin to connect them with their meaning. Children participate in the literacy events they find in their homes, events that are different for different children. For example, Hannah is only two years older than her brother Phillip, but they have had different literacy experiences. Hannah loves hearing books read aloud and has made her own books since she was four. Phillip also likes to be read to but not for nearly as long. Instead, he prefers to play games on the computer. At four, he was an expert at several games and could read difficult words like *shift*, *option*, and *delete*.

By participating in literacy, children discover written language and what it is for. When they enter kindergarten, children need rich literacy experiences that will help them move from their early approximations to more refined and precise concepts of how print works. They need abundant opportunities to read and write and to connect the two processes. Interactive writing, a group writing process, provides a demonstration of how written language works, how to make links between letters, clusters of letters, and sounds. Through shared reading of their own interactive writing as well as nursery rhymes, poems, and big books, children learn some of the basic early reading behaviors, such as moving from left to right, return sweep, and one-to-one matching with the support of the teacher and peers in a group.

In kindergarten, children also learn to recognize and name the upper- and lower-case letters so that the information letters provide is more available to them. Teachers have found that the most effective way to approach letter learning is to begin with children's own names, used many different ways, and to use interactive writing extensively, being sure to work explicitly on letters. *If children do not know letters, there is no need to delay their reading of text.* They can continue to learn more about letters and words as they encounter them in texts. But teachers will want to be especially vigilant in helping children who have low letter knowledge to build their competence.

As they approach first grade, most children will have a body of knowledge that they can use as resources for reading. They have developed language systems that allow them to think about whether something "makes sense" and "sounds right." They have some knowledge of what print looks like and the kind of information it contains. Usually, they know a few letters and can write and/or read their name and a few other words. This knowledge base is enough to begin reading for the precise message of the text, and that is where guided reading begins.

A Rationale for Guided Reading

Before children go to school, the process of being able to read text that is more and more decontextualized is guided informally by the responses of caregivers and preschool teachers. Some children focus a great deal of attention on reading and writing and quickly develop deep understanding, seemingly with little effort. Others have some basic knowledge of literacy—familiarity with the language of stories and with particular letters, sounds, and words—but they need help figuring out the complex process of reading text. As they work with text, children develop a network of strategies that allow them to attend to information from different sources. Information from these sources is, for the most part, implicitly or subconsciously held, but it is the foundation for reading text.

Clay (1993a) clusters these sources of information into three categories: meaning, structure, and visual information.

1. *Meaning cues* come from children's life experiences. Meaning is represented in their memories and in the language they use to talk about that meaning. This means that reading has to "make sense." As Holdaway (1979) says, if children have heard stories read aloud, they have formed high expectations of written language. They expect it to make sense and they expect to be intrigued by aspects of the text.

2. *Structure or syntax* comes from knowing how oral language is put together. Language is rule-governed; words are not strung together haphazardly but conform to rules. For example, "She wore a red dress" conforms to the syntactic rules of English. The sentence can be reconfigured in several ways and still "sound right" to an English speaker, but "she a red wore dress" is impossible. It doesn't match the rules we have all assimilated while learning to speak a language.

3. *Visual information* comes from knowing the relationship between oral language and its graphic symbols—the letters that are formed into words divided by spaces and arranged on the page, and the conventions of print such as punctuation. A child may have learned the distinctive features of a few letters, perhaps those in her name. She may even have developed the ability to produce these letters over and over in writing. The first letters serve as exemplars, helping the child "learn how to learn": she learns what to notice about letters and how to compare letters with each other.

Children have these sources of information at their disposal but may not know how to access and use them while reading extended text. It is one thing to recognize visual features of a letter or word in isolation. It is another to use visual information that is embedded in text. The teacher mediates the process for the young reader.

It is usually not enough simply to provide children with good reading materials. Teacher guidance is essential. A major decision is selecting the texts that children encounter while they are building their reading systems. First, children must have many opportunities to read all kinds of texts. A balanced program will provide a large variety of texts organized by level of difficulty. Book selection is discussed in depth in Chapter 10, but there are two basic questions teachers should ask themselves about the books their students read every day:

1. Is the text consistently so easy that children have no opportunity to build their problem-solving strategies?

2. Is the text so difficult to process that children get no real opportunity to read?

If the answer to the first question is yes, then children may be reading but not solving the problems a more challenging text would provide. An easy text that nevertheless introduces a few unfamiliar words or language structures allows the child to practice the "in the head" operations that build the system. It is not the words that are important but the thought processes required to figure out the new words while maintaining the meaning of the text. In the earlier *Spider, Spider* example, the pictures provided clear clues to the meaning, but readers had to look closely at the word *not* in the sentence "No, no, Spider, not me." They had to examine detail while maintaining the meaning and their own sense of how language was structured. The text provided a context for using word-solving skills and for checking the process by using knowledge of the story and sentence pattern.

A child who can carry out this process on beginning texts is on the way to learning "how to learn" in reading. The process has been described by Clay (1991a) as "learning how to access visual sources of information while reading for meaning with divided attention" (p. 286). The more children use problem solving while reading for meaning, the greater and more flexible their problem-solving repertoires become. It is the responsibility of the teacher, therefore, to be sure that children receive the support and guidance they need to read challenging texts every day. Guided reading is designed to support that process.

More commonly, the second question is answered yes—children are reading texts that are too difficult for them. Our rule of thumb is that if the reader, with an introduction and support, cannot read about 90 percent of the words accurately, the text is too difficult. The accuracy analysis here is not a test of the reader but a test of the teacher's selection and introduction of the text. A hard text for a reader does not provide an opportunity for smooth problem solving, and for meaning to guide the process. The process may break down into individual word calling (or frantic random guessing) that does not make sense and is not productive.

When children solve words using visual information, they need to be able to verify their success using meaning and structure cues. At the same time, they make predic-

tions from language structure and meaning (what the text is likely to say) while checking their predictions against the makeup of the word, asking implicitly, Does it *look* right? Accuracy of reading is not as important as learning the process of using different sources of information, self-monitoring, and cross-checking; the process is too difficult if the text is hard.

If the texts are extremely difficult, the situation is even more disastrous for the young reader. This can happen when the more inexperienced children are forced into "whole-class" reading or into reading basals that contain almost no texts a given group of children can read. In this case, the process completely breaks down and there may be bizarre responses such as "mumble reading." Children may also attempt to read along without looking at the print, trying to remember the entire text, or just read along one step behind all the other children with almost no independent processing. The situation for the child would be something like performing in a choir without knowing the music or words.

The answer is not to eliminate whole-class experiences but to use them for activities like shared reading and interactive writing, which are designed for the class community or a small group. Nor is it practical or even desirable to teach each child individually. Guided reading takes advantage of social support and allows the teacher to operate efficiently, to work with the tension between ease and challenge that is necessary to support readers' moving forward in their learning.

The Essentials of Guided Reading

Figure 1–1 outlines the essential elements of guided reading. It summarizes the teacher's and children's actions before, during, and after the reading.

What the teacher does

The teacher's actions emerge from (1) observing the children as they read and write

The Essential Elements of Guided Reading

	Before The Reading	During The Reading	After The Reading
Teacher	• selects an appropriate text, one that will be supportive but with a few problems to solve • prepares an introduction to the story • briefly introduces the story, keeping in mind the meaning, language, and visual information in the text, and the knowledge, experience, and skills of the reader • leaves some questions to be answered through reading	• "listens in" • observes the reader's behaviors for evidence of strategy use • confirms children's problem-solving attempts and successes • interacts with individuals to assist with problem-solving at difficulty (when appropriate) • makes notes about the strategy use of individual readers	• talks about the story with the children • invites personal response • returns to the text for one or two teaching opportunities such as finding evidence or discussing problem-solving • assesses children's understanding of what they read • sometimes engages the children in extending the story through such activities as drama, writing, art, or more reading • sometimes engages the children for a minute or two of word work
Children	• engage in a conversation about the story • raise questions • build expectations • notice information in the text	• read the whole text or a unified part to themselves (softly or silently) • request help in problem-solving when needed	• talks about the whole story • check predictions and react personally to the story or information • revisit the text at points of problem-solving as guided by the teacher • may reread the story to a partner or independently • sometimes engage in activities that invovle extending and responding to the text (such as drama or journal writing) • sometimes engage in a minute or two of word work

FIGURE 1–1   The essential elements of guided reading

and (2) studying and analyzing the available texts. The teacher's task is complex because he must constantly keep in mind text characteristics, reader characteristics, and a growing knowledge of the reading process and how people build this process in unique ways over time.

Before the reading

Knowing the individuals in the small group, the teacher selects a new text to introduce. He carefully matches the readers to a text that offers an appropriate level of support but also includes some challenges. Each new text provided to the group should have a few new things to learn but not so many that children have to struggle. The teacher's goal is children's successful problem solving on an extended piece of text.

Introductions are brief and vary with each book. They also vary according to the readers' interests and needs and the characteristics of the text. The teacher's goal is to interest the children in the story, relate it to their experience, and provide a frame of meaning that will support problem solving. He discusses the title and author and provides an overall sense of what the book is about. Based on his knowledge of the children, the teacher may suggest personal connections to the story. The introduction is conversational rather than a prescribed story review or series of questions. It uses new or important vocabulary and syntactic structures that may be unfamiliar to the group. Even proper names that may be difficult for children can be emphasized in the introduction. It "debugs" the book for the children by directing their attention to new text features they will need to use as readers.

The teacher does not "preteach" words although he may call attention to a word in context, asking children to locate it and notice specific features such as the beginning letter. The teacher guides the readers to look at the pictures and understand the structure of the story and critical aspects of meaning. When working with inexperienced readers, the teacher may go all the way through the story talking about each picture. Sometimes a briefer summary-like overview will provide enough support for children to read the text successfully. The teacher would rarely read the book to the children first: the goal is for them to read it themselves.

During the reading
Children who are just beginning to learn to read are asked to read softly to themselves; soon, they begin to read portions of the text silently. The ultimate goal of guided reading is independent silent reading. The teacher may "listen in" or ask a specific student to

read aloud softly. He looks for evidence of problem solving and intervenes as needed. His observations help him plan quickly what to teach after the first reading. This is a good time to take a few notes on a clipboard.

After the reading
After a brief response to the story, the teacher may decide to do nothing but send the group back to other literacy activities. He may, however, return to a part of the text to bring some example to the children's attention or to support children's growing strategies. He may talk with the children about the ideas in the story or ask them how they liked the story and what it made them think about. For a particular text, the teacher may want to talk about the meaning of the story more extensively. Routinely, some teachers take a running record with one reader after the others have left the area; others establish another time during the day to take several running records. The teacher keeps careful records of guided reading; these include books read, running records, and any notes on specific reading behaviors. Sometimes teachers take a brief time—no more than one or two minutes—right after the group meeting to jot down important observations while they are fresh in the mind.

What the children do
Before the reading
Children talk about the story, ask questions, and build expectations. The teacher's introduction supports their thinking about the story so that comprehension is foregrounded. Each child should be given a copy of the book to view while the teacher introduces it. They may look at the teacher's book during the introduction and then receive the book to begin reading if the teacher has a reason.

During the reading
Each child has a copy of the book and reads the whole text. The reading is usually soft or silent, but all members of the group are operating independently as readers at the same time. This is not "round robin" reading, in

which children take turns reading aloud. In guided reading each child has the opportunity to solve problems while reading extended text and attending to meaning. They construct meaning throughout the process, from their initial predictions about the story to examining the details of print in the text to their reflections after the story is read. Because their use of reading strategies are similar, the children in the group can read the carefully selected book at about the same rate and level of success, preferably with an accuracy rate above 90 percent. This procedure assures that children can process the words successfully without losing meaning; with a good introduction, they should need very little teacher help. Children sustain attention while problem solving an extended piece of text and, in doing so, build a system of strategies that they can use for reading other texts.

After the reading

Afterward children are invited to talk about the story they have read. Their individual responses are valued by the teacher. They may be guided to revisit portions of the text. The teacher selects one or two teaching points that will help the readers process more effectively, such as self-monitoring or using a source of information. Occasionally, children may be invited to extend the text through further discussion or activities such as writing, art, or drama, or to engage in a minute or two of word work.

Evaluating Guided Reading

As with any instructional approach, a teacher will ask herself, How do I know when I am using guided reading successfully? Ultimately, the test is whether the approach responds to the children's learning needs and helps them develop a self-extending reading system, one that fuels its own learning and enables the reader to continue to learn through the act of reading. Good readers have self-extending systems; they are independent. A teacher of guided reading does not have to wait for the results of end-of-year testing to know that

the instruction is successful. She will know that guided reading is effective if moment-to-moment observations and running records show that children are using effective reading strategies. She will also note that children are able to demonstrate effective reading behavior and read progressively more difficult texts accurately and fluently.

Children who are learning to read need to:

■ Enjoy reading even when texts are challenging.

■ Be successful even when texts are challenging.

■ Have opportunities to problem-solve while reading.

■ Read for meaning even when they must do some problem solving.

■ Learn strategies they can apply to their reading of other texts.

■ Use their strengths.

■ Have their active problem solving confirmed.

■ Use what they know to get to what they do not yet know.

■ Talk about and respond to what they read.

■ Expand their knowledge and understanding through reading.

■ Make connections between texts they have read and between their own world knowledge and reading.

We sometimes mistakenly assume that these needs can be met just by providing good books and encouraging children to explore them. In fact, what most young readers need cannot be found in books alone. The process of reading must be dynamically supported by an interaction of text reading and good teaching. Guided reading serves this important goal.

Suggestions for Professional Development

1. Over a period of two weeks analyze your daily schedule. Ask yourself:

■ How much time do I spend on reading instruction?

■ Where does reading instruction appear in my schedule?

■ How much reading instruction does each child receive each week?

■ How much time do children spend reading extended text at an appropriate level?

■ How much time do I spend in individual conferences? in whole-class instruction?

■ How many books does each child read each week? (You may want to count or estimate the number of words [in text] each child reads independently each week.)

2. After answering these questions, you will have a greater awareness of how much supported reading children do and a good idea of the amount of time you need to allocate for guided reading. You will also know where reading instruction fits into your schedule. Ask yourself:

■ Are my students doing enough reading?

■ What kinds of texts are they reading? Are they too easy? too hard?

■ Do I have at least an uninterrupted hour for working with small groups in guided reading?

3. Rearrange your schedule so that you have at least one hour per day for guided reading. Then begin setting up your management system (see Chapter 5).

Building on Early Learning

Helping greater numbers of children find meaning and success in school requires first that teachers understand how meanings are formed, why they sometimes are so difficult to communicate, and the crucial role language plays in both the formation and the sharing of meaning.   MARTHA L. KING

Children vary widely in the amount and type of literacy experiences they have had, but because they live in our print-rich world, all have some awareness of the function of written language. Encounters with literacy in school have meaning because children use their previously acquired knowledge of language and the world to make sense of printed symbols. Children who have had limited experiences do not need to wait to participate fully in classroom literacy; they will acquire knowledge quickly as they use reading and writing in functional ways. If literacy is personal, functional, and enjoyable, the young child will simultaneously learn what written language is, how it works, and how to use it for many purposes.

Language Is a Self-Extending System

It is sometimes said that no one has to "teach" children to talk; yet they master the huge and complex body of knowledge needed to use language by about age five. The young child's accomplishments are amazing. Every language has an infinite number of sentences, each with its own meaning, that are put together according to

rules. By encountering and using language in the environment, children learn the rules they can then use to generate this infinite number of sentences. Even typical early statements by children (*More juice* or *More cookie*) are not random utterances to "practice words." They are highly organized and meaningful statements that get results from the adults with whom the children interact. A language is redundant and highly predictable. For example, we know that in the English sentence "I can see three _____," the word to be filled in is probably a noun and it may be preceded by an adjective. Plurality is signaled both by the word *three* and the *s*, *es*, or other noun form that will follow.

As children use language, they reveal their working hypotheses about the rules and how to use them to put words and parts of words together in meaningful ways. A child who says *I runned here* shows she has a developing understanding of how to signal the past tense. Right now she is using the rule in a regular way by applying it to all examples, but later she will refine that use. All languages and dialects have these rules, which all children learn as they encounter and use them at home. Language is a self-extending system; that is, it allows the learner to keep on learning by using it.

There is no formal curriculum for teaching children language; they enter into conversation with other children and with adults, and through many examples derive the underlying rules. But the process is not random, and it is highly supported by adults. Everyone in the culture knows the special ways adults talk to babies. We know from language research that unconsciously, adults tailor their language interactions to support young children's ability to use language. By repeating words and phrases, altering sentence structure, and responding to what children say, they make language available and easy.

Parents seldom correct their children. Instead, they encourage children to produce whatever they can—one-, two-, and three-word utterances. Adults listen and respond as if the child has produced a fully constructed sentence; and indeed, it is constructed, even in those early attempts. At every level of language learning, children construct rule-consistent utterances, using adults as conversational partners to help them make sense of language.

As children produce more, caregivers produce less of the conversation, but at the same time expand children's speech as to both syntax and meaning. For example, caregivers accept what the child produces and repeat it, but as a fully grammatical utterance. Thus children learn the rules that their parents and community use in home dialect. Through learning language, children learn how to negotiate meaning. They also learn how to form hypotheses, test them, use feedback from interactions with others, search for more information, revise concepts, and connect sets of understanding.

A characteristic of language is that it varies by individual, family, neighborhood, region, and cultural group; there is infinite variety. Our first language is always that of the home and community in which we live as young children, but the learning opportunities—words, rules for generating meaningful statements and sentences, ways of pronouncing words and clusters of sounds—are there in every version of every language. Once children have learned to use any language, they have acquired a powerful self-extending system. Of the child entering school, Clay says,

He has learned how to learn language.

It is important for teachers to remind themselves of this when they seem to hear differences in a particular child's speech. The child may not know as much about language as some of his peers, or he may find the rules for talking in school are different from those in his culture or ethnic group, or he may see little similarity between talking in his family and the more formal teacher-pupil talk of the classroom, or he may even speak a different language from the teacher's. Yet in all these cases the child has already learned how to learn language. (1991a, 26–27)

Learning About Print Is a Highly Personal Experience

Children's experiences and interactions with a world of written language are infused with personal meaning. Shopping lists, telephone numbers, notes, and letters are written and then read. Just about everyone orders from restaurant menus, searches for items on grocery-store shelves, reads prices on sale items, uses recipes (or at least directions on the carton) for cooking, or fills out forms. Literacy is a tool for daily use.

The most important word a child learns is likely to be her name (Adams 1990; Clay 1991a). Children quickly make connections between their names and other words. Five-year-old Madeleine, for example, has just started kindergarten. She can write her first, middle, and last name (Madeleine Wayson Gifford). Recently, she told a friend on the phone about her new baby sister, Margaret. The friend said, "Oh, you two are the M and M's—Madeleine and Margaret!"

"And, Mommy!" Madeleine immediately said. Playing on the computer later, she noticed the M and made a lot of them. Then she said, "M is part of Daddy's phone number." The adults were puzzled until she explained, "When you call Daddy, you push mem one on the phone."

Madeleine writes *Mommy* as *ME*, noticing that it begins like her name; she hears the *e*. She can read very little, but she is beginning to match word by word on one line of print. In reading page 8 of the text in Figure 2–1, she can locate *my* by first thinking about what it would start with and then searching for the *m*.

The second time she read this little Keep Book (see Chapter 3), she read "I see a," then stopped, looked carefully at the word *my*, and returned to the beginning of the line, this time self-correcting her reading. On this simple text, Madeleine revealed that she could use visual information to check her reading, could search for more information by returning to the beginning of the line, and could make the whole meaningful message sound right and look right. She was using both her knowledge of meaningful language structure and her beginning and highly personal knowledge of visual signs.

Madeleine knows more letters and sounds, but her name has been a powerful exemplar in learning the process. Further learning is evidenced as she writes *BERB* and *KN* (*Barbie* and *Ken*) by saying the names slowly and thinking about the sounds. And in another small book, she was able again to locate and use the word *my* as an "island of certainty" to guide her reading (Clay 1991a).

The world is full of print. Even very young children will learn to recognize the symbols for their favorite fast-food restaurants or cereals. The context is powerful in helping children bring meaning to symbols, but they are also beginning to recognize features of the signs in their environment even though they do not yet know letter names.

In the classroom, a print-rich environment takes advantage of children's natural tendency to search for things that are meaningful to them. Thus, kindergarten and first-grade teachers can call children's attention to print in more deliberate ways, building from what is known to what is yet unknown. Working from children's names and words frequently used in interactive writing, teachers can help children recognize letters and sounds as they appear within words and alone. The process is systematic in that the teacher has in his mind the network of knowledge to be acquired and keeps careful records of children's progress. An important point is that children not only learn particular letters and words, they learn how to learn about and use these written symbols. Once a small repertoire of information is acquired, it is easier to learn a great deal more.

Writing and Reading Are Complementary Processes

Reading and writing are interrelated: what is learned in one area makes it easier to learn in the other. Children are quite willing to take small detours—learning words and how they work, hearing and recording sounds while constructing messages, or analyzing words while reading—if these activities are in the service of real reading and writing.

Processes are built up and broken down in both reading and writing, but the concept may be easier for children to understand in writing. During early writing experiences, children naturally and purposefully attend to the details of print.

Early attempts to approximate writing are valuable experiences for young children. At first, they scribble, produce letterlike forms, strings of letters, or their names and a few other words. As their knowledge increases, children gain full control of some words and construct others through their knowledge of letters and sounds as well as visual details (Bissex 1980; Dyson 1982).

Writing involves a complex series of actions. Children have to think of a message and hold it in the mind. Then they have to

FIGURE 2–1   The layout of a typical Keep Book

think of the first word and how to start it, remember each letter form and its features, and manually reproduce the word letter by letter. Having written the first word (or an approximation), the child must go back to the whole message, retrieve it, and think of the next word. Through writing, children are manipulating and using symbols, and in the process learning how written language works.

The process may appear tedious and labored at first, but when children want to write and are guided and praised for their efforts, they find it rewarding. Group or interactive writing, in which the teacher and children share the pen, is a powerful way to demonstrate writing processes for children—all the way from thinking of what to say (composing) to saying words slowly to determine sounds to quickly writing known words to comparing parts of words with other words.

Children in school need abundant opportunities to write; preschool and primary classrooms should have writing centers containing a wide variety of materials. In addition, writing materials can be available in other areas of the classroom—in the science center to take notes and keep records; in the house corner to make shopping lists; in the book area to keep records of books, to write responses, or extend texts; in the art center to annotate or label pictures; etc. It is helpful to children if teachers explicitly demonstrate appropriate writing processes. Through individual conferences, minilessons, and group writing (which we call interactive writing), teachers can provide feedback and instruction to help children expand their knowledge and skills.

Moving from Approximation to Strategic Silent Reading

By practicing literacy, children discover what it is for and what it is about, another advantage for the child entering school. Important early behaviors include "talking like a book" and approximated writing. "Talking

like a book" is the child's attempt to "read" by reproducing a text that has been heard several times. Sometimes such approximation appears spontaneously even when the child is looking at a book not heard before, but "talking like a book" usually happens with favorites heard over and over.

When Madeleine was three years old, she could "read" *Beauty and the Beast* by looking at the pictures and saying, " 'Oh, poor beast,' said Beauty." Like many modern children, her language had been acquired two ways—by hearing her mother read the story and by watching the Disney videotape. This twin encounter with a very long and complex text helped her acquire language structures that she would never use in everyday talk but could produce when cued by the illustrations in the book. She was using her assimilated knowledge of a particular kind of syntax, focusing on meaning but producing language that is different from oral language in significant ways.

Teachers can foster children's awareness of such linguistic structures by reading aloud stories that are rich in literary language, watching children for their response, rereading favorites many times, and placing these favorites in the classroom library where they are easily accessible when it is "reading time." Children need an opportunity to make some texts their own, controlling the language and reproducing it in different ways.

During reading time in Ida Patacca's kindergarten class, Kyeara and two friends sit together, each with a copy of *The Three Little Pigs*, which they have heard many times. They approximate the text as they dramatically read together, "I'll huff, and I'll puff, and I'll huff, and I'll puff, and I'll huff, and I'll blow your house in. . . ." They are enjoying the story; their focus is on the meaning and they are displaying their knowledge of language. They are not matching their language with the print on this difficult story and they may not notice many of the print details (such as letters or punctuation) unless they have particular meaning (such as enlarged letters or a big exclamation point). They are expanding and using two important systems of information that will help them become good readers—meaning and language structure.

Later in the day, Kyeara engages in a much more focused look at print as she rereads material that the group has produced through interactive writing, a retelling of *The Three Little Pigs* that includes the line, "The first little pig built his house of straw." On this simple text that the children composed, produced, and have read many times, Kyeara can point and match words, practicing early strategies such as word-by-word matching and moving left to right. She knows the words *the* and *pig*, and that knowledge helps her check and confirm her attempts. She can also read simple books with one line of print per page and will soon be able to track print while reading two or three lines of print per page, as in the Keep Book based on *The Three Little Pigs* shown in Figure 2–2.

Simple books like this one allow children to anticipate and look at each word, checking their predictions with the print. The topic is familiar; they already know just about what the book is going to say, so early literacy behavior is fully supported. Even in the early phases of learning to read, children can use a known word to act as a kind of anchor in reading, helping them to match their spoken words with the print appropriately or to realize when they are not reading the precise message of the print. Words are learned because children have had many opportunities to see and use words embedded in meaningful print. As they reread known texts many times and begin to write their own texts, beginning readers build up a repertoire of known words that are useful in strategic ways. Self-monitoring using these words is an early goal.

Rather than immediately moving to correct readers, an action that will foster dependence, teachers help young readers learn

how to use their knowledge to check on their own reading. Later, children will be able to use all systems together—meaning, knowledge of language structure, and the visual details of the print—as they read fluently.

Independent, Fluent, Strategic Reading

Good readers focus on meaning but use a range of information in balanced ways. When necessary, they can analyze an unfamiliar word, using visual detail and letter-sound correspondence, and they can then check that word with their own sense of language to be sure it makes sense in the story. This kind of cross-referencing or "cross-checking" is seen in the problem solving behavior of beginning readers; it is evidence that strategic work is going on "in the head."

Although it is not always an explicit or even a conscious process, good readers use powerful, in-the-head strategies such as (Clay 1991a):

▌ Searching for and using meaning, language structure, and visual information.

▌ Self-monitoring (checking on their own reading using meaning, syntax, or visual information).

▌ Cross-checking one source of information against another.

▌ Self-correcting through predicting, monitoring, and searching for additional information.

As teachers, we want to direct children's attention to using multiple sources of information in a skilled way. We can do this by giving children the opportunity to read many texts that offer just the right amount of challenge (not too hard and not too easy).

Children's use of cues and strategies becomes integrated as they read easy texts fluently. The processes are not used consciously but are more automatic, allowing the reader to give more attention to new information.

Once upon a time
there were three little pigs.

1

The first little pig built a
house of straw.

2

The second little pig built a
house of sticks.

3

The third little pig built a
house of bricks.

4

Along came a wolf.

5

The wolf blew down the
house of straw.

6

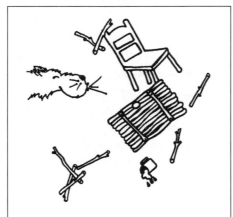

The wolf blew down the
house of sticks.

7

But the wolf could not blow
down the house of bricks.

8

FIGURE 2–2 *The Three Little Pigs* Keep Book

Fluency plays an important role in becoming a good reader. Good readers are fast, efficient problem solvers who use meaning and syntax as they quickly and efficiently decode unfamiliar words. Every day teachers make time in the schedule for children to engage in fluent, independent reading of familiar or easy texts.

Ultimately, children who are learning to read must construct the complex, in-the-head problem-solving processes that are characteristic of good readers and develop self-extending systems that enable them to keep on learning independently. As they read, they further their own learning, not only acquiring new words but making their reading more efficient and absorbing knowledge about the way different kinds of texts (such as narratives and informational books) are organized. As good readers read, they extend their own cognitive abilities.

Teaching Is Critical

Literacy is constructed by each child individually but this does not mean he does it alone. Literacy learning is facilitated by interactions with other, more knowledgeable readers. The role of caregivers and teachers is critical in children's opportunities to become literate. Adults demonstrate reading and writing and support children as they begin to participate in literacy events. Sometimes, they explain important concepts about written language; often, they encourage children by noticing evidence of effective processing. Parents and teachers demonstrate, explain, and support. They help children attend efficiently and meaningfully to visual information in print and to use that information in a dynamic way in connection with their knowledge about language. Through these assisted experiences, children construct internal control of the operations they need to match their thinking with the written words. The goal of all literacy teaching is independence and ongoing learning.

Suggestions for Professional Development

1. Even if you teach first, second, or third grade, make time to observe one kindergarten child closely as she pursues reading and writing activities. Find a child who does not yet know how to read. Identify behaviors that provide evidence of what the child knows about reading or writing.

2. You may also want to take a closer and more systematic look at some aspect of emergent literacy, such as the development of "book language." Select a text that is simple but interesting to children, such as *The Chick and the Duckling* or *Where's Spot?*

- Over a period of time, read the book to the child, inviting her to join in.
- After the second reading, ask the child to "read" the book. (Children sometimes say that they cannot read. If that is the case, invite the child to "tell the story" while looking at the pictures.)
- Take notes on the child's "reading" of the text. (Some teachers tape-record the reading and take notes immediately afterward. Others have created simple forms for themselves by placing the text and a small photocopy of the picture on one side of the page, leaving the other blank for the child's version of the story.)
- Repeat the above process twice each week for two or three weeks. Each time, read the book aloud to the child before asking her to read it.
- Examine several versions of the child's "reading" of the story.
- How does the child's language change over time as she becomes more familiar with the text? Consider specific words, syntax, and the structure of the story.
- What evidence is there that the child is noticing visual aspects of print? Consider specific letters or words,

following the layout of print, noticing punctuation, putting fingers on the print, etc.

3. Share descriptions of children's behaviors with your colleagues, noting changes over time in response to familiar text and finding similarities and differences. These comparisons will help to build a picture of the way children construct meaning from text and will also illustrate the value of rereading.

Guided Reading Within a Balanced Literacy Program

When teachers, librarians, and parents concentrate on plans to foster a love of reading in each child, communities become caring, literate places to live. CHARLOTTE HUCK

Guided reading is only one component of a balanced literacy program. A child might spend between ten to thirty minutes a day in a focused reading group that is organized, structured, planned, and supported by the teacher. During the rest of the day, that same student will participate in whole-group, small-group, and individual activities related to a wide range of reading and writing, almost all of which involve children of varying experience and abilities.

A Framework for Literacy Learning

A flexible framework is useful in conceptualizing the curriculum for teaching language and literacy in the primary grades. It is a way of thinking about the range of reading and writing activities that are essential for promoting early literacy; it also guides teachers in integrating instructional processes and the content of math, literature, science, and other areas.

The language and literacy framework presented here is useful throughout the first three or four grades of school. In its present form (see Figure 3–1) it has eight instructional components and emphasizes oral language across the curriculum, working with letters and words, the unifying aspect of integrated themes, observation, assessment, and the role of a home-school partnership. Flexibility is the key to implementing this literacy framework. *It is important to recognize that components are not separate elements but are linked together in two powerful ways: (1) through the oral language that surrounds, supports, and extends all activities and (2) by the content or topic of focus.*

Oral language across the curriculum

Oral language is the foundation of the primary curriculum. Throughout the day, children explore concepts and construct meaning by talking among themselves and with the teacher. As discussed in Chapter 2, language is a powerful system that children bring with them to their first school experiences. In both whole- and small-group activities, teachers encourage children to offer their ideas and comments. A basic assumption is that classroom talk for both teacher and children should have the quality of conversation, including:

▌ Making statements and asking questions.
▌ Elaborating and explaining.
▌ Listening.
▌ Responding.
▌ Expanding others' ideas.

The Ohio State University Literacy Collaborative Framework

The framework for early literacy lessons was developed by surveying the research and descriptive literature, examining research on language and literacy learning, and involving classroom teachers and Reading Recovery teachers in action research since 1984. The framework outlined below is a flexible organizational tool for classroom and reading teachers who want to engage children in a variety of literacy experiences and refine their teaching. The value of each component depends on the organization and the effectiveness of teaching within it. In each component, teachers observe children's responses carefully and draw their attention to powerful examples that illustrate critical processes.

Element	Values	Supportive Research & Descriptive Literature
1. Reading Aloud The teacher reads aloud to the whole class or small groups. A carefully selected body of children's literature is used; the collection contains a variety of genres and represents our diverse society. Favorite texts, selected for special features, are reread many times.	• Involves children in reading for enjoyment • Demonstrates reading for a purpose • Provides an adult demonstration of phrased, fluent reading • Develops a sense of story • Develops knowledge of written language syntax • Develops knowledge of how texts are structured • Increases vocabulary • Expands linguistic repertoire • Supports intertextual ties • Creates community of readers through enjoyment and shared knowledge • Makes complex ideas available to children • Promotes oral language development • Establishes known texts to use as a basis for writing and other activities through rereading	Adams (1990) Clark (1976) Cochran-Smith (1984) Cohen (1968) Durkin (1966) Goodman, Y. (1984) Green & Harker (1982) Hiebert (1988) Huck, Hickman, Hepler (1993) Ninio (1980) Pappas & Brown (1987) Schickedanz (1978) Wells (1985)
2. Shared Reading Using an enlarged text that all children can see, the teacher involves children in reading together following a pointer. The process includes: • Rereading big books, poems, songs • Rereading retellings • Rereading alternative texts • Rereading the products of interactive writing	• Explicitly demonstrates early strategies, such as word-by-word matching • Builds sense of story and ability to predict • Demonstrates the processes of reading extended text • Like reading aloud, involves children in an enjoyable and purposeful way • Provides social support from the group • Provides opportunity to participate and behave like a reader • Creates body of known texts that children can use for independent reading and as resources for writing and word study	Holdaway (1979) Martinez & Roser (1985) Pappas & Brown (1987) Rowe (1987) Snow (1983) Sulzby (1985) Teal & Sulzby (1986)
3. Guided Reading The teacher works with a small group of children who have similar reading processes. The teacher selects and introduces new books and supports children reading the whole text to themselves, making teaching points during and after the reading. Sometimes the teacher engages the children in an extension to further their understanding in a minute or two of letter or word work.	• Provides the opportunity to read many texts and a wide variety of texts • Provides opportunity to problem-solve while reading for meaning ("reading work") • Provides opportunity to use strategies on extended text • Challenges the reader and creates context for successful processing on novel texts • Provides opportunity to attend to words in text • Teacher selection of text, guidance, demonstration, and explanation is available to the reader	Clay (1991a & 1991b) Fountas & Pinnell (1996, 1999a) Holdaway (1979) Lyons, Pinnell, & DeFord (1993) McKenzie (1986) Meek (1988) Pinnell & Fountas (1998) Routman (1991) Wong, Groth, & O'Flahavan (1994)

FIGURE 3–1   The Ohio State University Literacy Collaborative framework

Element	Values	Supportive Research & Descriptive Literature
4. Independent Reading Children read on their own or with partners from a wide range of materials. Some reading is from a special collection at their reading level.	• Provides opportunity to apply reading strategies independently • Provides time to sustain reading behavior • Challenges the reader to work on his/her own and to use strategies on a variety of texts • Challenges the reader to solve words independently while reading texts well within his/her control • Promotes fluency through rereading • Builds confidence through sustained, successful reading • Provides the opportunity for children to support each other while reading	Clay (1991a) Holdaway (1979) McKenzie (1986) Meek (1988) Taylor (1993)
5. Shared Writing Teacher and children work together to compose messages and stories; teacher supports process as scribe.	• Demonstrates how writing works • Provides opportunities to draw attention to letters, words, and sounds • Enables children's ideas to be recorded • Creates written language resources for the classroom	Goodman, Y. (1984) Holdaway (1979) McKenzie (1986) Sulzby (1985)
6. Interactive Writing As in shared writing, teacher and children compose messages and stories that are written using a "shared pen" technique that involves children in the writing.	• Demonstrates concepts of print, early strategies, and how words work • Provides opportunities to hear sounds in words and connect with letters • Helps children understand "building up" and "breaking down" processes in reading and writing • Provides opportunities to plan and construct texts • Increases spelling knowledge • Provides texts that children can read independently • Provides written language resources in the classroom	Button, Johnson, & Furgerson (1996) McCarrier & Patacca (1994) Pinnell & McCarrier (1994) McCarrier, Pinnell & Fountas (2000)
7. Guided Writing or Writing Workshop Children engage in writing a variety of texts. Teacher guides the process and provides instruction through minilessons and conferences.	• Helps writers develop their voice • Provides opportunities for children to learn to be writers • Provides chance to use writing for different purposes across the curriculum • Increases writers' abilities to use different forms • Builds ability to write words and use punctuation • Fosters creativity and the ability to compose	Atwell (1987) Britton (1983) Calkins (1983; 1986) Giacobbe (1981) Graves (1983) Graves & Hansen (1983)
8. Independent Writing Children write their own pieces, including (in addition to stories and informational pieces) retellings, labeling, speech balloons, lists, etc.	• Provides opportunity for the independent production of written text • Provides chance to use writing for different purposes across the curriculum • Increases writers' abilities to use different forms • Builds ability to write words and use punctuation • Fosters creativity and the ability to compose	Bissex (1980) Clay (1975) Dyson (1982) Ferreiro & Teberosky (1982) Goodman, Y. (1984) Harste, Woodward, & Burke (1984)

FIGURE 3–1 *continued*

Letter and Word Study	Values	Supporting Research
Teachers provide minilessons to help children learn more about how letters and words work. Children work with letters and words at a letter/word study center and share their learning. Teachers help children notice letters and words throughout the language and literacy framework.	• Helps children become familiar with letter forms • Helps children develop phonological awareness. • Helps children learn to use visual aspects of print • Provides opportunities to notice and use letters and words that are embedded in text • Provides opportunities to manipulate letters and make words • Provides a growing inventory of known letters and words • Helps children link sounds with letters and letter clusters • Helps children use what they know about words to solve new words	Adams (1990) Cunningham (1995) Fountas & Pinnell (1999a) Pinnell & Fountas (1998) Read (1970; 1975) Schickedanz (1986)

Achieving Coherence Through Extensions and Themes
• Elements of the framework are integrated through the content of the curriculum. Teachers extend stories and link them together through art, drama, music, experiments, and mathematics activities. For example, children might make story maps, create a restaurant for daily dramatic play, make innovations on texts, plan their work with lists, write observations of change in nature, compare several versions of a text, engage in an in-depth study on a particular subject, or take surveys and analyze the results. Literature is an integral part of the process.
• Provides opportunities to interpret texts in different ways
• Provides a way of revisiting a story
• Fosters collaboration and enjoyment
• Creates a community of readers
• Provides efficient instruction through integration of content areas
• Enables children to express and extend their understanding using the processes of various disciplines

Documenting Children's Progress
• Teachers systematically gather observational data over time to document the progress of individual children. Some formal assessments are used; data are aggregated to assess overall effects of the program.
• Provides information to guide daily teaching
• Provides a way to track the progress of individual children
• Provides a basis for reporting to parents
• Helps a school staff to assess the effectiveness of the instructional program
• Provides children with evidence of their growth

Home and Community Involvement
• Parents participate in the school curriculum through receiving information, being welcomed in the school, participating in book-making workshops, and receiving Keep Books for children to read at home.
• Brings reading and writing materials and new learning into children's homes
• Gives children more opportunities to show their families what they are learning
• Increases reading and writing opportunities for children
• Demonstrates value and respect for children's homes

FIGURE 3–1 *continued*

- Taking turns.
- Thinking about and respecting alternative meanings.
- Repeating and restating ideas.
- Using language to investigate and wonder.
- Enjoying and sharing the play of language through poetry, rhyme, and humor.

In every component of the framework, children use language to learn and teachers use language to extend children's language and demonstrate new ways of using it. Reading aloud provides new models and meaning that can be applied in group and independent writing. Composing written text from a rich oral backdrop is demonstrated through interactive writing. In guided reading, teachers frame the selection orally before reading; ongoing conversation directs children's attention to examples that will move them forward. In literature circles, children learn how to listen to and extend each other's understanding. Writing workshop or guided writing provides a context for using oral language to support specific writing strategies and skills. In independent reading and writing and in center activities, children's conversations with each other support the process. With a balanced literacy approach, the classroom is orderly and quiet enough to work without distraction, but it is by no means silent. Oral language is the constant vehicle and support for learning.

Integrated themes

The talk varies as children focus on a topic of interest such as butterflies, folktales, or friendship. Integrated themes serve a larger purpose by creating an overarching web of meaning that helps children connect the various reading and writing activities in a purposeful way. Not all components of the framework are required to be part of an integrated theme. For example, guided reading is seldom connected to a theme. But where connections are possible, implementing a theme adds interest to the curriculum and helps children create meaning across reading and writing.

A piece of literature is sometimes the impetus for thematic learning that reaches across the curriculum. For example, *Peanut Butter and Jelly*, by Nadine Bernard Westcott, was the source of some limited but authentic connections in Ida Patacca's kindergarten class. Children enjoyed hearing their teacher read this fanciful rhyming song and joined in. They created a shopping list and made their own peanut butter and jelly sandwiches, an activity that involved mathematical reasoning as well as many aspects of literacy. A broader theme was sparked by reading several versions of *The Three Little Pigs*. Children compared versions, dramatized and wrote their own adaptation of the story, created a story map, and read it several times. They explored facts about real pigs and wrote an informational big book. Purposeful reading and writing permeated the thematic study.

Elements of the framework

The elements are not fixed and separate, and activity in the classroom moves smoothly around them. However, discussing them separately is a tool for planning how to use them. Each element requires a different level of support from the teacher and respects the level of control or independence of the children (see Figure 3–2). For example, the teacher is in full control of reading aloud, although the children are actually listening, commenting, and joining in on familiar parts. In shared reading the child shares the control with the teacher. In guided reading, the child is mostly in control, but the teacher provides a small amount of support. In independent reading, the child is in full control of the process, with little or no teacher support. The same applies to the different contexts for writing.

Figures 3–2, 3–3, and 3–4 summarize the four kinds of reading and writing, the level of support provided by the teacher, and the materials used.

Reading aloud

Reading aloud is the foundation of the early literacy framework. By being immersed in a

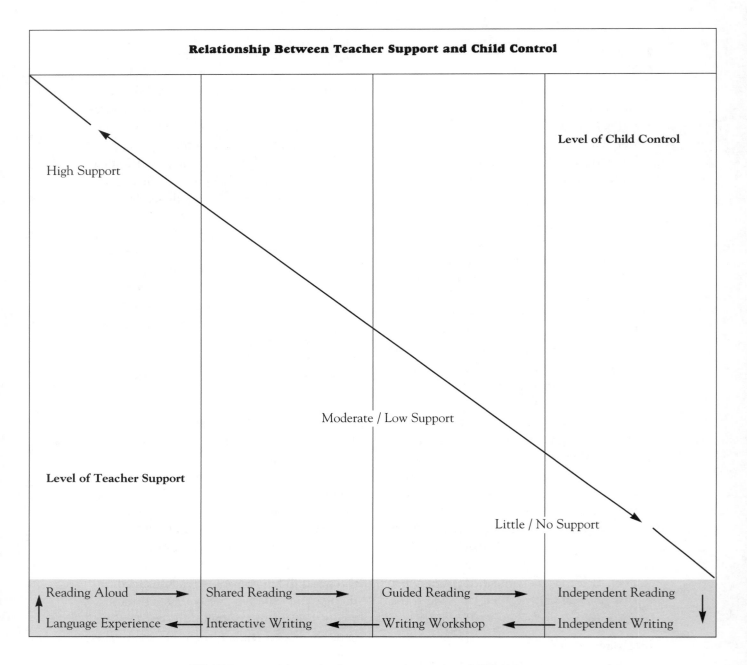

Relationship Between Teacher Support and Child Control

Level of Child Control

High Support

Moderate / Low Support

Level of Teacher Support

Little / No Support

Reading Aloud ⟶ Shared Reading ⟶ Guided Reading ⟶ Independent Reading

Language Experience ⟵ Interactive Writing ⟵ Writing Workshop ⟵ Independent Writing

FIGURE 3–2   Relationship between teacher support and child control

variety of well-chosen texts children not only learn to love stories and reading but they also learn about written language. Teachers in kindergarten and first and second grade often read the same story—a favorite that is rich in language opportunities—many times. Children assimilate a sense of the structure of written language and can produce it in a way that sounds like reading and approximates text. Just as

important, they learn how texts are put together—how stories work or how you look for the information in expository texts. They build up a repertoire of text structures and literary language structures that will support them in their independent reading.

Reading aloud begins the first day of school and continues throughout a child's school career. From hearing a text read,

Four Kinds of Reading / Four Levels of Support

	Four Kinds of Reading	Levels of Support	Materials
Reading Aloud	• The teacher selects and reads a book or other text to the children. Texts rich in meaning or language and class favorites are read again and again, and are used as a base for other activities.	• Teacher provides full support for children to access the text. • Children respond to pictures, meaning, and language. • They may join in but usually do not focus on features of print.	• Individual book for teacher.
Shared Reading	• The teacher introduces and reads an enlarged text or a small text of which each child has a copy. On refrains and in multiple readings, children join in, reading in unison.	• Teacher provides high level of support. • There is some group problem-solving and a lot of conversation about the meaning of the story. • Readers support each other.	• Large-print charts. • Big books. • Individual copies. • Easel. • Pointers.
Guided Reading	• The teacher selects and introduces a new text. • Children read the whole text to themselves.	• Some teacher support is needed. • Reader problem-solves a new text in a way that is mostly independent.	• Individual books. • Easel and chart paper. • Whiteboard. • Magnetic letters.
Independent Reading	• The children read to themselves or with partners.	• Little or no teacher support is needed. • The reader independently solves problems while reading for meaning.	• Big and little books. • Large-print charts. • Writing displayed in the room. • Classroom library. • Pointers.

FIGURE 3–3   Four kinds of reading/four levels of support

older children develop in-depth knowledge of characterization and complex plots. Reading aloud makes available rich content so that children can analyze texts and compare them. It allows the teacher to demonstrate ways to make personal connections and comparisons with books that children use for interactions in literature circles and forms a foundation for other reading and writing activities.

Shared reading

In shared reading, students join the teacher to read aloud in unison from an enlarged text—a big book, a poem, or any enlarged message or story. Texts enlarged on an overhead projector can also be used. The children must be able to see the print clearly so they can engage in the group reading process.

During the reading, the teacher or another student guides the readers by pointing to (or sliding below) each word of the text with a dowel rod or other long slender object. The technique was originally developed in New Zealand (Holdaway 1979) as a way to involve young children intensively in a story while inviting them to attend to print. As in the lap story, the text is initially read

Four Kinds of Writing / Four Levels of Support

	Four Kinds of Writing	Levels of Support	Materials
Shared Writing	• The teacher guides children to compose messages and acts as their scribe. The message is reread many times. • Teachers may use a combination of writing for children and interactive writing, being aware of time and pacing.	• The teacher provides full support. • The teacher models and demonstrates the process of putting children's ideas into written language.	• Large charts and markers. • Materials for making big books. • Individual slates (optional). • Magnadoodle or slate for the teacher. • White tape for making corrections. • Pointers for rereading. • Letter chart or letters for use as a model for formation.
Interactive Writing	• The teacher guides group writing of a large-print piece, which can be a list, a chart, pages of a book, or another form of writing. • All children participate in composing and constructing various aspects of the writing. • The piece of writing is read many times by the group during the process and as shared reading.	• There is a high level of teacher support. • The teacher models and demonstrates writing processes but also involves individual children. • The teacher selects letters, words, or other writing actions for individual children to do; the pen or marker is shared. • The message or story is composed by the group and then constructed word by word.	• Large charts and markers. • Materials for making big books. • Individual slates (optional). • Magnadoodle or slate for the teacher. • Whiteboard. • White tape for making corrections. • Pointers for rereading. • Letter chart or letters for use as a model for formation.
Guided Writing or Writing Workshop	• The teacher has individual conferences with writers, giving selected feedback. • The teacher may work with the whole class or a small group to provide general guidance and minilessons on any aspect of writing.	• Some teacher support is needed. • Children generally select their own topics and pieces but the teacher sets the scene and gives specific guidance and/or feedback as needed. • Children solve their own problems in writing with teacher assistance and/or feedback. • The teacher provides specific instruction in minilessons and conferences.	• Word wall, dictionaries, or other resources. • Paper, pencils, markers, staples, premade plain books, and art materials, including multicolored crayons, markers, and pencils. • Writing folders. • Hanging files for finished work.
Independent Writing	• Children write their own messages and stories, sometimes helping each other.	• Little or no teacher support is needed. • The reader independently composes and writes, using known words and constructing the spelling of unknown words • Children know how to use the resources in the room to get words they cannot write independently.	• Paper, pencils, markers, staples, premade plain books, and art materials. • Resources children use on their own such as the word wall or dictionaries. • Print-rich environment as a resource.

FIGURE 3–4 **Four kinds of writing/four levels of support**

by the teacher but the print is large enough that children can attend to it in incidental ways. Unlike home reading, however, teachers deliberately draw attention to the print and model early reading behaviors such as moving from left to right and word-by-word matching. Many texts used for shared reading in the early stages have a repeating refrain or rhyme to increase the enjoyment of reading them over and over.

Designed to be used with the whole class or a small group, this activity provides many opportunities for incidental learning about the way written language works. The context created by shared reading is totally supportive of young readers as they begin to attend to the details of print while still focusing on meaning and enjoyment. Shared reading:

■ Builds on previous experiences with books.

■ Provides language models.

■ Expands vocabulary.

■ Lays a foundation for guided and independent reading.

■ Supports children who are on the verge of reading so that they can enjoy participating in reading whole stories.

■ Provides an opportunity for the teacher to demonstrate phrased, fluent reading and to draw attention to critical concepts about print.

■ Provides a context for learning specific words and features of words.

■ Helps children become familiar with texts that they can use independently as resources for writing and reading.

Shared reading is highly complementary to the instructional goals of guided reading. It begins very early in the kindergarten year before children can read even a little. In shared reading, emerging readers get a chance to behave like readers and learn the process. After children begin participating in guided reading groups, however, shared reading does not stop. Many of the strategies needed for independent reading of a text can be taught during shared reading, especially when it is used with a small group rather than the whole class. For example, after several readings, when children are familiar with the text, the teacher can draw children's attention to various aspects of the text, such as letter-sound relationships, visual information, predicting and checking, or using illustrations. He can cover up a word with a stick-on note, for example, letting children predict the word and the first letter, and then uncover the word to confirm.

The approach can be varied by giving children small copies of the book and letting them follow along, reading their own copies. Books made through interactive writing can be reproduced in small sizes and photocopied so that everyone can take home a copy. Children can also do shared reading on their own (in small groups or with partners). Observation of children's use of reading strategies in one setting, shared or guided, informs the teaching decisions in the other.

Although there is some overlap, book selection is generally different for shared and guided reading. (Books introduced in both settings may be used for independent reading.) For shared reading, teachers can use a commercial big book, or a book, story map, or chart that the children have produced through interactive writing. Books children write in groups have many advantages. Children have attended closely to the print while producing the writing, and they have a strong feeling of ownership for the text. They go back again and again to the books they have made together.

The book selected should be one that children enjoy and will request again. Children's responses will indicate whether a particular book is a good choice. The print must be clearly seen by all children in the group, even those in the back. Some books may be appropriate for shared reading with a small group; others may have print that can be seen by a large group. Some books may have a refrain; the structure of repetitive texts helps children readily join in and supports their ability to use language pattern and syntax. Books with rhyme help children build an internal sense of the sounds of language.

A big book should have just a few lines of print on each page. For children just beginning to engage with print, one line on a page, with clearly defined spaces between words, is best. It is difficult for children to follow a text with many lines of print. The print should be clear and readable and there should be an easy-to-see but not exaggerated space between words.

Aside from the literacy learning involved, another value of shared reading is the role it can play in creating a community of readers who enjoy participating together in literacy events. Later on in school, shared reading becomes choral reading and readers theater. Over time the nature of the activity shifts and changes, but the shared experience still has much value.

Guided reading

Guided reading places the child in a more formal instructional reading situation. In kindergarten there is a smooth transition from shared to guided reading as children reveal that they are on the verge of reading. Teachers make the decision to move some children into guided reading by observing children's behaviors as they explore books independently and participate in shared reading. After hearing books read aloud, many children will begin to try to figure them out for themselves. Approximations come closer and closer to the actual text and they notice particular words or details of print. Shared reading demonstrates word-by-word matching, and children will begin to emulate this behavior as they read very simple books with natural language and only one or two lines of text per page.

In first grade, guided reading is a foundation of the literacy curriculum. To sustain forward progress, children need to take part in a guided reading group between three and five days per week in the early stages, reading a new book every time the group meets. Beginning books are relatively short (between eight and sixteen pages) so it is possible to build a large collection of books that children have read before, which can be placed in "browsing boxes" for independent reading. As children grow in their ability to read longer and more difficult texts, they may have to spend more than one day on a selection. There will also be shifts over time in the focus of guided reading. Throughout the grades guided reading takes on a variety of other purposes and forms: analyzing texts for character development and structure, comparing texts by theme, learning to read a variety of genres, or learning how to get information from texts.

Collections of books—leveled according to their support and challenge—are often shared by kindergarten and first- and second-grade teachers; collections may also be developed for intermediate teachers to share. Children do not read the same sequence of books; there are enough selections to meet the needs and interests of all. At all grade levels, teachers use dynamic, flexible, grouping rather than fixed reading groups.

Independent reading

Independent reading involves children not only in reading books but in using all the written materials in the classroom. A favorite activity is to "read the room," which means walking around with a pointer and reading everything that is displayed on the walls or on hanging charts. Poems, songs, pieces composed through interactive and shared writing, and big books are all grist for the mill.

Reading and rereading familiar texts has been shown to support young children's learning to read. Every child in every classroom, every day, deserves the chance to behave like and enjoy the pleasure of being a good reader. Achieving this goal requires us as teachers to be superb choosers of books for children and eventually to teach them to choose books for themselves. It also requires a large classroom library as well as well-stocked school libraries. Possibilities for independent reading are displayed in the chart shown in Figure 3–5, which is by no means exhaustive.

Further reading experiences

There are also other important structures or contexts that extend readers. Children need many opportunities to discuss books they have read or may not yet be able to read.

Literature circles. Literature circles are a means for more intensive talking or thinking about books, or "book talk." When children share their personal responses and interpretations of a book with one another, they are able to gain a deeper understanding of themselves and their world.

Book talks or literature circles can follow a read-aloud, as the children respond to story elements such as character, setting, plot, language, or illustrations. As partners, as a small group, or as a class, the children can make connections between one book and another, compare works by an author or illustrator, contrast versions of a story, or relate a story to their own lives. These same contemplations of a text can follow shared

Possibilities for Independent Reading

Location in Classroom

Variety of Texts to Read

Walls
- name chart
- nursery rhymes on large charts
- alphabet charts
- number charts
- songs (e.g., "Happy Birthday to You")
- labels or lists
- posters
- helpers chart and other management charts with names
- word wall
- interactive writing: story retellings, story maps with labels, alternative texts
- poster or poem charts
- pocket charts

Centers
- directions
- menus or recipes (restaurant or house corner)
- reference materials: encyclopedias, dictionaries, thesauruses
- informational books
- manuals
- reference charts, diagrams, maps

Classroom Library
- big books
- baskets of books sorted author, illustrator, theme, series, or other genres
- books arranged by level
- browsing boxes
- poem box
- class-published books
- paperbacks (novels)

FIGURE 3–5   Possibilities for independent reading

reading of a poem or story, listening to a story at the listening center, or guided reading of a book with many layers of meaning.

A common approach to literature circles is for partners or clusters of students to talk about their books. They may discuss the same title or different books they have read on a theme, by an author or illustrator, or of a particular genre. The teacher sets up a system for choosing books and schedules time for the students to meet. Partners or groups read their books, often noting parts they want to discuss, and gather to talk about them. This intensive, open-ended literature discussion provides the richness of literature experiences to all students regardless of current instructional reading level.

Reading workshop. The goal of any reading program is a child's ability to select, read independently, and think deeply about books. Reading workshop is similar to writing workshop: the teacher presents a short, focused lesson to support the effective use of reading strategies or to promote and broaden students' knowledge about books. Children generally choose their own books, confer with peers or the teacher, and share their reading with the group (there may be a designated reader's chair, for example). This structure is very powerful in developing readers who love books and who can choose, read, and discuss books in authentic ways.

Shared writing

For many years, language experience has been a useful technique in kindergarten and first-grade classrooms. Essentially, the teacher invites a child or group of children to compose aloud a written message. The message is usually related to some individual or group experience. The children talk and the teacher acts as scribe. The children are able to turn their ideas into written language, and the teacher can demonstrate the writing process. The stories are much richer than children can write themselves and are good material for children to read. Products

are usually displayed in the room as resources.

Interactive writing

Building on Holdaway's (1979) work in shared reading, Moira McKenzie, Warden of the Inner London Education Authority, created an approach that she called *shared writing* (now called *interactive writing*). The process drew from language experience but differed in several important ways. Instead of scribing verbatim exactly what children say, the teacher and children jointly compose a text, often modeling the structure of a piece of literature. For example, after hearing Bill Martin's *Brown Bear, Brown Bear* several times, a teacher and a group of children might create a text like: "White dog, white dog, what can you see?" The text is then written word by word, with the teacher demonstrating the process and the children participating in specific aspects of its construction.

1. Shared writing is especially useful in helping beginners make connections between oral and written language.

2. It involves more intensive attention to hearing the sounds in words and to spelling patterns.

3. It is one of the most powerful elements in the early literacy framework because the teacher is helping children develop the skills they need to become more proficient writers within a meaningful context.

Gradually, the teachers in the study groups we worked with began to involve children more, asking them to come up to the easel and fill in a letter or known word. Accordingly, they renamed the process *interactive writing* to denote the shared-pen characteristic.

First, the teacher and students work together to discover a reason for writing. Once the purpose is established, the teacher helps students gain control over the conventions of print that writers need in order to be able to communicate their messages in written language.

Sharing the pen begins in kindergarten with children filling in just a few letters, perhaps those that can be linked with the names of members of the class. They may also supply a few known words (*the* or *is*, for example). The technique gives teachers a chance to demonstrate saying words slowly and connecting the sounds that are embedded in words to the letters and clusters of letters that represent them.

Interactive writing provides an authentic setting within which the teacher can explicitly demonstrate how written language works. In kindergarten and first grade this approach eases the transition to literacy by engaging children in:

■ Cooperatively composing and negotiating a text.

■ Using literature as a basis for writing.

■ Constructing words through connecting letters (and clusters of letters) and sounds.

■ Learning how written language works.

■ Connecting writing and reading.

■ Producing a text that will serve as a continuing resource for reading and writing, particularly when children are working independently.

The subject of interactive writing may be anything—recounting a group experience; recording ideas from or about individuals; writing lists, letters, or messages; retelling stories; labeling; writing recipes; expanding on or developing a piece of literature; or creating a group story. The writing is based on the children's experiences, interests, strengths, and needs.

As children grow more knowledgeable about writing, teachers make different decisions about sharing the pen. For example, children who know the alphabet letters and many sounds will not need to link letters to their names but will be exploring more complex notions about the ways words work. There will be many words that all children know how to write quickly and automatically, so teachers will not take the time to share the pen in those instances but will write for the children. It is the teacher's responsibility to draw children's attention to elements of written language that challenge children and offer the examples that promote new learning.

There is no one way to conduct interactive writing, but the following procedures have proved effective with beginning writers:

1. The teacher and children negotiate a text, which the teacher helps the children remember as the writing proceeds. In the early stages of interactive writing, the negotiated message is repeated several times by the group. Additionally, it is reread from the beginning each time a new word is completed.

2. The teacher and children share the pen at various points in the writing. The message is written word by word, as the children reread up to the word for each new word attempted. Sometimes the teacher writes the word; often, different children contribute a letter, several letters, or a whole word.

3. Where appropriate, the teacher invites the children to say the word slowly (emphasizing but not segmenting sounds), predicting the letter by analyzing sounds. Children may come up with any letter in any order; the teacher fills in the rest.

4. Some words are known words that are written in quickly. Others are almost under control for most of the children in the class and can be called attention to as a "word we almost know." Still others can be analyzed later to help children learn how words work. Different kinds of words can be placed on a "word wall" to be used a resource for further learning.

5. As the teacher and children write the message, the teacher may help children

attend to important concepts about print such as spaces, punctuation, capitalization, or the features of a type of writing, such as a list or set of directions.

An important part of interactive writing is the way it makes visible to children how written language works. A neat, totally accurate product is not the goal, although the writing should be very readable, since it will be the basis of future shared or independent reading.

An interactive writing session will typically last from five to thirty minutes depending on the age, experience, and interests of the children involved as well as the purpose and topic.

Interactive writing can demonstrate the value of a continuing piece of work. Producing a piece of interactive writing may take days or even weeks. Conceptualizing, talking, and planning are part of the process. Not only do children like doing it over time, but they experience coming back to a project day after day, thinking about where they left off and where they will resume. An example is Ida Patacca's story map and retelling of the story of *The Three Little Pigs*. Ida read the Galdone version of the story many times to the children and they enjoyed joining in. Most children could approximate the text while "reading" it alone.

When they decided to make their wall mural, they first used interactive writing to list things they wanted to make and place on the map. Then, sentence by sentence, they created a text. Each word was written on individual cards and placed across the bottom of the mural to form a story of about ten lines, which would be read again and again as children chose to "read around the room." All children in the class could read the story, which had been reread many times during its construction, and they often used it as a resource for their own writing. The whole process took about three weeks and was the inspiration for other writing such as the

book about real pigs previously mentioned. At the end, children had a beautiful and constantly useful product of which they could feel proud.

The important thing, however, is the process. Many decisions are involved, and persistence and thought are required. Here is a timetable for a piece of interactive writing based on literature that might be used in kindergarten or first grade (other kinds of interactive writing may take much less time and follow different schedules):

■ *Days 1–4.* Read the selected piece of literature aloud each day.

■ *Day 5.* Read the selected text again. Negotiate the type of writing to be created (retell the story, create an alternative text, make a story map, etc.).

■ *Day 6.* Read the selected text again. Make a list related to the writing to be done.

■ *Day 7.* Read the text again. Write the first sentence on chart paper. Read the sentence together.

■ *Days 8–9.* Read a new story that is related to the interactive writing. Review the sentence written yesterday, and write several more sentences. Read together all sentences.

■ *Day 10.* Read a new story that is related to the interactive writing. Read together all sentences. Plan and begin art work.

■ *Days 11 & 12.* Read a new story. Complete art work and place in book (or on wall mural, etc.).

■ *Days 13 & 14.* Read a new story and begin to think about other kinds of interactive writing. Read together the previous book or wall mural created through interactive writing. Add details (such as labels or speech bubbles created by individual children). Read a "take home" book if the teacher has created one based on the interactive writing.

■ *Days 15 & 16*. Reread a selected story and begin to work on a new piece of interactive writing. Read together the previously completed piece of interactive writing. Encourage children to do independent writing based on the completed piece of interactive writing.

Interactive writing is a setting in which children become apprentices working alongside the more expert writer, the teacher. Everyone in the group gets a chance to contribute something, and everyone can see how it all fits together. Oral language is the foundation of the process. Children can participate in the complicated task of considering a range of language and ideas and shaping them into a piece of language that can be easily represented in written form.

It is very powerful for beginners to be able to put together skills to express a message. Even children who can read and write very little independently have a chance to participate in the process of making a book or other piece of functional writing. They can be authors and illustrators right away. By demonstrating and inviting children to participate, the teacher makes explicit the conventions of print—spacing, punctuation, organization of the page, beginning on the left.

Children can more easily see the purpose of these conventions because they are using them to produce their own text. Children begin to sense the relationships between the type of text being created and the form the writer selects. Often, the interactive writing is linked to other texts, giving children a chance to make meaningful connections between their own writing and other pieces of written language they have heard read or have produced themselves. Finally, interactive writing gives children a chance to create decontextualized language. The language they produce can be read and understood by others or, later, by themselves. They are assuming power over written language.

As children develop sophistication, interactive writing can still be used to illustrate more complex skills such as paragraphing. More accomplished writers explore different ways of structuring text for various genres. Teachers can illustrate the use of word analysis and teach spelling or complex forms of punctuation. Interactive writing can lead to group authorship. Group research projects, stories, and plays require interaction and cooperation.

Guided writing or writing workshop

Guided writing or writing workshop (Giacobbe 1981; Graves 1983; Atwell 1987) is another way for teachers to help children learn to write, but in this case the children are constructing their individual pieces of writing with teacher (and eventually peer) guidance, assistance, and feedback. The teacher may have individual conferences with children or call them together first for a minilesson on an aspect of writing from topic selection to composition to punctuation to letter formation.

To participate effectively in writers workshop, students need a simple, predictable structure that frees them to concentrate on their writing.

Minilessons (5–10 minutes). With students gathered on the carpet or in a circle of chairs, the teacher provides a short, focused lesson that provides assistance to the writers. These topics almost always emerge from what the teacher notices the students need to learn from observing their writing, conferring with them, and reviewing their writing folders. Topics for minilessons may be selected because they are fine examples of something writers do that will enable the students to develop their craft. When the minilesson is about something all writers need to do that day, the teacher may remind the students to attend to that particular topic in their own work. Mary Ellen Giacobbe, an expert in writing development, has categorized minilessons as *procedural*, *strategy/skill*, or *craft*.

A procedural lesson is a brief instruction on routines or materials that will enable writers to carry on independently. These minilessons are important early in the year because they show students how to manage their writing time. They might include such topics as organizing and using the writing folder, choosing paper and a cover, using the stapler, or conferring with a partner.

Strategy/skill lessons address the skills of a writer. These include saying words slowly and recording their sounds, leaving space between words, learning about word construction, and using capital letters for names or at the beginning of a sentence.

Craft lessons address what writers and illustrators do to communicate their message to readers. They include instruction on such topics as eliminating unnecessary information, adding information, providing detail, choosing a title, writing a good lead or ending, providing illustrations that enhance the story, and writing in a particular genre.

Writing and conferring time (30–40 minutes). During this time, all students are writing. One student may be composing, another revising by rereading and crossing out unnecessary information, another proofreading for spelling errors in a completed draft, another copying a story to make a published book. While students write, the teacher circulates, interacting with them in brief conferences or conversations that enable the writer to move the writing forward. For example, the teacher may first ask the student to read the piece, then tell the student what she understood or ask a question or two about something she didn't understand. Or the teacher may show a child how to say words slowly, write a simple frequently used word, or leave spaces between words. For a child who had trouble getting something down on paper, the teacher may simply listen to the child read what he has written. The teacher's focus is developing the writer, not simply improving the piece the child is writing.

Sharing session (10–15 minutes). The class gathers on the carpet or sits in a circle of chairs to share and support work in progress or to hear a writer read a finished piece. The teacher selects students to come to the author's chair, offering yet another opportunity for students to get response to their writing and to observe how to confer with peers. When a finished piece is being shared, no further suggestions are given, for the purpose is a celebration of the author's finished work.

The goal of writing workshop is continuous growth in the writers as they learn more about the writing process. They experiment with different styles, with editing and revising, with constructing both stories and informational pieces. They receive editorial feedback and guidance from the teacher and eventually from their peers. Teacher demonstration and articulation of the process of reading and writing is critical to children's understanding.

Independent writing

Independent writing is generated by the child and requires very little teacher support. Children have resources in the classroom, and they know how to use them. The walls are filled with writing that the children have produced and know how to read; pieces of art are annotated, and there are charts with familiar poems and songs. Particular words can be found in these known pieces. There are dictionaries, both personal and commercial. Younger children find the "word wall" particularly helpful. This wall is constantly being constructed and reconstructed by the group. Generally, it contains very useful words that children need to use in writing and also words that they have found to be alike in various ways (words that begin alike or have similar endings, for example).

Ideas for independent writing come out of the group sessions. Independent writing gives children an opportunity to write in various genres for various purposes across the curriculum: survey questions; letters to a friend; stories; informational pieces. Children may also have personal journals in which they write regularly. The literacy framework ensures that the teacher is constantly aware of the need for variety. Another way the teacher uses the framework is to help children see the relationship between what they are learning in interactive writing and how they encode messages in independent writing. Teachers show children how they can use their new learning independently and then observe to see whether the transfer takes place. Observing independent writing helps the teacher plan for guided writing minilessons and suggests teaching points to raise during interactive writing.

Classroom Snapshot: Use of the Language and Literacy Framework in Kindergarten

Kyeara is a typical kindergarten student in a culturally diverse urban school where 95 percent of the students receive free or reduced-price lunches. Ida Patacca is the teacher and for several years she has utilized the framework to conceptualize her teaching. The children in Ida's classroom spend their year together immersed in books and stories, first-hand experiences, and language. Every day they learn about how reading and writing works. By the time they leave this classroom, they are literate; they can read simple texts and write their own messages and stories.

Throughout their learning day, the children will engage in activities carefully designed and offered by their teacher to help them build and use their individual knowledge and strengths. Enabling children to use what they know to get to what they do not yet know is a basic principle of this education.

It is January in this kindergarten classroom. In the morning, children come in and begin their "reading time." Although a few students have chosen other projects, most are using the extensive classroom library. Kyeara and two of her friends, Sierra and Lindsay, read The Three Little Pigs together, laughing at the funny parts, knocking on the floor to represent the wolf, and saying to-

gether in fierce voices, "Little Pig, little pig, let me come in!" This could be called a "reenactment," for they are not matching print. However, their language is very close to the text. They have an internal sense of the syntax, the meaning, and the way the text is put together.

After the children spend some time in independent reading, Ida calls everyone together and selects a book to read aloud. While Ida reads The Three Little Pigs, she holds the book at the eye level of the children, who are seated close. As they listen, the children also discuss the story, making connections to other books and real life experiences. Without losing the momentum of the story, Ida judiciously pauses to give attention to children's observations and questions. Because this is the fifth time they have heard The Three Little Pigs read aloud, the children know the story so well they are able to ask in-depth questions. For example, one child points out the pig's *snout* and the concept—different kinds of *noses*—is discussed. This kind of attention to vocabulary would not be possible during the first reading.

Interactive writing

Often, children's literature is used as a base for interactive writing. Today, the children have decided that they want to retell The Three Little Pigs on a story map. After Ida suggests that they might want to make a list of what they will need to illustrate their map, the group agrees and children begin to suggest ideas. Kyeara says that they will need three houses, one of sticks.

This is one of the times when Ida helps children attend to the conventions of print. She asks the group to say the words slowly as they write them down. She finds this to be an extremely effective way of teaching sound/symbol relationships. By this time of the year, children are able to hear and record many sounds in words. They know that *pigs* begins with the letter *P* and ends with *S*. Figure 3–6 shows Kyeara reading the story map of The Three Little Pigs. Because she has had

FIGURE 3–6 Kyeara reading a story map

many experiences reading the first part of the map, she can read the story independently with ease.

At the beginning of the year, when children know less about sound/symbol relationships, one way that Ida helps them develop these relationships is by using a chart with everyone's name on it. She then links unknown words to known words—the names of students in the class. For example, had they been writing this list in the early part of the year, she would have linked the *P* in *pigs* to the *P* in *Patacca* saying, "Pigs, Patacca. Pigs starts just like Patacca, with a P." Now, later in the school year, the children don't need to refer to the chart for initial or final sounds, but they still notice things about their first and last names when analyzing more difficult parts of words. The

powerful demonstrations in interactive writing help children begin to write on their own.

Journal writing

Some mornings, Ida models the process of beginning a journal entry for her kindergarten students. She talks about and shows the supplies she needs. Then she says that first, she has to think of something to write: "If you are real quiet for a minute, I'll think of something I want to write." As the students look on, she demonstrates composing a sentence and beginning to write. She emphasizes thinking about the first word and saying the sentence out loud so that she can remember it.

Then, students begin to write for themselves. When Kyeara and her friends are writing in their journals, they can choose their own topics. Their teacher observes them closely to see who needs extra help. They write about what is happening in their daily lives and topics that are being studied in the classroom. Kyeara writes *I Like The house. I Like Miy MoM*. She draws a beautiful picture of her house, a rainbow, and the sun, which she labels *snu*. She reads it to Ida, who notices how she is saying the words slowly, really thinking about the sounds in *my*. Then, Ida works with her to say *sun* again and think about the last sound. Kyeara is well able to analyze words for the final consonant sound. She says words slowly, linking sounds and letters.

Moving to guided reading

On other mornings, Ida and her class read a few favorite poems that are printed on large chart paper. These poems are laminated for durability, and children often return to them during their independent reading time. After reading one particular poem, Kyeara locates the word *the*. Then Ida reads the big book *I Went Walking*. She has chosen this book in order to demonstrate checking the print with the illustration, but the children's attention was also drawn to other things in the text. For example, Kyeara notices that the punctuation was different on these two pages—one had a question mark and one a period. Ida and the children talk about statements and questions.

By January in kindergarten, Ida has begun to gather two or three children together for guided reading lessons. At that time she focuses on the particular instructional needs of that group of children. Today, guided reading for Kyeara is planned for the afternoon when children are working in the various centers in the room.

This classroom snapshot provides one example of literacy learning in a kindergarten in which the goal is providing every child with numerous opportunities organized around a flexible literacy framework.

Documentation of Progress

Assessment is an integral part of the framework. Chapter 6 outlines a variety of ways to assess and document children's reading behavior. The assessment system, however, encompasses the range of achievement across the curriculum. Teachers gather data that (1) track the progress of individual children and (2) assess the impact of instruction on the group. Marie Clay's *Observation Survey* (1993a) includes informative measurement instruments that when administered to individuals at systematically spaced intervals provide patterns of progress and also guide instruction. Running records are a powerful tool not only for assessing reading levels and matching children with texts but for analyzing reading behaviors for evidence of the development of independent reading strategies.

Home and Family Involvement

Home and family involvement enhances the work in the classroom and helps children use their literacy learning in different contexts. Teachers have found many ways to involve parents and family members in the life of the school, from visiting their homes to having parents work in the classroom to conducting workshops on children's learning. Three ideas that teachers in the literacy project have found helpful are described below.

Writing briefcase

The writing briefcase is a plastic carrying case that contains all kinds of writing materials—tablets, markers, pencils, crayons, loose paper, stapled books, note pads, envelopes, Post-its, scissors, etc. Many of these materials can be acquired free or at low cost. Children rotate taking the briefcase home, each time sharing what they produced at home when they bring the briefcase back to school the next day. Often, parents and siblings write notes or draw pictures for children to share. The briefcase has several positive outcomes. First, it helps children take their literacy learning into their homes and be recognized for their growing competence. Second, it helps parents give their children more opportunities to write and may suggest uses for printed material that might otherwise be thrown away. Finally, it communicates the value of writing to children and their families.

Keep Books

Inexpensive take-home books offer a way to expand children's opportunities to read at home. Teachers in the literacy project make sure that children have the chance to borrow books from the school—those for parents to read to them and those they can read themselves. It is widely known that school efforts are greatly enhanced when children have books in their homes. But because books are expensive and many parents don't know how to select and use them, it's difficult for many parents to provide home literacy. Children in lower economic areas, in particular, are at a disadvantage.

The Ohio State University staff has designed a home book program that simultaneously addresses the need for more books and creates positive communication with parents. These books do not take the place of the children's literature in the library, but they are an inexpensive way to increase the reading children do at home.

Keep Books are simple texts (although they will increase in complexity during first grade), inexpensively published, that sometimes have an interactive element. The books are simple, with black-and-white line drawings. Directions to children (and the front cover design) indicate that this is a different kind of book, one in which drawings can be colored with markers or crayons and in which their names (and sometimes some text) can be written. These books, in general, are intended to be read and reread by the children, although they are equally suitable for reading aloud by parents and siblings. Children are encouraged to put their names in these books and to keep them as a

collection. They fit in a shoe box, and teachers ask parents to make sure each child has a special place to keep her box of books.

The Keep Book program encompasses a wide range of books, including Spanish texts and books based on mathematical concepts, and a review process has been established to assess books for their text quality and potential for supporting beginning reading strategies. There is an accompanying teacher's guide provided with each book order and a videotape that may be ordered separately from Ohio State University. The guide provides step-by-step help for teachers in introducing and maintaining the program. Sample letters to parents are included, as well as a survey to assess the impact of books on the home. The videotape explains the purpose of Keep Books and shows their introduction and use; it is designed to be used at parent workshops. An initial order form is included in Appendix A. Additional order forms will be available as more books are developed.

Eventually we envision the collection including fifty preschool books, one hundred kindergarten books, and one hundred first-grade books. (Obviously, these can be used flexibly to fit different reading levels.) Presently, the books are available for $.25 per book. Thus, in the first three years of school a young child could conceivably read and own 250 books for an average per-year cost of about $20.00, just about the least expensive educational innovation we can think of.

Bookmaking workshops

Bookmaking workshops for parents are successful and popular. After only a few demonstrations, parents can easily write books for or with their children using plain sheets of paper and pictures from the Sunday paper or mail-order catalogs. These homemade books increase the variety of reading material for young children and create shared literacy for caregivers and children. They can be kept in the shoe box along with the Keep Books.

The Language and Literacy Framework

Development of the framework

We have organized this framework as eight major clusters of activity, all relying on oral language as a base and all focusing on building bridges between oral and written language. The components are not new; all have a long tradition and a research base. This particular organization grew out of our work with classroom teachers who had been involved in the Reading Recovery project in Columbus, Ohio. Reading Recovery was initiated in 1984 within a context that had fostered many years of informal collaboration between the university and the city school system. Reading Recovery training had a powerful impact on everyone involved in the project for several reasons:

1. Reading Recovery offered a convincing demonstration that even those children who appear to be struggling in classroom work could make accelerated progress and become good readers and writers with individual help of a particular kind.

2. The program confirmed the value of systematic and detailed observation as a basis of decision making.

3. The Reading Recovery procedures demonstrated the process of using a routine framework of activities within which observation and interactions could be tailored to the individual, enabling the teacher to work from the child's own knowledge base and strengths.

4. Reading Recovery lessons illustrated the powerful learning conversations that accompany reading and writing and are the heart of teaching.

5. Professionals involved in the program experienced colleague support during a long-term professional development program that involved observation, analysis, inquiry, demonstration, and self-reflection.

Beginning in 1987 and continuing to the present, study groups of Columbus area teachers and Ohio State University faculty met weekly to share and analyze their work. During the first years, professional development was mainly organized around sharing observations of children's behavior and products of their work. Teachers talked together to analyze and reflect on the process of teaching and they found observing each others' teaching to be productive. They also began to make use of videotaped examples of teaching. Ohio State University personnel worked in classrooms, teaching small groups and observing the process in order to continue the development of the framework. As they worked in first-grade classrooms, the need for an explicit focus on guided reading emerged and was confirmed. The framework was substantially revised, and selected videotaped examples were used as protocols for a training program. Since that time, Ohio State University's Literacy Collaborative has involved over five hundred additional schools in many different states. This initiative is further described in Chapter 15.

Using the language and literacy framework

The language and literacy framework is a conceptual tool for planning and organizing teaching. It includes four kinds of reading and four kinds of writing, connected through extensions and themes and applied through the teacher's observed evidence of children's progress. In using the framework, teachers consider a variety of factors:

■ The strength, needs, and experiences of the children they are teaching.
■ The nature of materials they have and can acquire.
■ The requirements of the curriculum.
■ Their own experience, background, and level of confidence.

The last factor—the teacher's own learning—is one of the most important. Each educator has to find his own point of entry to the framework. If teachers already use thematic teaching and a great deal of children's literature, they can immediately create a schedule that includes the four kinds of reading and writing. Usually, this would mean adding one or more elements and taking the time away from less productive activities. Teachers who are unfamiliar with using themes can start by selecting literature related to a theme and using interactive writing as an extension. Others might like to try each element separately before trying to implement everything at once. Adding any one of the literacy framework elements will increase instructional opportunities for children.

Each element is worth studying, trying with children, and reflecting on the results. Depth of understanding is more important than perfect implementation. The goal of such study is to increase the power of teaching and the literacy opportunities for children. The elements in the framework are flexible and are meant to provide opportunities to learn and teach. The quality and effectiveness of the interactions between teacher and children (and between children) within the framework are most important. It is not the elements themselves but

the teaching decisions within them that lead to new learning.

Suggestions for Professional Development

1. Form a study group of grade-level or primary-level colleagues to discuss the "balance" in your literacy program.

2. At each meeting, focus on one of the four kinds of reading or writing. Bring samples of work by your students and issues or questions you want to discuss. As preparation, everyone can read the same article or book that relates to that meeting's topic.

3. Bring a week's literacy plan or the record of a week's work in literacy. Discuss the different kinds of reading and writing as presented in the literacy framework.

- What elements received the most attention? The least attention?
- How can you eliminate or combine experiences to make your schedule more effective for the children?
- How did one element of the framework lead to another?

Designing and Organizing the Learning Environment

Getting students absorbed in meaningful, purposeful literacy activities requires a number of significant changes in the classroom—in the physical environment, in events and activities, and in the nature and quality of the interactions. NOEL JONES

A classroom organized for literacy learning invites children to use print in purposeful ways: wherever possible, written language—materials for reading and writing—are incorporated naturally and authentically. Individuals and groups of children are able to interact with the materials independently, regularly freeing the teacher to work with individuals or small groups. The setting is safe and supportive and enables all learners to develop confidence, take risks, learn to work independently, and develop social skills. In short, an organized and well-designed classroom enables the teacher to observe, support, and meet the learning needs of each child.

Underlying Theory

The classroom organized for literacy learning is built on the following theories about literacy:

I *All children can learn to read and write.* The teacher who expects all children to be able to learn provides many opportunities for literate behavior. Every day, every child in the classroom encounters materials that she can read and that are of interest.

I *Children learn about written language in an environment that is print rich.* The classroom organization makes it clear that print can be used in a variety of ways. Print is functional and informative, reflecting the rich diversity of language and literacy.

I *Learning is a social process.* Children learn by interacting with each other as partners and in small groups. The opportunity to talk with others while learning contributes to the rate and depth of understanding (Tharp & Gallimore 1988). The teacher observes and interacts with children, and children have space and convenient areas to work together in a small group or with a partner.

I *Learning is a constructive process.* Children learn to read and write through active engagement in authentic literacy. They learn to talk by talking, read by reading, and write by writing.

I *An organized environment supports the learning process.* Materials are readily at hand, and children know how to use them. The environment is truly supportive and moves children toward independence.

I *Powerful demonstrations are an important part of the learning process.* By observing their teacher and their peers, individual students develop resources on which they can draw.

■ *Children learn best when they are responsible for their own learning.* The classroom is organized for independence. The goal is for students to become self-managed learners who can take over the process for themselves.

Space

When the space and furniture are arranged with the activities of the classroom in mind, children can work more successfully and independently. Literacy-rich classrooms should have:

■ A large-group area for demonstrations and meetings that will develop a sense of community.

■ Areas for small-group, partner, and independent work.

■ Quiet areas separated from noisy areas.

Large-group area

Most teachers designate a large rug as the group meeting place. Some teachers prefer to make the meeting area central, with specific centers opening off it; others arrange a quiet corner of the classroom for the meeting area. Still others create a large classroom library that is also used for meetings.

In the large-group area, it is helpful to have at least two easels, one for group writing and one for shared reading of charts and books. There should be an organized supply area that includes everything needed for group writing and reading:

■ Pointers.
■ Magnetic letters organized on a cookie sheet or in a tackle box.
■ Markers of various colors.
■ Chart paper.
■ Scissors.
■ White correction tape.
■ Magnetic board and/or small white corkboard.
■ Sentence strips.

■ Masking tape or other tape.
■ Name chart of children in the classroom (for kindergarten and first grade).
■ Other writing resources—the ABC chart, word charts, etc.

Small-group areas

Bookshelves, tables, and other furniture can be used to create centers where materials can be stored and where groups of children can work together. Teachers usually prefer to group some desks to form a work table. It is not a good idea to create tall barriers in the classroom; tall bookshelves should be against the walls rather than in the middle of the room. Short dividers create a more open, un-cluttered look, and allow an unobstructed view. Divisions need only be suggested; for example, a cardboard back on a desk can create a space to work.

Dividers can do double duty by displaying instructions, examples of children's work, or reference materials. Some teachers use cardboard triangles, standing up, in the center of a group of four desks to designate a work center. Each surface of the triangle holds reference materials like word lists.

Small-group work areas should have enough space, materials, and chairs for the number of children who will typically be working there. Crowding makes it frustrating for children to work together productively. Whatever way the small-group areas are organized, it is important to have ample display space. Especially in kindergarten and first grade, children will want to "read the walls." Classroom display areas are resources. When walls are covered with bookshelves and static materials (such as helper charts or birthday charts) there is little room to display the rich array of print materials that children are producing and reading daily.

Independent work areas

For independent projects such as writing, children can work at a common table but each person needs sufficient space for his own materials. In addition, there should be some quiet places where individuals can work without distraction; a small study carrel can be created by circling three sides of a desk with cardboard that stands up eight to twelve inches. Again, this space provides more psychological than actual separation, and the divider can display resources for children to use.

Each child needs personal materials and a personal space such as a basket, bin, or cubbyhole. In addition, commonly used materials should be clearly labeled and accessible near the areas where children will be working independently.

Guided reading area

It is a good idea for there to be a particular space for guided reading, preferably in a quieter section of the room. The teacher can sit with the children in a semicircle on the floor or rug, or sit on a chair with the children in a semicircle of small chairs or stools or on the floor. Some teachers prefer to sit at a round or kidney-shaped table so they can observe all the readers. When there is no table and the teacher has a chair with rollers, she can quickly slide to any child in the group. Teachers who seat children at a table or in a semicircle like to move around behind children as they read to themselves.

Wherever guided reading takes place, teachers need to be able to scan the classroom as a whole so that they do not have to leave the group to identify children who need some help staying on task independently. There should also be a shelf or table nearby to store guided reading books, as well as some baskets of familiar books. The teachers' materials for this area include:

▌ A clipboard with running record forms.
▌ Sentence strips.
▌ Paper and writing materials.
▌ Student records.
▌ Markers or pencils.
▌ A whiteboard or easel with chart paper.

A print-rich classroom

From kindergarten through the grades, the classroom is filled with a variety of print resources. The level and type of material will vary, becoming more complex in second and third grade, but here is a general list:

▌ Big books in a range of genres.

▌ Leveled books for guided reading.

▌ Hardcover or paperback books for independent reading (includes "little" books for beginners and chapter books for older children).

▌ A range of quality children's literature for the teacher to read aloud and children to read independently.

▌ Charts of poems and songs.

▌ Labels and directions for materials.

▌ Informational books in study centers.

▌ Stories, messages, lists, and other written materials produced by children through interactive writing.

▌ A word wall, organized alphabetically, of frequently used words and other theme words that children can use as a resource (teacher and children create this wall together throughout the year).

▌ A name chart (first names for children beginning to read and more complex name-study charts for older children).

▌ Word charts that show different patterns of word study (phonograms, homographs, historical roots, usage, etc.).

▌ Published versions of children's independent writing for others to read.

▌ Alphabet charts and similar reference materials.

▌ Dictionaries.

▌ Children's personal collections of completed and in-progress stories and poems, all clearly labeled.

▌ Children's individual poem books for collecting and rereading.

■ Numerous pocket charts to hold a variety of print material (stories, lists, poems, etc.).

■ Magnetic surfaces for the manipulation of colored plastic letters.

■ A message board for a daily message to be read as children come into the classroom.

■ A sign-in sheet for children to use as they come in and later to use as a resource for spelling their friends' names.

■ Mailboxes for each child so that the teacher and members of the class can deliver messages.

■ A photo board (which can later become an album) that shows children in the class and pictures of their families or pets, with their names and sometimes a sentence about themselves.

If space permits, print should be at the children's eye level so they can "read around the room" and use reference materials easily. Teachers need to be especially critical of how they use display space. Sometimes "helper charts" or other management items take up so much room that there is little space to display group compositions created through interactive writing. Display space is a priority; management tools should be clear and easily seen but small enough so that children can point to and touch the items (see our work board in Chapter 5). A work board or other management item needn't be a permanent bulletin board. The work board can be on an eye-level easel or can lean against a wall; that way, it can be moved out of the way when not in use. Large display space is better used for a piece of well-loved writing that becomes shared reading the children go back to again and again. A good example is the retelling of *Goldilocks* shown in Figure 4–1. Children love to revisit and reread displays like this because they had so much fun making them.

Since much of the print on display surfaces will serve as reading material, the print should be in standard spelling. Children will use approximated spellings as they construct words in their journals and independent writing, and these may be displayed to honor children's work. Teachers can label these as "work in progress" to distinguish them from published work.

In the beginning months of kindergarten, the teacher will display children's art that includes some approximated spellings. These first attempts should be celebrated, but children should not be encouraged to read these pieces. Instead, their "reading around the room" should focus on the pieces of interactive writing they have produced together as well as on the charts and poems provided by the teacher. (For a description of interactive writing, see Chapter 3.) Later, children will be better able to produce standard spelling and to edit their pieces for publication.

Here are some criteria for displaying print that children will be expected to read:

■ The print is clear and legible, with well-formed letters. (When children are participating in the writing through the shared pen, the writing will not be entirely neat but will still be readable.)

■ There are clear spaces between words and also sufficient space between lines so that readers have no difficulty following each line of print.

■ For young children the displayed print is at eye level or at least reachable with a short pointer. (Older children will seldom be "reading the room" but they may be using the print in the room as a resource.)

Classroom library

The library is one of the most important areas of the classroom. An inviting classroom library resembles the best of public libraries, with a carpeted area and comfortable seating such as a soft chair, cushions, or a rocking chair, and many fresh-looking books of varying sizes displayed facefront across the tops of bookcases. (Plate stands are useful for this purpose.) There are places to browse, read

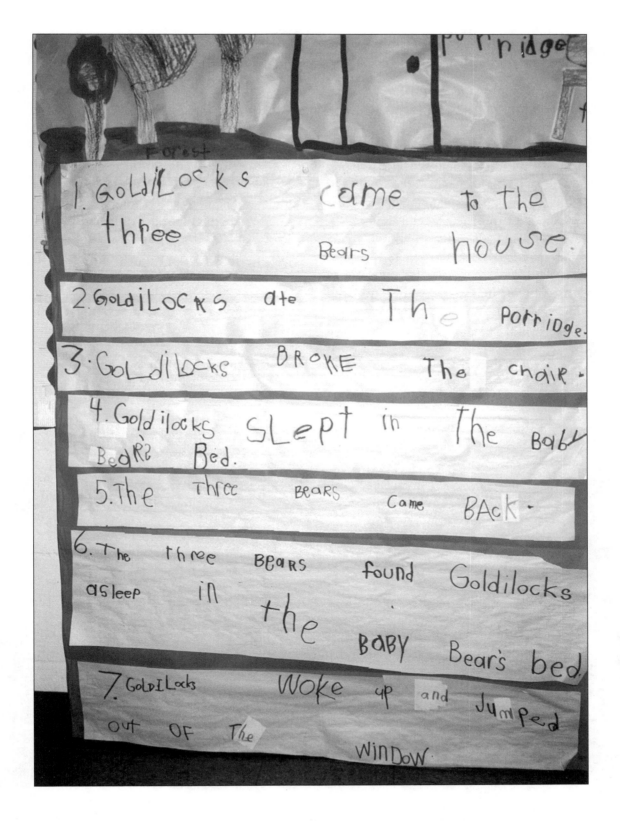

FIGURE 4–1   A retelling of *Goldilocks and the Three Bears*

on one's own, and share books with friends. Posters and charts are placed at young students' eye level.

Other books can be organized in colorful plastic baskets or tubs with clear labels (see Figure 4–2). Books can be arranged by author, illustrator, genre, series, theme, or topic. Genres should include wordless books, fairytales, fables, concept books, Mother Goose, alphabet books, number books, color books, and poetry. There should also be a variety of high-quality magazines for young children—*Ranger Rick, Cricket, Lady Bug,* or *Zoobooks.* Categories can be color-coded with dots or library tape so that even younger students can replace them correctly.

As time goes on, the children can help organize and label books. For example, when a new book is brought in, the teacher can ask children where it should go in the bas-

kets or in the library. New categories can be created during the year—a basket of dictionaries, riddles, math concept books, or student-published books, for example.

Independent reading is fostered by organizing "browsing boxes" or baskets of books that the students either have read in guided reading or are new books on the same level. There should be several browsing boxes at any one time as resources for guided reading groups; they may be identified by color or level. All students will have at least one of these collections that they visit every day for independent reading. Collections are added to and revised frequently.

It is important to add to the library collection each year and to include both hardback and paperback books. For a library to be attractive to children, many of the books should be fresh and new-looking—a dilemma

FIGURE 4–2   Book tubs in action

in these days of financial shortages. If teachers value the book collection and teach children to care for them, many of the books will keep their new look for a long time. Hardback books can be covered in clear plastic; this increases the book's life without detracting from its appeal. Parents or school volunteers can do some repairs to tattered and worn-out books, and children can then take them home.

If a classroom library has a large number of books, not all the books need to be on the shelves at one time. Consider beginning with a modest collection while children are learning how to use the library. With fewer books, students find it easier to learn the categories. All the books will be new to them at the beginning of school. Be selective, including those books that will be especially powerful for helping students learn how to use the library as well as those books that help introduce the curriculum. Later you can bring in new books a few at a time, giving short "book talks" as you add them to the collection. This will call attention to the books and prompt students to select them at independent reading time.

Centers

Primary classrooms often include a number of work centers. (We have not attempted an exhaustive description of every kind of learning center that can be used across the primary curriculum. See L. M. Morrow's 1988 article for more detailed information about classroom environments.) There may be some permanent centers, like writing and art, as well as centers that have a particular focus and change periodically—*caterpillars* or *trees*, for example. A center is a physical area set aside for specific learning purposes. The center has appropriate materials to enable children to explore and work independently (as individuals or with partners or small groups) and behave as active learners. Centers are task-oriented and there are clear expectations, but a center is not simply an "exercise," especially not a closed-ended

one. The best and most productive centers involve open-ended inquiry. For example, in a science center, children may check the growth of a plant, marking its progress and recording it in their journals. In art, they may produce parts of a mural. In a word study center, young children may make their names and as many of their friends' names as they can.

Centers work best when teachers are not under pressure to create new lessons or exercises each day. Centers have ongoing routines—that is, children know how to make use of the materials—and teachers are thus able to focus expectations in different ways. Chapter 5 describes a range of centers that particularly support the management of guided reading. Here are some general suggestions for making centers work:

1. As with every area of the classroom, the center and the materials in it should be organized and clearly labeled.

2. It is best not to have more centers than are needed and can be used within the course of a week. A center that sits idle most of the time is just taking up needed space.

3. Introduce centers one at a time, explicitly demonstrating and practicing the routines for using it with the children. A new center should not be introduced until the children fully understand how to use the one introduced before. Consider introducing or changing only one center each day.

4. Children need to know the specific tasks that are expected in the center for any given day or week.

5. Each center needs an adequate supply of necessary materials.

6. There should not be more supplies than needed.

7. Establish routines for participating in centers (for example, children may be assigned to centers on specific days or there may be a limit to the number of participants).

Storage for children's ongoing and completed work

Writing folders, portfolios, or any other records need to be stored. Children need space to keep work in progress as well as finished work that will be used to assess their progress. This problem can be solved in a variety of ways. Here are some suggestions:

■ Store daily writing folders for all members of the class in a labeled tub or a plastic or cardboard box.

■ Use a plastic crate with hanging files for finished writing work (and/or portfolios) for all members of the class.

■ Provide personal boxes for books children are reading, would like to read, or are using for reference.

■ Encourage each child to create a personal poem book over the course of the year, including photocopies of the poems that are used for shared reading or appear on charts; children can decorate and display their poem books, which can be stored in a labeled cardboard box.

■ Cut cereal boxes in half, cover them with contact paper, and have students store their journals, handwriting books, and other small items in them. These boxes can easily be placed in the center of work tables to designate the particular children who should work there.

Broader Use of Language and Literacy

All areas of the classroom can support literacy learning, even those that at first glance might not seem to be places for learning to read and write:

■ In the sand area, children can label their constructions; there might also be directions to read and utensils to put away in labeled areas. Books about sand and building can also be available.

■ The dress-up or drama corner can model household uses for literacy, like a note pad by the telephone. If this area becomes a doctor's office or restaurant, many more uses for literacy will be found (menus, charts, and books about food, for example). The literacy props will change according to the focus and purpose of the center.

■ A science center can focus on observation or categorization, with content that varies according to students' interests (magnets, a variety of objects that attract or repel them, and books about magnets, for example). There can be graph paper, blank paper, and pens for recording the results of experiments.

■ The art center is integrally related to literacy as children write about their creations and, alternatively, create visual images to illustrate their interactive writing, their own responses to reading, and their independent writing. Art is valued for its expressiveness, and we do not mean to imply that all art must be related to literacy; but there are many opportunities for a naturally occurring relationship.

In all of the above scenarios, children also use oral language in ways that support their thinking and develop new uses of language. Oral language supports literacy in a fundamental way.

Suggestions for Professional Development

1. The easiest time to design an organized environment is before the school year. If you have that luxury, you can make a floor diagram and gradually fill in each area. Discard or give away all nonessential materials and furniture so that you can create a clear, uncluttered space. Set up centers and view them with an eye for:
   ■ Ease of traffic flow.
   ■ Use of materials.
   ■ Display space.
   ■ Storage.

A Checklist for Analyzing the Classroom Environment

☐   1. Are there well-defined areas for large, small, and independent work?

☐   2. Is the classroom library inviting and well organized?

☐   3. Are books easy to find and return?

☐   4. Are there books integrated into the work centers?

☐   5. Are there numerous displays of written language at eye level—print for "reading around the room"?

☐   6. Are management tools such as a work board, helper's chart, or class rules located within easy view without usurping areas needed for "reading around the room"?

☐   7. Are pocket charts being used in several locations?

☐   8. Are all materials clearly labeled? Are there some simple, written directions where appropriate?

☐   9. Are there resources such as poems, charts, big books, and other print materials readily available for children to read?

☐ 10. Are all materials organized for easy access and return?

☐ 11. Are furniture and dividers arranged so that the teacher can have a full view of the classroom?

☐ 12. Is there a comfortable and well-supplied area for independent reading? writing?

☐ 13. Are noisy and quiet areas separated?

☐ 14. Are there neat, usable places to store, remove, and replace student work?

FIGURE 4–3   A checklist for analyzing the classroom environment

■ Essential materials rather than "overload."

2. Chances are, however, that you are reading this somewhere in the middle of the school year. Children in your class are already accustomed to one organizational pattern. You can still find a natural point at which to make some basic changes in organization and work gradually to reorganize the environment. The principles are the same; that is, with every change, children need the new routine to be taught and demonstrated. A new, tidily organized environment does not necessarily mean that children automatically know how to use it. Your classroom is a new setting in which the people who work there need to be initiated.

3. The best ways of operating are learned over time as teachers constantly reassess their learning environments and find new ways to work. Collegial support is invaluable. Ask one or two colleagues whether you can look at how they have set up their classroom, and invite them to look at yours. You are all bound to discover productive hints and suggestions. The checklist in Figure 4–3 may be helpful.

Managing the Classroom

The most lavishly appointed classroom may turn into a shambles if routines for using it

have not been established. NEW ZEALAND DEPARTMENT OF EDUCATION

When initiating guided reading, the first challenge for the teacher is to manage the classroom to be able to work in a focused, uninterrupted way with small clusters of students. A critical question is, While I am working with a group in guided reading, what are the rest of the children doing?

All other class members must be engaged in meaningful literacy. They must be able to function without teacher assistance, maintaining and managing their own learning. It will not be productive (or even efficient) for children to be doing busy work like coloring or fill-in-the-blank worksheets. Research does not support such activities, and too much learning time is lost when the management plan relies on them.

Granted the principle that all activities must be meaningful, productive, and usually related to literacy, here we will share some ways specific teachers manage their classroom for guided reading.

One second-grade teacher works with several small groups within the time the children undertake a series of tasks independently. First, they read a self-selected book silently. When they finish, they respond to the book in their reading journals and then share the journal entry with a friend. After

that, they add the title of their completed book to the record of books read. When that is finished, they select another text. This system works very well because the children are reading books that are interesting and appropriate for them. The teacher manages time carefully so that the activity does not go on too long.

At the beginning of the day, one first-grade teacher presents a list of tasks children are expected to accomplish. These tasks are not worksheets but established literacy routines that children know how to follow. For example, they might read several books from the browsing box, make a journal entry, and listen to a story in the listening center. When all assigned tasks are finished, children have a range of choices, including art, library corner, partner reading, or games. The way to make this system work is to be sure that the tasks are productive and that children know how to maintain themselves independently.

Another first-grade teacher has a large-print list of "Things to Do During Reading Time" (see Figure 5–1). Over time, she teaches children how to engage in each of the literacy activities on the list. Once they have a repertoire of activities they can engage in independently, she begins pulling

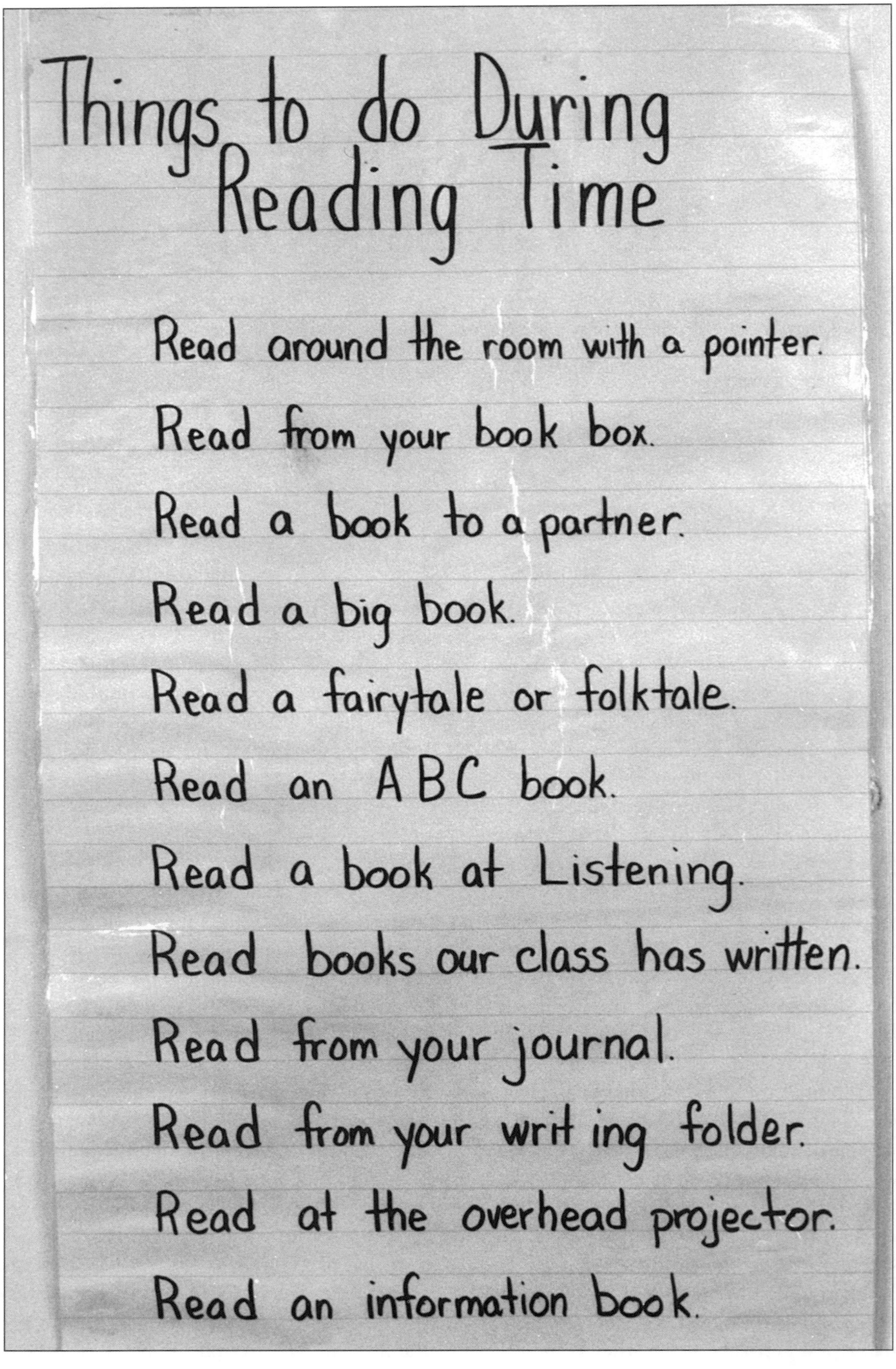

Things to do During Reading Time

Read around the room with a pointer.

Read from your book box.

Read a book to a partner.

Read a big book.

Read a fairytale or folktale.

Read an ABC book.

Read a book at Listening.

Read books our class has written.

Read from your journal.

Read from your writing folder.

Read at the overhead projector.

Read an information book.

FIGURE 5–1 Things to do during reading time

out groups of children for reading. Children not called for reading that day simply choose activities as long as reading time continues. If she wants to identify particular activities that are a priority for the day, she puts a red clothespin next to those tasks on the hanging chart.

One kindergarten teacher just getting started with guided reading lets children use the established work and play centers for a short time independently each day while she calls two groups for ten or fifteen minutes each. The centers include the full range of quieter activities like painting, clay, puzzles, writing, book corner, and magnetic letters. Since these activities have been well established from the beginning of the year, children are able to operate independently.

Using a Work Board

Many teachers use a work board to manage classroom activity. The work board is a large diagram that includes:

■ *Names of children in groups.* These are not ability groups or even guided reading groups but heterogeneous groups of children who have the same schedule of tasks for the day. These groups stay intact for a period of time, perhaps a month, before the composition changes.

■ *Names and pictures (icons) of routine tasks in the classroom.* These tasks usually involve literacy, though particular teachers may have a reason to include a greater range of activities.

■ *Flexible ways of rotating tasks and children's names on the board that provide variety and assure all children experience a range of literacy events.*

Making the work board
The work board may be made of heavy cardboard or some other strong material such as foam core or wood, or you can use a portable magnetic chalkboard or pocket chart. It is important for the work board to be at the children's eye level. The background of the board should be a plain color, the cards designating the group names and the activities a contrasting color—that way they'll be clearly visible.

Using icons
Icons are simple and designed so that the children will quickly recognize the activity being suggested. (We have included some sample reproducible icons in Appendix B.) While teachers are working with small groups in guided reading lessons, most of the independent activities will be directly related to reading and writing. We have, however, included some additional icons for teachers who wish to involve children in a wider range of activities (sand table, math, and science, for example). You may want to copy these icons on tagboard or other heavy paper and color them. You can also modify them to meet your needs or create your own. Effective icons:

■ Are large and simple.
■ Are clear rather than cluttered.
■ Indicate only one possible activity.
■ Are used consistently for the entire year.

The icons and the children's names can be mounted on cards that have Velcro or magnetic tape on the back, so they can be moved around the board. (Magnetic tape will stick to most chalkboards.) Rectangular business card–sized magnetic pieces (available at office supply stores) also work very well. A pocket chart provides equal flexibility for moving icons and names.

Organizing the work board
One way to structure the work board is illustrated in Figure 5–2. The group names are written on index cards placed in clear plastic pockets at the top of the board. The group name card can easily be rotated one place to the right each day, giving the group of children a new set of activities. It is also easy to make a new index card when the makeup of the group changes. We wish to emphasize that the groups are heterogeneous

FIGURE 5–2   A typical work board

work groups, not groups organized for guided reading.

The icons are changed each week to provide new sets of activities. On this work board, children use the browsing boxes for independent reading every day but other activities vary. Choices may reflect quite a wide range of activities, of which two or three are selected each week. If choice involves some special project, like doing something for Earth Day, the teacher can make a temporary icon.

An alternative version of the work board uses clothespins on which the children's names have been printed. The clothespins are easily clipped together into new work groups at the top of the board.

Using the work board

The work board is located at a central place in the room, usually where you have group meetings or read aloud. Place the chart at eye level so that children can refer to it easily, finding their names and tasks. They will also need to be able to see it from most areas of the room, so that they can quickly refer to it. Children find their names and follow the routine listed for their group. They complete the first task, then look below to find the next task. They make their way through the list until work time is over.

While the children are working, the teacher meets with guided reading groups. A child leaves his assigned work task, goes to his guided reading lesson, and then returns to the same center he left. Having the children accomplish the tasks in order helps manage the traffic flow.

How long do children stay in each activity?

When the teacher is teaching the routine to the children, he helps them understand about how long they should stay there. For example, using the browsing boxes means reading several books; using the listening center might mean listening to one story. For other centers, the time might be defined by the task. It is important that these routines be thoroughly taught and observed before the groups are left to work independently.

Do children have to move through the activities on a signal?

No, they move as individuals, because the time needed to complete each task varies.

What happens if there is no room in the center?

Children learn that there are limits to the number of children who can be in each area. If your classroom has a large number of children, you may need to paste a dot indicating the number limit on each icon. It helps if some centers, such as the art area, can accommodate more children than are normally in a work group. If one center is full, a child may move on to the next activity and return to the previous one later.

Will it take a great deal of teacher time to prepare each of these activities every day?

These activities require very little planning. The basic materials are there, and children know the routines. The teacher may add poems to the poem box, change the story at the listening center once a week, add more books to the browsing boxes, design a new but simple task for the ABC center, etc.; also, writing and art center activities are usually related to books the teacher has read aloud or extensions of guided reading or interactive writing.

These simple changes, which do not essentially alter the activity signaled by the icon, provide variety but take only a few minutes of teacher planning per week. And activities for some icons require no teacher preparation at all—"reading around the room" (a natural extension of the display of interactive writing) and independent reading.

What if the children do not finish all of the activities listed for their work group?

If they have been working hard, they simply do as much as they can during the specified time. They will have several other opportunities during the week to participate in an activity if they don't get to it on a given day. You may want to be sure that children are spending appropriate amounts of time on each task and not wasting their time. If individual children are managing their time in unbalanced ways (for example, spending all morning at the computer and not giving others a turn), you will need to remind them how they are to use their time in centers. Reteach the routines as often as necessary.

Why are there only four columns of icons when there are five days in a week?

Four columns seem to be enough, if the groups are of manageable size. Just keep rotating the children's names, moving from the fourth column back to column one. An alternative is to construct a five-column work board, allowing one column for each day.

Icons as Signals for Literacy Activities

Browsing boxes (Icon 1 in Appendix B)

In addition to the wide selection of books in the classroom library, there is a box of specially selected books for each guided reading group. These are usually cardboard boxes covered with contact paper, but you can also use plastic baskets, pots, or bins. The boxes hold about fifteen to twenty small books (and there should be several copies of most titles). Usually, the box is identified by color so that the teacher can direct children in each guided reading group to the appropriate box. The box contains several books that children have previously read in their guided reading group. In addition, the teacher places other easy books in the box that she is confident the children can read independently. During this activity, children go to a reading area and read and reread books from their assigned box. Because each group has its own box, several groups can work with the browsing boxes simultaneously.

ABC (Icon 2 in Appendix B)

The ABC center (for letter and word study) is organized on a table or in a corner of the classroom. Each week the teacher places letter or word activities in the center. Children may be asked to complete two or three assigned activities—for example, making their names in magnetic letters (for beginners) or playing around with word endings (for more sophisticated users of print). Word study activities are further described in Chapter 13 and in Pinnell and Fountas, 1998.

Listening center (Icon 3 in Appendix B)

The listening center contains a variety of stories on tape. Children can listen to stories using headphones if available; however, headphones are not necessary. Children can play a tape quietly and follow along in a copy of the book. Children also love to listen to tapes of their own shared reading sessions as they follow along on a photocopy of the text. It is not necessary to buy commercial tapes. You can ask parents and other volunteers to read stories into the tape recorder, building up a large collection at little cost. We also recommend asking well-known local celebrities (sports figures or newscasters) or the school principal, custodian, secretary, and music teacher to read books on tape. Children like to listen to someone they know or have seen on television, and it also helps them realize the wide range of people involved in reading.

The listening center should have labeled tapes and multiple copies of books organized in boxes or plastic bags. It makes sense to place the listening center at a distance from the guided reading area because children will undoubtedly do more than listen; they will join in enthusiastically.

There may be an extension activity of some kind that accompanies the book that children hear on tape. For example, they may be directed to draw a picture of their favorite part or compare the story to a similar one they have read. If you use an extension, select a story or stories for the week rather than let children choose from the entire collection; place the written directions in the center of the table or display them on the center divider.

Art center (Icon 4 in Appendix B)

The art center provides a place and materials for a variety of activities, including painting, drawing, collage, plasticine clay or play dough, etc. Often, art projects involve a response to the stories or poems introduced in read-aloud, shared, or guided reading sessions.

Writing center (Icon 5 in Appendix B)

The writing center is a clearly defined space that provides a range of writing materials and a place where the children's own journals are stored. The writing center may include small blank books, various kinds of paper, pencils, markers, scissors, stapler and staple remover, glue, and date stamp. Materials may be organized in trays in the middle of a large table or on nearby labeled shelves. Everything should be labeled and have a specified place to which it must be returned at the end of each use. Children write in response to any kind of reading in which they have been engaged; they also write about their own experiences and about what is going on in the classroom. Children may retell stories or write their own versions of stories. Writing for different purposes is essential because we want children to produce many different types of writing. For example, within several weeks a child might write:

■ Stories.
■ A letter.
■ A list of things to do or things to buy.
■ A set of directions.
■ Labels for pictures.
■ A poster.
■ Labels and a legend for a map.
■ A record of scientific observations.
■ A math survey.

The name chart, an alphabet chart, and the word wall should be visible from the writing area if possible. The writing area may also contain dictionaries and other resource materials.

Reading around the room
(Icon 6 in Appendix B)

As one activity, children may read all of the print displayed in the room. Baskets of pointers should be available near the material to be read. Teachers have found it effective to use chopsticks or rulers; however, the best pointers are dowel rods because they can be cut into different lengths. Shorter and longer pointers can be used based on the distance from the eye to the print on the walls. Sometimes teachers paint the dowel tip with brightly colored or fluorescent paint, or glue a small pom-pom on the end, in order to draw the young child's eye to the print and make it easy to read along. You can also purchase collapsible aluminum pointers at office supply stores. Some of these pointers even have "lighted" tips.

Every rich literacy classroom is "loaded" with print that is meaningful to children. Children can read their own group-written versions of favorite stories or their own variations on texts and poems. Young children enjoy reading the alphabet charts, word wall, lists, and the name chart. Even children who can read very little can read around the room when their own names as well as the number and alphabet charts are displayed. One may argue that the activity is not "real reading," but they are getting a feel for reading while pointing and matching. Appendix C may be enlarged to make a poster-size alphabet chart suitable for reading around the room. You can also build sentences and stories in pocket charts to introduce more variety.

Independent reading
(Icon 7 in Appendix B)

The goal of all classroom reading is to develop readers who select and read books independently. This icon signals time for free-choice silent reading from the classroom library. Kindergarten and first-grade children will not be silent but will be reading softly to themselves or their friends and will often be approximating texts that teachers read to them. During independent reading, children may also choose to read big books that they have encountered in shared reading. The most popular big books are those that children have made themselves through interactive writing. As children become more proficient as readers, teachers often require them to keep a list of books they've read independently.

Drama (Icon 8 in Appendix B)

Drama is a highly productive language activity and can include manipulating puppets, reading plays, and role-playing a story with some suggested costuming (masks, hats, or simple props). Drama can take place in the house corner or any area that can be transformed into a restaurant, hospital, doctor's office, or pet shop. Each focus will have built-in literacy opportunities. Supplies might include note pads, clipboards, paper, pencils, magazines (for the "waiting room"), menus, appointment and phone books, recipe boxes, price lists and labels, books, and empty food boxes or other storage containers that can be labeled.

The poem box (Icon 9 in Appendix B)

The class poem box is a collection of poems that the children have heard the teacher read or have learned to read during shared reading time.

You can also photocopy poems the children can read and let each child create his or her own personal book of poems during the year. Gluing photocopies in a notebook with the child's illustrations is an easy way to go about it. Children like to reread their own poetry books and to take them home.

The poems may be presented in a variety of ways:

- Large-print poems to read with a pointer.
- Poetry cards mounted on tagboard or other stiff material.
- Small books of poems.
- A class book of poems.
- Individual copies of poem books.
- Jig-saw poems for children to put together and read.
- Copies of poems to read and illustrate

Computer (Icon 10 in Appendix B)

Computers are available in many classrooms, either permanently or on a rotating sched-ule. The computer provides another way for children to use literacy. Commercially available word processing and book publishing software is readily available. Children can use the computer to:

- Write their own stories.
- Send electronic mail to each other and to other places.
- Interpret and expand on texts.
- Play games that require the use of language and literacy.

Overhead projector (Icon 11 in Appendix B)

The overhead projector is a little recognized but very useful activity center. When placed on the floor or mounted securely on a low box in front of a white paper screen, the overhead projector is a safe and flexible tool. The teacher can reproduce poems and short stories—including some written by children in the class—on plastic transparencies (stored in sheet protectors) and children can project and read them. One child can point to the words on the transparency while others read. Plastic letters can also be moved around on the overhead to make words come alive on the wall.

Buddy reading (Icon 12 in Appendix B)

Reading with a partner is a favorite activity for young children. You may introduce several options for buddy reading, demonstrating and practicing each one:

- Partners who each have a copy of the same book can read it to each other, one at a time.

- Partners who each have a different book can take turns reading the whole book while the partner looks at the pictures. It is important to teach children to hold the book so that both can see all of the time.

- Partners who each have a copy of the same book can read it together, switching back and forth on alternate pages.

- Partners may read a book in unison.

Many teachers bring in older children to buddy-read with younger ones. It is difficult to schedule this if buddy reading is an ongoing part of the morning rotation system; a ten-minute period at the end of the morning or in the afternoon works better in mixing age groups. Buddy reading can also use volunteers who are in the classroom on any given day.

If a child cannot find a partner, she can read her selection into a tape recorder and play it back. A stuffed animal can also become a partner. The best partner, though, is a classmate who provides encouragement and feedback.

Many teachers have been successful in teaching children to listen without jumping in and correcting each other. In partner reading, young children who have been intensively involved in guided reading begin to use some of the ways of listening that are common to teachers. Even young children are capable of showing respect for and praising each other's efforts.

Games (Icon 13 in Appendix B)

Games are an asset to the classroom. Many word and alphabet games are available from commercial publishers. You can also make simple games of your own that give children many opportunities to play with letters and words.

Reading journals (Icon 14 in Appendix B)

Each child may have his own small notebook in which he records titles of books he has read independently as well as his own responses to books. Record keeping and reflecting in writing are particularly important as children learn more about reading. For younger children, the record itself is impressive. It maps the journey they have taken. For older children, it is a link to writing and helps them become more aware of their own learning. The journal can be a combination of writing and drawing. Part of the routine for reading journals can be sharing with others or writing about what has been read in preparation for literature circles. The journal

is also a way to share reading progress with parents.

Literature circles (Icon 15 in Appendix B)

After children have read a book independently, they sign up for a literature circle. When the required number of students have signed up (usually three to five), the children gather on the rug with their books and talk about them. You can give a particular focus to their discussion (tell about the most interesting character or share your favorite part), or the discussion can be open-ended. Early on, the children tend to retell the story, but you can show them how to discuss different aspects of the book, how to make personal connections, and how to compare books. The goal is for children to talk more meaningfully about and dig more deeply into their books because of others' comments and questions.

Pocket chart (Icon 16 in Appendix B)

There are many ways to use pocket charts. One is to have a pile of sentence strips and individual words in a basket by the chart. Children can reconstruct favorite stories (or retellings of stories), poems, and songs on the chart and then read them—perhaps to a partner while using a pointer. They can insert their own names in familiar poems or in simple messages:

> Maya likes blue.
> Jerrold likes green.
> Taisha likes purple.

In kindergarten, work at the pocket chart can include rebuses (pictures) as well as words. As children become more familiar with words and text, they can construct stories in pocket charts.

Other centers

There are many different ways to select and establish centers that are useful within the school curriculum. The centers described above combine oral and written language and are appropriate for use within a focused language arts block. In classrooms using an integrated curriculum, however, teachers may want to encompass a broader view of learning. There is much language and literacy use in centers such as Building, Science, Sand Table, and Math, so we have also provided sample icons (17 to 20 in Appendix B) for them as well.

These centers require a wide range of manipulatives and artifacts specific to the discipline. Children can use learning logs, books on particular topics or concepts, and references as part of the materials in the center. A science center, for example, can include plants, magnifying glasses, a microscope, books about plants, a class observation log, a poem on the wall, diagrams of parts of the plant, graph paper for recording plant growth, and other items. Children can have specific tasks to perform in the center or be allowed open-ended exploration. Many primary classrooms involve children in cooking activities, which have enormous potential for learning about science, math, and literacy. Cooking needs adult supervision to be productive and safe; therefore, although it is rich in learning opportunities, it is probably not an appropriate independent work activity.

Choice (Icon 21 in Appendix B)

The star prompts the child to select one of the "choices" listed in a special section on the work board. The teacher usually changes these choices each week. All choices are activities that children have previously learned to engage in independently. Two or three choices are usually enough variety. Choices may grow out of themes that extend language and literacy across the curriculum. They often foster oral language development; for example, children working together to make illustrations for their own big book about snakes will discuss attributes of snakes such as size, length, and color. Most extensions like this will have been introduced in large-group or guided reading sessions.

Teaching Routines

Once the beginnings of an organized environment are in place, it is easy to teach children to use materials and activities in a systematic way. Every moment invested in teaching routines is time well spent, because it will save hours of instructional time later. There are two ways to think about teaching routines: (1) presenting a "big picture" of the entire year and (2) teaching specific tasks.

Presenting the big picture

At the beginning of the year, you will not want to use all centers and work areas immediately. You will need to introduce children to the classroom, gradually establishing ways of working there (see Figure 5–3). The important thing is to define clear expectations and be sure that children are comfortable with the routines before leaving them on their own.

Begin the year with large-group experiences that will establish the group as a learning community and build linguistic resources. During the first two weeks, the teacher and children can produce a great deal of the print that is needed on the walls. The teacher has already displayed songs, poems, big books, and other materials. It is necessary to enjoy these print materials with children many times so that they become familiar resources. In addition, interactive writing composed by the whole class is a source of printed materials that children can call their own (see Chapter 3).

Materials and work areas can be introduced one at a time so that children understand the operating procedures for using them. For example, in the classroom library, show children how to take out books and how to use them on the rug or at the table. For some groups, you may even want to show them how to turn the pages carefully so that books are not damaged and others can use them. You may want to show them how to share books with a partner so that both can see the pictures. Then, show them how to put away each book in its place. Be sure to notice and praise children's efforts.

The First Six Weeks:
Getting Started with Guided Reading, a Grade-One Example

Suggestions for Working with Children	Suggestions for Materials
Week 1–2 <ul><li>Use mostly whole-group activities—reading aloud, shared reading, and interactive writing.</li><li>Consider whole-class art projects that bring children together; give them a product that they can take home and that can lead to writing.</li><li>Show children the various parts of the room (such as the book corner) and demonstrate how to work in them.</li><li>Practice using the parts of the room; give explicit directions and observe progress.</li><li>Build up a collection of interactive writing that will fill the walls with print and be used as a resource the next week.</li><li>Read aloud often, introducing a core of books that are strong foundations for interactive writing and that children will revisit during the reading time.</li><li>Introduce independent reading time by demonstrating how to take out books, use them, and put them away.</li><li>Work with children's names.</li><li>Give children praise and encouragement for using materials in the room.</li></ul>	<ul><li>Have only basic materials very well organized.</li><li>Be sure there is an uncrowded place for whole-group work. (A rug is good.)</li><li>Have a large amount of print on the walls and use all of it in shared reading. (Rhymes and songs are good.)</li><li>Pre-select a collection of read-aloud books that are particularly appealing.</li><li>Have children's names up in every part of the room. (Name chart, helper chart, stories about them, name cards in the pocket chart, envelopes with their cut-up first names in them to put together, etc.)</li></ul>
Week 3–4 <ul><li>Open new areas one at a time; for example, the writing and art center if not already used. Provide explicit demonstrations each time. Show how to use materials and how to put materials away when finished.</li><li>Begin to have children work in smaller groups in the centers that are being used. Observe the process, praising them for self-management.</li><li>Begin to meet with individuals for assessment when children are working independently in centers.</li><li>Continue reading aloud and using interactive writing to establish the learning community and build up written language resources.</li><li>Teach children to use alphabet charts, the name chart, and a beginning word wall as a resource in their own writing.</li></ul>	<ul><li>Each time a new center opens, have materials organized in a standard way with materials labeled and a place for everything.</li><li>Create an assessment table for yourself with your own materials ready so that you can observe the whole class at once while working for a few minutes with an individual.</li><li>Designate a place and begin a simple word wall with children.</li></ul>

FIGURE 5–3   The first six weeks: getting started with guided reading, a grade-one example

Suggestions for Working with Children	Suggestions for Materials
Week 4–5 • Establish the routine of working in small groups in centers for a period of time—perhaps as much as one hour in the morning. • Emphasize independence during group work so you can work uninterrupted with one or two children. • Introduce the work board and help children follow it. Use only two or three activities at first. Circulate around the classroom to be sure that children understand the routines. • Use group time for individual assessment so that groups can be formed by week 6. Taking two or three running records per day will enable you to complete all children in two weeks. Other observation measures can be used at teacher discretion. • Teach children how to care for and keep some of their own records—putting away journals, etc.	• Introduce new materials gradually. • Display the products of group work so that print can be read. • Establish places for children's own materials and their individual records to be kept—for example, their journals and poem books.
Week 6 • Begin working with two small guided reading groups, at first for only fifteen or twenty minutes each. • Continue whole-group activities. • Introduce browsing boxes and observe children as they use them.	• Have a place for guided reading with all materials available. • Set up browsing boxes for each group from the beginning.

FIGURE 5–3 *continued*

In the listening center, teach children that there are five (or however many) chairs and that therefore only five people can work there. Show how to insert a tape, turn on the recorder, and use the earphones. Show specifically the level at which the volume should be set. (You may want to mark the machine at the appropriate place.) Demonstrate that it is easy to talk too loud when you have the earphones on, so listeners must be careful to use soft voices or whisper if they read or sing along. Have several children demonstrate and then have everyone practice. Show children where written directions will be when there is an activity to be completed after listening to a tape. You will probably have to read the directions to children in the beginning, so the activity should not change more than once each week early in the year. After that, children can read these directions to each other.

In demonstrating how to use a new area or type of material, it may help to follow this sequence:

1. Talk about and demonstrate it yourself.

2. Have one or two children demonstrate, and applaud their efforts (if necessary, have other children demonstrate as well).

3. If everyone can use the center at once, invite the class to participate and observe them, praising their efforts. If only a few children can use the area, keep an eye on it the first time it is used. Keep encouraging and praising children's self-managed behavior.

4. Observe the center until you are comfortable that children are habitually using the area independently and are being considerate of others and of the materials. This may take only one morning with some areas and a few days with others, depending on their complexity.

Initiating new tasks

After the basic areas of the room are established with working procedures, you will periodically want to add new tasks. As children grow in competence, they can expand their repertoire of independent activities. Eventually, this process leads to wide choice. In fact, toward the end of the year, children can be asked to select all of their own activities during a morning while you work with guided reading groups or supervise special projects. Once children understand the idea of learning centers and routines, they are easier to establish. While demonstrations will take some time at first, later in the year only a few suggestions may be needed. In a school where several teachers have been working together on management and guided reading, many children will come into the classroom at the beginning of the year already knowing how to use centers and how to follow a work board.

Introducing a new activity by teaching it well has productive value for the rest of the year. First-grade teacher Gloria introduced reading around the room this way: First, she made sure that a large amount of print was on the walls. She and the children had produced story maps, story retellings, lists of ingredients for recipes, alternative stories, directions, and class rules. She had displayed alphabet charts and charts of children's names, poems, and songs. At the beginning of the session, she demonstrated reading around the room herself. This was not difficult, because she and the children had been doing shared reading for several weeks. They knew how to point precisely under the words, moving left to right. Gloria showed them how to move from one part of the room to another. Almost anything could be read. Then, she gave several children chopsticks and invited them to demonstrate. That demonstration took only a minute or two before Gloria gave all children in the room chopsticks and allowed them to begin reading. She observed, helping and suggesting where necessary. Even children who could read very little used their own names, the alphabet charts, and number charts, and followed others' reading of more complex lines of print. From that time on, children were able to respond to the icon for reading around the room.

Making transitions

After children know how to engage in each activity, you may still need to teach them how to make the transition from one activity to another. Teach children to put away materials from one task, check the work board, and move to the new area. Talk about what to do if an area is full and how they can use their time.

Children need to develop an inner sense of how long to stay in each center, when a task is completed, and when it is time to move on, a self-regulating mechanism that will serve the individual well throughout school and life. You are teaching more than literacy. You are helping children understand how to conduct themselves as members of cooperative groups. They are learning how to fulfill commitments, manage time, manage tasks without constant reminders and supervision, conserve materials, collaborate with others, and respect others' rights.

Helping each other become independent

Establishing routines early in the year not only makes it easier to manage the classroom and work with small groups, it makes mobility less of a problem. Teaching new classmates how to use centers is a way for the students to make routines and operating procedures explicit to themselves.

Children also help each other complete daily tasks. Work groups should be heterogeneous, which means that there will be some children in each group who are more experienced and advanced in reading. They can help others with tasks that require reading. Others may share experiences they have had at home. The extent to which group members assist each other should be part of their self-evaluation.

Using the rotation system

The work board guides children through a series of tasks during guided reading time. Ideally, children should participate in a guided reading lesson every day; however, class schedules or size may make this impossible. The rotation schedule in Figure 5–4 assures that every child experiences guided reading a minimum of five times in every two-week period and that ongoing assessment takes place. (A blank copy of a similar form is provided in Appendix D; it may help you get started.)

Figure 5–4 shows the experiences one group of second graders had over a two-week period (it does not include choice or other centers). Members of each group used browsing boxes every day the first week to make sure they experienced easy, familiar reading that still offered some challenge. (Some children were reading early chapter books and more complicated pieces of children's literature.)

The first column shows the teacher's work with four guided reading groups. (Just to recap: members of guided reading groups are similar in their development of a reading process and can read about the same level of text successfully. When the teacher is ready to work with a group, she calls the children to the table or reading area. No matter what children are doing at the time, they are expected to join their group.) This teacher was just beginning to establish guided reading. Since these second graders were reading longer texts, she began by meeting with two groups each morning, ending each session by taking a running record and doing a bit of individual teaching as necessary. The first two groups had guided reading three times the first week, the remaining two groups had it three times the second week. Later on, if the teacher meets with three groups per day, the children will have six to seven lessons every two weeks.

Managing guided reading within a morning of literacy learning

Although guided reading may take place any time during the day, most teachers do it in the morning, because they prefer a large block of uninterrupted time—at least one hour (ninety minutes or two hours is even better). There are many ways to situate guided reading within the ongoing activities of a class.

In the sample management plan in Figure 5–5, the children start their independent reading as soon as they come into the room in the morning, selecting books from the classroom library. The teacher can talk with individuals and take attendance and lunch count during this time. Then the teacher assembles the group for a whole-class activity—reading a "morning message," talking very briefly about the calendar, reading aloud, shared reading, and/or interactive writing.

This morning, the teacher reads *Peanut Butter and Jelly*, by Nadine Bernard Westcott, for the fourth time. Children enjoy the language of this story and join in readily. After reading, they begin to make a list of the ingredients they will need to make a peanut butter and jelly sandwich. They use interactive writing to produce the list, first thinking about what they will need, and then writing the words one at a time. This activity gives the teacher a chance to have children say words slowly and think about the sounds. They produce the first part of the list and reread it each time they add a word. They will finish the list tomorrow and later in the week will check off ingredients, make sandwiches, and write directions.

Then children are directed to the activities listed for them on the work board while the teacher begins to conduct guided reading groups. It is important for the teacher to move quickly into group lessons. If children understand expectations related to the work board, they will be able to get right to work independently. This morning the children are using browsing boxes, working in the ABC center, reading around the room, and using the listening center.

After working with two groups, the teacher takes a few moments to complete records and put away materials while the children finish up the tasks on the work

Sample Rotation System for Guided Reading and Work Time

Day	Guided Reading Groups	Work Groups			
WEEK ONE		YELLOW	BLUE	GREEN	RED
Monday	Jenny's Group Ben's Group	Browsing Boxes Buddy Reading ABC	Browsing Boxes ABC Listening Center	Listening Center Browsing Boxes Buddy Reading	ABC Listening Center Browsing Boxes
Tuesday	Alex's Group Lamar's Group	ABC Listening Center Browsing Boxes	Browsing Boxes Buddy Reading ABC	Browsing Boxes ABC Listening Center	Listening Center Browsing Boxes Buddy Reading
Wednesday	Jenny's Group Ben's Group	Listening Center Browsing Boxes Buddy Reading	ABC Listening Center Browsing Boxes	Browsing Boxes Buddy Reading ABC	Browsing Boxes ABC Listening Center
Thursday	Alex's Group Lamar's Group	Browsing Boxes ABC Listening Center	Listening Center Browsing Boxes Buddy Reading	ABC Listening Center Browsing Boxes	Browsing Boxes Buddy Reading ABC
Friday	Jenny's Group Ben's Group	Browsing Boxes Buddy Reading ABC	Browsing Boxes ABC Listening Center	Listening Center Browsing Boxes Buddy Reading	ABC Listening Center Browsing Boxes
WEEK TWO:					
Monday	Alex's Group Lamar's Group	ABC Listening Center Read Around Room	Read Around Room Writing Center ABC	Writing Center ABC Listening Center	Listening Center Read Around Room Writing Center
Tuesday	Jenny's Group Ben's Group	Listening Center Read Around Room Writing Center	ABC Listening Center Read Around Room	Read Around Room Writing Center ABC	Writing Center ABC Listening Center
Wednesday	Alex's Group Lamar's Group	Read Around Room ABC Listening Center	Listening Center Read Around Room Writing Center	ABC Listening Center Read Around Room	Read Around Room Writing Center ABC
Thursday	Jenny's Group Ben's Group	Read Around Room Writing Center ABC	Read Around Room ABC Listening Center	Listening Center Read Around Room Writing Center	ABC Listening Center Read Around Room
Friday	Alex's Group Lamar's Group	ABC Listening Center Read Around Room	Read Around Room Writing Center ABC	Read Around Room ABC Listening Center	Listening Center Read Around Room Writing Center

Note: Each group participates in a guided reading session at least every other day and engages in productive reading and writing every day. On days when there are large blocks of time, the teacher can work with three or more groups each day.

FIGURE 5–4   Sample rotation system for guided reading and work time

Sample Management Plan 1
(150 minutes)

- Children begin independent reading as they come in—open choice (10 minutes of arrival time)
- Opening routines: morning message, calendar (5 minutes)
- Reading aloud (10 minutes)
- Shared reading or interactive writing (15 minutes)

- Guided Reading

- Two groups
  per day,
  alternating.

Work Time (60 minutes)			
Red Group	**Blue Group**	**Green Group**	**Yellow Group**
Browsing Box	Listening Center	Read Around Room	ABC
ABC	Browsing Box	Listening Center	Read Around Room
Read Around Room	ABC	Browsing Box	Browsing Box

- Reading aloud (10 minutes)
- Shared reading (5 minutes)
- Writing workshop (60 minutes)—includes minilesson, conferring, and sharing.

FIGURE 5–5   Sample management plan 1

board. Then, the whole group is assembled again for reading aloud and some shared reading. This morning they reread favorites such as *I Went Walking* and *Pumpkin Pumpkin*. They also reread a story map they previously produced in response to *Rosie's Walk*. The teacher has a new book to read aloud, *My Best Friend*, a book about children's getting to know each other.

Reading aloud is the lead-in to the next class activity, writing workshop. The teacher begins with a minilesson on how authors choose their topics and the children share ideas for choosing topics of their own. *My Best Friend* is a resource, helping children understand that a possible topic to write about is someone they know in the class or someone in their family. The topic is not prescribed, but the teacher helps children talk about the experiences in their lives that will help them generate topics.

The teacher distributes folders and the children go to tables to work on their stories. Each child has a writing folder in which to keep work in progress. The folders also contain resource materials such as an alphabet chart, a high frequency word list, and a personal dictionary. While the children write, the teacher observes and has short conferences with individual children. At the end of the morning, she calls the children together to share. One or two children sit in the author's chair and share their writing.

This morning (about a two-and-a-half-hour period) Carmen has heard two stories read aloud and joined in for shared reading of four more. She began to write her own story about her grandmother and shared her beginning in the author's chair. She also made a beautiful picture of her grandmother. In the ABC center, Carmen formed six words. At the beginning of the day, she read two books independently and looked through Galdone's *The Three Bears*, which the teacher had previously read to the group several times. She also read four familiar books from the browsing boxes and used a pointer to read around the room. Carmen experienced a new book in her guided reading lesson, one that offered some challenge. She listened and participated in the book introduction and then read the whole book to herself. She has had a productive morning of literacy learning.

The management plan in Figure 5–6 just moves things around a bit. The morning begins with a minilesson and writers workshop. Group time, including reading aloud and interactive writing, comes in the middle of the morning. Then children move into work time using the work board while the teacher calls guided reading groups. The morning ends with shared reading.

No particular sequence of events is better than any other. The teacher decides what is best for her based on her students' needs, the school context and schedule, and her own style of working.

Until routines are well established, it is best not to vary the management plan too much. Children respond to orderly and predictable environments and expectations that help them manage their time and behavior. You will not have to shout directions every few minutes, as you would if the routines were constantly changing. (Once children are self-managing their classroom activities, you can vary the routines as long as you communicate the change explicitly and teach new procedures.)

Sample Management Plan 2
(150 minutes)

- Children begin independent reading as they come in—open choice (10 minutes of arrival time)

- Opening routines: song, calendar (5 minutes)

- Writing workshop (55 minutes)

- Reading aloud or shared reading (10 minutes)

- Interactive writing (10 minutes)

- Guided Reading

- Two groups per day, alternating

Work Time (60 minutes)			
Red Group	**Blue Group**	**Green Group**	**Yellow Group**
Buddy Reading	Poem Box	Independent Reading	Writing Center
Writing Center	Buddy Reading	Poem Box	Independent Reading
Poem Box	Computer	Writing Center	Buddy Reading
Independent Reading	Writing Center	Buddy Reading	Computer

- Shared reading (10 minutes)

FIGURE 5–6   Sample management plan 2

Why Management Is Important

This chapter may seem to be stressing directed learning, perhaps even "top down" management. We do believe it is critical for the teacher of young children to establish an organized, predictable environment and teach children to use it. Responsibility for organization cannot be abdicated to young children who have no experience in group learning. In the beginning, the teacher will need to demonstrate routines explicitly and require that they be followed.

This very direction, though, creates independence because it frees both teacher and children from constant distractions related to management. It helps children become organized to learn and teachers become organized to learn alongside them. It helps children sustain productive behavior on their own, which is not only a literacy skill but a life skill.

After routines are thoroughly learned, they can be varied as the situation warrants because not only organization but trust has been established. In a classic article, R. P. McDermott (1977) describes "trusting relations" as a crucial subset of the working agreements people use to make sense of each other. This author says that in the classroom the teacher and child work to understand each other's behavior as directed to the best interests of what they are trying to do together. Indeed, once this trusting relationship is established, they can hold each other accountable for any breach of the formulated consensus.

McDermott is not referring to trusting relations in the ordinary sense. This is not "basic trust" but trust as a quality of social relationships, as a product of the work people do to achieve a shared focus. For example, he points out that success in getting organized for learning depends on how well the participants communicate to each other the importance of learning. Beyond that organization, there is an order or logic in the ways people relate to one another. They use this order to organize how they behave with one another. Interaction fosters this trust.

McDermott also talks about "whimperatives," the little questions and hints that teachers sometimes give to children (*"Would you like to put the books away now?"*). McDermott suggests that sometimes we fail to check whether children really understand that such statements are commands. Explicit understanding of a task may be important for children to get organized to learn. In the trusting relationship, there is an underlying understanding that the teacher is acting in a way that is in the best interest of what the teacher and child are trying to do together.

In a kindergarten classroom program, Ida Patacca establishes trusting relations by knowing what her children know and explaining activities and tasks that might be new. When Ida explicitly shows children how to hold paper, start at the upper corner, think of something to say, and begin to write the first letter, she is establishing trusting relations. Children know what to do, what is expected of them. The success of guided reading would not be possible without a context in which independent learning activity can take place. Children themselves must be able to understand and use these activities. Even when not working directly with the teacher, they are learning through a range of productive activities, both assigned and chosen, that have been carefully selected, demonstrated, and explained.

Suggestions for Professional Development

Here's how to make a management plan, step-by-step. You might want to do this with a colleague or the grade-level team.

1. List potential icons that fit your own situation. Select from the list provided here or make some new ones.

2. Carefully define the procedures for activities under each icon. List materials and process.

3. Looking at your class list, construct three or four work groups. Be sure:

∎ All children in the class are included in a work group.

∎ Children in each group can work well together.

∎ Groups are diverse.

∎ Groups are heterogeneous in terms of reading and writing ability.

∎ Groups are not too large to begin their work in one center or area.

4. Design a work board that accounts for the work groups and their activities. At first, you may start with only two activities. Eventually children should be involved in at least three activities per day over a four-day period. Be sure:

∎ No two groups are doing the same activity simultaneously (unless there are ample materials, as in browsing boxes).

∎ All activities involve some kind of literacy.

∎ Quiet and noisier activities are balanced, but there are no activities that will disrupt guided reading groups or children's individual work.

∎ There is some opportunity for children to make choices.

∎ There is a balance of reading and writing tasks.

5. Analyze how you will equip work areas signaled by icons. Some areas may be ready to use; others may need to be set up and supplied. List materials needed.

6. Develop a plan for teaching children to use the work board and engage independently in each activity.

7. Implement your plan over a three-week period. During the first week, teach the routines and develop children's use of the work board. During the next two weeks, work with guided reading groups.

8. With your colleagues, reflect on the success of the three-week pilot test.

Using Assessment to Inform Teaching

The logic by which we teach is not always the logic by which children learn.   GLENDA BISSEX

Rationale for Systematic Assessment

Assessment has a number of general purposes, moving from the kind of informal assessment that occurs in the classroom every day to the more formal reporting system that is required in the school arena:

■ Continually informing teaching decisions.

■ Systematically assessing the child's strengths and knowledge.

■ Finding out what the child can do, both independently and with teacher support.

■ Documenting progress for parents and students.

■ Summarizing achievement and learning over a given period—six weeks, a year, or longer.

■ Reporting to administrators, school board, and various stakeholders in the community.

Assessment begins with what children know; the evidence for what they know is in what they can do. For the teacher of reading,

assessment is an essential daily activity. The general purposes listed above apply to the assessments used in guided reading, but there are also a number of specific purposes related to literacy. The primary purpose of assessment is to gather data to inform teaching. If assessment does not result in improved teaching, then its value in school diminishes greatly. Assessment allows us to see the results of our teaching and allows us to make valid judgments about students' literacy.

Assessment is research. A researcher gathers evidence in ways that are reliable and valid and then uses this evidence to build a pattern of knowledge about the phenomenon being observed. Evidence (which we will sometimes refer to as data) is organized and categorized by the researcher in ways that reveal principles. Constructing these principles and testing them over time builds theory.

As teachers we have theories about learning and teaching that we refine and revise every day in our work with children. Our theories are incomplete in that we are continually testing them against our observations of

---

This chapter outlines what a teacher of reading needs to know about students in order to support their development of strategies. For a broader examination of assessment, see Johnston 1992; Anthony et al. 1991; Holdaway 1979; Rhodes & Shanklin 1993; Rhodes 1993; and Griffin, Smith & Burrill 1995.

and interactions with individual children. Every child adds to learning and enriches the theory. This theory is the base for our moment-to-moment decisions. As we experience more and learn more from teaching, our repertoires expand and the base is strengthened.

All of us have internal systems or sets of understanding that allow us to make decisions "on the run." Some of our instructional decisions seem automatic and we may not even be consciously aware of the process. We just know what to do because we have built our repertoire of responses over time and connected it with our observations and interpretations of behavior.

Yet we have to look closely at the strengths particular children bring to their literacy learning. There are many surprises in teaching; there is always some response we did not predict. Children make us revise our theories. Being a teacher is like being a scientist: we are obligated not to hold theory as static and unchangeable—a model into which all children must fit—when there is evidence to the contrary. One of the most important purposes of an assessment system, then, is helping us continually build theory that is the foundation of our instructional decisions.

Assessment has several essential attributes:

■ *It uses accessible information, most of which can be collected as an integral part of teaching.* The system must be practical and usable. It is not a separate and burdensome curriculum but is woven into daily practice. Of course, teachers may do some initial assessment of children and may have regular, focused assessment periods; however, the most powerful kind of documentation is that collected as a daily routine. As teachers, we have to make practical decisions about how we use our time. It is better to gather and record good information regularly than to have an elaborate and time-consuming assessment system that is so demanding and

impractical that one simply cannot find time for it.

■ *It includes systematic observations that will provide a continually updated profile of the child's current ways of responding.* A highly organized system ensures the information is handy for teachers to use. Clay (1991a) admits that it asks too much of a teacher with a full class of children to carry in her head the particular learning history of each child for the past two or three weeks: "It is helpful for the teacher to have some systematic observations to refer to. . . . She needs to be on the same track as the child and systematic observations of how the child is working with texts from time to time provide the teacher with necessary information" (p. 233). Sometimes we think about systematic assessment as a series of tests—the "unit tests" provided by basal systems and/or standardized tests that are a regular part of the district's reporting procedures. Observation that focuses on children's behavior can also be systematic and can provide more valuable information. Final assessment scores offer little to the teacher that can be put to practical use, because young children learn so rapidly. Systematic observation captures the shifts in responding that indicate instruction is working.

■ *It provides reliable information about the progress of children.* The system must be designed to yield consistent information. In other words, each time the assessment procedures are used they build a data base on an individual child, one that allows you to ascertain the results of teaching. According to Smith & Elley (1994), "Reliability means the consistency of the measures. If the same or a similar testing procedure is given after an extended period of time, or by another person, we would expect the results to be similar if the procedure is reliable. The results should be accurate" (p. 98). A reliable procedure is applied in a standard way so that it yields consistent results across items and with different children.

■ *It provides valid information about what children know and can do.* When inquiring about validity, we are asking, Does this test really measure what we are trying to assess? Many writers have referred to this as *authenticity.* It is impossible for all assessment tasks to be completely authentic in the sense that the task is one that the child has chosen for his own purposes and implements in an idiosyncratic way. Introducing a reliable and systematic approach inevitably leads to some contrived procedures. But assessment approaches must be as close as possible to the task being assessed. Children learn to read by reading; we must assess their reading progress by observing their reading. For children in the initial phases of learning to become literate we recommend some consistently applied measures that capture the child's beginning knowledge about literacy—the names of the letters of the alphabet or concepts about print (Clay 1991a, 1993a), for example. These assessments do not capture the process but do provide information on the child's knowledge about the items that support the process. The most powerful tool, however, is to observe and record reading behaviors on continuous text.

■ *It is multidimensional.* A multidimensional system provides the best chance to collect reliable and valid information on children's progress. The system should include both formal and informal measures; for example, a teacher might combine anecdotal records, lists of books read, running records taken every two or three weeks, a writing sample, and a criterion-referenced standardized test. A multidimensional system also allows the teacher to look across curriculum areas to find and use valuable information. For example, the assessment of a child's growth in writing can provide valuable information for helping him learn to read and vice versa.

■ *It provides feedback to improve the instructional program and the curriculum.* A feedback loop sounds complicated but it simply means looking at the combined results of assessment of student progress in a way that leads to improved instruction. The first part of the loop happens when a teacher works with an individual child. Behavioral evidence, as Clay (1991a) has said, "might cause a teacher to question her own assumptions and check them thoughtfully against what her children are actually doing, and to hold a watchful brief for when the child's processing behavior requires her to change her approach" (p. 344). This questioning and reflective process can occur whatever the teacher's philosophy or instructional approach, because children's responses rather than a prescriptive model directs the teaching. The second part of the loop takes place at the classroom level. In midyear, a teacher might assess all children using Clay's Observation Survey or a randomly selected sample of children on one or two similar measures. Or she might simply take a look at the last two weeks' collected observations in order to make some decisions about her program. If children are reading every day and yet there is little progress in the level of text they can read, something might be wrong with the way texts are selected for children in the group or stronger teaching with more explicit demonstrations might be required. A third and final part of the loop takes place at the school level. The primary team could, for example, conduct a study of their results, using the information to make decisions about further training they might need, materials they want to purchase, or new instructional emphases for the next year.

■ *It identifies and directs steps to meet the needs of students who do not achieve despite excellent classroom instruction.* Assessment is critical in identifying students who are not benefiting from the classroom program. Since intervention will be necessary for these students, assessment must occur early and be ongoing, so that no student moves on through the system without the level of support he needs to succeed. Clay (1991a) strongly recommends extra, individual, short-lived, high-quality help such as Reading Recovery for young students having difficulty in the initial phases of learning to read and write: "My special plea would be that we recognize that *some children need extra resources and many more supportive interactions with teachers* to get them through the necessary transitions of reading acquisition to the stage where they can pick up most of the different kinds of information in print" (p. 345, italics in original).

■ *It involves children and parents in the process.* Assessment is most powerful as a learning experience when the learner is involved. Even assessment systems for young children can provide the opportunity for them to reflect on their own strengths and goals for further learning. Involving the parents lets them learn more about their children's strengths and provides additional reliable, valid information for the teacher.

Guided Reading Assessment Procedures

Systematic observations—at the beginning of the year and at periodic intervals—give the teacher something to refer to when planning a guided reading program. Marie Clay's *An Observation Survey of Early Literacy Achievement* (1993a) provides the most practical procedures and the richest source of information currently available. Valuable information can also be obtained from the *Primary Language Record* used in England (see Barrs 1989). Many teachers use observation checklists. Word reading tests are another source of information, although the results should be considered in conjunction with other measures. Anecdotal records, when systematized and regularly used, are a final valuable resource.

Observation Survey of Early Literacy Achievement

The Observation Survey was created to help teachers observe young children just as they began to read and write. The survey has been reconstructed in Spanish (Escamilla et al. 1996) and is widely used by classroom and Reading Recovery teachers in daily teaching and as a tool for research. These measures are systematic, rigorous, reliable, and valid. How to administer and use the procedures is well detailed in Clay's book and will not be repeated here. We strongly recommend that you read the complete text and obtain the professional training that will let you use this comprehensive set of measures at their full potential.

The Observation Survey includes six measures. The first five will be described here, along with other procedures. The sixth, the running record, will be discussed in Chapter 7.

Letter identification

The child is asked to identify, by name, sound, or as the first letter of a word, the printed upper- and lowercase letters, as well as the typeset versions of *a* and *g*. The inventory of known letters is important as the child begins to take on reading and writing. Letter knowledge indicates that the child is familiar with some aspects of the visual details of print. Any knowledge of these details can be useful when the child begins to read simple texts. Children do not need to know all or even most of their letters before they begin to read texts for meaning; however, they need to learn more letters as they progress and use this visual information to monitor and check on their own reading. Even children who enter first grade knowing just one or two letters can begin reading, enjoying, and using early behaviors such as matching and moving left to right with simple caption books (see Chapter 9). Very often we find that when children confuse letters, their substitutions are visually similar. For example, if a child substitutes *h* for *n*, the error is a signal that the child perceives the distinctive features of the letter but has not yet refined his skills to the point that every detail is used in discriminating one from another.

Word Test

The child is asked to read a list of words in isolation. In the United States version of the Observation Survey, these words were drawn from a list of frequently used words. Recognizing words quickly makes it easier for children to move through text. It is useful for children to develop at least a small core of words they can use strategically while reading and problem solving. At first, when the child knows very few words, it helps the teacher to know precisely which words the child can read. The teacher might even use this knowledge when selecting the very earliest texts for individual children. When working with groups at the earliest stages, the teacher may look through the assessments to find the words that many children hold in common (there will almost always be some after children have been at school a few weeks). For example, the class might know *the*, *I*, *a*, *can*, *me*, *we*, or *to*. Children develop words in common through shared reading and interactive writing.

Children's attempts at words on the Word Test provide additional interesting information. By examining how they approach words in isolation, without the support of meaning or predictability in the text, teachers can learn more about children's ability to recognize features of words and also to take words apart. Often children will make an attempt that begins with the same letter as the word on the list or substitute a word that contains similar parts. For example, when Phillip substituted *love* for *over*, he showed his attention to a visual pattern and his search to link it with a word he knew.

Concepts about print (CAP)

In this assessment the teacher reads a small book while working with a child. The teacher says, "I'll read this book. You help me," and proceeds to read through the book,

asking the child questions that require him to act on critical concepts about print, such as which way to go, where to start reading, and where to go next. The measure is particularly valuable for assessing the literacy knowledge of kindergarten children and early first graders because it gives the teacher an idea of what children know about reading before many of them can actually read. It also assesses word-by-word matching in reading, book handling skills, locating words in print, distinguishing between the idea of letter and word, the meaning of punctuation, and other details of print. Information from the CAP assessment helps teachers decide when children have enough of an orientation to books and print to move into guided reading. CAP also helps teachers understand specifically what children know about print so that they can establish priorities in the early stages of guided reading.

Writing vocabulary

The child is asked to write all of the words he knows how to write, beginning with his name. The assessor may use a list of categories to prompt the child to think of words that he might know. The activity is not like a spelling test. Prompts are used as a support but the child writes the words independently. An inventory of words and parts of words that children know how to write is an indication of what the child controls. A word that the child can write easily (his name, for example) represents a "program of action" that can be performed again and again and becomes part of a network of information (words that start the same or sound like his name, for example). These networks form the basis for noticing more and more about the features of words. Of course, a child may write a word and not be able to recognize it when he encounters it embedded in text; but every word he can write has potential for later use.

Hearing and recording sounds in words

The child is read a short message of two sentences and is told that she should try to write it. Then the message is reread slowly while the child is given a chance to write the words, representing as many of the sounds as she can. Like the writing vocabulary, the assessment is not a spelling test but is a measure of the child's ability to hear and record sounds in words. (There are thirty-seven phonemes to represent in the short message.)

The value of this information lies in the teacher's knowledge of children's phonological awareness. The task requires children to move from sounds to letters; in reading, the child must coordinate two complex operations. In a first attempt at an unfamiliar word, she might think about what would make sense, look at the letters, and make the beginning sounds as a cue to give her an idea of what the word might be. Once she solves the word, she quickly confirms her response by checking the rest of the visual information. On the other hand, when stopped at an unfamiliar word, a child might make a prediction of what the word could be, given the meaning and the language of the story. Then she might confirm or reject her prediction by saying it (either aloud or to herself) and thinking what she might expect to see in terms of letters. Looking at the visual information in the word is a way to check. The process is complex and flexible, and the reader moves back and forth between sources of information, checking, checking further, and confirming. Even for young readers, this happens quickly and largely unconsciously. At the very beginnings of learning to read, the process will be overtly signaled by behavior. It is helpful to know the sounds that children can hear and link with a visual symbol.

Running record of text reading

A running record is a documentation of a child's actual reading of text, providing both quantitative and qualitative information. Running records are discussed in more detail in Chapter 7, since they are the most important tool in guided reading. Running records have a variety of uses:

- Finding the appropriate level of text for children to read.
- Grouping students for reading instruction.
- Checking on text selection and on teaching.
- Documenting progress in reading.
- Adding to the teacher's knowledge of the reading process.
- Suggesting ways to teach children who are having difficulty reading.
- Determining whether children are making satisfactory progress.
- Summarizing results of the guided reading program in the classroom or the school.
- Providing insights as to the child's use of meaning to guide his reading.

Comprehension

When we read, we construct meaning from written language. Comprehension is a recursive process in which the reader may construct new understanding cumulatively while reading or even later when reflecting on the text or connecting it to other texts. Comprehension is difficult to assess formally, yet teachers know every day whether or not children are understanding what they read. Some informal ways of knowing whether comprehension is taking place are:

- Asking children if they understand a story or an informational piece.
- Having conversations with the children about the material read.
- Observing children as they respond to the text both verbally and nonverbally.
- Observing children's behavior for evidence of using cues while reading.
- Observing children's responses to the text in art and writing.

Because comprehension is a complex and invisible process, it is easy to confuse methods designed to get evidence of comprehension with comprehension itself. Having a child retell a story or asking "comprehension questions" does not teach comprehension. It is only a fairly primitive way of gathering evidence of comprehension.

There are several ways to assess comprehension in a more formal and systematic way. We describe several approaches here, but we caution that no single assessment can fully inform the teacher of the child's understanding. We encourage you to make liberal use of the informal methods listed above. Anecdotal records can document information gained through observation and conversation that is often more powerful than the limited information one gains from artificial measures.

Retelling

After the student has read the story, the teacher asks him to reconstruct or "retell" the whole story in sequence. Sometimes, the retelling is tape-recorded, transcribed, and analyzed for:

❚ Knowledge of the gist of the story and main idea.

❚ Events accurately reported.

❚ Degree to which the sequence matches the text.

❚ Degree to which the reader uses phrases or words from the text.

❚ Degree to which the reader uses his own words and phrases.

❚ Ability to relate the information to personal knowledge.

❚ Presence of structures such as beginning, middle, and end.

❚ Use of precise vocabulary.

❚ Presence of elements such as characters and setting.

❚ Use of detail.

Retelling may be unaided or be done with teacher support. Sometimes the teacher uses questions to probe the reader's understanding. The information gained from a retelling is controversial. For one thing, it is an artificial task. The reader is asked to retell a story for someone the reader knows who has already read or heard the story. A natural tendency would be to leave out details, assuming that the listener knows the story. In addition, transcribing retellings is time-consuming and the time spent may not be worth the information received. When children have been taught about story structure and have practiced retellings, their scores generally go up. They learn how to "perform" by providing more accurate detail. Instead of reflecting comprehension, retelling may be a learned skill. However, as long as teachers keep the approach in perspective, it can provide information about how the reader approaches a text.

Questioning following reading

Asking "comprehension questions" following reading has limited value in helping teachers learn about children's understanding or in developing children's ability to comprehend. If questions are used, we recommend that:

❚ The questioning period be brief.

❚ The questions be more like discussion and conversation than like a test.

❚ The questions require children to make inferences rather than simply recall the text.

❚ The questions invite personal response to the material.

❚ The questions extend children's ability to make connections between the text and other experiences or texts they have read.

It may be helpful to think of this process not as asking questions but as demonstrating how to reflect on and explore text and inviting children to participate in the process. Lists of preplanned questions may turn into a ritualized quiz and lose their effectiveness. Instead, model the process. Make a few notes of the important ideas in the text or connections that you have made and share one or two of these with your students. Invite them to talk about what the text made them think about and encourage them to ask questions themselves about anything they did not understand.

Examining oral and written responses

Throughout a reading lesson, comprehension is the central and guiding focus.

Comprehension is foregrounded through the introduction to the story. Supporting prompts during reading keep children centered on the meaning of the story. After reading, discussion and personal responses not only help the teacher gather information about how children have understood the story but also extend their understanding. Readers bring different experiences and understanding to the reading and they take away different meanings. Interacting with one another and the expert adult can help them bring their understanding to conscious attention so that they can use it in many ways. When we see children writing their own stories modeled on favorite books or drawing pictures and talking about events in a story, we can get a much better idea of their interpretations and understanding. They might talk about their personal responses in a literature circle or record reflections in their journals. Looking across a range of responses is the best way to be sure that understanding is central in the whole process of reading.

Fluency, rate, and phrasing

It is easy to assess fluency, rate, and phrasing informally through observation and anecdotal notes. You will also be able to get important information from your systematic use of running records. At the end of each running record, make a few notes about how the reading sounds—whether it is smooth and phrased and whether the reader uses punctuation to aid the construction of meaning.

Assessing fluency, rate, and phrasing formally is time-consuming but does provide valuable documentation. Teachers might consider a formal assessment of these areas of reading once or twice a year for each child. These formal assessments will make informal assessments more reliable in that they force us to focus on and evaluate reading.

Here is a suggested formal technique that you can adapt for your own use. Ask children to read aloud a selection they have read twice before and can read with above 90 percent accuracy. (The entire class can read the same selection if you like, one that is very easy for all.) Tape-record the readings. Later, calculate the number of words read per minute. Then, preferably with a group of colleagues, listen to the tapes again, evaluating the readings according to the rubric in Figure 6–1. After ranking all tapes against the rubric, with all members of your team scoring each tape and discussing the results, you can reach a shared definition of reading fluency.

Fluency, phrasing, and rate of reading are related to performance on tests of reading comprehension. Some students make low scores on formal comprehension tests because they read slowly, attending too much to working out words and taking long pauses. Students who read accurately, quickly, and in phrased units usually do better on all assessments of reading. Moreover, their attitudes toward reading are more positive and they are more likely to read for pleasure (NAEP 1993). Those who read slowly, treating each word as a separate item to figure out, tend to have difficulty understanding what they are reading. Reading is not pleasurable for them; it is an activity to avoid.

You can pay attention to rate, fluency, and phrasing without a formal assessment. These characteristics of reading are particularly important in guided reading. You can observe, prompt, demonstrate, and teach for fluency during lessons. Another way to collect data on fluency and phrasing is to give each child an audiotape with his or her name on it. Audiotapes for an entire class can be kept in a labeled shoebox. On his "recording day," perhaps when he is reading from the browsing boxes (see Chapter 5), the child selects a book he has read before and reads it into the tape recorder. Teach the children the following procedures, and they will be able to do it independently:

Rubric for Fluency Evaluation

1. Very little fluency; **all** word-by-word reading with some long pauses between words; almost no recognition of syntax or phrasing (expressive interpretation); very little evidence of awareness of punctuation; perhaps a couple of two-word phrases but generally disfluent; some word groupings awkward.

2. **Mostly** word-by-word reading but with some two-word phrasing and even a couple of three- or four-word phrases (expressive interpretation); evidence of syntactic awareness of syntax and punctuation; although not consistently so; rereading for problem-solving may be present.

3. A **mixture** of word-by-word reading and fluent, phrased reading (expressive interpretation); there is evidence of attention to punctuation and syntax; rereading for problem-solving may be present.

4. Reads **primarily** in larger meaningful phrases; fluent, phrased reading with a few word-by-word slow downs for problem-solving; expressive interpretation is evident at places throughout the reading; attention to punctuation and syntax; rereading for problem-solving may be present but is generally fluent.

FIGURE 6–1   Rubric for fluency evaluation

1. Select a book.
2. Put your tape in the recorder and turn it on. Do not rewind; begin where your last reading left off.
3. Say the date and the name of the book.
4. Read the book.

When children first begin to use their tapes, check to be sure they understand how to start the tape in the right place so that previously recorded material is not erased. Taped readings are an excellent source of information for documenting reading over time. They are also useful for sharing in parent conferences. Sometimes parents will want a copy of the tape to keep.

Primary Language Record

A rich source of information on assessment may be obtained from the *Primary Language Record* (Barrs 1989). It is a comprehensive planning and record-keeping document based on the principle that records are needed to support and inform day-to-day teaching. It includes the involvement of parents and children, attempts to take account of bilingual development, and provides teachers with a framework for teaching language and literacy.

Observation checklists and anecdotal records

Checklists are useful for observing specific behaviors the teacher values. There are very few checklists in this book, because these tools are most valuable when they are a product of thinking about reading for your own students. Constructing the instruments yourself is a way to organize your teaching. The most useful checklist itemizes behaviors for teachers to notice and support, thus allowing them to focus on teaching, and has open-ended spaces in which to make notes on children's behaviors. Figures 6–2 and 6–3 are checklists that can be used while observing the reading of text by a guided reading group, the first with children who are just beginning, the second with children who already have control of early reading concepts.

The forms in Figures 6–2 and 6–3 combine anecdotal records and checklists of behavior. Checklists alone seldom provide enough information. A check is made at one point in time, as if a skill has been mastered; but strategic behavior changes over time and across more or less difficult levels of text. On the other hand, while anecdotal records are

Guide for Observing Early Reading Behavior

Behaviors to Notice	Children				
	Sara	Jessica	Jeff	Jeremy	Kayla
Behaviors indicating attention to features of print:					
• Is developing a core of known words • Can locate known and unknown words • Notices words and letters • Moves left to right across the line of print • Returns to the left for a new line • Matches word by word while reading a line or more of print					
Behaviors indicating early processing:					
• Uses information from pictures • Uses the meaning of the story to predict • Uses knowledge of oral language to predict • Checks one information source with another • Uses visual information (words and letters) to check on reading • Uses visual information to predict words • Notices mismatches • Actively works to solve mismatches • Uses knowledge of some frequently encountered words in checking and problem solving • Self-corrects some of the time					
Behaviors indicating independence and enjoyment:					
• Uses all sources of information flexibly • Actively searches to solve problems • Self-corrects most of the time • Shows enjoyment of books through talk or extension • Can sustain reading behavior alone					

FIGURE 6–2   Guide for observing early reading behavior

Guide for Observing Reading Behavior					
	Children				
Behaviors to Notice	Sara	Jessica	Jeff	Jeremy	Kayla
Behaviors indicating independence:					
• Gets started quickly • Works continuously • Makes attempts before requesting help • Actively searches to solve problems					
Behaviors indicating processing:					
• Rereads to confirm • Rereads to search and self-correct • Makes several attempts • Uses information from pictures • Uses language structure to predict and check • Uses visual information • Checks one cue against another • Self-corrects most errors • Notices mismatches • Recognizes many frequently encountered words quickly • Makes predictions using more than one cue • Reads with phrasing and fluency					
Behaviors indicating a positive response to reading:					
• Participates actively during story introduction and discussion • Discovers connections between personal experience and story • Participates with confidence and enthusiasm					

FIGURE 6–3   Guide for observing reading behavior

full of rich observations, it is easy to make them superficial and to neglect important behavior. These forms remind the teacher of priorities in the left-hand column but leave open space for teacher comments.

Other examples are a class list with days of the week across the top (Appendix E) or wide-open spaces for continuous notes (Appendix F). These forms enable the teacher to make notes as he observes children reading and also gives him a quick way to be sure he observes each child regularly. Appendix G is an even simpler form for keeping ongoing anecdotal notes.

Teachers successfully use a wide variety of forms, and each teacher finds his own efficient ways to keep records. The important thing is to find a way that is convenient and informative for you. Beginning, testing, and revising your record-keeping system over time will produce the best results.

Word tests

There are a number of standardized tests of word reading (e.g., the Burt, the Slosson, and the Botel). These tests assess decoding ability and word recognition, and are graded and normed. They offer an approximate indication of the child's ability to recognize isolated words quickly, provide basic information about attempts at unknown words, and give us a sampling of the child's reading vocabulary. This kind of test does not provide information about how children use other aspects of the reading process (meaning and structure) as sources of information to solve or confirm words.

If a word test is to be used, we recommend the Ohio Word Test included in Clay's Observation Survey. Three forms of the test are provided and they are easy to use. Most children will probably make perfect scores at about the middle or end of first grade. If word tests are needed for levels beyond that, other standardized lists may be useful.

Attitude and interests

Assessment is a difficult organizational task and teachers should be careful not to load themselves down with too many forms or formal procedures. We believe that conversation and ongoing observation are equal to the task of assessing children's attitudes and interests. Some teachers find a set of simple interview questions, used several times during the year, to be helpful. The value of the activity is that it requires systemization. With a class of thirty children, it is easy not to notice that some children are reluctant to read or have little interest in it. Setting aside a time to look at affective factors may provide useful information on all children.

On your own or with your colleagues, develop a set of three questions (four at most) that you think your students can answer. Be careful interpreting the results, since children often say what they think adults want to hear. The goal is to find out as much as possible about what interests your students and how they perceive themselves as developing readers.

Record of text level progress

Marie Clay (1991a) and other New Zealand teachers have used simple charts to graph reading progress over time along a gradient of text difficulty. Appendix H can be used to record individual progress (a completed form can be seen in Figure 14–2); Figure 6–4 (Appendix I) is a composite form on which to monitor the text level progress of an entire class (you'll need two or three sheets).

Summarizing and Reporting Children's Progress in Reading

Assessment is the ongoing process of observing and recording children's behavior. *Evaluation*, on the other hand, involves summarizing and reporting on children's progress. Evaluation ultimately requires teacher judgment; but it is also true that teachers make judgments—better termed decisions—almost every moment of the day. We could also talk about *formative* evaluation (data gathered for the purpose of adjusting a process for better outcomes) and *summative* evaluation (undertaken in order to report the outcomes to an-

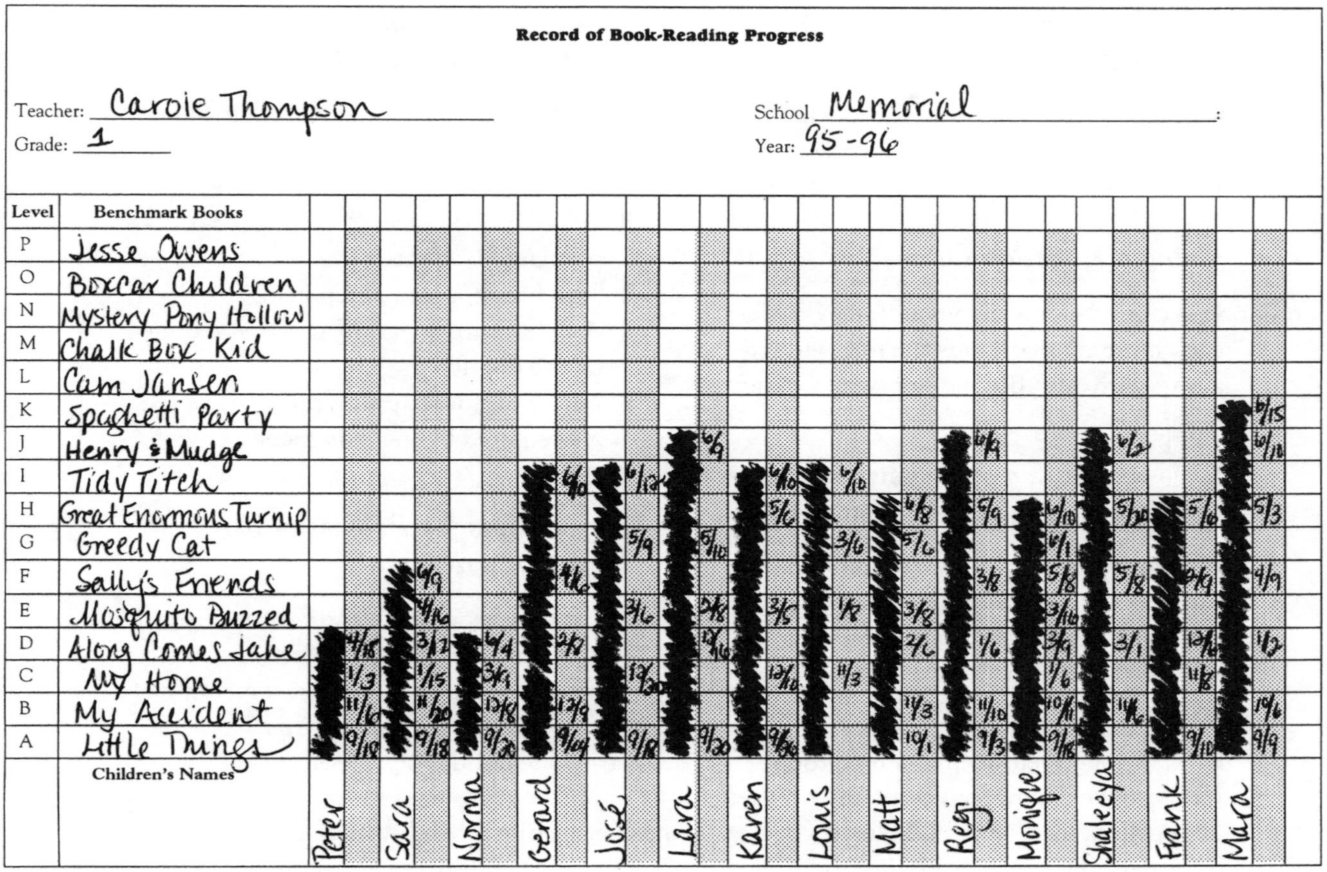

FIGURE 6–4   Sample of a completed group chart

other entity). Whatever the distinctions, there will always come a time when teachers must summarize their research findings and report them to others—parents, the school administration, the community, and the students. This summing up can be constructive for both teachers and their audiences.

For guided reading, the summing up includes:

■ The level of text the child can read at the time of the reporting period.

■ A description of the strategies the child shows evidence of in his behavior.

■ A description of the child's reading behavior in terms of fluency, rate, and phrasing.

■ Evidence of the child's understanding of the texts read.

■ An inventory of "item" knowledge—number of letters the child can name, sounds she can represent with letters, and words she can associate.

■ Level of development of the child's reading vocabulary.

■ An inventory of the conventions of print under the child's control.

■ A description of the child's personal interests in and attitudes toward reading.

■ A measure of the volume of reading completed by the child (e.g., a list of books read during both guided and independent reading).

■ A description of the range of reading, both in level and in breadth, undertaken by the child during the current assessment period.

■ An individual book-reading graph showing the child's progress.

■ A description of the degree to which the child can maintain his own behavior in independent activities.

Using a Literacy Folder

It is a good idea to have a literacy folder for each child that contains the following items, along with any district- or school-required tests:

■ Observation Survey. Observation Survey test forms and summary of information

■ Running record forms. A sampling of running records taken for each child over time with complete information as to accuracy, self-correction, and analysis of cue use.

■ Anecdotal records. If you use group forms, make a copy for each child on them, or cut them into strips and glue the information for one child onto individual cards or paper.

■ Record of fluency assessment. A summary sheet that describes the assessment, shows the rubric, and records the child's score along with any observations. Also include the audiotape on which the child has periodically recorded her reading.

■ Individual book list. A list of books read independently (this is most appropriate after the child is reading longer books and can keep this list independently).

■ Book graph. A book graph that shows progress over time (see Appendix H).

■ Other assessments of literacy. Informal writing and spelling assessments, and similar items.

This folder is meant as a teacher record, although some of the items (the book list, for example) would also be appropriate for the child's literacy portfolio. The literacy folder is a source of organized information that can be used in a variety of ways:

■ To make decisions about grouping and placement.
■ To prepare for parent conferences.
■ To analyze the strength and needs of particular students.
■ As a basis for formal reporting.
■ As a basis for assigning grades if required by the district.
■ As a basis for letters on progress, which are required by some districts.

Suggestions for Professional Development

1. After working with the concepts in this chapter and designing and testing some of your own procedures, arrange a meeting of your grade-level team. Have each teacher bring one child's folder (selected at random or according to a predetermined criterion—high-achieving or low-achieving, for example) and share the assessments.

2. Build a shared definition of fluency among your primary literacy team by investigating the fluency of children in an age cohort.
   a) Select three benchmark texts as well as a sample of children who can read each text with an accuracy level of at least 90 percent. You now have three groups of children. (At this point, do not try to assess every child in the class. It is useless to observe for fluency if texts are too difficult for children. For those who cannot read the benchmark texts, work later to find a level at which they can read fluently.)
   b) Assign appropriate texts to children and tape-record their reading of the text. If the benchmark text is too easy or too hard, try another.
   c) With your team, listen to five tapes, individually using the rubric and then discussing your ratings. Add detail to

each rating if needed to assure that members of your team are looking at the reading in the same way. When you are confident that you are using the ratings with reliability, score five more tapes independently.

d) Compare your results on the next five tapes. Repeat the process until you are achieving reliable results, with about 80 percent to 90 percent agreement.

3. Use this activity to prompt an in-depth discussion of fluency and the strategies that contribute to fluent reading. Your team will become more aware of fluency and be able to use the rubric reliably as part of the assessment portfolio.

4. Calculate the words read per minute for each reader of the benchmark books.

Using Running Records

*Authentic assessment practices . . . hold enormous potential for changing
what and how we teach and how children come to be readers and writers.*

RICHARD ALLINGTON AND PATRICIA CUNNINGHAM

A running record is a tool for coding, scoring, and analyzing a child's precise reading behaviors. Marie Clay's book *An Observation Survey of Early Literacy Achievement*[1] contains a complete and thorough description of this technique and provides a running record form to be used for this purpose. We recommend that you purchase Clay's book as a companion to this one, as we give only an introduction to the basic principles.

Taking running records of children's reading behavior requires time and practice, but the results are well worth the effort. Once learned, the running record is a quick, practical, and highly informative tool. It becomes an integral part of teaching, not only for documenting children's reading behaviors for later analysis and reflection but sharpening the teacher's observational power and understanding of the reading process.

Taking a Running Record

Taking a running record involves sitting beside the child while he reads a text, usually one he has read once or twice before. (Occasionally a teacher will take a running record on text the child has not seen before. In Reading Recovery [see Chapter 15], for example, releasing children from the program is partly based on their performance on a running record taken on text not seen before.) The text is one the teacher has predicted will offer a bit of challenge but not be so difficult that the child's processing will break down.

Both teacher and child are looking at the same text. (The teacher does not need a separate copy of the text; that would take too much time to type, duplicate, file, and retrieve the needed forms. Typing out texts would also get in the way of the teacher's flexibility in selecting texts and in recording complex behavior.) The process is quite simple. The teacher watches the child closely as he reads, coding behaviors on a separate form or a blank piece of paper. The teacher does not intervene; her role is that of a neutral observer. When the child needs help to move on, the most neutral thing to do is to tell him the word. This process offers an opportunity to observe what the child can do on his own without adult support.

The teacher records all the accurate reading with a check for each word read accurately. Mismatches are recorded with a

---

1. Marie Clay is credited with creating the concept of running records.

line, children's behavior above the line, and text information and all teacher actions below the line. This principle will become evident as the coding system is explained. The codes for significant behaviors are shown in Figure 7–1. When the teacher has coded all the behaviors, he makes a short note about how the reading sounds.

Scoring and Analyzing Running Records

Quantitative analysis

In scoring the running record quantitatively:

∎ A substitution counts as one error.

∎ If there are multiple attempts at a word, only one error is counted.

∎ Omissions, insertions, and "tolds" count as one error. Repetitions are not considered errors and are not counted in the scoring.

∎ Self-corrections are not errors.

∎ Running words includes all the words in the book or passage, not counting the title.

To determine the accuracy rate, subtract the number of errors from running words, divide by the number of running words, and multiply it by 100. As a short cut, you can divide the number of running words by errors, achieve a ratio, and refer to Clay's Calculation and Conversion Table in *An Observation Survey of Early Literacy Achievement*; this chart can be photocopied and taped to the bottom of the clipboard you use to take running records.

To determine the self-correction rate, add the number of errors and self-corrections and divide by the number of self-corrections to calculate a ratio.

You should also indicate whether the text is easy, instructional, or hard, according to the following criteria:

Below 90% = hard
90% – 94% = instructional
95% –100% = easy

Reading at 90 percent or above provides good opportunities to observe reading work.

Figure 7–2 is a running record of Sara's reading of *My Dog Willy*. Sara read seventy-one words with five errors: her accuracy rate is 71 minus 5 divided by 71 multiplied by 100, or 93 percent. Her self-correction rate— 5 errors plus 2 self-corrections divided by 2 self-corrections—gives a ratio of 1 to 4 (3.5 was rounded up to the closest whole number). The running record of Peter's reading of the same text in Figure 7–3 also shows five errors and two self-corrections, resulting in the same accuracy rate, 93 percent, and the same self-correction ratio, 1 to 4. Their use of sources of information is also quite similar.

The accuracy rate lets the teacher know whether she is selecting the right books. The text should be neither too easy nor too hard. A good guideline is that the children should be reading with more than 90 percent accuracy. The point is not accuracy per se but whether the teacher has selected a text in a range that provides opportunities for effective processing. Stretches of accurate reading mean there are appropriate cues that allow the child to problem-solve unfamiliar aspects of the text.

When the text is too hard, children cannot use what they know; the process becomes a struggle and may break down to using only one source of information. The child may stop attending to visual features of print and invent text, or the child may rely on labored sounding that makes it difficult to read for meaning. We have all observed children produce nonsense words when struggling with hard text.

When text is too hard, it is nonproductive in helping the child become a strategic reader. To become a good reader, the child must sustain effective behavior over long stretches of meaningful text.

The accuracy rate also helps the teacher group children effectively. For example, if a particular level of text is "right" for six to eight children, they can work effectively together even though they have differences in the ways they process text.

Coding a Running Record

Behavior	Code	Description
Accurate Reading	√ √ √ √ √	Record a check for each word read accurately. The line of checks matches the layout of print.
Substitution	$\dfrac{attempt}{text}$ $\dfrac{attempt \mid attempt \mid attempt}{text \ \ \mid \ \ \ \ \ \ \ \ \mid}$	The reader's attempt is placed over the accurate word on a line. When the child makes multiple attempts, each is recorded above the line with a vertical line in between.
Told	$\dfrac{-\quad\mid}{text\ \mid\ T}$	When the reader makes no attempt, he is instructed to try it. If there is no attempt, the word is told and a T is written below the line.
Appeal and Told	$\dfrac{-\ \mid A\ \mid\ √}{text\ \mid\ -\ \mid}$ √ √ √ √ √ $\dfrac{-\ \mid A \mid}{text\mid-\mid T}$	The reader's appeal, either verbal or nonverbal, is recorded with an A above the line. If the child reads correctly, a check is made. If the child makes an attempt it is recorded above the line; if he doesn't or it is incorrect a "told" is recorded.
Omission	$\dfrac{-}{text}$	A dash is placed on a line above the word in the text.
Insertion	$\dfrac{word}{-}$	The word inserted by the reader is placed above the line and a dash is placed below.
Repetition	√ √ √ √ R √ √ √ R √ √ √ √ R2	Place an R after a single word repeated; for a phrase or more of text repeated draw a line to the point to which the child returned. The number indicates number of repetitions.
Self-Correction	√ √ $\dfrac{attempt}{text}$ SC √ √ R	The symbol SC following the child's corrected attempt indicates SC at point of error. A small arrow can be used to indicate that the SC was made on the repetition.

FIGURE 7–1   Coding a running record

Pg.	MY DOG WILLY Level C
1	My dog Willy likes to wake me up in the morning.
3	My dog Willy likes to eat breakfast.
5	My dog Willy likes to say hello to our neighbors.
7	My dog Willy likes to ride in the car.
9	My dog Willy likes to go shopping at the store.
11	My dog Willy likes to play ball.
13	My dog Willy likes to take a bath.
15	And my dog Willy loves to make new friends.

RUNNING RECORD SHEET

Name: Sara   Date: 10/95 D. of B.: 4/23/89 Age: 6 yrs 6 mths
School: Memorial   Recorder: Tessie Davis

Text Titles	Running words Error	Error rate	Accuracy	Self-correction rate
1. Easy _____		1: ____	____ %	1: ____
2. Instructional My Dog Willy	71/5	1: 14	93 %	1: 4
3. Hard _____		1: ____	____ %	1: ____

Directional movement Controls left to right movement and return sweep

Analysis of Errors and Self-corrections
Information used or neglected [Meaning (M) Structure or Syntax (S) Visual (V)]

Easy _____

Instructional Substitutions consistently reflect use of meaning and structural cues. Self correction results when attention is directed to visual cues.

Hard _____

Cross-checking on information (Note that this behaviour changes over time)
One self-correction results from cross-checking a visual cue with meaning and structure.

Analysis of Errors and Self-corrections (see *Observation Survey* pages 30–32)

FIGURE 7–2   Running record of Sara's reading

Finally, the accuracy rate lets the teacher know whether his book introduction and other kinds of support he offered during the first reading were effective. The introduction is especially important in helping children read text independently. High accuracy and self-correction rates indicate that the teaching was helpful to the child's developing independence in reading.

Qualitative analysis

Qualitative analysis involves looking at reading behavior and thinking about how the reading sounds. The teacher looks for evidence of cue use and of the use of strategies such as cross-checking information and searching for cues. She examines each incorrect attempt and self-correction and hypothesizes about the cues or information sources the child might have been using. In Clay's analysis, cues refer to the sources of information. There are three major categories:

■ *Meaning.* The teacher thinks about whether the child's attempt makes sense up to the point of error. She might think about the story background, information from the picture, and meaning in the sentence in deciding whether the child was probably using meaning as a source.

■ *Structure.* Structure refers to the way language works. Some refer to this information source as syntax because unconscious knowledge of the rules of the

Pg.	MY DOG WILLY Level C
1	My dog Willy likes to wake me up in the morning.
3	My dog Willy likes to eat breakfast.
5	My dog Willy likes to say hello to our neighbors.
7	My dog Willy likes to ride in the car.
9	My dog Willy likes to go shopping at the store.
11	My dog Willy likes to play ball.
13	My dog Willy likes to take a bath.
15	And my dog Willy loves to make new friends.

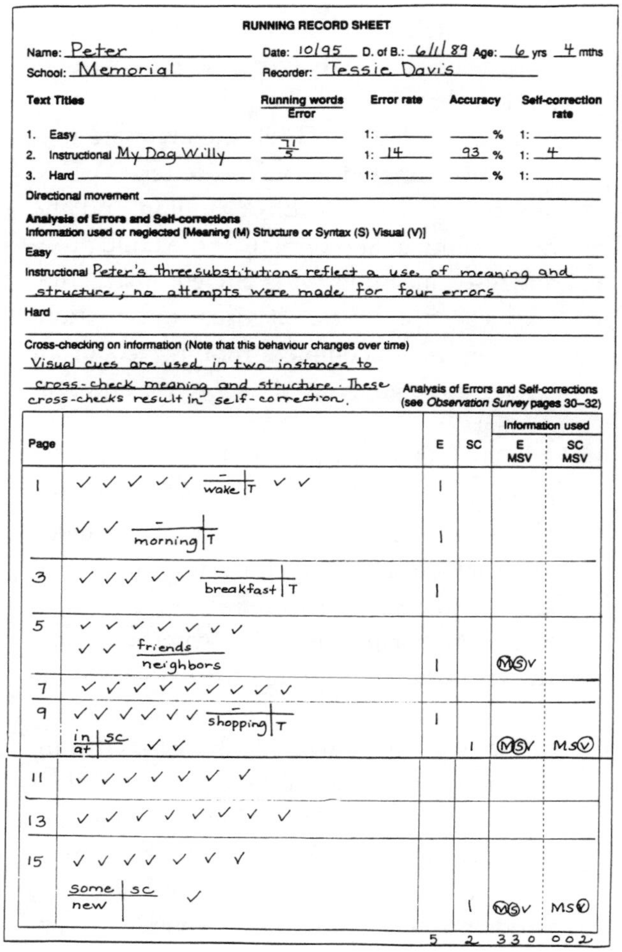

FIGURE 7–3   Running record of Peter's reading

grammar of the language the reader speaks allows him to eliminate alternatives. Using this implicit knowledge, the reader checks whether the sentence "sounds right."

❚ *Visual information.* Visual information includes the way the letters and words look. Readers use their knowledge of visual features of words and letters and connect these features to their knowledge of the way words and letters sound when spoken. If the letters in the child's attempt are visually similar to the letters in the word in the text (for example, if it begins with the same letter or has a similar cluster of letters), it is likely that the reader has used visual information.

Readers use all these information sources in an integrated way while reading

for meaning. For example a reader might look at a word, make the sound of the first letter, search for a word that would make sense and sound right in the sentence, and check this prediction against other visual features of the word. In this case, the reader has initially used visual information, searched for and used meaning and structure, and then checked against visual information. Of course, all of this happens very quickly and most readers are not aware of the process. The result is accurate reading, but the operations reflect a complex integration of ways to use information. The reader's focus remains on the meaning or message involved.

The running records of Sara's and Peter's readings in Figures 7–2 and 7–3 demonstrate how a teacher codes errors and self-corrections as he thinks about the sources of information the child was probably using at that point in reading. For each incorrect attempt and self-corrected error, the letters M S V are indicated in the Error column and the SC column, as appropriate. If the child probably used meaning, M is circled; if structure (syntax), S is circled; if visual information, V is circled. A complete running record includes these analyses of each error and self-correction.

The value of this activity is to look for patterns in the child's responses. You should not spend a great deal of time trying to figure out each miscue, searching for the "right" analysis. The idea is to reflect on the child's behavior, make your best hypothesis, and then look at data through the whole reading and over time.

What you are really looking for is an indication of the kinds of strategies the child is using. An important thing to remember about errors is that they are partially correct. They indicate strategic action and provide a window through which the teacher can observe successful use of information while reading. The teacher can observe whether the child is actively relating one source of information to another, a behavior that Clay (1991a) calls *cross-checking*, because the child is checking one cue against another. At the top of the form, the teacher notes cues used, cues neglected, and evidence of cross-checking behavior. She summarizes how the child used cues and the pattern of behavior that is evident.

Once cues are analyzed, the teacher might think about questions like these:

❚ Does the reader use cues in relation to each other?

❚ Does the reader check information sources against one another?

❚ Does the reader use several sources of cues in an integrated way or rely on only one kind of information?

❚ Does the reader repeat what he has read as if to confirm his reading thus far?

❚ Does the reader reread to search for more information from the sentence or text?

❚ Does the reader reread or use additional information to self-correct?

❚ Does the reader make meaningful attempts before appealing to the teacher for help?

❚ Does the reader request help after making an attempt or several attempts?

❚ Does the reader notice when cues do not match?

❚ Does the reader stop at unknown words without actively searching?

❚ Does the reader appeal to the teacher in a dependent way or appeal when appropriate (that is, when the reader has done what he can)?

❚ Does the reader read with phrasing and fluency? Does he use punctuation?

❚ Does the reader make comments or respond in ways that indicate comprehension of the story?

These kinds of behavior (the list above is not exhaustive) provide a description of the child's reading processing system. They will reveal whether the child is using internal strategies, which include:

❚ *Self-monitoring*. These strategies allow the reader to confirm whether he is reading the story accurately. Readers who are reading accurately are consistently using meaning, structure, and visual information to confirm their reading. This is not a conscious process, but the internal system tells them whether the reading makes sense, sounds right, and looks right.

❚ *Searching*. Searching is an active process in which the reader looks for information that will assist problem solving in some way. Readers search for and use all kinds of information sources, including meaning, visual information, and their knowledge of the syntax of language.

∎ *Self-correcting.* This is the reader's ability to notice mismatches, search for further information, and make another attempt that accomplishes a precise fit with the information already known.

Let's now look at Sara and Peter as readers, noting behaviors that provide evidence of the way they are processing print (see Figures 7–2 and 7–3). Although the quantitative analyses of their reading records were quite similar, each is building a reading process in a different way.

Both Peter and Sara use meaning and structure cues most of the time and cross-check with visual information, which leads to some self-correction. However, Peter's running record shows that he often stops when he is unsure and most of the time does not make an attempt. Twice in the text he made an incorrect attempt and fixed it, and later he tried something that made sense and sounded right, though it didn't look right. When Peter is unsure, he usually waits for adult assistance and does not reread to search further. He does not initiate much problem solving when he runs into difficulty.

In contrast, Sara consistently rereads, makes several attempts and tries everything she knows how to do. When she has made her best effort to puzzle it out, she asks for help, and then rereads to confirm and put the whole text together. Her errors show that she is attempting to use more visual information along with meaning and structure to solve unfamiliar words. She demonstrates active monitoring, searching, and cross-checking, and is very successful at self-correction.

Developing a Self-Extending System

Sara and Peter are beginning readers. As shown in our analysis, they are beginning to use cues in integrated ways. The goal of reading (and what we want for Sara and Peter) is to develop a self-extending system. As described in Chapters 12 and 14, a self-extending system is an integrated network of understanding that allows the reader to discover more about the process while reading. As teachers observe children's behavior, they will be looking for evidence that shows children are on their way to a self-extending system and are able to apply the strategies of self-monitoring, searching, using multiple information sources, and self-correction on more difficult texts and for longer and longer stretches of print.

Suggestions for Professional Development

1. Instead of beginning with Clay's standard coding system, you would benefit from making your own *grounding observation* by observing several readers closely, noting behaviors that you think are important. For each reader, select the text that you are currently using for reading instruction, but also have the reader try an easier text and one that is just a little harder. If you can work with two or three colleagues, all observing the same child, you will collect a great deal of significant behavior in just two or three readings. Try to be detailed in your observation, noting and describing behavior rather than making any judgments about it at the time. Write down only what children do, not what you think the behavior means.

2. Make a rough inventory of behavior, categorizing the ones that are similar. If you are working in a small group, use chart paper. Once you have completed your list of observations, have a discussion in which you hypothesize about what is going on in the child's head. Ask:
   ∎ What kind of information does the child seem to be using at the point of error?

- Is the child actively sorting and relating cues?
- What led to this error?
- Is there evidence that the child made an attempt using a cue source and then checked it against another cue?
- What might the child have noticed?
- What led to self-correction of an error?
- Is self-correction at the point of error or does the child go back in the text and repeat?
- What evidence is there that the child is searching for information?
- Does the child stop and wait for help or try something?
- Is there evidence of repetition to search, self-correct, or confirm?
- How accurate is the reading? Is the text easy? hard? about right?
- How phrased and fluent is the reading?

3. At this point, you will have a good idea of what to look for, so the coding system you eventually use will have meaning. After completing your grounding observation, compare your list of behaviors with the coding system we have presented here. Chances are, you will have already recorded every behavior we suggest. Taking running records of many readings over time will build up a large body of data on each child. Behaviors that seldom occur may be recorded with a brief note right on the record. The main goal is to develop a system that teachers on your team can share and understand and that can be part of children's long-term records.

4. Purchase Marie Clay's *An Observation Survey of Early Literacy Achievement* and read the chapter on running records. Find a local source for training in how to use running records and build your skill so you can use them efficiently and easily to capture the changing reading process of each child you teach.

Dynamic Grouping

Grouping allows children to support each other in reading and feel part of a community of readers.

It also allows for efficient use of a teacher's time. JOHN SMITH AND WARWICK ELLEY

There are three assumptions at work when a primary teacher is getting ready to group children for guided reading: (1) there will be a wide range of experience, knowledge, and skills among any group of primary-age children; (2) every child will be different from every other child in some levels of knowledge and skill; and (3) children will progress at varying rates. Given those assumptions, how does a teacher organize groups for teaching reading? And added to the logistic difficulties are the documented dangers of grouping, against which we must always be on guard. *Dynamic grouping* enables teachers to group children effectively for efficient teaching.

Concerns About Grouping

In 1991, a committee of the Massachusetts Reading Association thoroughly reviewed the research on grouping and found that:

1. Assigning students to self-contained classes or tracks within classes according to achievement or ability does not enhance achievement. Once a child is assigned to a low group, the chances of moving to a higher group is very low (Hiebert 1983; Good & Marshall 1984). Assigning a

student to an ability group does not seem to meet individual needs very well and may actually cause harm.

2. Students in high- and low-ability groups receive different instruction. For example, Allington (1983; also see Allington & McGill-Franzen 1989) found that children in low groups have fewer opportunities to read. Moreover, they spend more time practicing "item" tasks like decoding individual words. Students in higher groups spend more time on critical thinking, focus more on meaning, and read two to three times as many in-context words as children in low groups. For lower-group students, the pace is slower and they are more likely to be off-task.

3. Students' self-confidence and self-esteem are damaged by their assignment to low groups. No matter how carefully teachers name groups, everyone always knows which is low and which is high (Filby, Barnett & Bossart 1982). This situation is particularly evident when children follow each other through the same books in the basal system, the low group finally reading the book read by the high group months before. Moreover, minority groups are more likely to be assigned to low groups (Eder 1983;

Good & Marshall 1984; Sorenson & Hallinan 1986).

4. Interaction among students of a variety of ability levels appears to increase achievement (Slavin 1987). If students, particularly "low group" students, benefit from being in contact with a variety of achievement levels, then we need to make opportunities for children of all levels of experience to mix. When cooperative learning groups made up of students of different experience and abilities work together toward a goal there are significant increases in learning (Johnson et al. 1981; Slavin 1983a, 1983b).

5. Supplementing heterogeneous groups with smaller needs-based groups may contribute to achievement. Ability groups are effective when students are placed in them for specific instruction rather than as broad ability categories and when the composition of the group is flexible and fluid. The fluidity of the needs-based group works against the dangers of tracking.

Based on these findings, the Massachusetts task force recommended that teachers:

■ Create opportunities for interest-based, multiability reading groups.

■ Increase opportunities for noncompetitive student-student interaction.

■ Use peer tutoring and cooperative learning pairs.

■ Introduce cross-grade "buddies."

■ Create opportunities for needs-based groups.

■ Implement flexible grouping using a combination of whole-group instruction and needs-based smaller groups.

Rationale for Grouping

Like most teachers, we are concerned about the catch-22 created by the harmful effects of grouping and the necessity for children to read material that is right for their skills and abilities. As a way of resolving this dilemma, we propose combining grouping by similar reading processes and text level with a wide range of heterogeneous grouping for other purposes:

■ Maintain heterogeneous whole-group activities for reading aloud, shared reading, literature circles, readers workshop, science and social studies, interactive writing, and other curricular activities.

■ Promote heterogeneous small-group activities in these same areas.

■ Convene interest groups around literature and curriculum study.

■ Assess individual students using a wide range of measures.

■ Form small guided reading groups of students who have similar reading processes and can read about the same level of text.

■ Meet with these small guided reading groups about three to five days a week.

■ Regularly assess children in guided reading using running records.

■ Re-form guided reading groups based on this ongoing evaluation.

If young children are to learn to read, they must encounter material that supports their development. In the beginning, even small details are important. For example, children who are just beginning to understand important concepts about print need clear words with spaces between them and only one or two lines of text. To force them to read complex texts with three or four lines and without clear picture clues would confuse them. Sometimes teachers select books for and have conferences with each child individually. While it is possible to teach guided reading this way, for most teachers it simply isn't practical given the number of children in many classes. In addition, social interaction enhances children's learning to read; they learn how to support and help each other, and when instruction is handled effectively, they learn from the teacher's interactions with individuals and the group.

The Observation Survey scores in Figure 8–1 illustrate our concern about the consequences of not grouping for needs-based reading instruction. If the teacher uses whole-class instruction for reading, with everyone in the same book on the same page:

■ Students like Kara, Karin, and Ray will day after day read material that is too hard for them. Faced with several lines of print, which they cannot match word by word with spoken language, they will have difficulty seeing individual words and will find it almost impossible to use what they know about words and letters. They may develop wrong concepts such as the idea that reading means listening to what is said and "remembering" rather than solving problems using many sources of information. They may "mumble along," a nonproductive behavior.

■ Students like John will be completely lost during instruction, not able to attend or participate.

■ Students like Casey and Molika will day after day read material so easy that they do not have the opportunity to increase their processing power. Moreover, reading along with slower readers who are struggling with the text can undermine their fluency and integrated problem solving.

Traditional Versus Dynamic Grouping

While we are convinced that whole-class reading does not provide the context needed for guided reading, we want to avoid the mistakes of traditional reading groups. Figure 8–2 shows important differences between traditional grouping and dynamic grouping in terms of underlying assumptions and the processes of grouping, teaching, and evaluation.

Traditionally, only one kind of grouping—based on ability—was used for classroom work. In dynamic grouping for comprehensive literacy, many kinds of groups are used for reading and for other activities, with only guided reading based on achievement or experience. Matching children to texts is tentative and cautious, because young children learn very quickly. Any particular grouping is a hypothesis that is continually being tested. Groups are expected to change. Moreover, in dynamic grouping, children do not read a fixed sequence of books. Texts are chosen for their appropriateness for the group.

There are also differences in the teaching provided to groups; using appropriate-level texts avoids the slow progress through texts experienced by many "low" groups. It was typical in the past for the low group to spend many days on a story that the middle and high groups spent only one or two days reading, part of the reason being that the text was so hard (and the exercises that accompanied it even harder) that the teacher had to spend many days going over the material.

With dynamic grouping, all children can read many books; children making slower progress have easier books but they are building experience. Evaluation is based not on unit tests or progress through a fixed sequence of texts, but on running records and teacher observations that are documented through notes (the reading graph described in Chapter 6 is an effective way to document individual children's progress).

The Process of Dynamic Grouping

Let's talk through the initial grouping of the class listed in Figure 8–1. First, how many reading groups should we form? Three groups for twenty-six children would give us too many students in each group and a range within groups that might be difficult to cope

Observation Survey Data
Grade 1
Ms. Baker

Name	Letter Identification	Word Test	Concepts About Print	Writing Vocabulary	Hearing & Recording Sounds in Words	Text Reading Level	Percent of Accuracy
1. Casey	54	20	21	47	36	D	93
2. Molika	54	17	22	51	34	G	92
3. Rashon	52	8	19	21	23	D	96
4. Carrie	54	9	16	29	25	C	100
5. Laura	53	4	19	15	20	C	92
6. Shawn	49	10	17	17	32	C	94
7. Heather	53	2	16	31	30	C	95
8. Kayla	54	3	11	20	19	B	95
9. Steven	49	2	13	13	16	B	100
10. David	49	2	13	8	12	A	100
11. Michael	53	4	16	6	5	B	100
12. Amber	47	0	11	1	9	A	80
13. Cameron	38	0	13	7	14	A	93
14. Ashley	40	0	12	1	1	B	80
15. Talisha	42	0	12	3	4	A	90
16. Terry	21	0	11	3	5	A	85
17. Curtis	5	0	10	3	1	A	75
18. Nicky	21	0	3	0	0	A	60
19. Sherrell	12	0	5	0	0	A	80
20. Courtney	10	0	0	0	0	A	55
21. Maria	2	0	0	0	0	A	75
22. Kara	1	0	5	0	0	A	63
23. Ira	6	0	1	1	0	A	20
24. Karin	0	0	0	3	0	A	20
25. John	2	0	0	0	0	A	35
26. Ray	3	0	2	1	0	A	40

FIGURE 8–1 Observation survey data

Comparison of Traditional and Dynamic Grouping

	Traditional Reading Groups	Dynamic Grouping for Guided Reading
Assumptions	• General ability as determining factor • Progress through same phases with established rate; change not usually expected • One kind of grouping prevails	• Ability to use sources of information to process text is determining factor • Change on a continuous basis is expected • Different groupings for other purposes are used
Process of Grouping	• Grouped by general determination of ability • Static; usually remain stable in composition • Progress through a fixed sequence of books • May not skip materials	• Grouped by specific assessment for strengths in the reading process and appropriate level of text difficulty • Dynamic, flexible, and changeable on a regular basis • Books chosen for the group from a variety on the appropriate level—some overlap but generally not the same for every group • Difference in sequence of book level expected
Process of Teaching	• Words pre-taught • Skills practice follows reading • Limited number of selections buttressed by skills practice in workbooks or worksheets • Limited variety of selections • Controlled vocabulary • Selections usually read once or twice • Heavily focused on skills • Round robin reading; children take turns; each reading a page or line	• Introduction foregrounds meaning and language with some attention to words in text • Skills incorporated into reading; skills teaching directly related to selection • Unlimited number of selections; skills taught during reading • Wide variety of selections • Many frequently used words but vocabulary not artificially controlled • Selections reread several times for fluency and fast problem-solving • Balanced focus on reading for meaning and the use of flexible problem-solving strategies to construct it • All children read the whole text to themselves
Process of Evaluation	• Evaluation based on progress through set group of materials and tests	• Evaluation based on daily observation and regular, systematic individual assessment

FIGURE 8–2   Comparison of traditional and dynamic grouping

with. Based on the wide range of scores on this class list, we could form five, six, or even seven groups; however, we have to weigh our need to match children's reading levels against the time we have. Too many groups means the teacher spends too much time on guided reading to the detriment of other important areas of the curriculum (process writing, art, mathematics, etc.), cuts down the time spent with each group, or meets groups less frequently. Whichever alternative is chosen, teaching opportunities are limited. So, for this group of children, we recommend four groups.

Since we need to meet with each group for about twenty or thirty minutes, we could expect to meet with three groups within a daily ninety-minute block. A rotation system like the one described in Chapter 5 and the variety of productive independent activities we provide assures that all twenty-six children will engage in focused reading and writing for about ninety minutes every day and will meet in a guided reading group three or four days a week. In the beginning of first grade, group meetings may take somewhat less time because the selections are quite short, but time needed will increase as text length increases.

The rotation system in Chapter 5 provides for two groups per day; as you begin meeting guided reading groups, that's realistic. Two groups a day in a class with three reading groups guarantees guided reading time for each child five times during a two-week period. Three groups a day in a class with four groups guarantees each child in-

struction every other day. It is better to have high-quality teaching than brief, rushed periods that accomplish little. Over time you will find that you will become even more efficient and can meet with more groups each day, and your students will make even faster progress.

For Ms. Baker's class, our goal is to get some initial groups started and then revise and regroup based on our experience with these groupings. (Figure 8–3 illustrates the chain from observing individuals, to grouping, to selecting an appropriate text that supports the reader's use of strategies but offers opportunity for new learning.)

We decide to place Casey, Molika, Rashon, Carrie, Laura, Shawn, and Heather in one guided reading group. We feel comfortable having seven children in this group because they will probably be able to work with a great deal of independence. All these

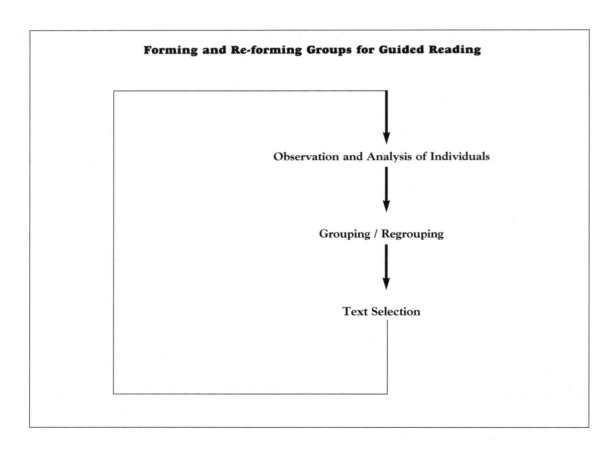

Forming and Re-forming Groups for Guided Reading

Observation and Analysis of Individuals

Grouping / Regrouping

Text Selection

FIGURE 8–3   Forming and re-forming groups for guided reading

children can already read print that has several lines of text. They can represent a majority of the sounds with letters and all know many words (their word tests and writing vocabulary assessments show that they can write many words independently, spelling them accurately). All of them can match word by word in reading and their Concepts About Print assessment indicates they have the early strategies under control. All these children will most likely be able to read texts at level C. (Refer to the book list in Appendix M). Molika will need supplemental reading to challenge her but will enjoy the work with the group even though the texts are easy.

We will begin our guided reading in this group with a relatively easy text, give it a rich introduction (see Chapter 11), and observe children closely. If their behavior confirms that the book is too easy, we'll select a slightly more difficult book the next day, repeating this procedure until we are sure that the level is about right. Given appropriate selections and introductions, this group will move rapidly through the text levels. The challenge will be to continue offering them texts that stimulate problem solving. The goal for these children is not so much to move up levels but to assure their enjoyment, expand their experiences and understanding of books, and increase their strengths as readers with a greater variety of texts.

Next, we look at some children who will need extra attention. We place Ray, John, Karin, Ira, Kara, and Maria in another guided reading group. This group of children needs to concentrate on early reading behaviors like directionality and word-by-word matching. We will begin this group with very simple caption books. (See the level A book list in Appendix M.)

The members of this group don't know many letters, but that does not mean reading needs to be delayed. They can start to enjoy reading from the very beginning and learn about letters, words, and sounds as they go

forward. We'll take this group through a gradual transition from shared to guided reading. A priority will be to help them use what they know to create "anchors" (familiar or known words) in the text that they can use to monitor their reading. We will try to meet this group every day, perhaps varying their activity by including some group shared reading or interactive writing, which is a powerful way to help them learn letter names, develop phonological awareness, and build up a store of known words, all of which will be important to use while reading. We will do a great deal of explicit demonstration and modeling for them, and they will read their selections many times. All these children will be placed on the list for Reading Recovery (see Chapter 15), with John, Ray, and Karin receiving top priority.

In another group, we place Courtney, Sherrell, Nicky, Curtis, Terry, and Talisha. These children know a few more letters than Karin's group but will still need a great deal of work on early strategies. We will also begin their reading with simple caption books.

Our final group has Kayla, Steven, David, Michael, Amber, Cameron, and Ashley. Most of these children can read very simple patterned texts and their Concepts About Print scores indicate awareness of how print works. Even though Amber's text reading score indicates that she is not really reading, she does know the names of almost all the letters and quite a few of the sounds associated with them, so we believe that with a few demonstrations she will be able to participate successfully in the group. Ashley may have more difficulty even though her score on text reading indicates that she can read level B texts; she could be using meaning and structure to predict in patterned text but not attending much to print. We will observe her closely to be sure she is building a reading process that uses all sources of information.

For the two groups of children who have little knowledge about literacy, our guided reading lessons will, in the beginning, look much like shared reading; we will probably do a lot of writing work with them as well. But we will certainly introduce them to many texts. All children in this classroom will build up a large number of books that they can read and reread.

It is obvious that specific "item knowledge" such as letter names, concepts about print, writing vocabulary, and hearing and recording sounds in words played heavily in our initial placements. But we must fight our inclination to think of grouping as a housekeeping detail that we want to accomplish so that teaching can begin. We need to remember that grouping is a continuously developing process based on observations of literacy-related activities. It is as much a part of teaching as is text selection and deserves constant attention and evaluation.

Therefore, our last decision related to these initial groupings is to watch closely for needed changes. *We expect changes*, so our initial decisions are tentative. Some children may have had very few experiences with print but will learn quickly once they receive instruction. Others may need a longer period. We will monitor children's progress closely as they work in their small guided reading groups. We will also take running records regularly. Change in groups does not have to happen all at once, nor is it a "big deal." When our observations and records indicate a change is needed, the child in question can be moved that day. Another possibility is to ask the child to attend two groups for a week or so and then decide which group is best. What matters is that the individual child reads an appropriate level of text. Children should become accustomed to a fluid situation in which groups change often.

Skilled teaching, which begins with observation, is the key to successful dynamic grouping. The chart in Figure 8–4 (adapted from McCarrier, Henry & Bartley 1995) shows the changes Ms. Baker made in six guided reading groups during a six-week period. The dotted lines show children who moved to other groups and the dates the changes were made. David and Becky exchanged places for two weeks and then Ms. Baker put them back with their original group. Though Jake and Tiffany were reading at a level far beyond the other children, they were able to participate in heterogeneous groups at other reading times. Juan, Bobby, and Mara received Reading Recovery in addition to their regular guided reading instruction.

Revisiting Purpose

Here's how dynamic grouping fulfills the purposes of guided reading:

1. *To facilitate the teaching and learning of individual children.* Although children are working in groups, they are being observed as individuals; often, the teacher has an opportunity to make critical notes on individual behavior or interact briefly to bring a good example to a child's attention. Because the text is selected within the appropriate range, it offers the maximum chance for individuals to use their developing skills.

2. *To help children understand reading as a thinking process.* A guided reading group provides an opportunity for children to discuss reading with each other and with the teacher and to support each other as they encounter new material that demands new strategies. Because the children have a few challenges in the text, there are opportunities for the teacher to call their attention to examples of effective problem solving.

3. *To make efficient use of time and materials.* Grouping gives the teacher a way to approach reading instruction systematically so that each child's needs are met. With their ability to learn constructively, almost all children can learn from skillfully managed group practice. Making a totally individualized program is not necessary or desirable; children learn pleasurably together.

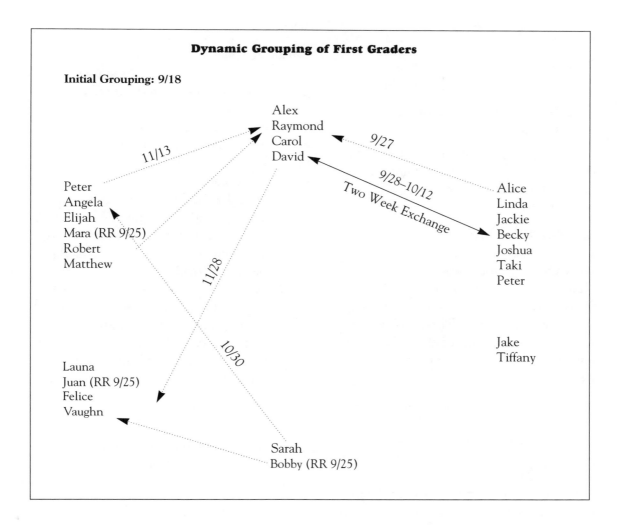

FIGURE 8–4 Dynamic grouping of first graders

4. *To move toward the goal of each child selecting and reading books independently.* The goal of every group teaching session is independent reading of the new book introduced and, eventually, of books that children pick up on their own. The teacher can instantly evaluate the book selection and introduction by watching individuals in the group as they read through the whole text on their own.

Supporting Guided Reading

It is clear from this chapter that we strongly favor needs-based grouping for guided reading. It is based on ongoing, systematic observation for the purpose of gathering small clusters of students who are similar in their development of a reading process. But guided reading is only one part of the literacy framework. There are many other kinds of grouping that support guided reading and we would expect other groupings to take place in primary classrooms:

■ Interest groups to listen to literature selections read aloud and extend them through discussion.

■ Author, illustrator, theme, or genre study by the whole class or small groups.

■ Literature circles or book clubs for discussion and closer attention to the meaning of texts.

■ Research "clubs" to investigate areas of interest in science or history.

▮ Cooperative learning groups of all kinds.

▮ Readers workshop for self-selected reading.

Suggestions for Professional Development

1. Form a group of colleagues interested in developing a deeper understanding and greater skill in dynamic grouping. Set a time to meet.

2. Using the Observation Survey results or your current assessment measures, form two guided reading groups, each made up of four children who show evidence of similarities in their reading processes and read at about the same level of text. (These groups can later be expanded, but it helps to begin with a very small group in order to gain experience.)

3. Select three texts for each group, one you think will be easy, one you think will offer some challenge but will be within their control, and one that you think is a little bit too hard. Try out the three texts with each group, first introducing the text and then observing them as they read. Take a running record for every student on that same book the next day. At the end of the period, evaluate your grouping and text selection:

▮ What were the strengths in each child's processing of the text? What did each child do when he or she encountered difficulty or made an error? What will each child need to do to process a new text more successfully?

▮ How did children in each group compare with each other? Were the results consistent? Is the composition of the group workable? Do changes need to be made?

▮ Were your text selections appropriate? Did most children in the group find the texts, in order, easy, just right, and difficult? (Here you are checking whether you were able to judge the level of text for the group you had in mind.)

4. Work at the above exercise until you get the feel of forming groups. Then expand the existing groups and form more groups.

5. Share your running records, texts, and insights with your colleagues.

Creating a Text Gradient

For nearly two generations we have relied upon graded, sequential programs to match the difficulty of materials to children's abilities. Even then we have too often failed—we still see children struggling with material that is far too difficult for them. Abandoning controlled vocabulary for ungraded literature would seem to be an act of sheer madness. DON HOLDAWAY

A critical aspect of guided reading is matching books to individual children. To accomplish this goal with efficiency, it is necessary to organize the books so that teachers' decisions can be easier, faster, and more effective. The books for guided reading are categorized on a continuum. These books are usually not available for children to select until they appear in browsing boxes or are used for extensions after being read in guided reading groups. If a classroom is very well equipped with books, it is a good idea for children to have their own boxes or resealable plastic bags that contain some previously read books for independent reading.

A group of primary teachers can work together to (1) select books that are suitable for guided reading; (2) place each book along a continuum; (3) create descriptions of each category on the continuum; and (4) establish a system for sharing books among classrooms and grade levels so that children have maximum access to books. Our list, included in Appendix M, is a starting point.

Selecting Books for Guided Reading

Building a good collection of books for guided reading is not just a matter of investing resources. Selecting books requires the same care one might take in acquiring any valuable collection. Think about a collection of fine pottery, jewelry, or art. Each piece is chosen with care; its attributes—both artistic and technical—are analyzed; the purchase is carefully considered. Adding new pieces means reexamining the existing collection to see where the addition will fit in the whole.

When we buy classroom books, however, we sometimes make hasty decisions. Often we are forced to purchase a set of books without having the opportunity to examine and try them with children. Whenever possible, we recommend selecting individual titles, adding to the collection one book at a time. Some publishers package assorted titles in a way that forces the consumer to accumulate a collection of mixed quality. If you select individual titles, you get better books for the money.

Some characteristics to consider in creating a good collection are:

❚ Enjoyment, meaning, and interest to children.
❚ Accuracy and diversity in multicultural representation.
❚ Breadth of type or genre.

- Depth in the number of titles at each level of difficulty.
- Links across the collection (common characters, authors, settings).
- Quality of illustrations and their relation to the text.
- Content.
- Length.
- Format.

Enjoyment, meaning, and connection to children's lives

Books in the collection are selected because they will provide enjoyment for and engage children through humor and interesting stories. All books in the collection should provide interesting information, good stories, or ideas that young readers can relate to their own lives. *Where Is Miss Pool?*[1] takes place in a school and describes children's reactions when their teacher is absent. *Cookie's Week* realistically depicts the antics of a house cat. A book on the same level with more text, *Saturday Morning*, is about a family completing their weekend chores and having a picnic together. Pat Hutchins's *The Doorbell Rang* is a more complex story about making cookies and having company. Chapter books that children enjoy include *The Dog That Pitched a No-Hitter* and *Second-Grade Friends Again*. The books on our list represent a rich collection of experiences and a fund of enjoyment for children.

Multicultural representation

The collection of books should reflect the multicultural world in which we live. They should not only include characters of different races but contain accurate information about a variety of cultures. People of color should be depicted in all roles and in everyday experiences. *The Stories Julian Tells*, *Daniel's Dog*, and *Worms for Dinner* are good examples. A few years ago, it was difficult to find books that were at appropriate levels for children learning how to read and that also reflected a variety of cultures. With the explosion of new books currently available, however, there is no excuse for an ethnocentric collection. Books should be examined rigorously for any kind of stereotyping, particularly race or gender.

Breadth

The collection includes many different kinds of books: natural language texts, stories, informational books, and various genres. Natural language texts (sometimes called *transition texts*) are modeled on children's oral language and are especially designed to support beginning reading by creating links between written language and the way children talk, thus creating a bridge to more literary texts (Clay 1991a).

A special kind of natural language book is the *caption book*, in which the text is very short and directly related to a simple picture. Caption books are designed for children's very first independent reading experiences. They are short and simple, have clear print that is separate from the picture, and good spacing. They have a top-left starting point on the page, and each page usually has one or two lines of highly predictable text. Figure 9–1 is a good example. In this text the line "I can hop" is easy for the child to read. Often the words *I* and *can* are already known. The picture provides a clear clue to the meaning and the word *hop*. The exclamation "Watch me! Watch me!" is typical of young children.

A more difficult story book is *Grandpa's Cookies*. In this story (two pages are shown in Figure 9–2) Grandpa sends cookies to a little girl named Lisa but all the animals sample them so that the box is soon emptied. The solution Grandpa comes up with is to make more cookies.

For younger children, the collection might include teacher-made books, which are especially valuable for children's first in-

---

1. All children's selections mentioned in this book are included in the guided reading book list in Appendix M.

I can hop.

Watch me!

Watch me!

4

5

FIGURE 9–1   A simple caption book: *Watch Me*

Bear gobbled up a cookie.
Then he hurried on his way.

"Frog, please take these cookies
to Lisa," he said.

"Me again?" said Frog.

"You may have just one," said Bear.

FIGURE 9–2   A more difficult story book: *Grandpa's Cookies*

troduction to guided reading. These are simple texts accompanying pictures from magazines or colorful stickers. When teachers make simple books for children, they can carefully consider topics of interest, familiar language structure and vocabulary, and letters and words that will support early reading.

The collection will also include a rich variety of literary texts in a number of genres. *Red Ribbon Rosie* and *The Three Blind Mice Mystery* are typical chapter books. *The Day the Giants Came to Town* is a collection of short stories, and *How to Ride a Giraffe* is a set of directions.

Depth

A high-quality collection includes many selections at each level of difficulty so that teachers have the flexibility to select books that particularly suit individuals in the groups and so that some children are able to read many books at a given level. There should also be multiple copies of each title (five to eight copies, depending on the class size.) Our list includes a large number of books on each level for levels A through P, encompassing kindergarten through grade three. It is certainly not necessary to have every book on the list, but a good sampling is essential.

Links across the collection

An important part of reading is making connections between texts. Children love to encounter familiar material over several texts; there is a natural attraction to "series" books, and quality ones can easily be a part of the guided reading collection. By including different kinds of books with common elements, we support young children's ability to search for connections and comparisons.

They like to meet the same characters again and again (Nate in the *Nate the Great* series, for example). Younger children enjoy the sequels to *Mrs. Wishy Washy*, *The Hungry Giant*, and *Greedy Cat*. The PM storybooks distributed by Rigby show one family and friends through several books.

Children also like to meet the same au-

thor again and again. Favorite authors for young children include Joy Cowley; one child met Joy Cowley and asked her, "Did you write all the Joy Cowley books?"

Settings may also connect texts; after children have read *Stories Julian Tells*, they will love the adventures in *More Stories Julian Tells* or *Julian, Secret Agent*, which take place in the same setting.

Another good way to help children link texts is to use different versions of the same story. For example, at the beginning of the year a first grader will enjoy reading a very easy version of *The Three Little Pigs*, a story she has heard read aloud in a more complex version. Later, she can read harder versions of the same story with equal enjoyment.

Experiencing such connections between texts supports children's learning about and analyzing characters, developing a sense of setting, learning to compare and contrast texts, and developing critical reading skills.

Variety of genres

By studying different kinds of literary texts, or *genres*, children learn to appreciate the language and devices authors use in creating them. The study of genres is broader than guided reading and is perhaps more appropriate for whole-class instruction or small-group literature circles. In guided reading, however, children can be introduced to many different genres, including:

■ Informational texts on a variety of topics.
■ "How to" books.
■ Mysteries.
■ Realistic fiction.
■ Historical fiction.
■ Biography.
■ Fantasy.
■ Traditional folk and fairy tales.
■ Science fiction.
■ Humor.

At first, genre is not a major consideration, because children are just beginning to learn how print works. Simplicity and appeal are important criteria, and narrative text provides the most support early on. But as children gain experience, the selection of books becomes broader, offering opportunities to look at texts in different ways. A masterful volume on children's literature by Charlotte Huck, Susan Hepler, and Janet Hickman (1993) provides extensive support for developing literature study in the classroom.

Illustrations

Books in the collection should have attractive, clear illustrations that capture young readers' interest, contribute to the enjoyment of the story, and provide valuable information that they can use strategically. In selecting books for a collection, remember Huck's (1994) admonition that "a picture storybook . . . must be a seamless whole conveying meaning in both the art and the text. An illustration does not merely reflect the action on that page but shares in moving the story forward" (p. 241). Even in simple storybooks without elaborate artwork, you must still consider the meaning that the illustrations convey. Most books in the collection will be picture storybooks. At higher levels, however, children begin to read books in which important incidents in the story are illustrated to create more interest. Illustrations can either support or detract from the child's ability to construct meaning. Even some natural language texts, which are designed specifically for early reading, have outstanding illustrations (Nadine Bernard Westcott's illustrations in *How to Make a Mud Pie* and Brian Wildsmith's *Cat on the Mat*, for example).

Content

The books in the collection must cover a wide range of topics that mesh with young children's life experiences and interests. Your own experience will tell you which topics are especially appealing. Young children especially enjoy stories that are humorous (*How to Make a Mud Pie*) or reflect their own experiences (*Chicken Pox* or *The Hole in Harry's Pocket*).

At the lower levels especially, be sure that familiar topics are explored. A simply written book focusing on a large number of concepts that are well beyond some children's experiences (a book about shellfish, for example) is not really simple or easy. In spite of few words and lines of text, the book would be quite difficult to read. The higher-level books in Appendix M (levels J to P) extend children's life experiences by introducing less familiar topics. For example, *Keep the Lights Burning, Abbie*, set in 1856, is a piece of historical fiction, and *Molly's Pilgrim* is a story about Russian immigrants. However, many of the chapter books also focus on activities children enjoy in their daily lives. An example is *Martin and the Teacher's Pets*, in which a young boy takes home the classroom fish.

Length

Books should vary in length as well as difficulty so that there are opportunities to read shorter and longer texts at each level. At first, children need texts that are both easy and short; but the development of effective strategies requires that children sustain reading behavior over an extended time. It helps both teacher and children if there are some longer books at each level. *Goodnight Peter* is a level G book that is easy and short; there are four lines of text on each page. *Greedy Cat* is a longer book at that level, with more lines of text on each page.

Toward the end of first grade and into second, children need to be able to read longer texts and hold on to the meaning over several days. Some chapter books that probably would not be read in one sitting are *Nate the Great* and *Cam Jansen and the Mystery of the Monster Movie*. *A Hippopotamus Ate the Teacher*, on the other hand, can probably be read in one day. You need to have both options available within the collection.

Format

Format refers to the way a book is designed—size, shape, typography, text layout, illustrations, cover design, binding. Like the books in the classroom library, books used for guided reading should vary in size, appearance, and cover design, at a glance communicating rich variety rather than boring sameness.

Text layout is very important. Sometimes books that have excellent stories and illustrations are not appropriate for early stages of guided reading because they have very small, crowded print or a tricky layout. More complex layouts are appropriate as children learn more about how print works and develop as readers. Then different layouts are valuable, because they help readers become more flexible. The page in Figure 9–3, from *How to Ride a Giraffe*, illustrates a more complex format.

Typography and layout are important in different ways in higher-level texts. *How to Eat Fried Worms* has tiny print with many lines on a page and few illustrations, while *A Book About Your Skeleton* has a small amount of print and a picture on every page. *Molly's*

Pilgrim has larger print but full pages of text, with illustrations every four or five pages. Examining text formats will help you plan how to introduce these books and pace the reading. Working in a supported way with different kinds of layouts helps children develop flexibility in the way they cope with challenging texts.

Part of guided reading is helping young readers understand how authors are presenting information. Knowing how to analyze a text's inner workings will build a foundation for the large amount of informational material students are expected to read in upper elementary grades. For example, in second and third grade, teachers should be sure to introduce a number of informational texts to children and teach them how to use text features peculiar to this genre: table of contents, charts and diagrams, picture captions, glossary, etc. Readers who are accustomed to the structure of narrative texts often find informational texts difficult simply because no

FIGURE 9–3   A complex page layout: *How to Ride a Giraffe*

one has shown them that the information is presented differently.

Finally, you want to be sure that children are working with what Clay (1991a, p. 262) calls "information-rich texts" that offer support at every level of language development. They are rich in meaning that children can access and relate to, and the relationships among words (pronouns and their antecedents, for example) are clear. Information-rich texts offer the redundancy that supports reading. Meaning is signaled in several ways—through syntax, through print conventions such as punctuation, and through words. Children have the opportunity to check sources of information against each other. When they have to search for information in words and letters, the task is made easier if meaning is constantly accessible.

Creating a Gradient of Text

It is impossible for a teacher to provide a literature-based guided reading program for children without carefully considering what makes texts difficult or easy for individual children. A gradient of text reflects a defined continuum of characteristics related to the level of support and challenge the reader is offered. To create a leveled collection of books, teachers evaluate texts against the characteristics for each level. Our gradient has sixteen levels encompassing kindergarten through third grade. There are nine levels through kindergarten and first grade, four levels across second grade, and three levels for third grade. Within each level, there are many more choices than one school would ever need.

To create a continuum of text levels, teachers need to analyze the supports and challenges inherent to each text. In doing so, the teacher considers how individual readers might respond to these supports and challenges in reading the text. Each text has specific features that support a child's use of strategies and offer new opportunities. For

example, some early books support the use of phrasing by laying out the text so that each sentence begins a new line or certain words are grouped on a separate line. These details can make a big difference for the beginning reader.

Easy and *hard* are relative terms. We cannot classify books themselves as easy or hard; they can only be designated that way in relation to an individual reader. Creating a text gradient means classifying books along a continuum based on the combination of variables that support and confirm readers' strategic actions and offer the problem-solving opportunities that build the reading process.

A gradient of text is not a precise sequence of texts through which all children pass. Books are leveled in approximate groups from which teachers choose particular books for individuals or reading groups. No text sequence will suit every child, but efficiency requires a leveled set from which to choose. The teacher who recognizes the convenience of the gradient yet reminds herself of its limitations will be able to make cautious choices and test her decisions against children's behavior while reading each text.

Getting started

There are many ways to construct a suitable text gradient. You can begin with any leveled set of books you are comfortable with (a publisher's starter set or the district basal, for example), then look critically at the texts to see whether any are misplaced. With most basals, you will need to look carefully at each story. After using a series for several years, most teachers know the texts that are harder than they should be for their place in the series. Eliminate or change the level of those texts. Then gather other books that are suitable for guided reading and place them on the continuum using your original set of books as prototypes.

A more complicated but very useful way to create a gradient of text is illustrated in the procedures below, another example of the productivity of colleague support:

1. All teachers gather examples of books available in the school. Each teacher brings to the initial meeting those books that he or she knows well and has used successfully with children.

2. From these books, select all those that are appropriate for guided reading. Eliminate books best suited for content area study or literature circles and those of poor quality.

3. Place books in groups by difficulty. Compare a few books at a time and consider factors such as:
   ■ Length.
   ■ Size and layout of print.
   ■ Vocabulary and concepts.
   ■ Language structure.
   ■ Text structure and genre.
   ■ Predictability and pattern of language.
   ■ Illustration support.

4. Create formal descriptions of the books in each group, noting the general characteristics (these are often expressed in comparison to the level below).

5. Identify the control of reading strategies children would need to read the texts in each level successfully and the opportunities each level provides for new learning.

6. Test the leveled book collection with students for several months.

7. Reconvene the group. Share running records of children's behavior while reading texts and observations about the supports and challenges in particular books. ("This book is harder than it looks." "This book had difficult concepts that I had not anticipated." "This book has a lot of print, but it's actually quite a bit easier than other books at this level.")

8. Make adjustments in the leveled collection, moving some books to higher levels and others to lower levels. Create new levels if necessary.

9. Test the collection again.

10. Meet periodically to reevaluate the collection and add new books.

Benchmark books

An important step in creating a gradient of text is to select benchmark books for each level. A benchmark book is stable for the level and highly reliable; that is, the book will be appropriate, at about 90 or 95 percent accuracy, for a large majority of children who demonstrate similar behaviors at a particular point in time. There may be several benchmark books at each level. These are the books teachers have found to be most reliable with children at a particular level. Benchmark books serve as prototypes. Designating some benchmarks will help teachers new to the process and identify reliable texts to use in ongoing assessment (see Chapters 6 and 7). In more formal systems, a few benchmark books can be removed from the guided reading collection and used only for systematic assessment.

Some frequently asked questions
Should children choose their own books for guided reading?
As the teacher, you use your expertise to select the texts children will experience in guided reading. No young child can be expected to select a series of books that will adequately support learning to read. All children deserve and need expert help. Choice comes into play when they reread familiar material from browsing boxes, choose books for literature circles or readers workshop, and use the classroom library. Even in those activities, you may want to narrow choices for particular children at certain times. As children grow more expert in reading, they learn to recognize books that will be easy or a bit more challenging and not to struggle with material that is far too difficult. You need to make teaching how to make choices part of the curriculum.

How can I develop skill in determining the level of books?

Expertise is built through practice. Expect to test all of your texts with many children. Running records are the most powerful tool we know for this process. It is difficult initially to learn the procedure, but you will become proficient with time and the knowledge you gain makes it well worth the effort. After using texts with several different groups of children over a year, determining levels becomes much easier. You will build up a repertoire of known texts that are easy to think about in relation to individual children. Characteristics of benchmark texts will become second nature, making it easier to place new books on the continuum. Collaborating with colleagues is essential if you are establishing a schoolwide program. Plan to spend one or two years creating your system and learning how to use it.

Is the gradient described in this book the same as that used in Reading Recovery?

No. Reading Recovery requires a finer gradient because teachers are working closely with individuals who have very little experience with print and may need very small increased challenges to support their reading. Reading Recovery teachers need to recognize, record, and build on the slightest indications of progress. They choose one particular book at a time for one child and they take a running record every day.

In a guided reading classroom such a fine gradient is not practical or necessary. Groups involve children with different strengths, so broader levels are needed to accommodate the differences within the group. Also, children who are making average and above average progress have greater flexibility than children who are having the most difficulty.

Having slightly broader levels also makes it easier for a group of teachers to organize and use texts and to add to the collections. The range of books within a level is obvious, and teachers choose selections to fit particular groups. Our book list (see Appendix M) is de-

signed so that there are finer gradations for kindergarten and early first grade, slightly broader categories for later first grade, broader categories for second, and even broader categories for third and fourth grade. (See Fountas and Pinnell 1999a and Pinnell and Fountas 2002 for extensive book lists.)

What makes the guided reading text gradient different from published reading programs?

Different sets of leveled texts are based on different criteria. For example, most traditional basal readers use the same words over and over, with only a few new ones added in successive stories. Sentence length is also controlled. Meaning takes second place. The result is a text that contains easy words but whose language is unnatural and whose meaning is often distorted. Texts that look easy are actually hard.

Another way to control the gradient of text is to use phonemic elements as a guiding principle. So-called linguistic readers use words that can be sounded out using learned letter-sound associations, but the resulting sentences are often extremely distorted in terms of language structure and meaning. For example, the sentences "A pig in a wig did a jig. Did a pig jig?" are centered around the short *i* sound and the phonogram *ig*. Children who have practiced using these phonemic elements may be able to read the words, but we question whether they will find reading enjoyable and meaningful. If this is the only kind of text they encounter, they may not realize how a reader has to check one information source against another with flexibility; they can develop a narrow view of the reading process.

Our gradient of text recognizes that children need to use a variety of sources of information while problem solving for meaning. Therefore, a much more complex set of text characteristics are used to determine level.

Are all books in a guided reading classroom organized by level?

Most books in the classroom library are not organized by level. Most books in the classroom library, for example, can be organized by topic, author, genre, and other categories, with only some baskets organized by difficulty level. For guided reading, however, books need to be organized by level of difficulty. The leveled set of books allows the teacher to provide texts that support the successful acquisition of reading skills and processes by every child in the class.

Can books in the guided reading collection be used for other purposes?

Yes. Some titles are good selections to read aloud; in that case, the level designation would not apply. Some big books are appropriate for shared reading. All levels of books that are easier than the one in which children are working can be available for free-choice reading. Children at more advanced levels occasionally enjoy reading books they're familiar with, and doing so is valuable and highly motivating. You don't need to be too rigid about using books in different ways, however; keep in mind that children do need experience processing new texts.

How can I afford to purchase the books needed for guided reading?

It may seem at first glance that we are recommending a large expenditure for this essential collection of books. This isn't the case. (See Fountas and Pinnell 1999a.)

First, the collection is built over time. You will begin by analyzing the books you now have, probably finding more appropriate titles than you think. If you pool your efforts with colleagues, you'll be able to create group sets, because each of you may have one or two copies of the same title.

Second, you can begin guided reading with a relatively sparse collection, adding to it year by year.

Third, you are buying individual books instead of expensive anthologies that quickly become outdated. Your guided reading collection never needs to be replaced; you only need add to it or replace worn copies. And you can use your anthologies if they contain

good selections: just categorize individual selections by level of difficulty. Some teachers have even cut old anthologies apart, put new covers on the usable portions, and added good selections to their leveled sets that way. Book clubs, in which points accrue for use on reduced-price or free books, are another good way to add to the collection. Specific book club ordering information can be found in Fountas and Pinnell, 1999a.

Where can I find more information on using leveled books and more titles at each level?

You can find 7,500 titles and word counts along with ten chapters dedicated to the use of leveled books in *Matching Books to Readers* (Fountas and Pinnell 1999a), and 6,000 titles for grades 3–6 in *Leveled Books for Readers, Grades 3–6* (Pinnell and Fountas 2002)

Suggestions for Professional Development

1. An excellent professional development activity is to follow a procedure similar to the one suggested in this chapter for creating a leveled booklist. If that is impractical, try using the procedure with books in your own classroom.

2. Use the form in Appendix K to participate in evaluating and revising the lists presented in this book. Fill in the form and mail it, fax it, or e-mail it to us. We welcome and appreciate a growing network of teachers who would like to communicate about the level of books.

Irene Fountas
Lesley University School of Education
29 Everett Street
Cambridge MA 02140
ifountas@mail.lesley.edu

Gay Su Pinnell
Ohio State University
29 W. Woodruff Avenue
200 Ramseyer Hall
Columbus OH 43210
pinnell.1@osu.edu

Using a Leveled Set of Books

If children could work on literacy tasks most of the time at a level of success, we would have solved the biggest problem in learning to read and write. DON HOLDAWAY

Below is a general description of the important characteristics that define each level of our book list. Not every book at a level will have all the attributes listed here, but these descriptions will help as you begin using the books. As you examine and evaluate books, closely observe children's reading behavior, and take running records, the characteristics at each level will become second nature.

Whether a text is easy or hard for a child depends on more than the characteristics inherent to the text. The way the text is introduced and the supportive interaction during reading play important roles as well. The teacher is constantly balancing the tension between text level and the amount of support he will provide to readers. His knowledge of individual children and the way they approach texts is the most valuable tool; hence, we provide examples of important behaviors to notice and support for each level. Our list is not exhaustive; it is a general heuristic for a teacher's observations of complex behavior.

Levels A and B

Examples
Dad (Level A) (see Figure 10–1)

At the Zoo (Level B) (see Figure 10–2)

Description
Level A and B books are very easy for young children to begin to read. Many of these books focus on a single idea or have a simple story line. There is a direct correspondence between the text and the pictures, and children can easily relate the topics to their personal experience. The language, while not exactly duplicating oral language, includes naturally occurring syntactic structures. Teachers can use books at these levels to introduce children to word-by-word matching and locating known words.

The format is consistent; print appears at the same place on every page. Layout is easy to follow, with print clearly separated from pictures. Print is regular, clear, and easy to see and there is a full range of punctuation. There is ample space between words so that children can point and read. Several frequently encountered words are repeated often throughout the text. Most books have one to four lines of text (one or two sentences) per page or illustration. Many one-line caption books are included in level A, while level B books usually have more words, more lines of text, and a slightly greater range of frequently used vocabulary.

Dad is reading.

14

FIGURE 10–1   *Dad*

I like the giraffe and the giraffe likes me.

I like the tiger and the tiger likes me.

FIGURE 10–2   *At the Zoo*

Important behaviors to notice and support

■ Handling books—moving through the text from front to back, turning pages.

■ Controlling left-to-right movement and return sweep.

■ Noticing and interpreting detail in pictures.

■ Using oral language in relation to the text.

■ Matching word by word (indicated by precise pointing).

■ Paying close attention to print—noticing some features of letters and words.

■ Locating familiar and new words.

■ Remembering and using language patterns.

■ Using knowledge of language syntax as a source of information.

■ Using oral language in combination with pointing—matching voice with words on the page.

■ Predicting what makes sense.

■ Self-monitoring—checking one's reading by using word-by-word matching, noticing known words in text, or noticing mismatches in meaning or language.

Level C

Examples
Trolley Ride
Wake Up, Dad (see Figure 10–3)

Description
Books at level C also have simple story lines and topics that are familiar to children. They tend to be longer than level B books but still have only a few (two to five) lines of text on a page. At this level more of the story is carried by the text, but pictures are still very important in supporting meaning and there is a direct correspondence between text and pictures. Print appears on both left and right pages but it is still clearly separated from text. Oral language structures are used and often repeated, and phrasing is often supported by print placement. Frequently encountered words are used more often, and there is a full range of punctuation.

Patterns and repetition are used in some books; others support prediction through natural language and meaning. There is more variation in language patterns, requiring children to attend closely to print at some points. Sentences are a little longer but the syntax is simple and easy to control; there are more words than in level B texts.

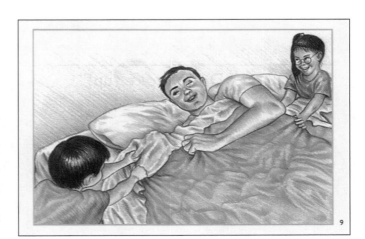

James said,
"Wake up, Dad."

"I am asleep," said Dad.

8

9

FIGURE 10–3 *Wake Up, Dad*

Important behaviors to notice and support

■ Using visual information to help predict, check, and confirm.

■ Controlling word-by-word matching of voice with print.

■ Using illustrations to predict meaning as well as particular words.

■ Predicting from events what will come next.

■ Checking illustrations with print.

■ Using known words as anchors.

■ Moving fluently through the text while reading for meaning.

■ Solving some unfamiliar words independently.

■ Engaging independently in same behaviors listed for level B.

■ Accumulating a reading vocabulary—a group of known words, usually those frequently encountered, that are recognized from book to book.

Level D

Examples
Greedy Cat Is Hungry (see Figure 10–4)
Tom Is Brave

Description
Stories are slightly more complex but still very easy for children to understand. Concepts are within children's experience. The illustrations are supportive, but more attention to the print is required. Most texts have clear print; spacing is obvious. Most texts range from two to six lines of print per page and have more words than the previous levels. Sentences are generally a

Greedy Cat sat
on a mat
by the fridge.
Meow, meow, meow!

6

"No!" said Uncle.
"You're a greedy cat!"

7

FIGURE 10–4 *Greedy Cat Is Hungry*

little longer than level C. There is a full range of punctuation; words encountered in previous texts are used many times. The vocabulary contains more inflectional endings—*ing, ed, s*—so that children have an opportunity to notice the variations in word structure.

Important behaviors to notice and support

■ Controlling early strategies (word-by-word matching and directional movement) on longer stretches of text.

■ Moving away from finger pointing as eyes take over the process.

■ Using pattern and language syntax to read with phrasing.

■ Checking on one's reading using knowledge of letter-sound relationships, words, and parts of words.

■ Rereading to confirm reading or problem solving.

■ Checking one source of information against another to confirm, make another attempt, or self-correct.

■ Moving more fluently through the text.

■ Actively reading for meaning.

Level E

Examples
Baby Bear Goes Fishing
At the Seaside
Mrs. Wishy-Washy (see Figure 10–5)
Pat's New Puppy

Description
The amount of text is gradually increasing; most stories have three to eight lines of text per page and text placement varies. Stories

FIGURE 10–5 *Mrs. Wishy-Washy*

are more complex; where repeated language patterns are used, they vary within the text. The ideas in stories are more subtle and may require more interpretation. Illustrations strongly support the story but contain several ideas; the text carries the story line. Problem solving is needed to figure out new words and to relate the illustrations and text.

The reading vocabulary requires skill in word analysis; words are longer and have inflectional endings. Texts at level E build on and extend children's vocabulary of frequently used words. Taking words apart will help children problem-solve. A full variety of punctuation is evident. Some concepts may be less familiar to children. Texts may look easy (having only one line or few words) but the ideas require more control of aspects of print.

Important behaviors to notice and support

❚ Tracking print with the eyes except at points of difficulty or on novel text.
❚ Using knowledge of language syntax and meaning to read with phrasing.
❚ Reading fluently.
❚ Solving new words while maintaining a focus on meaning.
❚ Rereading to check, confirm, and search.
❚ Cross-checking one source of information with another.
❚ Self-correcting using multiple sources of information.
❚ Predicting what will happen next and reading to confirm.
❚ Using known words to get to words not yet known.
❚ Relating one text to another.
❚ Using more information from print to construct the meaning of the story.

Level F

Examples
Cookie's Week
The Hungry Giant (see Figure 10–6)
Just Like Daddy

Description
Texts are slightly longer than level E; the print is necessarily somewhat smaller. There are usually between three and eight lines of text per page. Pictures continue to support reading although the text carries more of the meaning. Literary language is mixed with typical oral language structures, but the syntax of the text reflects patterns peculiar to written language. The variety of frequently used words continues to expand. Story lines include more episodes (actions or events), which follow one another chronologically, and some characters are more fully developed. Generally the text has a distinct beginning, middle, and end. Dialogue has appeared at earlier levels, but at this level there is greater variety in the way it is signaled and presented. Punctuation supports phrasing and meaning. There are many more opportunities for word analysis.

Important behaviors to notice and support

❚ Being aware of punctuation and using it for phrasing and meaning.

❚ Searching visual information to figure out new words while reading.

❚ Using the syntax of written language to predict, then checking the accuracy of the prediction.

❚ Analyzing new words and checking them against what makes sense or sounds right.

❚ Controlling early strategies even on novel texts.

❚ Reading with fluent phrasing and attention to meaning.

❚ Moving quickly through text.

❚ Using known words and parts of words as well as letter-sound relationships to get to new words, and checking against other information such as meaning.

❚ Using multiple sources of information to self-correct.

FIGURE 10–6   *The Hungry Giant*

Levels G and H

Examples
The Carrot Seed (Level G)
Greedy Cat (Level G) (see Figure 10–7)
Ben's Tooth (Level H)
Rosie at the Zoo (Level H) (see Figure 10–8)

Description
Books at level G contain more challenging ideas and vocabulary. Most books still have between four and eight lines of text per page, but the sentences are longer. As at level F, literary language, structures, and concepts are integrated with natural language. A greater range of content extends children's experiences. The reading vocabulary continues to expand; new vocabulary is introduced. Stories have more events; occasionally repetition is built into the episodic structure to support reading. Level H is very similar to G, but the language and vocabulary are even more complex, the stories longer and more literary, and there is less repetition in the episodic structure.

Important behaviors to notice and support

∎ Moving through the text using pictures and print in an integrated way while attending to meaning.

∎ Solving new words by using word analysis, then checking the words against meaning.

∎ Monitoring one's reading (accurately reading long stretches of text with intermittent hesitations and repeats).

∎ Self-correcting close to the point of error.

∎ Rereading to check and search.

∎ Discussing ideas from the story in a way that indicates understanding.

Mum went shopping
and got some bananas.

8

Along came Greedy Cat.
He looked in the shopping bag.
Gobble, gobble, gobble,
and that was the end of that.

9

FIGURE 10–7   *Greedy Cat*

Dad took us to the zoo.

"Let's go and see the monkeys,"
said Dad.

"Me, too!" said Rosie.

2

We lifted Rosie up.
"I like monkeys," said Rosie.

"Let's go and see the lions,"
I said.

"Me, too!" said Rosie.

3

FIGURE 10–8   *Rosie at the Zoo*

■ Discussing characters in a way that indicates understanding and interpretation.

■ Effectively managing a variety of texts, including fiction and informational texts.

■ Connecting text to other texts.

Level I

Examples
Happy Birthday, Sam
Henny Penny
Leo the Late Bloomer
The Princess, the Mud Pies, and the Dragon
(see Figure 10–9)
Tidy Titch

Description
At level I there are a variety of texts, including some informational ones. Story structure is more complex; episodes are more elaborate; and themes are varied and sophisticated. Illustrations provide low to moderate support, extend the texts, and assist children in interpretation. Readers are asked to understand different points of view. Texts offer many opportunities to discuss new ideas.

Texts are generally longer than the previous level, with more sentences per page. Specialized, unusual, and challenging vocabulary is evident. Texts include a large number of words that by now will be familiar to most children; problem solving will be needed only for unfamiliar words. Characters are memorable. There are many possibilities for comparison with other texts, those previously read and those children have heard read aloud.

Important behaviors to notice and support

■ Fluent and phrased reading, especially when rereading.

■ Competent problem solving of new words on initial reading.

In a land far away, a sweet princess lived in a castle with her mother the queen and her father the king.

The princess had toys of gold and toys of silver.
But she never played with them.
All day long, the princess made mud pies.

FIGURE 10–9 *The Princess, the Mud Pies, and the Dragon*

❙ Flexibly checking one's reading against meaning.

❙ Using information sources (meaning, syntax, and visual information) in integrated ways while focusing on meaning.

❙ Making connections between texts through discussion, art, or writing.

❙ Demonstrating an understanding of and empathy with characters through discussion, art, or writing.

❙ Moving toward easy, fluent reading even of unfamiliar and difficult texts, demonstrating less overt problem solving.

❙ Self-correcting at the point of error with fewer returns to the beginning of sentences or phrases.

❙ Coping with unfamiliar concepts.

❙ Gaining momentum while moving through the text because knowledge is being constructed about how this text works and what it is likely to say.

Level J

Examples
Danny and the Dinosaur (see Figure 10–10)
Henry & Mudge
Not Now, Said the Cow

Description
Level J approximately marks the beginning of second grade; however, advanced first graders will already be reading books at this level. Other children, especially if they have

It got late and

the other children left.

Danny and the dinosaur

were alone.

"Well, goodbye, Danny,"

said the dinosaur.

"Can't you come

and stay with me?"

said Danny.

"We could have fun."

"No," said the dinosaur.

"I've had a good time—

the best I've had

in a hundred million years.

But now I must get back

to the museum.

They need me there."

"Oh," said Danny.

"Well, goodbye."

FIGURE 10–10 *Danny and the Dinosaur*

not had much reading experience over the summer, will need easier books. Texts at this level and the next allow children to orchestrate their reading strategies on a greater variety of texts, consolidating and extending what they know.

Stories are longer and more complex, although they still deal with subjects of interest to young children. Most concepts and themes are familiar, from either personal experience or previous experience with books. There are a variety of texts—nonfiction, folktales, realistic stories, and more.

Some books are beginning chapter books that let children sustain reading. These long books (thirty to sixty pages) may use shorter sentences and familiar vocabulary so that readers can move through them rapidly, still sustaining problem solving and fluency. Some will be too long to read in one sitting, so children will need to sustain interest and meaning over a period of time. Others will involve much harder text but be shorter.

The language is appropriate for the type of text; many stories have literary language, with which children are by now familiar. They will still need to figure out new styles, particularly the way certain characters reveal their personality or development through the way they speak.

Important behaviors to notice and support

▌ Using skills and strategies effectively on a variety of texts.

▌ Sustaining interest and fluency through a longer text.

▌ Easily coming back to a text if it requires more than one sitting.

▌ Solving unfamiliar words or concepts "on the run" without detracting from meaning.

▌ Self-correcting when necessary to support meaning, but showing a general forward thrust (checking and self-correcting behaviors become less overt and more internal).

▌ Reading silently much of the time, no longer finding it necessary to vocalize every word.

▌ Demonstrating an understanding of the story or text through discussion, art, and writing.

▌ Moving flexibly from nonfiction to fiction and vice versa.

▌ Using ideas from one's reading in one's writing.

▌ Summarizing or extending a given text.

Level K

Examples
Nate the Great and the Pillowcase
Keep the Lights Burning, Abbie (see Figure 10–11)

Description
Level K includes a variety of texts. Some books contain long stretches of easy text so that children strengthen their ability to read longer selections. These easy chapterlike books usually have pictures on every page or every other page. The amount of text on a page varies, some pages having text only and others having text and pictures. Print is laid out with clear spaces between words and lines. Illustrations support and extend the text and enhance interpretation. The stories have multiple episodes related to a single plot.

Literary picture books that can be read in a single sitting are also included in level K. These picture books generally have large illustrations and about ten or fifteen lines of print on each page, although some pages might have only one or two lines depending on the layout. There are a few traditional tales that children will have heard read aloud in kindergarten or first grade; now they will take them on as independent readers.

Much of the reading is silent; at other times, particularly in group sessions, children read aloud (usually favorite, interesting, or important parts rather than an entire text).

Abbie sat on a rock and watched them.
"Now listen, Hope, Patience, and Charity,"
she said.
"Don't eat it all too fast.
There is not much corn left.
But Papa will bring you more."
Abbie sighed.
"I hope he gets home today.
I am a little afraid
to care for the lights alone."
Patience pecked Abbie's shoe.
Hope turned her head.
Charity ruffled her feathers.
Abbie laughed.
"You three always make me feel better."

18

FIGURE 10–11   *Keep the Lights Burning, Abbie*

Important behaviors to notice and support

▌ Using multiple sources of information in an integrated way.

▌ Reading silently much of the time.

▌ Effectively and efficiently analyzing longer words.

▌ Using a variety of word analysis strategies without losing meaning or fluency.

▌ Reading in a phrased, fluent way over longer stretches of text.

▌ Demonstrating through discussion, writing, or other media that they can understand and interpret the stories from different perspectives and empathize with the characters.

▌ Using text structure (both narrative and logic) to predict a likely sequence of events or to analyze and critique the text.

▌ Sustaining characters and plot over several days.

Level L

Examples
Cam Jansen and the Mystery of the Monster Movie (see Figure 10–12)
The Dog That Pitched a No-Hitter

Description
Level L marks a big shift in material. Many texts are longer chapter books with only a few illustrations. The pictures provide much less support. More characters are involved in the plots, and there are more sophisticated language structures, more detail, and more description. Stories are more involved, and

ders on the poster and each has eight legs. That's forty legs." Cam opened her eyes. "Am I right?"

"Yes," Eric said. "Now come on. Your parents are way ahead of us."

Cam and Eric caught up with Cam's parents at the ticket window.

"Two adults and two children," Mrs. Jansen said. Then she passed some money through the window.

"How old are the children?" the ticket seller asked.

"They're both ten."

The ticket seller gave Cam's mother two purple tickets, two green tickets, and some change. Then Cam, Eric, and Cam's parents went into the theater.

The lobby was crowded and warm. A few people were standing and talking. Others were waiting in line to buy popcorn and soda.

"We can get food later," Cam's father

6

said. "I want to get good seats. And I don't want to miss anything."

They went through the swinging doors and into the theater. Soft music was playing. People were sitting in many of the seats. Cam's father found four empty seats near the front of the theater. Cam and Eric took off their coats and sat down. Then they looked up at the dark, blank screen and waited.

FIGURE 10–12 *Cam Jansen and the Mystery of the Monster Movie*

the vocabulary is challenging. Text size is smaller and word spacing is narrower.

In general, the texts require higher level conceptual work to understand the subtleties of plot and character development. Reading a book must be sustained over several days and is supported by group discussion during and after. Reading will be primarily independent, mostly silent but with some parts read aloud for emphasis or interest.

Important behaviors to notice and support
The same behaviors noted for level K, but exhibited in connection with

❚ Longer stretches of text.

❚ More difficult vocabulary, ideas, and language structures.
❚ More complex ideas and topics.
❚ A greater range of genre.

Level M

Examples
What's Cooking, Jenny Archer?
Molly's Pilgrim (see Figure 10–13)

Descriptions
Books in level M are long, with lots of text per page, smaller print, and narrower word spacing. There is a wide variety of texts but they all have complex language structures and sophisticated vocabulary. They are highly

I started to run. When I got to our apartment, I burst into tears. It was all right. I could cry in front of my mother.

She put her arms around me. I leaned my head against her chest. She felt like a big, soft cushion. *"Shaynkeit,* what's the matter?" she asked. My mother didn't speak much English. She talked to me in Yiddish.

"Mama, let's go back to New York City," I said. "In this third grade, there aren't any other Jewish children. I don't talk like the other girls. They make fun of me. I hate going to school."

FIGURE 10–13 *Molly's Pilgrim*

detailed and descriptive and present more abstract concepts and themes. The subtleties of these texts require more background knowledge. Many characters are involved in more complex and expanded plots; character development is a prominent feature.

Important behaviors to notice and support
We note the same behaviors listed for levels K and L, but exhibited in connection with

❚ Longer stretches of text.
❚ More difficult vocabulary, ideas, and language structures.
❚ More complex ideas and topics.
❚ A greater range of genres.

In addition, watch for indications that children:

❚ Can use texts as references.
❚ Can search for and find information in texts.

❚ Can interpret texts from a variety of perspectives.
❚ Can read critically.
❚ Can understand subtleties of plot and humor.
❚ Can reflect on their personal response in relation to how others see the text.

Levels N, O, P, Q, R, and S

The titles at each of these levels identify third-grade and some fourth-grade texts. The texts become much more complex in terms of a variety of added characteristics (see Fountas & Pinnell 1999a).

The Teacher as Mediator of the Text

The selection of any book begins with the children's strengths, interests, and needs. A critical factor in children's ability to read a text successfully is the way the teacher mediates or intervenes to help them. Chapters 11 and 12 describe how to support reading by introducing stories and teaching for strategies using appropriate demonstrations, prompts, and reinforcements. The diagram in Figure 10–14 illustrates this integrated process, sometimes called *teaching from behind*. The teacher's foregrounding is critical to the child's work on the text, as are her brief and highly selective interactions during reading. The idea is for the child to learn the strategies he needs to read the text as independently as possible.

Coordinating gradient text with grade-level expectations

The text gradient described above and exemplified in Appendix M applies broadly across the primary grades from kindergarten through second and third grade. The list is a continuum; it implies progress from very simple

texts and early reading behaviors to self-extended reading of a wide variety of complex texts. The tentative grade-level approximations are exactly that and not meant to be rigidly applied. Each school needs to adjust these levels to fit its particular community.

The levels will be applied in different ways based on particular children's backgrounds and previous experiences. Figure 10–15 illustrates one way to think about difficulty levels in relation to grade levels. The grade levels overlap, but even within this flexible arrangement, some children will need supplemental materials; others may have experienced problems in learning to read and need material that is simpler than usually expected at the grade level. As teachers we want to be especially aware of children who fall outside an average range of progress. A child in second grade who is reading at level A or B needs texts at those levels but will

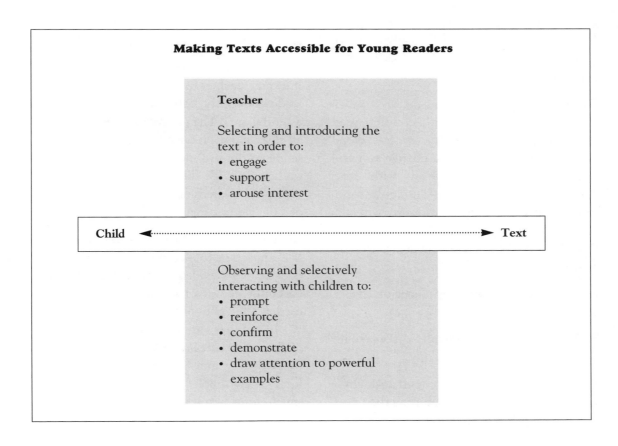

FIGURE 10–14   Making texts accessible for young readers

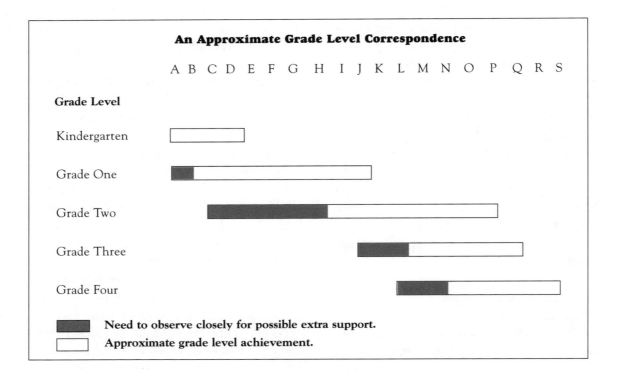

An Approximate Grade Level Correspondence

A B C D E F G H I J K L M N O P Q R S

Grade Level

Kindergarten

Grade One

Grade Two

Grade Three

Grade Four

    ■ **Need to observe closely for possible extra support.**
    □ **Approximate grade level achievement.**

FIGURE 10–15   An approximate grade level correspondence

also need extra support. The first-grade Reading Recovery program (see Chapter 15) is an excellent way to prevent such wide discrepancies.

Revising the levels

Any text gradient used with children year after year is always in the process of development. We expect our list to change and encourage you to try the levels with your students and give us feedback using the form in Appendix K. In appreciation, we will add you to our mailing list for further information about books. As you evaluate the books, answer these questions:

■ Is the book appropriately placed on the level?

■ Are there points of difficulty that make it harder than it seems?

■ Is the text supportive in ways that might not be noticeable when examining the superficial characteristics and therefore easier than it seems?

■ Are there other books that you feel are appropriate for guided reading at this level?

Storing the collection

If several teachers in a school are using guided reading texts, the collection can be stored in a central area. The room can have shelves on all sides and even have freestanding units resembling library "stacks." Cardboard or plastic boxes on the shelves can house multiple copies of hundreds of titles organized by level of difficulty (see Figure 10–16).

Including books for other purposes

It is important to mention again that not all books can be leveled for difficulty; they may be better placed in separate categories and used as references or for literature circles.

In another category are whole-class sets of literature titles used in connection with the language arts or social studies curriculum. These books may be pulled out for small-group literature study but can also be used for a common literature experience for the whole class.

FIGURE 10–16   A book room

In addition to the common collection, you should have a good quantity and range of natural language texts in your own classroom at all times. Classrooms also should have books children can take home.

Labeling books for use by several teachers
Teachers using a common collection should establish a clear convention for labeling the boxes and the books. A sample book box is shown in Figure 10–17. The title or titles of the books appear on the outside of the box, with the level of difficulty in the upper right-hand corner. If several titles are stored in one box ("little" books that do not require much space, for example), we recommend placing each set of copies in a resealable plastic bag so that they can be easily grabbed and returned. Use a permanent marker to write the title of the book on the outside of the bag as well as the number of copies and the level.

As a checkout system, you can use clothespins. Teachers clip a clothespin with their name on it on the box when they take a set of books and remove the clothespin when they return them.

We have presented one example of a gradient of text that will require constant revision. We urge readers of this book not to take the list as a static resource but to check all recommended selections against what you know and are finding out about your own students. The list is available as a starting point for your own investigations and development. The most valuable resource here is observation of children and colleague support.

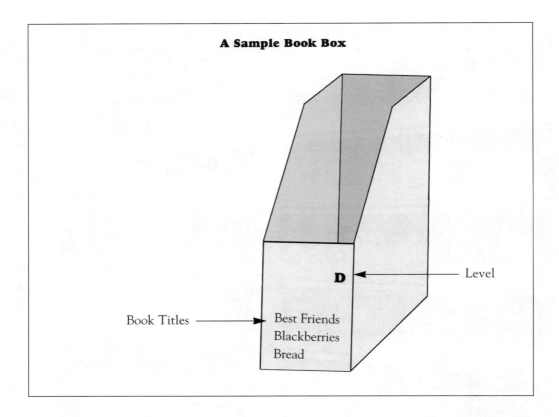

A Sample Book Box

Level

Book Titles

D

Best Friends
Blackberries
Bread

FIGURE 10–17 A sample book box

Suggestions for Professional Development

1. With colleagues in your school, establish a beginning leveled collection using procedures like those described in this chapter. Then work to establish benchmark books at each level. Start by trying out appropriate levels with children and collecting about ten running records of children's reading of each text.

2. Convene a session to suggest benchmark books for several levels based on your beginning observations and running records. Then devise a systematic way of testing the benchmarks by identifying a large number of children who are reading at the designated level for the potential benchmark. Have these children read the books, again taking a running record and recording accuracy

and self-correction rates and then analyzing reading behavior.

3. Bring running records to another session and discuss the texts one at a time, noticing the stability of the text across a range of children who are at about the same level and also noting the ways the text supported and challenged children's reading strategies.

4. Continue to test benchmarks over time until your group feels comfortable with several texts at each level.

5. You may want to consider purchasing more copies of those books that serve as benchmarks or exemplars because they will probably be read by most children during their progress through the grades and represent stable texts that can be used to place children on reading graphs (see Chapter 6) and for assessment.

Selecting and Introducing Books

As the child approaches a new text he is entitled to an introduction so that when he reads, the gist of the whole or partly revealed story can provide some guide for a fluent reading. MARIE CLAY

Guided reading has two essential elements. First, the text must provide the right level of support and challenge for the children's current processing abilities: it must include language and concepts that they either control or can get to with their present strategies while providing a few new things to learn. Second, the text must be introduced in a way that gives children access to it while leaving some problem solving to do. Both elements depend on the teacher's knowledge of the children in the group, the texts, and the reading process.

Before children begin to read a book in guided reading, the teacher (1) selects a book that will suit the children in the group and (2) introduces the story by talking with the children about aspects of the text. Some important principles to keep in mind are:

■ Varying levels of support are built into the process. The teacher can provide more support for a challenging text and a briefer introduction when the text is easy, fine-tuning the text gradient to provide just the right amount of challenge.

■ The teacher mediates the text. By preselecting and previewing the book, the teacher helps children use their strengths while approaching new texts.

■ There will be change over time as different texts are selected and the level of support changes.

■ Children's background knowledge and the language they bring to the process will affect a teacher's selections and mediations.

■ Children's knowledge of letters, of the way words work, and of the conventions of print (like spacing and direction) is also a factor in the books chosen for guided reading and in the way they are mediated.

Selecting Books

First, select books that will appeal to and delight children. This is true whether you are building a general collection or selecting a book for a particular group to read the coming week.

Your leveled set of books is the starting point. If the children are reading well and finding new learning opportunities on a particular level, the selection is probably about right; however, there are more factors to consider:

■ Are the concepts in the book familiar to children or can they be made accessible through the introduction?

■ Is the plot interesting? Will it appeal to this group of children?

■ Does the text provide opportunities for this group of children to use what they know?

■ Are some words in the book known to children?

■ Are other words accessible through children's current ability to use strategies such as word analysis and prediction from language structure or meaning?

■ Does the text offer a few opportunities to problem-solve, search, and check while reading for meaning?

■ Do the illustrations support children's search for meaning? Do they extend the meaning of the text?

■ Is the length of text appropriate for the experience and stamina of the group?

■ For emergent and early readers, is the text layout clear? Is the print clear? Are there an appropriate number of lines of text? Is there sufficient space between words?

Obviously the book's level of support and challenge will not be the same even for all children in one guided reading group. They bring different experiences to the book, so they will search for meaning in different ways. Even if they have been exposed to about the same frequently encountered words, they will have paid attention in different ways and each will have an idiosyncratic store of word knowledge to bring to any particular text. Nevertheless, with social support, all members of the group can process the new text successfully.

Introducing Books

The key to children's access to the book is your introduction. A book introduction is defined by Holdaway as "a brief and lively discussion in which the teacher interests the children in the story and produces an appro-priate set for reading it" (1979, p. 142). Sometimes teachers are afraid of "giving away" too much when they introduce stories to children, but Clay asks us to think about it in terms of two people in conversation. For the listener to understand, the speaker must either key in to the listener's prior knowledge or provide some kind of scenario or introduction. Clay says, "This is not a case of telling the children what to expect. It is a process of drawing the children into the activity before passing control to the children and pushing them gently towards problem solving the whole first reading of the story for themselves" (1991b, p. 265).

Clay's admonition to allow children to read the whole story for themselves is related to building independence in approaching novel texts. The introduction supports and sparks independent problem solving that helps young readers build self-extending systems. The balance of support is adjusted for different readers. The diagram in Figure 11–1 illustrates Clay's discussion of teacher involvement in storybook introductions. The teacher shifts up or down this gradient according to the characteristics of the text, her knowledge of the children in the group, and the relationship between the two.

A teacher rarely reads the story to children, because that provides so much support the children could become dependent. Even worse, they might think that reading a new text means listening and remembering as the only strategy. Rich introductions will make more challenging texts accessible to a group of children. At other times the teacher may need to provide only a short, focused introduction or "a few moves to increase accessibility of a new text" (Clay 1991b, p. 272). When children have developed independent reading systems and they are engaged in taking on many new texts that are well within their control, they introduce texts to themselves, making the "task an unseen, unshared, unhelped activity" (ibid., p. 272).

Drawing from Clay (1991a, 1991b) and Holdaway (1979) we have compiled a list of

Introducing Stories
Gradient of Teacher Involvement
(Clay)

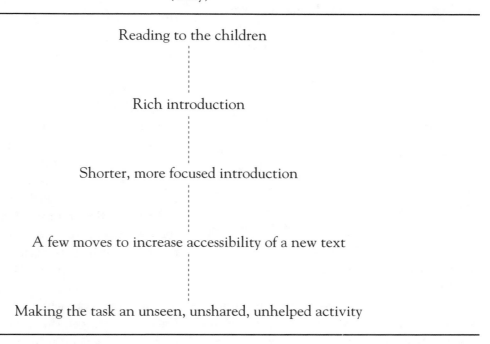

Reading to the children

Rich introduction

Shorter, more focused introduction

A few moves to increase accessibility of a new text

Making the task an unseen, unshared, unhelped activity

FIGURE 11–1   Introducing stories—gradient of teacher involvement

actions teachers take during book introductions. These characteristics are not a checklist but a repertoire of options. You need to think carefully about a particular group of children so that the introduction can flow much like a conversation among people who are interested in the same thing. The process leaves "room for child input to inform the teacher and for the teacher to make some deliberate teaching moves" (Clay 1991b, p. 267).

In introducing stories to children, you might:

▮ Draw on the children's experience and knowledge.

▮ Leave room for the children to bring their experiences to bear on the story.

▮ Explain important ideas and concepts.

▮ Discuss the plot or theme of the whole story.

▮ Say (and sometimes have children repeat) language patterns that are unfamiliar and are critical to the story.

▮ Talk about the meaning of the whole story.

▮ Talk about the illustrations and help children discover information in them.

▮ Discuss the characters in the story.

▮ Draw children's attention to the structure of the text and help them understand "how the book works."

▮ Occasionally address letter-sound relationships or clusters in the pronunciation of unfamiliar words (proper names, for example).

▮ Use some of the new and challenging vocabulary found in the story.

▮ Draw children's attention to specific words and punctuation.

▮ Explore any aspects of text layout that

affect the meaning of the story or would be tricky for children to follow.

■ "Leave the children with one or two clear questions that will drive them into the text and serve as a continuing impulse to seek meaning when they read" (Holdaway 1979, p. 143).

Examples

Below are five examples of teacher book introductions. The five texts being introduced are intended for five different groups of children. The introductions reflect the characteristics suggested by Clay (1991b) in her article on introducing stories to children.

Ron's introduction of *I Can* (see Figure 11–2)

Ron is working with a group of kindergarten children who are just beginning to read. They can match word by word on a single line of text and are highly motivated to read for themselves. He begins by setting the scene for the children; he talks about the title, the theme, and the characters. The "big idea" of the story (that the little sister always says she can but really can't do everything the big sister can) is foreshadowed in his brief comments. He also links the story to the children's own experiences.

In subsequent pages, Ron uses some of the language of the story, repeating important patterns. He is careful, though, to turn over some of the investigation to children: after setting the pattern and letting children know about the story structure, he prompts them to look through the pictures themselves and find out what else the big sister can do. The teacher also directs children's attention to aspects of print. He selects two important words, *can* and *here*. *Can* appears on every page and is a frequently encountered word that will be useful for children to learn. *Here* is a new word and is the first in the sentence. It would be difficult for children to recognize and use this word

without some prior attention to the beginning letter *H*.

Ron does not preteach the words or drill them in isolation. His goal is for children to begin to recognize these words as they encounter them in text and use them to monitor reading. As these frequently used words are encountered over and over again, children will learn them so that they can recognize them anywhere. In addition, the same words are being used in writing in this classroom. They are learning how to use their knowledge of the visual features of words as a tool for moving through text.

Finally, Ron returns children's focus to the meaning of the story and asks each child to "read it with your finger." This reminder is not by chance. Ron knows that these children need to practice word-by-word matching. As Clay says, "when a teacher says read it with your finger, she is demanding an integration of several responses. She is saying, 'Remember the ideas, retell them, find them in print, and move correctly across print.' That integration is the heart of early reading success" (Clay 1991a, p. 105).

As the children read the story aloud to themselves, Ron will receive feedback on how his introduction provided a scaffold for a successful first reading. His observation of children's reading will inform succeeding book selections and introductions.

Susan's introduction of *The Hungry Kitten* (see Figure 11–3)

Susan sets the scene for this book by asking her first graders whether they have a kitten and talking about the hungry kitten looking everywhere for food. She uses the language of the story in several places throughout the text. At one point, she acquaints children with the unfamiliar expression "look after you."

She prompts children to search for meaning in the pictures and to predict what will happen in the story. She accepts children's partially correct responses but pushes them to go further in describing the characters.

Introduction of *I Can* to a Group of Kindergarten Children

Title Page

- Sets the title, author, characters, and theme
- Relates topic to children's own experiences

Teacher: Today we are going to read a story written by Catherine Peters. The story is called *I Can* and it's about a little girl and her little sister. How many of you have a little sister or brother?
Andrea: I do, a little sister.
Michael: I have a baby brother. He's two months old.
Carlos: I don't have any. . . .

Pages 1–2

- Elaborates the theme
- Encourages children to use pictures
- Provides some of the language

Teacher: Michael, you have a new brother, don't you? What were you going to say, Carlos?
Carlos: I have a little cousin.
Teacher: You know, sometimes little brothers or cousins try to copy but they can't really do what the big kids can do. That's what happens in this story. The big sister says, "I can jump." See how she is jumping in the picture? And her little sister always says she can do the same thing. Look, she's jumping too. But it's hard for her to jump, isn't it? But she says . . .
Andrea: I can jump too.
Teacher: Yes, that's what she says, "I can jump, too."

Pages 3–4

- Reinforces the language pattern and the use of information in the pictures
- Prompts children to locate an important word

Teacher: Now look what they're doing. The big sister is swimming. What will she say to her little sister?
Peter: I can swim.
Teacher: That's right, and little sister is going to say, "I can swim, too," isn't she? Let's point and read what the little sister says.

Together, children point and read the words, "I can swim, too."
Children locate can *and the teacher checks to see that all are pointing under the word.*

Teacher: Put your finger under the word *can*. Yes, that's *can*. You found *can*. Find *can* on this page.

Children locate can *quickly.*

Pages 5–14

- Encourages children to examine the text for information
- Leaves opportunities for problem-solving
- Passes control to the readers

Teacher: Now look at the rest of the pictures. On every page the big sister is doing something and the little sister says that she can too. Find out if she really can do what the big sister can do.
Andrea: She can write.
Michael: But she can't (pointing to the little sister).
Carlos: *(pointing to singing)*: What's that?
Michael: Singing!
Carlos: Her book is upside down.

FIGURE 11–2 Introduction of *I Can* to a group of kingergarten children

Page 15

- Confirms use of information in pictures
- Calls attention to a letter form within a word
- Prompts locating a new word that starts a sentence with a language pattern
- Returns to the plot and meaning
- Signals the pattern change, says the phrase several times, and gets children to repeat it
- Confirms children's thinking about their own experiences

> Teacher: They can both ride their bikes, can't they? Look, little sister's riding. Now, they're saying, "Here we go!" *Here* starts with an uppercase *h*. Put your finger under *here* and say "here."
>
> *All children locate* here.
>
> Teacher: "Here we go!"
> Andrea: She can ride a bike (pointing to the little girl).
> Several children: "Here we go!"
> Teacher: They're going to have fun now because they can both ride a bike. Here we go!
> Andrea: My little sister can ride her bike with me.
> Teacher: I bet she can. Now go back to the beginning of the story and you read the whole story softly to yourself. Read it with your finger.

FIGURE 11–2 *continued*

She also writes "Are you hungry?" on chart paper so that the children can look closely at the details of the written language, notice the punctuation, and practice reading the inverted sentence structure used here to ask a question. Twice she prompts them to notice quotation marks.

Susan asks children to locate the word *went* in the text, after first prompting them to predict the letter at the beginning. *Went* is a new and important word; moreover, some of the children in the group might not be able to predict this word from the meaning and the language structure. At the end, Susan provides a model for anticipating the outcome of the story.

Although Susan expects some challenges for members of the group as they read through the story for the first time, she does not use or call attention to all the unknown words in the text (*big, little, away, after,* and *said,* to mention a few). She expects that the children will be able to solve these words by anticipating the language and meaning and

then checking their predictions against the visual information.

Amy's introduction of *The Three Billy Goats Gruff* (see Figure 11–4)

Amy gives her group of first graders a shorter, more focused introduction because they are already familiar with several versions of this folktale. Also, they have demonstrated good control of the types of language patterns (dialogue, for example) in the text. They are able to use a variety of sources of information while reading, checking one source against another. They have developed a substantial reading vocabulary, and this text includes a number of known words. Amy believes the children can get to most of this text using their current strategies (using the known word *go* to get to the inflectional *going,* for example).

Level of text is not a factor in Amy's decision; she could provide a rich introduction at any level. Children's reading behavior and knowledge are the deciding factors. Here she chooses a shorter introduction to find out

Introduction of *The Hungry Kitten* to a Group of First Graders

Cover, Title Page

- Sets the scene
- Relates to children's experience

Teacher: We have a lovely new story today called *The Hungry Kitten* by Beverley Randell. Do you have a kitten?
Sara: I have one cat and two baby kittens.
Teacher: Does anyone else have a kitten for a pet?
Shamal: I used to have a dog, and I wish I could get a kitten for my birthday.
Mark: I don't have no pets.
Aneeca: Not me.
Robert: Not me.

Pages 2–3

- Sets the topic, theme, and main character
- Provides the meaning and language
- Draws attention to punctuation and relates to meaning
- Draws attention to meaning in the picture

Teacher: This little kitten is very hungry and looks everywhere for food to eat. What did she see?
Several children: Milk!
Teacher: When she sees the milk, she says, "Miaow." You say that.
All children: Miaow!
Teacher: Do you see the marks that show us the kitten is talking (pointing to the quotation marks)? You point to those marks in your book.

Children point to quotation marks.

Teacher: Do you think she likes this milk?
All children: Yes!
Teacher: I think so too. But this milk belongs to someone else. Who does it belong to?
Aneeca: A cat!

Pages 4–5

- Uses language from the story
- Confirms children's interpretation
- Probes for prior knowledge and understanding
- Accepts a partially correct response

Teacher: Yes, a big cat. The big cat tells the little kitten to "go away."

Pages 6–7

- Uses language from the story
- Encourages prediction and searching
- Prompts construction activity
- Asks children to confirm

Teacher: Now the hungry little kitten finds some more food. He likes this food too. But it doesn't belong to him. Let's find out who that food belongs to.
Shamal: That's dog food. That's the dog's food.

FIGURE 11–3 Introduction of *The Hungry Kitten* to a group of first graders

Pages 8–9

- Uses language from the story and involves children
- Prompts children to predict
- Models the language structure

> Teacher: Was Shamal right? *(Children nod.)* The dog said "Grrr . . . grrr. Grrr." You say that.
> Children: Grrr.
> Teacher: The dog tells the little kitten to "go away." What do you think he did?
> Robert: He goed away.

Pages 10–11

- Prompts children to attend to letter-sound relationship at the beginning of a word
- Prompts locating a word in text and noticing the first letter

> Teacher: Yes, that's what he did. He went away. What would you expect to see first in *went?*
> Aneeca: W
> Several other
> children: W
> Teacher: Find *went. (Observes to see all children pointing under* went.*)*

Pages 12–13

- Calls attention to punctuation
- Asks children to predict and use pictures for meaning
- Guides children to use the question language structure while pointing and reading text
- Probes to find out what the children know

> Teacher: There are some of those talking marks again. Now who's talking to the little kitten?
> Children: A boy.
> Teacher: The boy says "hello" to the kitten and asks, "Are you hungry?"
>
> *The teacher writes "Are you hungry?" on a piece of chart paper on an easel, and asks children to read while she points. They discuss the question mark and locate the first word,* are. *Children read and point out the punctuation and the word.*
>
> Teacher: And what do you think the little kitten says?
> Shamal: That's miaow. He says, "miaow."

Pages 14–15

- Presents new knowledge
- Prompts children to think about the meaning and interpret the text
- Provides a model for anticipating the outcome

> Teacher: The little boy's mother came along and she said, "We will look after you." What does that mean? *(No response.)* It means that the boy and his mother will take care of the little kitten. They will "look after" the little kitten. Do you think they like kittens?
> Children: Yes.
> Teacher: What do you think the kitten is thinking now? You read to find out. Go back to the beginning and read the story softly to yourself.

FIGURE 11–3   *continued*

Introduction of *The Billy Goats Gruff* to a First Grade Group

Title Page

- Sets the scene and provides information about the genre
- Confirms children's use of prior knowledge

Teacher: Today's story is a folktale, an old story that has been told over and over for many years. This time the story is retold—that means "told again"—by Susan McCloskey. *The Three Billy Goats Gruff*.
Matthew: I know this. You read it.
Kayla: I do too.
Several children: I heard this story.
Teacher: Yes, I've read several versions of this story to you. This one you're going to read. In lots of folk tales, the characters are animals who talk and act like people.

Page 2

- Introduces the characters
- Checks on children's knowledge of the story

Teacher: In this story there are three billy goats and their name is Gruff. Which one is little billy goat? Who are the others?
Sara: There's little billy goat, and big billy goat, and middle-sized billy goat.
Teacher: What was the problem the goats had?
Kayla: They wanted to go across the bridge.

Page 3

- Probes to find out what the children know
- Prompts constructive activity to understand the plot

Teacher: Why did they want to go across the bridge?
Kayla: To eat grass.

Page 4

- Maintains interactive ease
- Promotes enjoyment of the story

Teacher: There goes little billy goat, trip, trap, trip, trap.
Children repeat: Trip, trap.

Pages 5–14

- Prompts constructive activity to access prior knowledge
- Probes for prior knowledge and understanding
- Passes control to the reader
- Asks children to confirm events in the story using the pictures

Teacher: Every time a billy goat goes across the bridge, you know who they meet?
Matthew: The troll!
Teacher: Yes, the troll, and he wants something, doesn't he? Look through the pictures and find what happens to the troll.

Children look through the pages.

Kayla: He's going off the bridge.
Teacher: Is Kayla right? Do you all see him going off the bridge?
Children: Yes!

FIGURE 11–4 Introduction of *The Three Billy Goats Gruff* to a first-grade group

- Provides a model for reflecting on the story
- Draws children's attention to the letter-sound relationships within an unfamiliar word
- Promotes reflection on the meaning and conclusion of the story

Teacher:	Do you think it was a good idea for the billy goats Gruff to cross the bridge? What would you expect to see at the beginning of the word *idea*?
Several children:	I.
Sara:	There's *idea*.
Teacher:	That's right. You're all pointing under *idea*. (*Says the word* idea *slowly as she writes it on a white board.*) You can hear all of the sounds in that word, can't you?
Children:	(*Slowly*) Idea.
Teacher:	It was a good idea, wasn't it? They look like they're having a good time eating grass.

FIGURE 11–4 *continued*

whether the children can take on the text with less support.

This focused introduction clearly takes less time, and Amy leaves a considerable amount of work for the children to do as they read the text for the first time. Even though Amy does not discuss every page, she communicates the plot and ideas. The characters are well known to the children from having heard the story before, so Amy merely confirms their prior knowledge. She asks probing questions and lets the students know their own experience has value. She provides a model for reflecting on the story and prompts constructive activity to understand the plot. She draws children's attention to an unfamiliar word, *idea*, that did not appear in the versions previously heard. This word has regular letter-sound relationships that make it useful for demonstrating word solving while reading text.

Claire's introduction of *Keep the Lights Burning, Abbie* (see Figure 11–5)

Claire is introducing a longer book to a group of second graders. Her introduction is rich and highly supportive, but not all texts need such an elaborate prereading conversation. If you are confident that readers can control most elements of the text, you can give a brief overview and let readers begin.

Then, after some of the text has been read, discuss that section before having the students continue.

Keep the Lights Burning, Abbie is historical fiction. Claire's students have not encountered this kind of text before, so she introduces the title, setting, theme, and characters, making it clear the events took place long ago. (Some groups might need an even more elaborate introduction to get a sense of history, in which case the teacher might show them illustrations or pictures from the period.) Since the island setting is unfamiliar, Claire mentions it again and introduces potentially difficult names. Next, she asks children to work with their new knowledge by finding the long and difficult name *Matinicus Island*. As children offer their own observations of the word, Claire tightens the criteria. She wants them to notice the word and analyze its parts. The goal here is not to learn the word *Matinicus* but to learn how to approach those long and difficult words that often turn readers off as they begin a text.

Claire also probes students' prior knowledge. She asks, "What do you think it would be like to live over a hundred years ago on a small island?" The predictions they make will drive them into the text and will help the children understand the plot. Finally,

Introducing Second Graders
to *Keep the Lights Burning, Abbie*

- **Introducing the title, setting, theme, and characters**

  Teacher: Let's look at the cover of the book while I tell you a bit about our new story. This is a true story about a young girl named Abbie. Abbie lived a long time ago on an island with her parents and three younger sisters. Her father got stuck in town during a terrible storm and Abbie had to keep the lighthouse lit for all the sailors. She had to be very brave and work very hard while her father was away.

  Becky: This is real? She really did this? Where was it?

- **Expanding upon the setting and introducing potentially difficult names**

  Teacher: Yes, Abbie Burgess really did this. The island is called Matinicus Island and it is off the coast of Maine.

- **Calling children's attention to some orthographic features of text.**

  Teacher: See if you can find *Matinicus* on this page. What do you notice about it?

  Sheila: It has a capital letter. It's like a name.

  Teacher: Uh-huh. Anything else?

  Becky: It's a really long word.

  Tiffany: It has "mat" and "in."

  Sheila: And "us" too at the end! Cool! It's all parts.

  Teacher: Those parts can help you if you have trouble with the name.

- **Probing to access/assess children's prior knowledge**

  Teacher: What do you think it would be like to live over a hundred years ago on a small island?

  Tiffany: There was no TV or electricity and all the kids had lots of chores to do.

  Sheila: Yeah, they might not even have any schools.

  Becky: I bet they had boats instead of cars to get places.

  Sheila: It looks really cold and windy there. Everything's blowing.

  Teacher: You're right. That's how it was for Abbie and her family. Let's take a look through the book and see what happened.

- **Prompting the children to constructive activity (to understand plot)**

  Teacher: Here's Abbie's father telling her he has to leave for town. What do you think he's telling Abbie?

  Becky: To make sure the lights stay burning.

  Tiffany: Maybe to take care of her sisters, too.

  Teacher: Now that Papa is gone, Abbie is doing all of her chores.

  Sheila: She's feeding chickens! Cool!

- **Increasing accessibility to difficult names**

  Teacher: Yes, and their names are Hope, Patience, and Charity.

  Becky: One, two, three. (Counting hens in illustration.)

  Tiffany: Look, now she's cooking, too. Is that her? Yeah, she's the biggest and those are the sisters.

  Teacher: Her sisters' names are Esther, Lydia, and Mahala. Let's practice saying those. They're tricky.

  Sheila: Mahala is the hardest one! (Others agree.)

- **Providing a model of reflecting on story**

  Teacher: Now the storm is coming and Abbie is heading to the lighthouse. I bet she's pretty scared being in there all alone in the dark. I don't know if I'd like that too much. She had to keep checking on the lights all night and blow them out each morning.

  Sheila: All night? How does she sleep?

  Tiffany: She probably doesn't until her father gets back.

FIGURE 11–5   Introducing second graders to *Keep the Lights Burning, Abbie*

- **Maintaining interactive ease**

  Teacher: It was a hard job. I bet she was pretty tired from it.
    Becky: REALLY tired!
   Tiffany: Look. She fell asleep at the table here. *(Pointing to illustration.)*

- **Prompting constructive activity to understand plot**

  Teacher: The storm got worse and Abbie kept working, until finally her father came back with all the supplies.

- **Pausing for the children to generate the ending**

  Teacher: Abbie was so happy to see him. She gave him a big hug and he told her . . .
    Sheila: You did a good job with the lighthouse, Abbie.
    Becky: I'm proud of you.
   Tiffany: You were really brave and a hard worker.
    Sheila: Let's read it now!
    Becky: Are there other books about Abbie we can read next??

FIGURE 11–5 *continued*

she demonstrates how to reflect on the story. She implies that Abbie is probably scared being in there all alone in the dark.

Throughout, Claire invites comments from students and responds to them, and she allows children to generate the ending. By the end of this introduction, they are poised to read the story.

Glenda's introduction of *Amelia Bedelia and the Baby* (see Figure 11–6)

Glenda's brief introduction makes the most of the fact that students have read other books in the series. She states the title, setting, theme, and characters, using the phrases "this time" and "as usual" to signal that the students have encountered Amelia before. Knowledge of similar texts helps readers interpret new texts. In explicitly connecting this new story to the kinds of situations in which Amelia always finds herself, Glenda helps these young children make such connections for themselves. Glenda did not need to give a rich introduction; her brief summary is enough.

Assisting Learning

The text selection and story introduction work together to help the reader attend to information from different sources while main-

taining a strong sense of meaning. Teacher actions related to the text selection and introduction are consistent with the concept of "guided participation," as explained by Rogoff (1990). Rogoff describes how routine activities support children's ability to focus attention on new aspects of a task. Additional features of guided participation include tacit communication, supportive structuring of novices' efforts, and transferring responsibility for handling skills to novices. Teachers support children's learning through tacit as well as explicit communication. In the introductions modeled above, the teachers demonstrate processes that are important in taking a stance toward a text. The conversational tone as teacher and children wonder together what will happen stimulates thinking. In both the selection and introduction, teachers support the novice's efforts. Children can bring their own ideas to the text and use them. Even in rich introductions, teachers begin to transfer responsibility to the young readers.

Careful book selection and thoughtful story introduction continue to be important even as children grow older and more competent. As adult educators, we often profit from recommendations and introductions by colleagues. It is a mistake to think of teach-

Introducing Second Graders to *Amelia Bedelia and the Baby*

(a brief introduction to a book from a series previously read by the students)

- **Introducing the title, setting, theme, and characters**

    Teacher: I think you're really going to enjoy our new book, today. It's a very funny story about Amelia Bedelia called *Amelia Bedelia and the Baby*. This time, Amelia is baby-sitting and she gets herself into some very funny situations. But as usual, she manages to work things out in the end.

    Patrice: Oh, I've read lots of these stories. She's always doing crazy things. These are really funny.

    Seth: Yeah, me too.

- **Probing to find out what children know**

    Teacher: Do you remember the other Amelia Bedelia story we read in school?

    Alice: The baseball one. *Amelia Bedelia Plays Ball*.

    Teacher: Yes, it was about baseball; *Play Ball, Amelia Bedelia*. What types of things did Amelia do in that story?

    Sara: She did exactly whatever people told her to do, instead of what they meant for her to do. Like really stealing the base like a robber instead of just stealing the base, like, uh, like in baseball.

    Patrice: I loved when she tagged the boy with a tag instead of the ball!

    Sara: And when they told her to run home, she ran all the way to her house.

- **Linking new text to previously read text**

    Teacher: Well, in this book, Amelia does the same types of things. She gets a list of directions for taking care of the baby. But instead of figuring out what each direction really means, she does exactly what it says. Like on one direction it says it's playtime until five o'clock, so Amelia sits down and plays with the baby's toys until five o'clock. Is that what the direction really meant?

    Alice: No! It was supposed to be time for the baby to play, not her!

    Students: *(Giggling.)*

    Teacher: Even though she does all these crazy things, the baby likes her and the parents are very happy with her baby-sitting. Did *Play Ball, Amelia Bedelia* end like this too?

    Sara: Yeah, they were happy with her because they won the game.

    Patrice: She never gets in any trouble. She's always the hero.

    Teacher: Well, let's take a look at what Amelia Bedelia is up to in this book.

FIGURE 11–6   Introducing second graders to *Amelia Bedelia and the Baby*

ing as only what the teacher does when the child is reading text. The selection and book introduction set the scene for successful processing of the text and support children's ability to sustain effective reading behaviors for increasingly longer periods of time. The truest test of a teacher's selection of and introduction to a book is the child's reading of it, which will provide evidence that he understood the text and was able to use it to develop more effective reading strategies (see Clay 1991a, p. 202).

Suggestions for Professional Development

1. Select a text for one of your guided reading groups and record your introduction on audio- or videotape.

2. The next day, take running records of four group members as they read the new book.

3. Then, preferably with a colleague, listen to or view the introduction and

use the running records to reflect on the success of the students' first reading. Guide your discussion with these questions:

- To what extent did children understand the story? Were their substitutions meaningful? Did they read with high accuracy and some phrasing and/or fluency?
- Where were the points of difficulty for each child? Is there evidence that the introduction helped them in their problem solving?
- Were there opportunities for each child to engage in problem solving ("reading work") rather than simply reading the text perfectly?
- What sources of information did children use in their problem solving on the new text? Did they initiate problem solving on their own?
- Was the text the right level for these children? How do you know?
- Is there evidence that children used processes modeled in the introduction?
- In retrospect, how would you have introduced the text differently?

Teaching for Strategies

Teaching . . . can be likened to a conversation in which you listen to the speaker carefully
before you reply. Marie Clay

All learners have in-the-head processes they use to integrate new information with what they already know. Readers have the particular challenge of applying their cognitive processes to text. Clay (1991a) describes strategies as operations that allow the learner to use, apply, transform, relate, interpret, reproduce, and re-form information for communication. Through this "network of unobservable in-the-head strategies the reader is able to attend to information from different sources" (p. 328). The network is flexible, allowing the reader to change direction as needed. Inner control, Clay says, is built as the young reader becomes increasingly able to deal with information in the brain.

As teachers it is difficult for us to think about these complex in-the-head strategies. We cannot observe them but must hypothesize that they are being used. We can observe behavior, though, and as Kenneth Goodman (1982) has said, children's reading behavior gives us a "window on the reading process."

We are tentative in the way we talk and think about children's in-the-head strategies because we are never certain what is going on there. We must rely on behavioral evidence, and that evidence must be collected over time. The teacher who is systematically taking running records of children's reading, ideally about one every two to four weeks, is building a pattern of evidence from which he can make fairly reliable hypotheses. He might want more frequent records (about every one or two weeks) on children who are making slower progress and need fewer records on children making very fast progress.

Just as strategies cannot be directly observed, neither can they be directly taught. We teach *for* strategies. Experience is a powerful influence on the construction of reading strategies. Anyone who has taught someone to swim knows that merely explaining the process does not work. Even modeling and showing is insufficient. The future swimmer must get in the water. When we talk about teaching for strategies in this book, we are not talking about a specific teaching approach to each new strategy but about a repertoire of interpretations and responses you can apply at any time to help the child learn from reading text. Your moves must be focused and supportive, designed to bring forward examples that will help children learn "how to learn" in reading.

There are many different strategies for reading. Clay discusses some of them by providing examples in three categories: (1) strategies that maintain fluency, (2) strategies that detect and correct error, and (3) strategies for problem-solving new words. Each function involves a network of *cues* provided by meaning, language structure or syntax, and visual information. The important thing about these cues, however, is how readers access and use them. Let's look at what good readers do in each of Clay's broad categories.

Strategies for Maintaining Fluency

When good readers read aloud, they are fluent and use phrasing. We infer, therefore, that silent reading is also fluent and phrased, that readers rapidly access meaning and apply it to the text (Does this make sense? Does this sound right in terms of what I know about language?). A fluent reader doesn't get bogged down in the details. A fluent reader is also flexible, varying her speed with the difficulty of the text. Less fluent readers rigidly use the same "reading voice" whether there is a great deal or very little problem solving to be done. Students who read slowly with little reflection of syntactic patterns are probably not accessing all sources of information and may, in fact, be losing comprehension.

Fluency is a critical factor in reading control. A study of over one thousand fourth graders' oral reading fluency (Pinnell et al. 1995) found that rate, fluency, and accuracy were all highly related to comprehension. The story the students in the study were asked to read was very easy, so they all read with high accuracy, but rate and fluency were critical factors in comprehension.

Readers' oral language is their primary source for anticipating what may happen next in the text and checking whether their reading makes sense. Oral language is a complex, rule-governed system. Before they come to school, children have learned rules by which they can generate an infinite number of oral sentences. Entering school, their knowledge of language expands rapidly, not just in vocabulary but in the kinds of structures they can produce.

Initially, it helps young readers if the texts they read resemble their oral language. As they read more (and also hear written language read aloud) they become aware of the way written language "sounds," the syntax, the way it is organized. This knowledge is a rich source of information for them as they move through text.

The example in Figure 12–1 is from Matthew's reading of *Worms for Breakfast* (level I). (This was an easy text for Matthew;

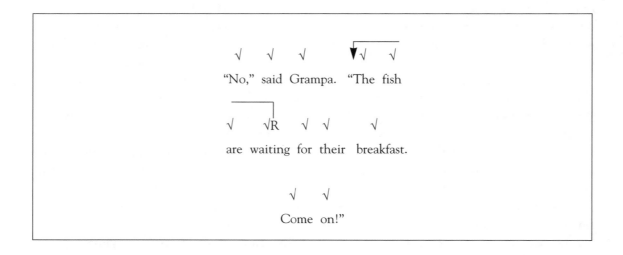

FIGURE 12–1 Matthew's reading

he finished with an accuracy rate of 96 percent.) Matthew is reading accurately in this passage, but his behavior also indicates a strong sense of language and meaning. He reads up to the word *waiting* without phrasing. He then hesitates, goes back and puts the phrase "the fish are waiting" together as a phrased unit. He then reads "for their breakfast" and "come on" as phrased units. Matthew as a reader is using his oral language as a cue to maintain fluency.

The child's prior knowledge and understanding of the world is another basis for fluency: children anticipate what will happen in stories or the way information will be presented in expository texts. This framework makes the reading more quickly accessible.

Fluency is also supported by the reader's ability to process visual information rapidly, including the use of punctuation. Being able to recognize words without slowing down helps maintain fluent processing. Fluent readers also recognize features of words that they know and use these features to get to words that are unknown. Fluent reading means solving problems "on the run," something all readers must do if they are to gain understanding.

Teachers need to give special attention to phrasing and fluency and to the use of punctuation because "when the reading is phrased like spoken language and the responding is fluent (and some people say fast), then there is a fair chance that the reader can read for meaning and check what he reads against his language knowledge. And his attention can go mainly to the messages" (Clay 1993b, p. 51).

The book selection and introduction are critical factors in helping children read fluently. The teacher makes sure that the text is well within the child's control, that the words and language are accessible. The child's background, his system of oral language, his store of words, and the way he solves words all work together if the texts are just difficult enough but not so difficult that the child cannot "put it together."

As the reader moves through the text gradient, he becomes fluent at each level; the process is always whole and integrated. In the introduction, the teacher demonstrates the links between the new text and the children's own knowledge of the world and the structure of language. She first engages the children with the text by talking about it and using some of the language. These teaching moves support the reading of text with phrasing and fluency.

Strategies for Detecting and Correcting Error

Good readers read accurately but not necessarily perfectly. When they make errors, they have strategies for detecting and correcting them. This behavior indicates a combination of effective anticipation based on meaning and syntax and fast, efficient use of clusters of visual information. Young readers, at first, are coping with the print code and making connections between print and their own language systems. They may need to work on accuracy in order to match spoken and written language.

In the example in Figure 12–2, Moneisha stops when she says the word *me* while

| √ | √ | monkeys | and | monkeys | like | me. |
| I | like | the | monkey | and | the | monkey | likes | me. |

FIGURE 12–2 Moneisha's reading

pointing under the word *monkey*, indicating that she knows something is wrong. She notices it doesn't match. She is using her own language and re-creating a text close to that in the book, but she knows that oral language must match the words printed on the page. At this point, Moneisha is not using particular aspects of words. She probably hasn't noticed the discrepancy between *me* and *monkey*, but she is beginning to monitor her reading, in this case the clusters that make up words, as she moves along the line. While she is familiar with the word *the*, it is overridden by her strong sense of language and she does not use this known word to check herself.

When a reader uses information from any source to check his own reading, he is *self-monitoring*. When the information encountered is not consistent with his understanding of what the text means, his sense of language structure, or the visual features of words, he wants to eliminate the dissonance. As adults, we also check on ourselves when we read, although we notice it only when there is dissonance. For example, if you are reading a long, complex novel with many generations of characters, you may suddenly find you do not remember how two people

are related. If the relationship is vital to understanding the plot, you might search back through the text (or refer to one of those handy "family trees") to resolve the dissonance.

Young children like Moneisha who notice a mismatch of whatever kind take steps to get rid of the dissonance. They may return to the beginning of the line, stop and make several attempts at an unknown word, or indicate by other behavior that they are bothered by the dissonance and want to solve the problem. This behavior is more productive than simply going on without trying to make a fit between meaning and visual cues. Although the behavior may not always result in self-correction, nevertheless it indicates a beginning inner control of strategic processes.

In the example in Figure 12–3, Karl reads accurately up to the word *waited*, when he substitutes *wanted*. This substitution provides evidence that Karl is using language, meaning, and visual information. The sentence made sense and sounded right up to that point and *wanted* is very similar visually to *waited*—the two words begin and end alike and both have a *t* in the middle. In fact, they differ by only one letter. When

√	√	√	√	√	√	√	√
They	put	big,	fat,	juicy	worms	on	their

√	√	√	√	√	√	√
hooks	and	dropped	them	into	the	water.

	√ √	wanted	SC	√ R	√	√	√	√
Then	they	waited			for	the	fish	to	bite.

FIGURE 12–3 Karl's reading

Karl reads the word *for*, he probably notices a dissonance, a mismatch among his sources of information. His behavior indicates his awareness of the mismatch, and provides evidence that he is monitoring. His substitution no longer makes sense, and it is syntactically not a likely sentence in English. He goes back to the beginning of the line and this time corrects the word to *waited.*

The important observation about Karl's self-correction is not accuracy per se. It is his process of control. First he had to notice the dissonance and then search for sources of information that he may have previously neglected. The process of checking, searching, and self-correcting builds the reader's network of strategies. Early readers begin bringing together sources of information by checking one kind of information against another, a process Clay calls *cross-checking.* As readers practice cross-checking, they begin to use multiple sources of information.

In Figure 12–4 Karl shows by his behavior that he is actively processing. He reads

accurately but notices when he makes a substitution. The two substitutions are meaningful and fit with his knowledge of syntactic patterns (the structure of English language) but do not "look right." His knowledge of visual features of words prompts a further search of the visual information and self-correction. We can infer that Karl is also checking back with his own knowledge of language to be sure that his self-correction "sounds right" and "makes sense." Karl's teacher is pleased with Karl's initial, partially correct attempts—*cried* for *called* and *whispers* for *whispered*—because of the competence they reveal. Not only do they make sense and sound right, they are visually consistent with the beginning and ending of one word and with the first letter of the other.

Why did Karl search further? We might hypothesize that Karl is actively noticing and working on words and searching to make all systems, including visual information, fit together. Also, Karl self-corrects at the point of error rather than going all the way back to the beginning of the line, indicating that he probably is able to keep the

√	√	√	√	cried │ SC	√	
" Here,	fish!	Here,	fish!"	called │	John.	

√	√	√	√	√	√	√
" Come	and	get	your	worms	for	breakfast! "

√	√	√
" Shh,"	said	Grampa.

√	whispers │ SC √	
" Okay,"	whispered │	John.

FIGURE 12–4   Karl's further reading

meaning and structure in his head while attending to the particular word.

The important insight here is that Karl is doing effective processing. What we notice is not so much that Karl reads correctly but that he works on the printed message using all sources of information at his disposal.

This checking, searching, and confirming process is in itself rewarding to young readers because it works—they are able to read text successfully. Much of the behavior indicating monitoring, checking, and self-correction is overt as young readers sort out the complexities of written language while reading out loud. For self-extending readers, self-correction becomes more covert and is used efficiently when needed. Helping young readers develop this self-extending system is the goal of reading instruction.

Strategies for Problem Solving New Words

The redundancy in extended texts (that is, the notion that information is communicated in multiple ways) allows the reader to solve new words. Perhaps not all the information is needed, but the reader uses it selectively to check and confirm.

For example, a text might say, "Two kittens ran away fast." Plurality is signaled by two words, *two* and *kittens* (the *s* ending). The meaning of the word *fast* is supported by the meaning of the action, *ran*. The reader doesn't really need all these cues to know that there were more than one kitten and that they ran fast; she usually samples some of the information available, just enough to be sure that there is no inconsistency. The word *two* signals that *kitten* should end in *s*, and the reader automatically predicts this ending rather than having to decode the word *kittens* precisely. By using language, the reader has reduced the number of likely alternatives, made her reading more efficient, and made word solving "on the run" easier. (Readers who are just putting the process together might overtly notice the *s* as a con-

firming strategy.) For competent readers, the process is so fast and efficient that the *s* needs minimum attention.

Texts for young readers usually have pictures that provide an additional resource for checking and confirming. In text selection, one of the factors teachers consider is the degree to which illustrations help the reader. Good readers read for meaning with "divided attention," focusing on the meaning but simultaneously paying attention to visual information.

As teachers of reading we promote children's ability to solve words while reading extended text. The text itself becomes a support for taking words apart to solve them.

In the example in Figure 12–5, Susan predicts the verb *get* instead of *try*, a syntactically consistent substitution that makes sense unless one knows that the story is telling about steering the giraffe to the right, to the left, and forward. The text warning not to "back up" can be predicted from the sequence of events and from noticing the picture, which shows the rider already on the giraffe (not "getting back up") and a rhinoceros standing right behind the giraffe. Susan is not pointing to words, so we do not know exactly when she notices the *b* in *back*, but we hypothesize that she does notice it and that the letter, perhaps in conjunction with the other information from the story, prompts self-correction. Susan is using redundant sources of information in her word solving.

In the next error, Susan substitutes *back* for *backing*, but moving to the next words, *up* and *could*, creates a dissonance. In the previous text, "Do not try to back up," *back up* was signaled as being a verb phrase. Turning this verb phrase into a noun (gerund) signals that *ing* will be present. In Susan's implicit understanding of language syntax, "back up could" doesn't fit as well as "backing up," so she returns to the word and self-corrects. There are also redundant sources of information here. Susan may be using knowledge of language syntax to monitor and prompt searching, but she may also be noticing the

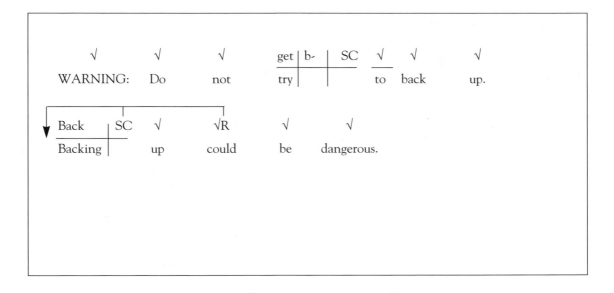

FIGURE 12–5   Susan's reading

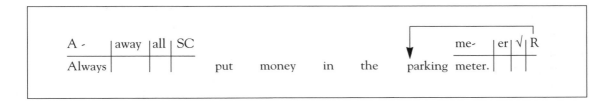

FIGURE 12–6   Susan's further reading

ing in *backing* or simply noticing that the word is longer than *back*. The process is different from solving words in isolation, because there are multiple sources of support.

Sometimes readers encounter words that are completely unfamiliar and the meaning and language in the text do not provide strong enough support for predicting the word with any accuracy. In this case the child needs his knowledge of how words work and letter-sound correspondences as cues. The clearest example of this circumstance for the young reader is a word at the beginning of a line of print—there is no syntactic information available and little meaning except for previous text and the picture. We would not encourage beginning readers to "read on" because it is a behavior that can interfere with meaning and detracts from the efficient use of all sources of information.

In Figure 12–6, Susan uses word-solving skills on the first word of the sentence, *always*. Her processing is overt; she appears to notice the first letter, uses a word she knows to be similar (*away*), then notices the initial word part (*al*) before she puts it all together to achieve a response that fits precisely with her knowledge of the way the word looks.

Readers also need word-solving skills when they encounter unfamiliar words later in the sentence, as Susan does here on the word *meter*. We can hypothesize from her overt processing that she has noticed the first part of the word as being consistent with a part she knows, *me*, but she is not satisfied with that attempt. She then notices the *er* ending, with which she is also familiar. Finally, though, when she puts it together as the word *meter*, which is the precise word on the page, she repeats *parking meter* as if to confirm her work.

Clay (1991a) has noted many ways children solve unfamiliar words while reading text. Some are useful to think about here:

■ *Using the meaning of the story, sentence, and/or language* to anticipate the word and confirming it with the visual information (does it make sense and look right, for example).

■ *Repeating the line up to the problem word and making the sound of the first letter* is a productive strategy for beginners because it allows them to use the preceding meaning and structure while getting a cue from the first letter. This is a very early strategy, and children need to move well beyond this.

■ *Sounding parts of words and then linking them to known words*, eliminating unlikely alternatives on the basis of meaning and structure, helps children narrow the possibilities until they can come up with the precise word.

■ *Noticing part of a word that is like another word* (the *to* in *together*, for example) speeds up solving the new word and is much more effective than letter-by-letter analysis.

■ *Solving words by cumulative letter-by-letter analysis* allows children to sample some of the information and quickly link it to prior knowledge (for example, the word *idea* in a previous example).

Reading as Comprehending

Reading is the construction of meaning. Comprehending is not a product of reading; it is the process. The child is continuously making sense of the world; when reading, he is making sense of text. It is obvious from the previous examples that meaning is a strong support in maintaining fluency, detecting and correcting error, and solving words while reading text. Comprehension has a central role in constructing the network of strategies that are the foundation for the self-extending system (see Askew 1991). Researchers (see, for example, Clay 1991a; Goodman 1996; Holdaway 1979; Tierney 1990) have found that:

■ Readers have high expectations of text—that is, they expect it to have meaning for them.

■ Readers want—in fact, are driven—to make sense of the process.

■ Readers' understanding is influenced by their prior knowledge.

■ Comprehension begins before reading as readers make predictions and anticipate the text, and continues after reading as they use their experience and extend it.

When you use running records, you are looking for behavioral evidence of comprehension. The accuracy rate is one indication: it may be that a high rate of accuracy (generally above 90 percent) is necessary. When the text is too hard, comprehension is simply impossible. The process breaks down for any reader, no matter how competent.

The use of cues is a second indication. When Karl read "then they wanted for" instead of "then they waited for" and then corrected himself, he was using meaning, syntax, and visual information to rethink a response that did not make sense or sound right to him.

Third is behavior that indicates an active search for meaning: repeating as if to confirm an attempt, repeating to search further, making different attempts at a word until one seems to fit either the story meaning, the structure, or the picture.

A fourth indication is fluency and phrasing. Good readers can dip down to the word level when they need to, but they tend to operate at the sentence and phrase level. A broad and reliable rubric for assessing fluency is included in Chapter 6.

A final indication is conversation with children following the reading, in which they reveal their expectations of text and their responses to it. If you need more evidence, it is always possible to ask the child some questions about the text or even have him retell it. It may be, though, that Bill's comment, "I guess that troll learned not to pick on somebody his own size," is evidence enough that he understood *The Three Billy Goats Gruff*.

Teaching to Support Readers' Developing Strategies

Good readers self-monitor, search for cues, discover new things about text, check one source of information against another, confirm their reading, self-correct when necessary, and solve new words using multiple sources of information. A self-extending system is a system of strategies that work together so that by reading, readers continue to learn more about the process of reading. Once children are able to use several sources of information fluently and effectively while reading, they apply their knowledge and skill to less familiar language, to novel and more difficult texts, and to longer and more complex pieces of written language. A reader must develop a self-extending system for himself and to do so requires appropriate texts that are rich in information.

When we prescribe reading instruction, as we must, we need to include a certain amount of control and support for beginning readers, but not of the type that requires teaching one item (a word or a letter, for example) at a time in a tightly controlled sequence. Such tight control reduces children's opportunities to put together the process. Information-rich texts at the right level of difficulty allow children to use what they know (words and parts of words, meaning, and language) in strategic ways as they problem-solve their way through many books. This "reading work" builds the processing system. Books that are initially difficult become easy; strategies like self-monitoring and checking, tedious at first, require less attention, freeing the reader to engage in more complex operations.

As teachers, we have a range of options after introducing the story. Once the reading begins, we look for evidence that reading strategies are being used, focusing on each reader's strengths. For an example, let's look at Susan's guided reading group reading *The Hungry Kitten*.

In the sentence documented in Figure 12–7, Erica reads accurately but inserts *milk*. She is trying to make the text fit the meaning she sees in the accompanying picture but by her hesitation shows she is aware of the mismatch between her meaning and the print. Susan intervenes briefly to help Erica focus on the punctuation as an important source of information. Erica then repeats the sentence, using Susan's intonation patterns. Brief instructional conversations like this direct a reader's attention just for a moment to

---

√   √ √ √   milk

Erica: "Miaow, I like this," — (*She hesitates and shakes her head*)

Susan: Milk would make sense but remember those talking marks? They mean the kitten stopped talking right there (*points to end quotation marks*). It would sound like this, "I like this."

Erica: I like this (*repeats with more appropriate intonation*).

FIGURE 12–7 Erica's reading

an example that will help her learn "how" to process not only the book at hand but all future books.

Brian's reading is documented in Figure 12–8. It is clear he knows some words and is using meaning; however, when he approaches a word he does not know, there is no active searching. He skips *hungry* after just hearing an introduction that mentioned the title of the book and emphasized how hungry the kitten was. He has apparently missed connections that could have helped him. When he comes to *away*, he says part of the word, hesitates, and goes on. This is not nearly as powerful as actively searching to make the whole message come together.

Later in the text, Brian again says *a* for *away* but this time stops and asks the teacher for help. Susan says, "Are you thinking about the story and what the big dog told the kitten to do?" "Go away?" Brian responds tentatively. Susan confirms the response but in a way that reiterates a strategy: "Does 'go away' make sense and look right?" Brian then reads the sentence correctly.

The reading documented in Figure 12–9 shows Sarah engaging in self-monitoring and self-correction. She predicts *like*, then, after checking the word, corrects to *will*. Still using meaning and syntax, she predicts *take* but checks it with visual information and self-corrects to *look*. It appears that Sarah is cross-checking one or more sources of information.

During this group's reading, Susan listens in, captures samples of reading behavior, confirms children's problem-solving attempts and successes, interacts briefly with individuals, and takes notes. The children each concentrate on her or his own reading, moving through the text in a way that is, for the most part, independent. After the reading, Susan makes two teaching points.

First, she asks the children how they thought the kitten felt; several children talk briefly about how happy the kitten was to have found a home. Then Susan writes *"Hello, little kitten," said a boy* on the board. She says, "This is a sentence from the story and there are little marks that will help us read it. These little marks [*pointing to quotation marks*] tell us that the boy is talking.

	√		√		√		√		
"Miaow,			I			like			this,"

	√		√		−		√		√
said			a			hungry			little			kitten.

	√		a-		√		√		√		√
"Go			away,"			said			a			big			cat.

	√		a- | A		√		√	
"Go			away,|			little			kitten."

FIGURE 12–8   Brian's reading

<table>
<tr>
<td></td>
<td>√</td>
<td colspan="2">like | SC</td>
<td colspan="2">take | SC</td>
<td>√</td>
<td>√</td>
</tr>
<tr>
<td>Sarah:</td>
<td>We</td>
<td colspan="2">will |</td>
<td colspan="2">look |</td>
<td>after</td>
<td>you,"</td>
</tr>
</table>

	√	√	√	√
	said	the	boy's	mother.

Carol: Good checking. That makes sense and looks right.

	√	√	√	√	√	√
Sarah:	"We	like	kittens,"	said	the	boy.

FIGURE 12–9   Sarah's reading

Down here [*pointing to the comma*] is a mark that means when we read, we stop and take a little breath. It's a comma. I'm going to read it." She reads the text with appropriate pausing and intonation, modeling the process. "Now you read it with me."

All the children read the sentence in unison, using pauses and phrasing. Susan then asks them to turn to page eight in their books, which has text that provides good opportunities for children to read with phrasing and expression:

"Grrr . . . grrr . . . grrr.
Go away," said a big dog.
"Go away, little kitten.
Grrr . . . grrr . . . grrr."

The group reads the page together, pausing at commas and making the whole page sound like a story.

Susan has also noticed that two of the children had difficulty with the word *stay*, so she takes a minute to write the word *stop* on chart paper. She says, "You know this word." Several children say *stop*. Then Susan writes *day* on the paper, and again, children read the word easily. Susan knows that these two words are generally known in the classroom. They have appeared in writing many times. She says, "This word starts like *stop*," and she writes *st*, "and ends like *day*," and she writes *ay*. The children come up with the word *stay* right away. Susan then has them open their books to page sixteen, where the text "I will stay here" appears, and has them locate the word *stay* in the text. Finally, she asks Sarah to read the whole page just the way the little kitten would have said it. Sarah's reading is phrased and fluent, and she uses the punctuation marks. Susan praises Sarah, asks Erica to remain (Susan will take a running record of her reading of the story), and sends the rest of the group off to reread the story to a partner before rejoining their work groups.

It is obvious that even when groups are reading the same text, teaching points will vary according to a particular group's strengths and needs. Susan chose these today; for another group on another day, her teaching points will be different. Also, in a guided reading approach, groups do not "follow each other" through books. The other groups in Susan's class might never read *The Hungry Kitten*.

Using Running Records to Assess Teaching for Strategies

Susan will take a running record on one child's reading of *The Hungry Kitten*. She has the children in the group on a rotation schedule so that she is sure to systematically assess them. Teachers usually take between three and five minutes to take a running record on a book. For shorter books the time may even be less than three minutes. When children are reading very long texts, the teacher may select a part of the text for the record to get an adequate sample of the processing behavior (from 100 to 200 words). There are many options that accommodate taking running records during class time:

■ Some teachers find a time in the morning (perhaps first thing when children are doing some kind of independent work) to take two or three records.

■ Others dismiss the guided reading group, keeping one child to take a record while the other children go off to read to a partner, respond or extend the story, or return to work board activities.

■ Another option is to call one child from the group, take a record on the last new book introduced, and then call the rest of the group for their guided reading lesson.

■ Still another option is to call the entire group, ask children to reread books from the browsing box (sometimes specifying one or two of the newest titles) while taking a running record on one child from the group.

Prompts Used in Teaching for Strategies

In the examples in this chapter, teachers use questions or prompts to help children learn how to think about different sources of information as they put together a flexible system of strategies they can apply on increasingly difficult text. The teacher listens carefully, observes the precise reading behavior, and when appropriate, makes a facilitating re-sponse. The list in Figure 12–10 is a sampling of suggested prompts or questions for facilitating the effective use of information sources by beginning readers (Clay 1993b; Goodman 1996; Routman 1991; Department of Education [New Zealand] 1985).

The goal is for children eventually to consider these questions themselves as they use all sources of information in an integrated way to read with phasing and fluency. The teacher needs to learn to prompt with just the right amount of support. As the child gains more strategic control, the teacher's level of support will lessen. This change over time will enable the child to take over the processing for himself.

Assisted Learning During and After Reading

In guided reading, our decisions are based on group work, both for reasons of efficiency and social value. But even though we are working in a group context, we are developing the individual reader's processing systems. We focus on what individual children can do and help them use their knowledge to get to what they do not yet know. We assess individual behavior. The teacher must know how individual skills develop and the many paths to learning that individuals may travel.

Jerome Bruner (1974) has described how young children develop skilled actions: they anticipate them; attempt them; and adopt them (if they have been successful) or modify them based on corrective feedback. With practice, they establish subroutines, which free their attention, allowing them to concentrate on new aspects of the task. Throughout the process accuracy, speed, and fluency increase.

Early reading behavior may at first require a great deal of a child's attention. Learning is helped by the child's natural eagerness and by feedback from the teacher, who suggests, points out, draws attention to, and sensitizes. In the process, young readers develop the systems that help them achieve greater

Prompts to Support the Use of Processing Strategies

To support the control of early reading behaviors:
Read it with your finger.
I liked the way you pointed under each one.
Did you have enough (or too many) words.
Did it match?
Were there enough words?
Did you run out of words?
Try _____. Would that make sense?
Try _____. Would that sound right?
Do you think it looks like _____?
Can you find _____? (a known or new word)
Read that again and start the word.
Try that again and get your mouth ready to start the tricky word.

To support the reader's use of self-monitoring or –checking behavior:
Were you right?
Where's the tricky word? (after an error)
What did you notice? (after hesitation or stop)
I liked the way you stopped.
What's wrong?
Why did you stop?
What letter would you expect to see at the beginning? At the end?
Would _____ fit there?
Would _____ make sense?
Do you think it looks like _____?
Could it be _____?
It could be _____, but look at _____?
Check it. Does it look right and sound right to you?
Check it. Does it make sense and sound right to you?
You almost got that. See if you can find what is wrong.
Try that again.

To support the reader's use of all sources of information:
Check the picture.
Can the picture help?
Does that make sense?
Does that look right?
Does that sound right?
Does that make sense and look right?
Does that sound right and look right?
Does that make sense and sound right to you?
That makes sense but does it look right?
That looks right but does it make sense?
That sounds right but does it look right?
You said _____. Can we say it that way?
You said _____. Does that make sense?
What's wrong with this? (Repeat what the child said.)
Try that again and think what would make sense.
Try that again and think what would make sense and look right.
Try that again and think what would sound right.
Try that again and think what would sound right and look right.
Try that again and think what would look right and make sense.
Do you know a word like that?
Do you see a part that can help you?
Do you know a word that starts with those letters?
What could you try?
Do you know a word that ends with those letters?
What do you know that might help?
What can you do to help yourself?

To support the reader's self-correction behavior:
Something wasn't quite right.
Try that again.
I liked the way you worked that out.
You made a mistake. Can you find it?
You're nearly right. Try that again.
You worked hard on that.

To support phrased, fluent reading:
Can you read this quickly?
Put your words together so it sounds like talking.

FIGURE 12–10   Prompts to support the use of processing strategies

efficiency. Over time, using these systems becomes automatic.

As an example, let's take a child who is just beginning to match word by word. His teacher demonstrates and reminds him to "read with his finger." Just how much demonstration, what kind, and with how much repetition depends on the child's ability to understand and control the action. But over time, the direction to "read it with your finger" is no longer needed; both teacher and child direct their attention to other aspects of the process.

Children have been developing these processes from infancy; it is how they learn to learn. The reading teacher's responsibility is to help children use their knowledge of the world, of language, and of print to read simple stories and to interact with students moment to moment.

The kind of help given is critical. *Making it easy to learn* does not mean simply *making it possible for the child to get it right.* Too often, the impetus behind a book introduction is, How can I help Debbie get this word right? or, If I can get Paul to read with 90 percent accuracy, my reading graph will go up. That kind of thinking doesn't lead to powerful teaching that enables readers to develop the operations they need to read new text for themselves. Making errors gives readers a chance to develop effective procedures for searching, checking, and self-correction.

These problem solving opportunities, surrounded by a backdrop of successful reading, are what enables young readers to build a reading process. It is the quality of assistance given by the teacher that directs the child's attention to efficient, effective ways of learning how to solve problems for themselves.

Suggestions for Professional Development

1. Form a small study group consisting of a grade-level team or a number of primary teachers.

2. Have each member of the group take running records with a child of his or her choice (preferably one who is making average or above-average progress) every week for six weeks. Be sure the texts are ones the child can read with an accuracy rate of between 85 and 95 percent.

3. At the end of six weeks, bring the records to a session and work together to examine them for evidence of strategic processing:

- Was the text an appropriate level of difficulty for this child?
  - Was it too easy?
  - Was it too hard?
  - Did it provide the opportunity for problem solving?
- Did the overt problem-solving behavior provide valuable information?
- What sources of information (cues) did the child use or neglect?
- Did the child notice error and actively work to make cues match? What does he do at the point of error?
- Did the child's further attempts after error lead to a correct response? Did they provide evidence of the use of a variety of sources of information?
- How did the child's behavior change from week 1 to week 3 to week 6? What did these changes indicate about possible changes in the development of a reading process?
- Is there evidence of fluency?
- Is there evidence that the child is reading with understanding?

4. If your group finds this activity helpful in understanding how children develop reading strategies, continue taking records on these same children for another six weeks and repeat the discussion session.

Learning About Letters and Words

Good teachers are aware of the need for drawing children's attention to words and letter combinations. . . . At the same time, there is no substitute for children's own reading of real books and their own questions about how words work.   DAVID BOOTH

To read print we need to relate clusters of letters to sounds and individual words. Some researchers (Smith 1994; Goodman 1982) have suggested that readers only sample this kind of visual information. Others (Adams 1990) insist that the eye scans every letter. For us as teachers, the important aspect of the task is the amount of attention readers need to give to individual letters or clusters of letters in order to read for meaning.

Our view of guided reading is based on Clay's theory of reading continuous text (1991a). Letters and words within continuous text offer different kinds of informational support than they do when isolated. The syntactic patterns of the language narrow the possibilities and make it easier for children to select and use the graphic symbols.

Clay's phrase "reading for meaning with divided attention" is a useful way to think about the process. The story or message is the focus of the reader's attention. While focusing on meaning, the reader will also:

❙ Monitor to be sure the message makes sense.

❙ Monitor to be sure the different sources of information are consistent with each other (that verb tense is maintained, for example).

❙ Make predictions based on the text and previously encountered syntactic patterns.

❙ Check predictions.

❙ Solve unfamiliar words as they are encountered in text.

❙ Search back in the text to confirm or facilitate word solving.

Good readers use many strategies to solve a word while reading for meaning:

❙ Recognize it as a familiar word and check whether it makes sense and sounds right.

❙ Derive the new word by analogy to a word or words they already know (using *my* and *tree* to figure out *try*).

❙ Search for meaning in pictures and text.

❙ Predict based on meaning or syntax and check against visual information.

❙ Think about what would make sense and sound right given some aspect of the word.

❙ Partially sound letters of the word and fit this partial information with meaning and language structure.

■ Sound out parts of the word and link them to known words or parts of words.

■ Analyze the word letter by letter, using larger clusters as much as possible.

The challenge for teachers is to help children develop a repertoire of flexible strategies for solving words while reading for meaning. In fact, *to read* means to use graphic symbols (letters clustered into words) embedded in continuous text. Children may know enough about the written code to recognize letters and words in isolation, and this is useful. However, to read for meaning they must be able to decode words strung together in sentences, paragraphs, stories, and informational texts. And, they must be able to relate the words in one text to other texts they have read. Further, the more texts they read, the more the phonological and visual information becomes available. Through repeated readings, the reader has more attention for the way words look and is able to learn more about phonics and word patterns.

Guided reading, in connection with a number of other classroom learning experiences, nurtures the ability to use visual information in collaboration with the way language is organized to convey meaning.

1. During *interactive writing*, children's attention is directed to aspects of words, perhaps even to how to construct words letter by letter or in parts.

2. During *their own writing*, children construct words, hear and record sounds, use known words to get to words they don't know, and notice parts of words.

3. Through *reading aloud* and *conversation*, children build up their store of known words and how they sound.

4. In *centers* (see Chapter 5) and *minilessons*, children focus on letters and words and how they work.

The Role of "Phonics"

The relationship between the phonological aspects of language (the sounds) and the graphic signs (the letters and combinations of letters) is an important source of information for readers. According to Clay (1993a) a competent reader

> uses not just the sounds of letters but phonological information from several levels of language. He can provide phonological identities for letters, digraphs, clusters, syllables, prefixes and suffixes, root words, phrases, and nonlanguage strings. He will select a larger rather than a smaller unit for efficiency and may check one source of information against another. (p. 290)

Much of a child's familiarity with the graphophonological system is developed in settings other than the specific guided reading lesson. Children have opportunities to work on print in many ways. During interactive writing they construct words in conjunction with other students and their teacher. They say words slowly, becoming aware of the sequence of sounds, and then link these sounds to the letters they know. As they reread the group messages they produce, their knowledge expands rapidly.

The center activities described later in this chapter (as well as in Chapter 5) expand children's experience in using written language. You can use children's own names to draw attention to letters, teaching not only the letter names but the features of letters and how to recognize one from another. The goal is learning to use information from letters that are embedded in text.

Words that are written, located, and read many times become strategic "anchors" for children as they begin to recognize them in text and use them to monitor their reading. A known word can also be used to decode unknown words. Clay's work (1991a; 1993a) suggests that through experience, and with good teaching, children become readers of three categories of words in English:

1. Words with sound sequences that can be predicted from the letters (*can*, *went*, *but*). Children learn to connect both letters and parts of words that they recognize and check their decoding against what would make sense in the sentence being read.

2. Words that have alternative letter-sound correspondences because there are two or more ways of saying the same spelling pattern (*ow* in *owl* or *ow* in *slow*). The child uses a combination of letter-sound information, knowledge of spoken words, and syntactic language patterns to solve the word.

3. Words that are orthographic (spelling) sequences rather than sound sequences (*could*, *eight*).

The process is systematic in that teachers have in their minds the body of information that will be useful to children. They have assessed what children already know and help them coordinate two complex sets of activities—decoding sound sequences and decoding letter sequences—while reading text with fluency.

The interplay between writing and reading is especially important for the beginner. During writing, the child constructs words (a building-up process) while composing and then writing a text. During reading, the child takes words apart (a breaking-down process). Combining reading and writing activities allows the child to coordinate and use both processes.

Phonological awareness, letter recognition, spelling patterns, letter-sound relations, and words that do not have predictable letter-sound relationships are also taught in guided reading lessons:

■ During the story introduction, teachers call children's attention to aspects of individual words.

■ At any time during a guided reading lesson, but usually after the reading of a new text, teachers incorporate writing to help

children analyze words. An easel is always on hand; teachers demonstrate using white boards, pocket charts and sentence strips, and chart paper.

■ During or following reading, teachers call attention to letters, letter-sound relationships, letter clusters, and parts of words within the context of meaning. Every text provides ample opportunity to examine and analyze words. Teachers select particularly useful examples to explicitly teach for word-solving strategies following the reading.

■ At the end of a lesson, teachers may spend a minute or two on word work.

■ As children encounter challenging new texts every day, they practice putting together the process of searching, checking, and using phonological information in connection with meaning and syntax.

For further information, see Pinnell and Fountas 1998.

Learning Vocabulary

Vocabulary is integral to reading. If children do not understand the meaning of the words they read, the process becomes meaningless decoding. No student should ever have to struggle along producing nonsense. As teachers, we want students to understand a wide range of words. An important part of comprehending is quick, fluent access to word meanings.

What does it mean to "know" a word? Experts (see Beck et al. 1987; Dale 1965) have identified a continuum ranging from being completely unfamiliar with a word to having a rich network of meaning attached to it. We all sometimes have the feeling that an unfamiliar word "has something to do with" a word or concept with which we are familiar. This partial recognition, supported by context, often lets us read on without losing the meaning. In fact, encountering a partially known word in context and relating it to the meaning of a whole text enhances our knowledge of that word and helps us move it along the continuum toward a richly known word. Beck has suggested that when readers truly know a word, they are able to use it in a decontextualized way, extending it to other situations and perhaps even using it metaphorically.

Readers are able to connect words with other words and to understand the connotations attached to them by virtue of their various uses. That is, every word has a social history that continually attaches meaning to it. Encountering words again and again in text builds a fabric of meaning that makes it easier to learn new words.

As teachers, we want to help students:

■ Use the meanings they know while reading text.

■ Recognize words quickly and automatically while reading for meaning.

■ Figure out partially known words by making connections and using context.

■ Call up related concepts when they encounter a partially known or narrowly known word.

■ Learn when they need to consult an authority (a dictionary, for example) and when other cues can be used effectively.

■ Notice the structure of a whole text as a clue to meaning.

■ Monitor their own level of comprehension.

■ Realize that connotation can be an important part of understanding a piece of writing.

■ Use the words they read in their own writing.

What is the best way to teach children the meaning of words? Traditionally, students copied, looked up, and memorized definitions and then used the words in sentences. (Some of these sentences were remarkably constructed, using as many of the assigned words as possible!) However, learn-

ing vocabulary words one at a time like this is not only ineffective, it is impractical. As Anderson and Nagy (1992) have pointed out, students must learn about three thousand words a year to keep up with demand. Moreover, there is good evidence that students do learn from context, although some students may not have enough background knowledge to be able to use context alone. In other words, vocabulary acquisition is fostered not by one approach but by a combination of approaches.

Some guiding principles for effective vocabulary instruction are:

■ New words should be integrated with familiar words and concepts.

■ Students should experience words in repeated, meaningful encounters.

■ Students should apply the words they learn, using them in other contexts and associating them with other knowledge.

■ Instruction should engage students in active processing of word meanings.

Letter and Word Study in the Guided Reading Lesson

When selecting new text

Readers should be able to control most features of the new text, and that includes having the strategies to access the words. In selecting a new text, consider children's language, vocabulary, and experience. Because children do not know some particular words or concepts is not a reason to discard a text; however, a book with too much unfamiliar material (an informational text, for example) might be inappropriate for a given group.

Books for emergent readers need to include words they will be able to recognize. Those words can be used as anchors to help them begin to monitor their reading. This consideration is temporary but important: a text that contains some known words helps children match what they think the text says with the print displayed on the page. Later, known words are much less important, but there must always be enough of them (along with words clearly indicated by pictures or strongly predictable through meaning) that the reader does not have to solve very many.

In the introduction
While the purpose of the introduction is to support the meaning of the text as a whole, you may also draw attention to specific words and letters within words in order to make unfamiliar words accessible to students using their present strategies. This is not the same as "preteaching" new words: the purpose of drawing attention to word features is not simply to get the word right. It is to help children learn a *process* for figuring out a word while maintaining their reading momentum.

For example, *The Three Little Pigs* (Figure 2–2) is a very easy text that would be used with early readers. In introducing this text, you might point out the word *there* because:

1. It is the first word of the text and therefore critical to getting started.

2. It cannot be predicted from the pictures and although it fits with syntax, the structure might be difficult for many children; therefore, some visual information must be used.

3. It is a good opportunity to use a known word to help figure out a new word: "In this story, *there* were three little pigs. The word *there* starts like a word you know, *the*. Look on this page to find the word *there*. It starts like *the*. Put your finger under it."

Another word you might single out is *Along*, because it is the first word on a new page and the language structure on this page is more literary and less like natural talk. Being able to figure out the word will help the children keep the reading going.

Sometimes it's necessary to point out words that will help emergent readers match and monitor. Ron's introduction of *I Can* (see Chapter 11) is for a book with only one line of text per page, a predictable sentence structure, and clear picture support. His beginning readers are learning to match language and print as it is laid out on the page. A known word can be very helpful in the process. In his introduction, Ron says, "Put your finger under the word *can*. Yes, that's *can*. You found *can*." On the next page, he again asks the children to locate *can*, building the process of noticing and using known words.

When children are reading more complex texts, attention to particular words is still an option. For example, in Claire's introduction of *Keep the Lights Burning, Abbie* (see Chapter 11), she points out a long and difficult name, *Matinicus Island*. The students examine and analyze its parts, thus learning a way to approach long words that sometimes seem too hard for readers who lack confidence. Or again, in Amy's introduction of *The Three Billy Goats Gruff*, she had children locate the *i* in *idea*, a word that had regular letter-sound relationships and was useful as an example of using word-solving skills.

During the reading
For the most part, children will be reading the text independently without teacher intervention, but you will often help individuals make small detours focusing on problem solving.

For example, Peter stopped at the word *of* while reading "The first little pig built a house of straw," attempted it by saying *on*, and asked "What's that word?" His teacher wrote *on* on a blank piece of paper and said, "You almost have it. There's an *f* at the end of the word." She said *of* as she wrote it under the word *on*. Peter repeated the word *of* and returned to the text, reading the whole page independently.

This individual attention to one reader is typical in the guided reading lesson. Other children continue reading, paying little attention to the interaction. If several children in the group showed similar difficulty in using a known word to get to an unknown word, you could bring this bit of problem solving up after the reading.

Approach individual interventions with caution; you need to be very selective and very quick. Although these brief detours may be productive, taking children away from the text interrupts their construction of meaning. If you've chosen an appropriate text selection and given it a good introduction, you won't need to interrupt the process very often. Most important, remember that visual analysis is only one type of word-solving strategy; direct children to a variety of strategies as appropriate.

After the reading

Carefully observe how individual readers use all information sources as they process text and use this information to guide your teaching after the reading. The goal is for each reader to use various information sources while reading text, focusing more closely on the parts of words as needed, in order to construct meaning.

When you observe that one or more readers in the group have had difficulty taking words apart to solve a problem while reading, you may want to spend a few minutes after the reading taking a careful look at how a word works. You can use magnetic letters on an easel, write on a chalkboard or white board, use a Magnadoodle, or simply draw children's attention to a word in the text by using a card or mask. The degree of explicitness will depend on children's familiarity with print and the nature of the demonstration.

For children who are just learning to locate words in text, it is a good idea to be sure that the example is in very clear large print on a piece of chart paper on the easel or on a white board. Since the idea is to work with something you have observed children wrestle with, you cannot preplan. Having chart paper and markers handy enables you to bring forward a quick example. Even with more experienced children who can easily locate words in the text, it is still useful to put the example on the easel or white board.

In the example in Figure 13–1 the teacher is not only helping children learn how words work but is also fostering their ability to orchestrate several different kinds of cues, or information sources. The important point is that these children are not only learning how to solve a particular problem while reading text by looking at some examples, but they are then asked to apply what they learned by rereading. Further, the children will be able to use the analysis strategy while reading other texts. This procedure contrasts with practicing the analysis of words in isolation, a situation in which many children will not immediately realize how their skill can be applied.

Clay (1993a) found that good readers focus on larger parts of words but can use letter-by-letter analysis when needed. Reading larger chunks or letter clusters is more efficient. When readers learn how words and parts of words work, they use their understanding to "take apart" new and unfamiliar words. The teacher's goal is to help each reader develop this set of strategies.

The important difference between teaching children to "sound out" words and word analysis is that the reader may use any word part or may read only some of the letters and figure out the rest of the word. The reader is learning how to use as much of the visual information as necessary and how to check the visual information (the letters) with the text to be sure that the word also makes sense and sounds right.

Attention to words and how they work involves a brief, clear, focused look in which readers take a very active role. The teaching activity leads them back to the text. *A key question for teachers to ask themselves is, What are children learning from this example that they can use in reading other texts?* Your teaching is

Example of a Teaching Point
to Help Children Learn How Words Work

After the children have finished reading the whole text individually:

Teacher: Yes, every time the family is doing their work, Jake comes along and causes trouble. Turn to the part that you think was the funniest and show it to the person next to you.

Children in pairs, talk together briefly.

Teacher: There was a tricky word in this story. Let's take a look at how we can think about a tricky word. What's this word?

Teacher writes the *on chart paper.*

Children: The.

Teacher: If I add one letter to *the*, it says *then*. You can put a letter at the end of a word to make a different word. *The* becomes *then*. Turn to page 5. Find *then*.

Children put fingers under then.

Teacher: Read what happens after Ben helps Mom.

Children: "And then along comes Jake!"

FIGURE 13–1   Example of a teaching point to help children learn how words work

not incidental; you are consistently directed toward the goal of independent, rapid reading of text. Many readers figure out a great deal about how words work through reading and writing; however the teacher's role is to make sure that each student can use many word-solving strategies.

To emphasize the brevity of these kinds of teaching moves, we call them *teaching points*, but we do not mean to imply that the process is casual. Teaching for word analysis immediately after reading a new text is powerful in that it offers clear examples of some of the critical processes that enable readers to strengthen their word-solving strategies over time.

In addition, you may want to plan for a minute or two of isolated work with letters or words to help particular groups of readers learn more about how words work. This preplanned word work helps to de-

velop automaticity and flexibility in using word parts.

At first, it may seem difficult to use this moment-to-moment teaching effectively. Over time, using running records and working every day with small groups of children, you will build up a repertoire of moves. Through many supportive encounters you can ensure that your students have built up the key strategies they need.

Letter and Word Study as an Element of a Balanced Literacy Curriculum

Children learn about how letters and words work by reading and writing. Focused attention from you assists them in the process. Most teachers plan systematic work that focuses on letters, letter-sound relationships, and word study. This focused attention is brief and simply conceptualized in the beginning of kindergarten, but by second or third grade children can use words and study them in sophisticated ways.

In addition to focusing on word study during guided reading lessons, you can use other times in the school day to build children's understanding of how letters and words work. The more children use words (that is, the more they read them, write them, play with them, or talk about them), the more likely they will be to develop the understanding and flexibility necessary to take words apart while reading or construct words for writing.

During shared reading

As you and your students read poems, chants, or stories from enlarged text, you can invite students to revisit the text for different purposes, one of which is to learn about letters or words. This brief attention to the way letters and words work in the author's construction of a message gives children new insight to bring to their independent reading and writing of text.

During interactive writing

During interactive writing, you can effectively use the names of children as resources in writing group stories. "Sharing the pen" not only helps children use what they know but draws their attention to the features of letters. They learn many words as well as powerful strategies they can carry over into their own writing. This group setting in which the purpose is to produce a group-composed, coherent piece of text is an ideal opportunity to show children the inner workings of words so that they can complete their product.

For example, children in Ida Patacca's classroom wanted to write the word *use* in a note to be placed on the school oven: "Please do not use the oven. Room 6 is using it." After they had written and read the message up to the word *use*, several children suggested that the way to spell *use* was *yous*.

Ida said, "I like your thinking. That makes sense. You know the word *you* and

added *s*. That might be one way to spell it." She wrote *you* and then *s* on the white board. Then she said, "I don't know why but in books they spell it another way," and she wrote *use* under the previous attempt while saying it slowly.

The children looked at both words. They could hear the /u/ sound in *use*. Tracey said, "If you take off the *e*, it would be *us*. Andy noticed, "It could be *U.S.* if you take off the *e*." Tasha connected the word to *USA*. Ida had recognized the analytic work they did when they were attempting to construct the word and had showed it to them visually. These children were learning to take words apart; they were learning how words work.

During writing

Children learn much about words as they use them to convey messages in writing. During writing workshop, you can explicitly demonstrate the processes, strategies, and skills of writing through minilessons and conferencing that support independent work. As children begin to write, it is useful for them to have a bank of known words that they fully control and can write quickly. This store of words can also be built through interactive writing and assisted independent writing. Using the word wall to display some frequently used words will help students recall and use these words. As they write more and read more, they will know more words and be able to produce text more easily and concentrate on constructing new words.

The strategy children learn during interactive writing (saying a word slowly as they try to write it) carries over into independent writing, where they begin to produce more and more parts of the word. It is not as simple as sounding out the word letter by letter, however. As they write more, children will see patterns among words. They will learn to write letter clusters to represent sounds and meaning chunks, such as *er*. You can support this process through minilessons and individual conferences. In the early stages, each child can keep a list of words she or he knows; this list can be conveniently stored in the writing folder. One word-solving strategy is to link unknown words with words the writer already knows. Thus, every known word becomes a resource.

Letter and Word Activities

Letter and word learning is most effective when children see purpose and authenticity in the task. The real task for a reader is using letters and words that are embedded in text. We do not recommend extensive practice on letters and words in isolation, especially if children do not have the opportunity to learn the purpose of this information. And we certainly would not support the fairly common practice of not having children read and write until they know all the alphabet letters. We agree with Clay:

> If the learner already knows letters (the set of symbols), this is a good start for the new task. If he does not then he can learn letters at the same time as he is learning other kinds of new visual information. (1991a, p. 260)

Learners may begin reading and writing through guided reading as we have suggested while at the same time building their knowledge of letters and words. Activities that draw children's attention specifically to letters and words will be helpful in the beginning phases of literacy learning. As children grow more sophisticated in their knowledge of written language, word study continues to be an important part of the curriculum.

Frequently used words

While the texts on our book list do not have controlled vocabulary and the emphasis is on a variety of language patterns and good stories, it is obvious that many words occur over and over. These words are useful to beginning readers and writers:

■ Because they appear over and over, knowing them facilitates fluent reading and

allows the reader to pay attention to new words.

■ They may be the springboard to solving unfamiliar words.

■ They add speed and fluency to writing and can be used to construct new words.

Often teachers in the early grades compile a list of one hundred or so words on which to focus in reading and writing in the first two to three years of school (see Figure 13–2).

As children read the easiest books (levels A–C), it will be important for them to learn how to recognize and use some of these frequently encountered words. Knowing them fosters the important early behaviors of matching words, one by one. You may help children attend to known or almost known words by pointing them out in the text and using them in charts or sentence strips.

Cunningham (1995) gives wonderful directions for creating and using different kinds of word walls, which are useful resources for writing and reading. The words are used as a reference as well as the focus of many different word activities. Figure 13–3 is an example of a word wall that is used for many different activities in a primary classroom.

There are many different ways to help students develop their vocabulary for both reading and writing. Stephanie places a small pocket chart of words children use often in the center of each table for children to refer to as they write. Joan writes a list of frequently used words on the round, fat coffee can for pencils at the middle of each table and places a list in each child's writers workshop folder.

Word study or ABC center

A classroom word study center includes many opportunities for children to work with letters and words. Elsewhere we have called this kind of area the ABC center, but it can also be called a word study center. The center is not simply a loosely structured storage area for magnetic letters and other

Frequently Used Words

a	day	if	old	this
after	did	in	on	three
all	do	into	one	to
am	don't	is	or	too
an	down	it	our	two
and	for	just	out	up
are	from	keep	over	us
as	get	kind	people	very
asked	go	know	play	was
at	going	like	put	we
away	good	little	ran	went
back	had	long	run	were
be	has	look	said	what
because	have	looked	saw	when
before	he	make	see	where
big	her	man	she	will
boy	here	me	so	with
but	him	mother	some	would
by	his	my	that	you
came	house	no	the	your
can	how	not	then	
come	I	now	there	
could	I'm	of	they	

FIGURE 13–2   A list of frequently used words

materials that children use for play. The initial exploratory activities may seem like play, but from the teacher's point of view the center is carefully planned to extend children's learning.

If the center is used as an independent activity during the guided reading period, there will be specific tasks for children to perform there, tasks that lead them to explore the features of letters and to make and break words. Often, the activities require minilessons in which the teacher demonstrates the process, after which the children follow through with independent work. Here are some activities that might be demonstrated and then included in an ABC Center.

Alphabet linking chart

For beginning readers, many teachers use a chart of clear letter forms and simple pictures that provide a clear letter-sound link to key words. You may want to copy the chart in Appendix C for individual students or place enlarged copies in many areas of the classroom for children to refer to or to read when they "read around the room."

A small group of children who need more letter name and sound experiences can be asked to do a choral reading of the chart a number of times over several days or weeks. The reading would sound like this: *Aa apple, Bb bear, Cc cat, Dd dog.*

The chart can be used in many different ways:

■ Read every other box.
■ Read only the letters.
■ Read only the words.
■ Read only the vowels.
■ Read only the consonants.
■ Read the pictures.

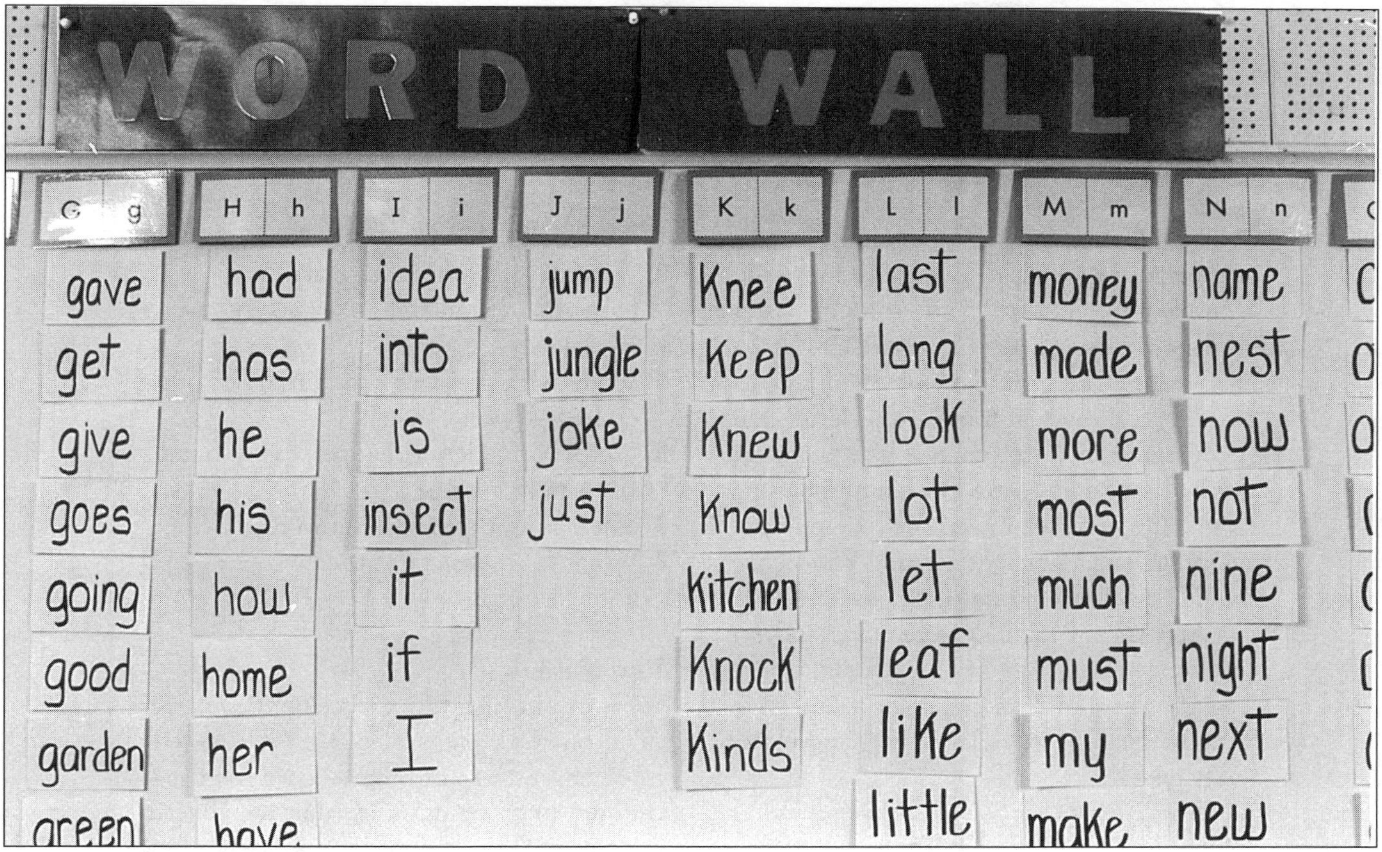

FIGURE 13–3   Word wall

❚ Have one group read the vowels and
another group read the consonants.
❚ Have the class or group sing the chart.
❚ Cover some letters with Post-its and ask
for predictions, then remove the stickers.

Alphabet books

Collect a wide range of simple alphabet
books for children to read to themselves or
with a buddy. This activity will provide much
practice in using letter names, recognizing
letter forms, and developing many new letter-sound associations.

Children can also use magnetic letters to
make the words that are associated with each
letter, checking their constructions against
the words in the book.

Children enjoy making alphabet books;
the alphabet provides an organizing frame.
At first, you may want to use interactive
writing to model making a group alphabet

book. Alphabet books can reflect a theme,
such as clothing, animals, or food. It is not
necessary for every book to include every
letter. You can make a book with selected
letters, such as those that begin children's
names or five favorites.

Sue Hundley started off one year with a
big empty alphabet book. Each time her
class was introduced to a new read-aloud,
she asked them for two or three items they
wanted to place in their class book. When
they read *Five Little Monkeys*, they added
monkeys, and when they read *The Three
Bears* they added *Mama Bear*, *Papa Bear*, and
Baby Bear. Then each time they reread the
big book, they reminisced about their rich
story history.

Individual letter books

One way to get acquainted with letters and
begin to connect them with words that reflect

letter-sound relationships is through individual letter books. Many commercial companies produce colorful books focusing on a single letter; for example, a whole book about the letter *a* might have the letter in clear print on each left-hand page, with each right-hand page having a picture of an object beginning with *a*. Even children who know few letters can "read" through letter books with just a little guidance. The books have the advantage of drawing children's attention to the visual form of the letter and encouraging them to practice a sequence of words that start with the corresponding sound. Children who need extra help in developing fast, efficient letter knowledge should be able to take letter books home.

Appendix J includes directions and reproducible masters for twenty-six eight-page letter books. Children can color them, have an individual set in a plastic bag, and eventually take them home.

Matching and sorting letters

Children enjoy matching and sorting, and these activities are very useful in helping them attend to features of letters. Children can match upper- and lowercase letters, find all the *e*s or *m*s, find letters with circles, find letters with tails, sort tall letters and short letters, sort letters by color, find the letters in their name, put the letters into alphabetical order, etc. Another useful activity is to have children sort letters three or four ways and tell how they are alike.

Making words

Children can make groups of words with many different kinds of letters—magnetic letters, tile letters, foam letters. There are numerous possibilities:

■ Words from a set of letters (*c, n, t, a, p*).
■ Words with the same first letter (*box, bat*).
■ Words with the same final letter (*up, hop*).
■ Words of which one is included in the other (*but, butter*).
■ Words with some of the same letters in them (*once, twice*).

■ Words with a particular letter sequence (*sh, ch*).
■ Words with a letter cluster at the beginning (*stop, clay*).
■ Words with a letter cluster at the end (*sand, rust*).
■ Words with *e* in them (*egg, clean, tree*).
■ Words with a letter that makes a particular sound (the *s* in *sun* or *bus, was,* or *treasure*).
■ Words with the same root but varied endings (*looking, looks*).
■ Words with a letter that makes no sound (*here, meat, make*).
■ One-, two-, or three-letter words.
■ Words in a category or theme (colors, animals, names).

Sorting words

You can also use the pocket chart, magnet strips on word cards placed on a magnetic easel, or a list of words on a board to engage children in grouping words that are alike in some way. Your demonstration of each new way of sorting words is an important element in children's being able to take on the task; after learning many different ways to sort words, children will invent new categories themselves. Sorting words gives children practice in attending to many different features, including the way they look or sound and the way they are similar to or different from each other.

At an ABC center small groups of partners can work together to sort and read words in a given category. They can work individually, share with each other, write their list on a card, and put it in a box for you to highlight with the class at sharing time. Here are some possible categories:

■ Rhyming words (*cat/fat, we/me*).

■ Words with the same initial or final letter or letters (*hot/him, lip/jump, who/what/when, sugar/vinegar*).

■ Words with initial or final letter clusters (*spring/sprout, last/fast*).

■ Words with the same number of syllables (*dog/bus/toy, baby/looking/dragon*).

■ Types of words (*into/fireman/butterfly/ outside/doghouse, can't/we're/I'm*).

■ Categories of words (colors, children's names, places, food, things to do).

■ Words with inflectional endings (*playing/walking, runs/jumps*).

■ Words with the same sequence of letters (*black/track/snack, fat/fatter/fattening, airport/ airplane/fairy, tree/see/green, sky/skate/ski*).

■ Words with similar letters that have different sounds (*took/food/flood, the/they/then, cow/snow, bear/near*).

■ Words with the same vowel sound (*sky/shine, play/weigh, me/feet/mean*).

After sorting a selection of words, children can identify the principle that makes them the same and give them labels.

Sort and label

Children can also sort a selection of words and then identify the principle that makes them the same. They create and label categories. For example, *treasure, pet, fell, sent,* and *kept* all have the short /e/ sound, while *seat, feel, we, keep,* and *chief* have the long /e/ sound. Further, as shown in Figure 13–4, the children can work with an open-ended pile of words and create their own piles, sorting the same words in many different ways. The children at this center have sorted words by number of letters, number of syllables, colors, and by silent *e* endings.

Word ladders

Working from a word they know, children can add and remove letters to construct a ladder of words:

in	as	do	net	an
pin	has	dog	nest	and
pen	ham	dig	next	sand
open	hat	digging		candy
opens	hit			
opening	hits			
reopening	hitting			

Using analogy

When children understand how words work, they can use what they know about one word to construct or take apart another. For

FIGURE 13–4   Word sort

example, when children know *my* and *tree*, they might be able to put together *try*. Using analogy means knowing some words very well and using them as examples, noticing parts of them and putting the parts together in flexible ways. You can demonstrate the use of analogy and leave several examples for children to perform themselves in the center during independent work. After a number of examples, many children will begin using analogy in other circumstances.

Achieving Balance

The ultimate goal of learning about letters and words is for children to use this knowledge as they read and write text. Children vary in the amount of experience and practice they need to be able to use visual information fluently and flexibly. Some children come to school already very familiar with the visual forms of letters. They easily distinguish one from another and even if they do not know all of the names, they learn them quickly. Others need much time and opportunity to manipulate letters until they are familiar enough to recognize the distinguishing features.

Keep an ongoing inventory of what children know and can do, so that your teaching can be more efficient. Two circumstances are nonproductive:

■ The learner cannot do the task because it is too difficult.
■ The learner can already perform the task so easily that it is tedious.

In a large classroom, a few students will likely be susceptible to either circumstance. Here are some general principles to help you avoid them as much as possible:

1. Don't work on letters and sounds that most children already know; instead, take some children aside as a small group for extra work on those letters and sounds.

2. Provide opportunities for children to make connections themselves between sounds and letter clusters and between words

that they know. Teach them how to use what they know as a resource for new learning.

3. Demonstrate new tasks explicitly so that children having difficulty will understand and be able to perform them.

4. Leave room for some children to go beyond the given task (for example, by exploring the principles further in the ABC center).

5. Do not allow work on letters or words to become so prominent that it takes time away from reading and writing extended text; while specific attention to visual elements is useful, it should be considered a brief encounter for a particular purpose.

Suggestions for Professional Development

1. Convene a group of colleagues to discuss what children at your grade level understand about letters and words.

2. Give each group member a copy of the writing vocabulary task of the Observation Survey as completed by a high-achieving child. Talk about the variety of relationships the child understands about words.

3. Bring some running records to a session and discuss what you notice about the children's knowledge of how to solve words by the way they attempt unknown words.

4. Bring children's writing samples and discuss what they show about their understanding of how to construct words.

5. Bring a tub of magnetic letters and spend time sorting the letters in as many ways as possible.

6. Bring a tub of letter tiles or word cards and sort words in different ways.

7. Together, following your hands-on experiences, make a list of important aspects of letters or words that can be integrated into guided reading lessons, writers workshop minilessons, or the ABC center.

Shifts Over Time

Many children learn to read by the time they are seven or eight years old; but to become truly literate, they will go on learning to read throughout their lives. MOIRA McKENZIE

Guided reading is not a static concept; the materials, teacher decisions, and interactive framework change over time as children grow in knowledge, skill, and independence and teachers become more experienced. One way to demonstrate this development is to follow one child—we'll call him Reginald— as he goes from being an emergent reader to becoming the originator of his self-extending literacy. No one school offers every support system described in Reginald's story. His story combines the stories of many children we know; his experiences are a composite of the many opportunities available. Every school, however, has the potential to mediate a rich journey like Reginald's.

Reading Development

But first, to frame the picture, let's look at an outline of reading development. Figure 14–1 charts four broad categories of readers: emergent, early, transitional, and self-extending. These categories are not discrete stages but a continuum of learning that varies with the complexity of each individual's development. Behavior relative to each category also varies with the task and the material. Nevertheless, the chart is an overall map that helps

teachers and administrators make instructional predictions.

While these categories are roughly age related, it is obvious that experience and attention are major factors and that there is a great deal of overlap. At the same time, a self-extending system must be in place by grade three. (Later we discuss the need for early intervention for those students who do not appear to be making satisfactory progress.) The behavior in each category requires a different guided reading emphasis.

Emergent readers are just beginning to control early behavior such as directionality and word-by-word matching. They use pictures to support meaning and rely on language as a strong cueing system. With emergent readers, teachers move from shared to guided reading, focusing on helping children independently read texts that are easy for them and that they have read before.

Early readers are in full control of early strategies and can read appropriately selected texts independently once the teacher has introduced them. Their teachers are concerned with helping them more fully develop their ability to search, check, and use multiple sources of information.

Transitional readers take on novel texts

Guided Reading Development Over Time*

	Emergent Readers	Early Readers	Transitional Readers	Self-extending Readers
Description	• use mostly information from pictures • may attend to and use some features of print • may notice how print is used • may know some words • use the introduced language pattern of books • respond to texts by linking meaning with their own experiences • are beginning to make links between their own oral language and print	• rely less on pictures and use more information from the print • have increasing control of early reading strategies • know several frequently used words automatically • read using more than one source of information • read familiar texts with phrasing and fluency • exhibit behaviors indicating strategies such as monitoring, searching, cross-checking, and self-correction	• have full control of early strategies • use multiple sources of information while reading for meaning • integrate the use of cues • have a large core of frequently used words • notice pictures but rely very little on pictures to read the text • for the most part, read fluently with phrasing • read longer, more complex texts	• use all sources of information flexibly • solve problems in an independent way • read with phrasing and fluency • extend their understanding by reading a wide range of texts for different purposes • read for meaning, solving problems in an independent way • continue to learn from reading • read much longer, more complex texts • read a variety of genre's
Age & Grade Range	• approximately age 2 to 7 Preschool to early Grade 1	• approximately 5 to 7 Kindergarten to Grade 1	• approximately 5 to 7 Kindergarten to Grade 2	• approximately 6 to 9 Grades 1 to 3
What might guided reading be like?	• Reading will be moving from shared to guided reading. The teacher prompts children to use pictures and to use language. The focus is on early strategies such as one-to-one matching and directionality.	• After the introduction, children independently read the whole book, solving difficulties with little help	• Each child reads the whole text independently after the introduction. Often, children can read the whole text with just a summary overview. Teachers continue to provide a fuller introduction when a text with new features is introduced.	• Children read the whole text independently with a brief overview or provocative introduction. New text features are carefully introduced. They may come together to discuss particular aspects of text (like characters or setting) at appropriate breaks in the reading (for example, of chapter books) or they may extend reading in responsive ways.
What might the introduction be like?	The introduction: • is rich, providing children with language and patterns of the book • may draw attention to frequently used words • covers the whole book • as a transition from shared reading, may include a complete reading by the teacher, with children joining in, before children read on their own	The introduction: • ranges from fully covering the book to just providing a brief overview before reading • focuses on particular words by locating them • introduces unfamiliar language structures • provides a strong support for meaning	The introduction: • may involve brief support that enables independent reading of the text • may include less detail but continues to provide a good framework for reading • familiarizes readers with new concepts, particular vocabulary words, and unusual language structures • assures that students are tuned in to the meaning of the selection	The introduction: • may be provocative in terms of arousing interest or questions in the reader's mind • may be geared to helping children notice aspects of text or understand the structure of different genres • may build an understanding of the importance of previewing a text before reading • has the goal of enabling children to introduce books to themselves

*Development is unique and complex, so these provide only a broad frame for observing changing patterns.

FIGURE 14–1   Guided reading development over time

with more independence. The teacher is still responsible for introducing the text, but a rich, detailed introduction often may not be necessary. A brief summary and overview provide the needed support.

Self-extending readers have developed a system that itself fuels further learning. Every time they read, they learn more about reading. Guided reading takes on an added purpose in that it is designed to help readers attend to different and varied features of text. The introduction may simply arouse interest and prompt questions. The goal is silent reading and complete independence, when readers introduce books to themselves.

Reginald's Journey to Literacy

Reginald brought a rich home experience with him to school. He enjoyed building with blocks and made up dramatic stories using his toy cars and plastic animals. He loved playing with cousins in his large extended family; one of his greatest interests was watching his father repair machinery like the family car and the VCR.

Reginald was an active child who had spent little time sitting and listening to stories, although he enjoyed listening to music. He owned few books himself. Most of all, Reginald had developed skill in oral language. He could repeat the lyrics of many songs; he had learned to play with language, recounting stories to his friends and imitating his heroes. Like all children, his language was a rich store of knowledge about the way syntax works and how meaning is mapped into words, phrases, sentences, and texts.

Preschool experience

Reginald's introduction to school literacy began before he entered kindergarten. His mother and father attended several outreach-to-parents meetings welcoming them to the school community and helping them prepare Reginald for the transition to school. They were given *Reading and Writing—Where It All Begins* (Oxley et al. 1991),

as well as a series of Keep Books especially designed to be used at home. Reginald's mother read the books to him, and he kept them in a shoe box. His mother also attended a workshop on how to make books at home. Reginald was eager to begin "real" school and had high expectations.

Kindergarten

When Reginald entered Mrs. Snow's kindergarten he knew eight letters. He could write *REGI* and the words *A* and *I* in uppercase letters. He could represent three phonemes with letters, /r/, /m/, and /t/. He controlled some aspects of early print knowledge; for example, he recognized that print carried the message and he knew where to start. He did not have full control of left-to-right text direction, could not yet match word by word while reading, and had not sorted out the difference between letters and words.

Mrs. Snow's kindergarten was filled with opportunities for Reginald to engage in literacy. From the beginning of school, Reginald's name was displayed in many ways on the walls of his classroom. For example, he could find his name on the helpers chart, on the story map that he helped to make, in a big book about colors that all the children in the class liked, on his cubbyhole, and other places. He could find connections to his name in the alphabet chart (*R* for *ring*) and in other words that started with *R* or were linked in some way with his name. The web of understanding around his name gradually grew. In interactive writing sessions with Mrs. Snow, Reginald was able to see how written language is composed and constructed word by word. His first contribution in interactive writing was to write the /r/ for *red* in the story about colors.

He worked on letters in many different ways. In the ABC center, he used magnetic letters to make his name and other words; often he sorted letters using different categories—color, shape, upper- or lowercase, letters with circles and letters with tails, tall and short letters. He made his full name,

Reginald, by finding the letters to match his name on a card that the teacher had made. In time, he began to write his full first name and then his last name, although he learned to write his best friend's surname before his own.

He noticed the features of letters and was able to see what made a letter distinct from every other letter. He used fold-up letter books that he was able to take home, and he could read the alphabet charts displayed in various places in the room. By midyear, he knew the letters and many letter-sound relationships, and he had begun to notice important things about words such as endings.

Reginald loved reading. His teacher read to the class several times a day, and Reginald had favorite picture books that he liked to look at, approximating the stories. He was beginning to take on the language of the books because he had heard these favorite stories many times. He always joined in on repeated refrains. His teacher used many enlarged texts—big books made by the class, charts of nursery rhymes and songs, sentence strips—and Reginald enthusiastically read along with the pointer in shared reading. He repeated this activity independently by "reading around the room," using a chopstick or long pointer. He participated daily in interactive writing that contributed to his writing skill but also helped him learn about reading. He often volunteered to write particular letters in the message or to use the pointer while his classmates reread the text.

By frequently encountering the same words in shared reading, interactive writing, and the ABC center, Reginald developed a repertoire of ten or fifteen words he could quickly recognize. He used some of these words in his writing, developing the ability to write them automatically. Controlling these words helped him begin to monitor his own reading.

Mrs. Snow introduced children to the work board in October of their kindergarten year. Reginald was eager to participate in all the activities, but at first he moved quickly from one to another without sustaining his learning. After more practice and some demonstrations by Mrs. Snow, he was able to manage his work better; he continued to improve, becoming generally productive even while working independently.

By April, Mrs. Snow was working with a few children in guided reading. Reginald participated in a small group. Mrs. Snow would introduce a simple caption book and then the children would read it. At first, they tended to read together much as they had in their shared reading of big books. They pointed under each word while Mrs. Snow observed. After they became accustomed to working with small individual books in this way, Mrs. Snow advised them to read softly to themselves, and each child began to work more independently.

In this classroom Mrs. Snow had a read-aloud book bag. Each Monday children could take home a book for their parents to read to them. In addition, her PTA had purchased Keep Books: each child received twenty-four books, one a week from November to May. Eight of the titles were nursery rhymes, which Reginald learned and could read right away. The rest were simple caption books and stories. After midyear, Reginald could read these stories given Mrs. Snow's introduction and some practice. He was behaving like a reader.

By the end of his kindergarten year, Reginald was reading independently at level B with Mrs. Snow's introduction. On the Observation Survey, he knew forty-five out of fifty-four letter forms, had a Concepts about Print score of 16 (indicating that he controlled most critical early behavior), could represent eighteen phonemes with letters on the hearing and recording sounds in words task, and could write fifteen words accurately. Mrs. Snow and Reginald assembled a small literacy portfolio of work to pass on to his first-grade teacher. It included his book-reading graph (see Figure 14–2), a list of books he had read independently, a list of words he knew how to write, the titles of sto-

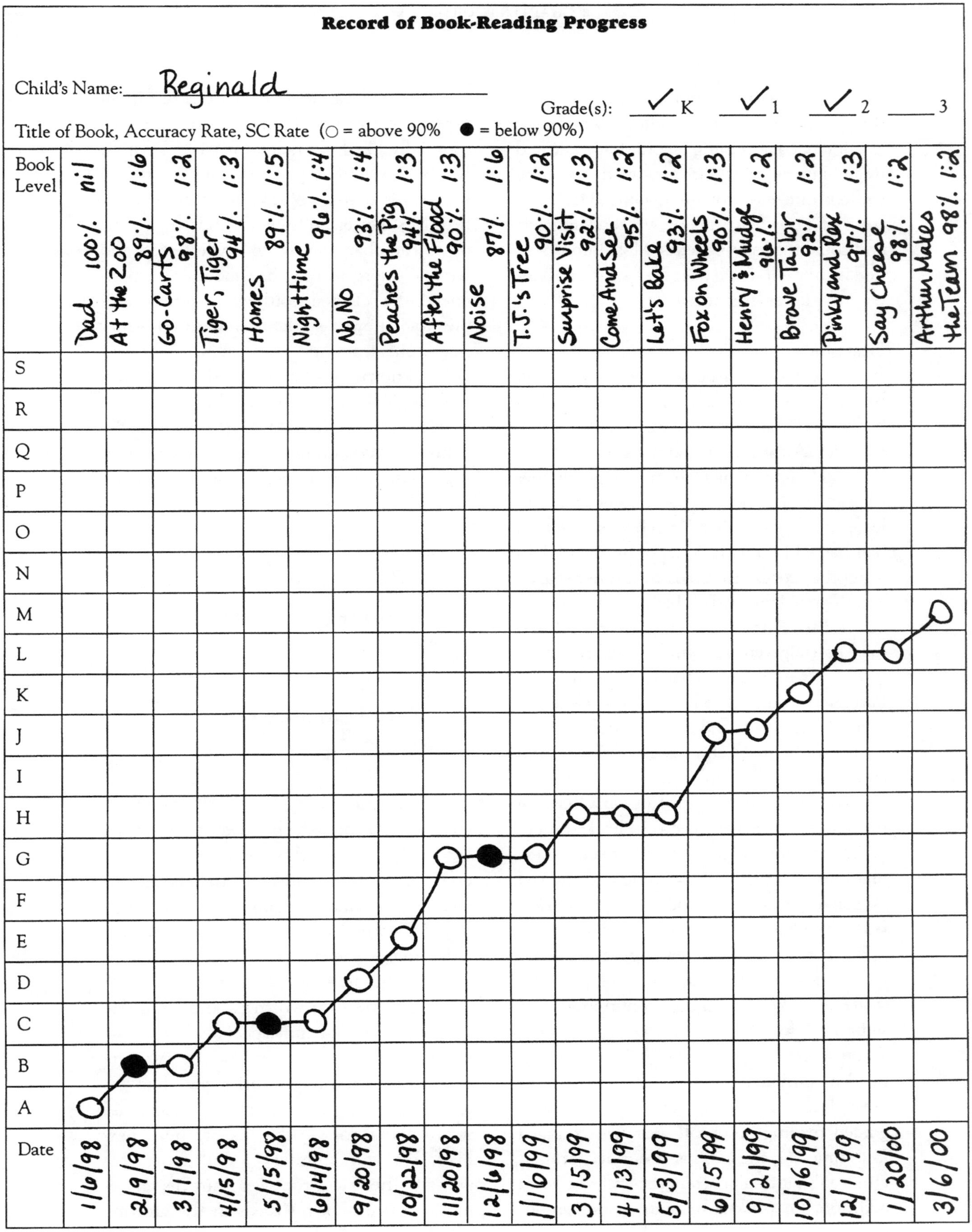
Record of Book-Reading Progress
Child's Name: Reginald
Grade(s): ✓ K ✓ 1 ✓ 2 ___ 3
Title of Book, Accuracy Rate, SC Rate (○ = above 90% ● = below 90%)
Book Level
Dad 100% nil
At the Zoo 89% 1:6
Go-Carts 98% 1:2
Tiger, Tiger 94% 1:3
Homes 89% 1:5
Nighttime 96% 1:4
No, No 93% 1:4
Peaches the Pig 94% 1:3
After the Flood 90% 1:3
Noise 87% 1:6
T.J.'s Tree 90% 1:2
Surprise Visit 92% 1:3
Come And See 95% 1:2
Let's Bake 93% 1:2
Fox on Wheels 90% 1:3
Henry & Mudge 96% 1:2
Brave Tailor 92% 1:2
Pinky and Rex 97% 1:3
Say Cheese 98% 1:2
Arthur Makes the Team 98% 1:2
S
R
Q
P
O
N
M
L
K
J
I
H
G
F
E
D
C
B
A
Date
1/6/98
2/9/98
3/1/98
4/15/98
5/15/98
6/14/98
9/20/98
10/22/98
11/20/98
12/6/98
1/16/99
3/15/99
4/13/99
5/3/99
6/15/99
9/21/99
10/16/99
12/1/99
1/20/00
3/6/00

FIGURE 14–2 Reginald's book-reading graph

ries he had written, and one writing piece that he chose as his best effort. Mrs. Snow also included a running record that indicated Reginald was using word-by-word matching to help him monitor his reading. He had a store of knowledge about written language and could read simple texts. Most important, he saw himself as a reader and a writer. Reginald was an emergent reader.

First grade

When he entered first grade the following fall, Reginald again had high expectations. He had had an active summer, playing outside most of each day. Although he had not gone to the library, the school had given him a summer pack of books and by this time he had collected a shoe-box full of Keep Books. His mom had helped him write some of his own books using the grocery store ads in the newspaper, and Reginald had added them to the box.

In Mrs. Patterson's first-grade class, Reginald participated in a guided reading group three or four days each week. Typically, Mrs. Patterson would introduce a book while the group examined it and talked with her about it. Then, Reginald and his classmates would read the whole book on their own. He quickly gained full control of early reading behaviors and began to cross-check sources of information to monitor his reading. He maintained a focus on meaning and showed evidence of solving words on these new texts. Gradually, he expanded his ability to solve new words while reading text. His behaviors revealed that he was using powerful strategies like searching, confirming, and self-correcting. Mrs. Patterson observed the group members' progress closely and, when needed, provided minilessons in particular areas. Reginald did not remain in the same guided reading group all year. He changed four times as the groups re-formed around children's particular strengths and needs. In addition, he worked in many other groupings, working with several of his classmates on an author study and taking part in literature circles.

Reginald was an active participant in all aspects of the rich literacy curriculum. He especially liked interactive writing. By now, he could write many words and liked to notice words that were alike in some way. At first, Mrs. Patterson invited children to come up to the chart and write single letters and letter clusters; as they became more experienced, she selected words as powerful examples and showed students how to construct new words from ones they knew. The easier words, known by all children, she wrote herself. Reginald especially liked to make new words with magnetic letters in the ABC center; he took on more and more challenging tasks. For example, about midyear, he made this ladder of words:

can
candy
sandy
andy (name of a classmate)
and
an
man
dan (character in a book)
man
many

Using the work board, he guided his own activity through the reading period (he especially enjoyed the computer). In general, he became more able to manage his own learning and to monitor his own behavior. He learned to collaborate with several close friends. He even provided "orientation tours" to children new to the class.

Reginald's own writing ability grew. He wrote in a journal and especially liked writers workshop. By the end of the year, he had written fourteen stories and had selected three of them to publish. Reginald wrote about topics like his brother's new bike, his grandmother in Baltimore, his grandmother's cat, the sweatshirt his grandmother gave him, his seeds in the growing center, his seventh birthday, and his own version of *The Three Little Pigs*. In writers workshop, he learned to select his own topics, choose interesting titles, add detail to his pictures, elaborate using details, and to use capitals and punctuation. Being an author motivated him to take more time and care with his work.

He read more at home this year. Mrs. Patterson continued the home book bag program and also provided twenty-four more Keep Books for Reginald to add to his collection. Ten books created by the class through interactive writing were also published for every child in the room to take home. In addition, at the end of the year he took home his personal poetry book, which he had created throughout the year by pasting in photocopied poems.

Reginald finished first grade reading at level J. The last book he read was *Nate the Great*, and he wanted to read more books in that series. His literacy portfolio was expanded. Still present were the book-reading graph, the list of books read, his best piece of writing, a long list of words he could write and read, and a sample running record from a level J text.

Second grade
Reginald's second-grade teacher, Ms. Thomas, provided many opportunities for word study. He compiled a personal dictionary, worked with the word wall, and took words apart and made new ones. He could deal with multisyllable words, homonyms, antonyms, and onomatopoetic words. He liked to explore the complexities of language and consciously used interesting words in his own writing.

Reginald worked independently, guided by the work board, and also was highly skilled at initiating activities to extend his own learning. For example, he worked for a week to create a map of his own neighborhood. He continued to develop as a writer, illustrating longer stories. About midyear, he compiled a group of stories about his grandmother into a volume titled *My Special Granny*.

Reginald finished the *Nate the Great* se-

ries, read all of the *Cam Jansen* series, and many other books. Some books he read with his guided reading group. Others he selected himself for independent reading. He liked to read and look at informational texts, especially those about snakes. He signed up for literature circles several times each month and was an active participant. As a reader, Reginald extended his understanding by reading a wide range of texts—stories, information books, simple biographies and history books, and magazines. He was able to write his own newspaper articles. He was especially interested in animals and eagerly awaited each new issue of *Zoo Books*, to which the class had a subscription. He constructed his own report on African animals using many of the text features of the *Zoo Books* articles.

Reginald was a fluent reader who knew when to read quickly, focusing on the meaning, and when to slow down briefly for problem-solving detours. He could solve new words in independent ways as needed. He read silently during independent reading and was able to sustain his interest in reading long texts, coming back to them over several days. Reading workshop supported his independent reading. Ms. Thomas scheduled one week of reading workshop and three weeks of guided reading each month.

At the end of the year, Ms. Thomas and Reginald decided to include both his story collection and his animal report in his literacy portfolio, along with the year's book graph and list of books he had read and two sample running records from readings at level N. By now, he could write and read so many words that a list was not needed, but his proofreading list from his writing folder showed what he could do as a writer. Reginald was a reader who knew how to use literacy as a tool for learning.

Reginald's progress as a reader
Reginald's progress from emergent reading to using a self-extending system (see his book-reading graph in Figure 14–2) is substantiated

by looking closely at parts of the running records in his literacy portfolio.

His kindergarten reading record (see Figure 14–3) provides evidence that Reginald was using his awareness of aspects of print to monitor his reading. He relied heavily on meaning and on his knowledge of the structure of sentences. While pointing, he accurately read the first two lines. On the third line, he repeated a pattern he expected but noticed at the end of the line that he had "run out of words." He stopped and repeated to make his reading match. Reginald was probably not making use of known words although he could use words like *I* and *a* to confirm his reading.

The running record taken midyear in first grade (see Figure 14–4) shows that Reginald was self-correcting, using multiple cues, and paying attention to aspects of words. He noticed the *st* in *stuck*, said it aloud, and then immediately said the word. He predicted *plates* for *dishes* and immediately noticed the beginning letter of the word, a clear example of cross-checking. At the end of the line, he repeated it, reading fluently.

The running record in Figure 14–5 is from Reginald's reading at the end of first grade. Here Reginald read most of the text accurately; his substitutions made sense and

his self-corrections indicate he was attending to word endings. He also showed his competence in taking words apart while reading; for example, when hesitating at the word *clever*, he noticed *cl* as a letter cluster and used that information to solve the word. Mrs. Patterson also noted that during the reading Reginald read dialogue with expression. He used a full range of punctuation to guide his reading; the reading was smooth and phrased.

Our final sample, Figure 14–6, taken about the end of second grade, shows that Reginald had become a strategic reader. He read fluently, with phrasing, making only slight detours for problem solving. He was developing power as a reader. He did not exhibit much overt self-correction but he knew how to solve complicated pieces of text. He ignored some minor errors; when he encountered the word *mustache*, which he knew was unfamiliar, he made an attempt but stopped and appealed when he knew he could not solve the word. He self-corrected at the point of error when necessary to preserve syntax and meaning, but we can hypothesize that much searching, checking, and self-correcting was happening covertly since Reginald was reading fluently for meaning.

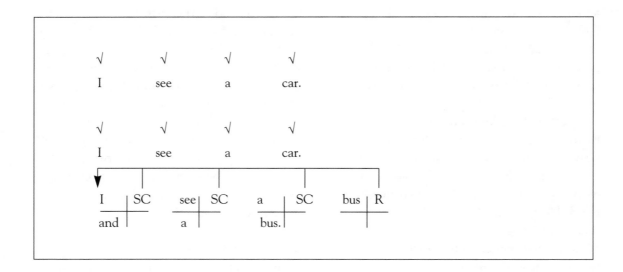

FIGURE 14–3   Reginald's reading of *Traffic*

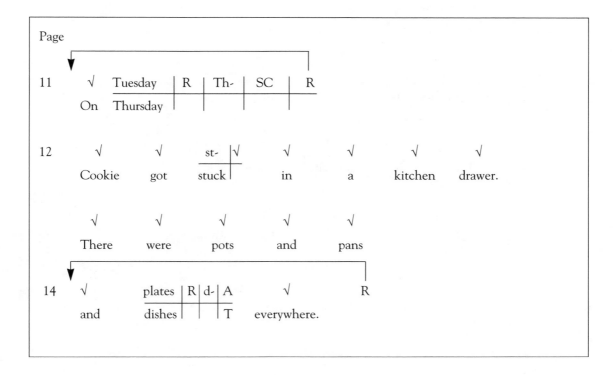

FIGURE 14–4   Reginald's reading of *Cookie's Week*

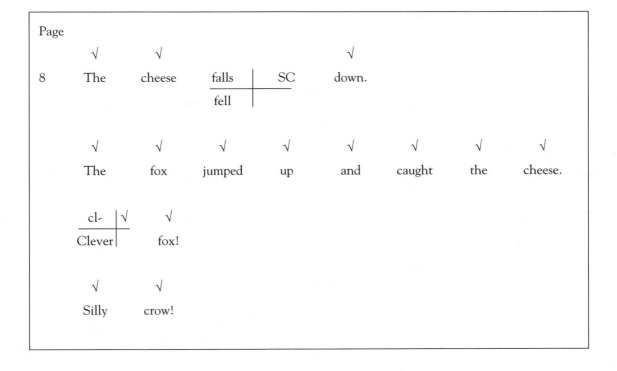

FIGURE 14–5   Reginald's reading of *The Fox and the Crow*

√   √   √   √   √   √   √   √   √

A   big   tall   man   was   standing   on   top   of

√   √   √   √   √   √   √   √   √

the   mound   of   dirt.   He   was   wearing   an   ugly

√   √   √   √   √   must | A √   √

green   tie   and   had   a   mustache | T that   curled

(must/mustache over A/T)

√   √   √   √   √   √   √R   √

up   at   the   ends.   It   was   the   runner.

√   √   √   √   √   √   √

"Well,"   he   growled,   "look   who   we   have

√   √   √   √   √   the   √

here—the   baby   sitter   and   her   baby.

(the over her)

Where is   √   √

Where's   your   boyfriend?"

(Where is over Where's)

He's | SC   √   √   √

"He . . . | he   went   home."

(He's/SC over "He . . .)

√   √   √   √   √   would h- | SC   √ √ √ √ √ √

"If   you   were   smart   you   would've | done   the   same   thing.   Let's   go."

(would h-/SC over would've)

√   √   √   √   √   √   √   √

Cam   carried   Howie   up   the   front   steps   of

√   √   √   √   √   √   √

the   house.   Inside,   the   house   was   musty.

FIGURE 14–6   Reginald's reading of *Cam Jansen and the Mystery of the Stolen Diamonds*

The Complexity of Development Over Time

Reginald's progress as a reader helps us understand development over time, but each reader makes his or her own journey. Any chart, however useful, is simplistic when matched against the complex progress of an individual reader. Remember that Figure 14–1 provides broad guidelines, showing some overall characteristics and some milestones to help you think about reading progress through a comprehensive literacy program. Each teacher must look closely at each reader's individual journey.

Teachers Reflecting on Teaching and Learning

Each of you as teachers of guided reading will develop and refine your understanding of the organization of material, classroom management, grouping, lesson components, text selection, story introductions, teaching points, engagement of children, and pace. As a tool to help you review and refine your effectiveness in guided reading, Appendix L, Guided Reading Self-Assessment, provides a scale of descriptions for you to use to identify and reflect on your level of development at various points in time. With your colleagues, you may wish to identify specific areas for further professional development or as a focus for a study group.

Suggestions for Professional Development

1. As a primary literacy team, select three to five readers at each grade level to follow over the course of one year, building simple literacy portfolios as described in Chapter 6.

2. Build a collection of running records taken at various levels over time as a resource for your school.

3. At the end of the year, place running records on a continuum categorized roughly by levels of text. Notice how readers differ and how they are similar in their behavior at each level of text.

Good First Teaching with a Second Chance to Learn

In schools that have high-quality classroom instruction and Reading Recovery,

almost all children, including the high-risk children, achieve high levels of literacy.

DOROTHY HALL, CONNIE PREVATTE, AND PATRICIA CUNNINGHAM

The critical factor in a child's literacy education is the support, direction, demonstration, and encouragement toward independence that she receives from her teachers. It is important to think about the entire series of experiences that a child will meet (see Figure 15–1). There are many excellent teachers in our schools; but good schools are not made by isolated "star teachers."

The primary literacy team will vary by school and may include preschool, kindergarten, first-grade, and second-grade teachers; a Reading Recovery teacher; a Title I teacher; a reading specialist; the special education teacher; the principal; and other educational personnel whose responsibility it is to ensure that every child becomes literate.

Figure 15–1 is set up according to traditional grade levels; however, more and more schools are moving to ungraded progression and multiage classrooms. We favor these approaches as long as professional development and long-term planning ensure that these changes will be successful. Another innovation that fits well with the ideas in this book is for a first-grade teacher to move with her students to second grade, then move back to first and take another group through two years of literacy education. (This would work with kindergarten and first grade or second and third grades as well.) We also have seen many schools successfully reduce class size for a ninety-minute literacy block by engaging all literacy teachers with the children for guided reading.

The important elements in comprehensive primary literacy education are:

■ An outreach program for the parents of preschoolers that includes books for the home. Parent outreach and books for the home continue in succeeding grades.

■ A dynamic, rich kindergarten that introduces children to the reading and writing processes in authentic, enjoyable ways.

■ An extensive literacy program in first grade, with Reading Recovery as a safety net for the lowest achievers.

■ Additional in-class small group support for other children as needed.

■ Continuation of Reading Recovery in second grade for those who entered late in the spring and did not finish their program.

■ Continuation of a balanced literacy program in second and third grade classrooms.

Thinking Comprehensively
About Primary Literacy Education

Continuous Professional Development	PRESCHOOL	• Parent Outreach • Workshops • Keep Book Program
	KINDERGARTEN	• *Balanced Literacy Program* • Parent Outreach • Keep Book Program
	FIRST GRADE	• *Balanced Literacy Program* • Parent Outreach • Keep Book Program • *Safety Nets:* 　—Reading Recovery (for lowest children) 　—Additional classroom support for other children as needed
	SECOND GRADE	• *Balanced Literacy Program* • Parent Outreach • Keep Book Program • *Safety Nets:* 　—Reading Recovery (for children to finish the program) 　—Additional classroom support for other children as needed 　—Special Education Services
	THIRD GRADE	• *Balanced Literacy Program* • Special Education Services

FIGURE 15–1   Thinking comprehensively about primary literacy education

■ Special education services for a very small number of children in second and third grade who require long-term support.

■ Continuous professional development for all teachers.

Materials span the grades; each classroom has a rich collection, but there is also a central primary book collection that provides an abundant supply of guided reading selections. Professional development is continuous. A school just starting to build a comprehensive literacy program should make an intensive start and develop local leadership. As staff members become more experienced in working together they can take over much of their own learning, but they will still need a professional support network.

What Is It Going to Take?

Piecemeal approaches and quick fixes will not bring us to our goal of making every child a competent, independent, joyful user of literacy at an early age and extending this literacy to the levels of sophistication needed in our society.

Workshops, even a series of good workshops, do not provide enough support for teachers. Materials alone will not do it, although they are necessary. We need programs that are based on a dynamic theory of literacy learning and that comprehensively support every child at the level needed. If we do not get it right in the first years of school, many children may never receive the effective education to which they are entitled.

The most important group of educators a child will ever meet is the primary literacy team. Ideally, this team is nurtured by a school literacy coordinator who teaches children in classrooms daily but also assists peers. The primary literacy team meets together and mutually takes responsibility for the literacy achievement of each child who enters the school. They help each other by sharing resources and ideas and sometimes providing feedback. It is critical to the future of children's education to develop the knowledge and skills of this team.

Turning around the sense of failure that permeates schools today will take decisive policy and professional will. Allington and Cunningham (1996) offer a somber warning followed by an encouraging note:

We always seem to be searching for the single quick fix that will solve the problems of American schools. We mandate, bandwagon, proselytize, and alienate and continue our ever-reforming educational innovations. Perhaps it is time for us to realize that:

1. There is no quick fix.
2. We have actually learned quite a lot about schooling and teaching reading to all children.
3. Achieving literacy for all children isn't such a simple matter that we can blame the method of teaching or the type of curriculum, though those are about all we ever debate.

Policy changes and broad institutional goals are useless unless they are put into operation in a quality way in schools. To do that, teachers place themselves on the line.

They need support and training of a quality that has not been attempted before. Our experience and research suggests that the following components are needed:

1. Long-term professional development for teachers.
2. The development of local leadership to support professional development.
3. Materials that support the process.

The Ohio State University's Literacy Collaborative provides long-term professional development that is integrated with research. Figure 15–2 outlines the phases of this initiative.

Developing a comprehensive literacy program takes time, collaboration, and effort. Although resources and support systems such as Literacy Collaborative are available, we wish to emphasize again that professional development and good first teaching, while necessary, are not enough to serve all children fully.

Safety Nets

For most students, early success in literacy depends on rich, dynamic, well-taught classroom programs in preschool, kindergarten, and first and second grade. Improving classroom teaching for all students is the first goal. But many students, approximately 20 percent (more in some areas), need extra help in spite of excellent classroom programs. Any prudent educational designer, therefore, will make provision for the extra help low-achieving students need.

Compensatory programs have addressed the problems of low achievers; however, most of these efforts have fallen far short of the desired goal—to assure literacy to virtually every student. Evaluation of compensatory programs reveals poor results: students who are behind their peers almost never catch up. Moreover, much time is wasted removing students from classrooms and providing programs that are ineffective and inconsistent with classroom instruction. Students who "go down the hall" to reading spend a great deal

Phases of Development in the Literacy Collaborative
(Primary and Intermediate Grades)

PHASE 1: Awareness and Planning

- Stakeholders investigate the models for curriculum and professional development
- Broad ownership is achieved
- A local plan is developed
- An option is to hold a series of four to six start-up seminars, with planned tasks between sessions to develop knowledge, create interest, and build commitment to a long-term plan

PHASE 2: Leadership Development (can occur simultaneously with Phase 1)

- Train an in-school leader called a literacy coordinator (for the primary and/or intermediate grades)
- One year of training focusing on classroom processes and teacher leadership. Literacy coordinators in training receive university credit and:
  —participate in six to seven intensive weeks (four to five during the school year and two in summer) at Literacy Collaborative training site to develop skills, observe in classrooms, and learn theory and rationales
  —use the literacy framework in classrooms all year with visits, videotaping, and feedback from university trainers
  —experience teaching other adults
- Build a school book collection
- Collect baseline data

PHASE 3: Intensive Inservice Course for Literacy Teams

- Literacy coordinator provides a structured course for classroom teachers (may involve university credit, continuing education credit, or noncredit)
- Literacy coordinator provides regular coaching and analysis of teaching
- School adds to book collection to support guided reading and other parts of the framework
- School creates home outreach and home book program
- Literacy coordinator and literacy team collect data and analyze for reporting and self-analysis

PHASE 4: Professional Development; Involvement of Intermediate Grades

- Literacy teams meet together regularly
- Literacy coordinator continues to provide training sessions for the team as updated by the university training center through institutes
- The ongoing staff development program is collaboratively designed by the literacy coordinator and staff to meet their needs; the literacy coordinator continues to help new staff on a systematic basis
- Literacy teams complete design of the guided reading program and assessment systems for the school
- The team analyzes book needs and completes book acquisition
- School continues parent and home book programs
- Teams plan miniconferences with other schools in literacy project
- Literacy coordinator and literacy team collect data and analyze for reporting and self-analysis

PHASE 5: Independent Implementation

- Literacy coordinator and the literacy team continue professional teamwork
- The school goes forward with development work in the intermediate grades
- New books are added to enrich the school collection
- Literacy coordinator and the literacy team collect data and analyze it for project report, comparing entry levels of children across the years

FIGURE 15–2 Phases of development in the Literacy Collaborative

of time doing just that; some researchers have even suggested that they would profit more from spending the time in their classroom instructional programs.

At the same time, it is foolish to expect students to sit day after day in classroom programs pitched to an average range (a necessity of group instruction), struggling, failing, and falling into behavior patterns that will not serve them well in their future education or their lives as citizens.

Early intervention is necessary to move the greatest majority of students into literacy easily, before they feel the weight of failure. Early intervention is a wise investment of our tax dollars; each dollar spent early in a student's career can prevent long years of expenditure on remediation, special education, and other costs related to low levels of literacy. Early intervention does not guarantee continuing achievement; but *not* providing early intervention guarantees failure for many students throughout schooling.

Providing just any early intervention program will not necessarily meet our goal. The lowest-achieving children in the early grades are often off-track or confused; they need expert, high-quality intervention to help them get back on track as achievers in reading and writing. The intervention must help students learn from the excellent classroom literacy program and must make sure that students achieve accelerated progress in learning the critical skills of literacy. That means it must be well timed and intensive.

Finally, while a high-quality early intervention program will put most at-risk students in the mainstream of literacy, further services in special education will be needed for a much smaller but more needy group of children.

Intervention, admittedly, is a controversial idea in literacy education. Some writers advocate changing society and schools rather than providing extra levels of support for young children, saying that if we give up the notion that everyone should read by age six, there would be no need for early intervention programs like Reading Recovery. The idea is that with good classrooms where children learn to read "naturally," some children might not learn to read until age nine. We cannot agree.

First, our experience with hundreds of Reading Recovery children indicates that even these children have interest in books; they want access. Most kindergarten teachers recognize that children may know little about print but they want to experience books. We cannot wait so long for children to read; rather we advocate providing the level of support needed to help them.

Imagine what life is like for a fourth grader who cannot read. Even in the most humane classroom, that student will feel at a disadvantage. For several years, he has not been able to use literacy as a tool for learning in science, mathematics, or other content areas. He depends on someone else to read to him the good stories he might like to enjoy himself.

Reading Recovery demonstrates that we know enough about the reading process to ensure that the great majority of children, even those who initially experience difficulty, can become good readers and writers. *Learning with teaching is natural*; all of us have teachers of various kinds throughout our lives. We do not wait; we teach and work toward the vision of ensuring that everyone learns to read.

The primary years are our chance to alter the trajectory of failure, make a difference in students' lives, and in turn make a difference in our educational system. This is a critical time, and we only have one chance at it; therefore, we must take great care in what we do. We suggest the following intervention criteria:

■ *The intervention is delivered by the best teachers*. Too often, remedial help, especially for young children, has been delivered by uncertified personnel. Children in difficulty require expert teaching if intervention is to succeed.

■ *The intervention has a strong diagnostic component.* Systematic diagnosis is a critical component of successful early intervention efforts. Every child has a different background and knows different aspects of literacy. Teachers must be expert in finding out what children know, even if that is very little, and using strengths to overcome deficiencies.

■ *The intervention provides an alternative program that focuses on the individual child.* The lowest-achieving children follow idiosyncratic paths of progress; they attempt to use what they know but their competencies do not match the school curriculum. So they spend their days in activities that are meaningless to them, and they appear to be incompetent. A prescriptive program will not work. The early intervention offered these children must be systematic and intensive but it must be systematic in terms of each child. The process seems simple—find out where the child is and take him where you want him to go—but requires an instructional approach tailored to the individual; each moment-to-moment interaction can be very powerful in helping these young children make sense of reading and writing.

■ *The intervention provides abundant practice in reading and writing.* People learn to read by reading and to write by writing. Children who are low achievers, however, get fewer chances to read and write. They may be given plenty of drill and practice but spend little time actually reading stories and informational material. Drill and practice are especially meaningless to children who do not understand the purposes or the joy of reading and writing. An effective intervention will have at-risk children reading and writing daily.

■ *The intervention helps young children develop phonemic awareness and a knowledge of graphophonemic relationships and visual aspects of print.* Young children enter school

knowing language; most can easily apply meaning and syntax to reading and writing. For some children, connecting language to print is difficult. They must learn letters and the visual aspects of letters and words. An effective early intervention effort will give specific attention to the connections between oral language and print.

■ *The intervention has a teacher-training program that ensures excellence.* Teaching at-risk children presents a challenge even to the most experienced teachers. Teachers need a high-quality training program to enable them to help these children make accelerated progress.

■ *The intervention accounts for every child.* An intervention program must be based on solid research and must include record keeping that documents progress in every child with whom it is used.

Reading Recovery, A Primary Safety Net

We know of no more powerful intervention than Reading Recovery; research is continually underway to refine the procedures of this early intervention program and to improve its implementation.

Reading Recovery is designed to help lowest-achieving first graders develop effective strategies for reading and reach average levels for their particular class or group. The goal of Reading Recovery is to help children become independent readers with internal self-extending systems. The idea is to help children construct the inner control that will enable them to continue to develop reading ability independently as they encounter more difficult and varied texts.

The current program in the United States involves first graders only, but continuing the instruction at the beginning of second grade is recommended if children have entered Reading Recovery late in first grade and haven't had time to complete the program. Children are selected for Reading Recovery through a combination of teacher judgment and independently administered assessments (Clay 1993a, 1993b). They receive individual tutoring until they show evidence of independent, strategic reading of texts and demonstrate an ability to participate in classroom reading instruction at adequate levels for their class or school. Then the program is "discontinued" for that student and another enters the program.

Reading Recovery has four key elements: (1) inservice training for educators in how to use the program; (2) intensive daily one-to-one thirty-minute instruction; (3) a network of professional support for teachers and administrators involved in the program; and (4) a research program to monitor program results.

One-to-one instruction

The child receives an individual lesson for thirty minutes each day *in addition* to the normal classroom literacy experiences. In the context of continuous text, the Reading Recovery teacher directs the child's attention to "the clearest, easiest, most memorable examples with which to establish a new response, skill, principle, or procedure" (Clay 1993b, p. 8). Because Reading Recovery is an individual program, the teacher works from the child's responses and knowledge base.

This powerful moment-to-moment child-teacher interaction occurs throughout a lesson that is structured around seven general components, each of which is present every day:

1. Reading many known stories.

2. Independently reading a story that was read once the previous day while the teacher observes and assesses progress.

3. Using magnetic letters to work on identifying letters and making and breaking words.

4. Writing a message or story, with the teacher helping to construct words.

5. Putting together a cut-up sentence from this message or story.

6. Listening to and talking with the teacher as she introduces a new story.

7. Reading the new story introduced by the teacher.

The Reading Recovery lesson has been described as "a highly organized, intensive, and, it must be stressed, enjoyable occasion. Moreover, it is not confined to reading alone—writing and good deal of speaking and listening also features strongly" (HMSO 1993, p. 5). The teacher's goal during these tasks is to help children become independent, strategic users of literacy. Only by using strategies in connection with the support of a more expert other will the child be able to take over the learning. "Acceleration is achieved as the child takes over the learning process and works independently, discovering new things for himself inside and outside the lessons. He comes to push the boundaries of his own knowledge, and not only during his lessons" (Clay 1993b, p. 9).

Initial training and ongoing professional development

Reading Recovery inservice for teachers is a yearlong after-school program of weekly classes during which live lessons are viewed from behind a one-way glass screen. Teachers take turns teaching while their peers observe and, guided by the leader, talk aloud about the lesson. This process of talking while observing is a hallmark of Reading Recovery training both during the initial year and in the continuing education in which teachers participate as long as they are involved in the program. There are also Reading Recovery conferences for teachers and an annual institute for teacher leaders.

The key person in Reading Recovery is the *teacher leader* (in the United States and Canada) or *tutor* (in New Zealand, Great Britain, and Australia). Teacher leaders are based in school districts or, in some cases, in county offices of education or universities.

They teach daily Reading Recovery lessons but spend the rest of their time offering the training and providing on-site coaching and assistance to teachers. Teacher leaders complete a yearlong course at a university.

Implementation and quality control

Reading Recovery is disseminated through a long-term, structured process. School districts begin by training a *teacher leader* who will in turn train individual teachers and oversee the program. (Teacher leaders are prepared at one of twenty-three university training sites in the United States and at two sites in Canada.) At the same time, a *site coordinator* administers the program in a given school district or consortium of districts. As part of the agreement with the regional training center, the sponsoring school district or consortium agrees to follow the *Guidelines and Standards for the Reading Recovery Council of North America* (1993), in order to ensure quality services to children.

The name *Reading Recovery* has been a trademark/service mark of The Ohio State University since December 18, 1990. Reading Recovery programs that meet essential criteria are annually granted a royalty-free license to use the name. Every district that has a Reading Recovery program is reviewed annually to determine if the district has met the standards and guidelines.

Reading Recovery programs are supported by a network of several hundred Reading Recovery sites representing over five thousand schools that span North America. Personnel at these sites provide training and continuing contact, coordinate the collection of data on Reading Recovery children, disseminate awareness information, and develop program guidelines. Reading Recovery was pilot-tested in the United States in 1984–85 and has been adopted by schools representing various regions, economic groups, cultures, and linguistic backgrounds. From 1984 through 1996, over twelve thousand Reading Recovery teachers have been trained and over two hundred thousand children have received Reading Recovery tutoring. Each year over 80 percent of these initially low-achieving students attain at least average reading levels for their school after an average of seventeen weeks of daily lessons.

The Ramifications of Reading Recovery

Learning from Reading Recovery

Reading Recovery is not a classroom program and we would not want to base a classroom program on Reading Recovery. It is a specially designed program for providing *individual* help to the very lowest achieving readers. However, teachers who have worked with Reading Recovery have found that this close, intensive look at children makes a difference in their views of learning and teaching:

◼ They have learned to be sensitive observers of children's behavior.

◼ They have thought long and hard about what children's responses tell them.

◼ They have learned that teaching means knowing children and working from their base of understanding.

◼ They have seen powerful learning conversations between teachers and children that support their becoming independent readers and writers.

◼ They have learned the value of providing abundant opportunities for young children to read and write.

◼ They have especially learned the value of teaching—demonstrating, explaining, encouraging, praising, and supporting independent, flexible use of reading and writing strategies.

◼ They have learned that they must approach change as researchers—systematically and rigorously. They must be in it for the long haul.

Connections between Reading Recovery and the Literacy Collaborative

No extra program, not even one as powerful as Reading Recovery, works alone. It is the partnership between the classroom teacher and the Reading Recovery teacher that makes it possible for the lowest achievers to make accelerated progress, catch up with their peers, and succeed. All children, including those who receive extra services, need a sound, balanced classroom literacy program. Figure 15–3 highlights important differences between Reading Recovery and the Literacy Collaborative.

But classroom teachers and Reading Recovery teachers share many goals and approaches. Both:

■ Base decisions on a strong theory of learning.

■ Create abundant opportunities for reading and writing extended texts.

■ Provide opportunities for children to read and write whole texts.

■ Help children connect reading and writing processes.

■ Select texts from a gradient in order to match texts to children.

■ Teach how to use strategies in reading and writing.

■ Teach children to use the visual information in print, including letter-sound relationships.

Comparison of the Literacy Collaborative and Reading Recovery

Literacy Collaborative	Reading Recovery
• Classroom planning and instruction	• Individual observation, planning and instruction
• Whole and small groups with systematic attention to individuals	• Individual instruction
• Teacher-group interactions	• Teacher-individual interactions
—use of powerful examples	—use of powerful examples
—observe group response with attention to individuals	—observe individual response in detail
—foster peer assistance	—untangle confusions
• Wide range of literacy-related activities	• Reading, writing, and letter/word study
• Assessment is systematic, including ways to examine individuals' progress within the group and to determine each child's level of need.	• Assessment is daily and systematic to note and tailor instruction to each child's idiosyncratic path of progress.
• Comprehensive approach	• Specific approach
—includes Reading Recovery as a safety net	—safety net for lowest achievers
—collaboration is valued	—part of the comprehensive effort
	—collaboration is valued

FIGURE 15–3 Comparison of the Literacy Collaborative and Reading Recovery

■ Carefully observe, analyze, and monitor children's behavior and progress.

■ Attend to their students' critical literacy concepts: personal response to written language, ability to notice print detail within meaningful text, and efficient, effective strategies for reading and writing.

■ Participate in continuous professional development.

In both contexts, teaching is the key to children's success. Teachers demonstrate, explain tasks, and look for opportunities to help children develop strategies that have generative value. In both situations, the teacher may have to go the "child's way" in achieving the goals of literacy (Clay 1991a).

Good First Teaching

We began this book by talking about good first teaching and what it means. Without it, many children will not achieve their full potential as contributing citizens.

Children want to become readers and writers, and it is our job as teachers to know that there are many routes by which literacy can be achieved. Though there is great diversity in the experiences that individual children bring to reading, all can attain self-extending systems by using their strengths, reading extended text, and receiving quality teaching in their first few years of schooling. With guided reading as an essential component of a quality program we can assure the right to literacy for every young child.

From the Literacy Collaborative

KEEP BOOKS™

at The Ohio State University

___ (CB) Caption Book Set *(level 1,2 & A,B)*
- *Dinosaurs*
- *Trucks*
- *What Do I See?*
- *Traffic!*
- *Look at Me!*
- *Balloons*
- *The Farm*
- *Watch Me!*

___ (NR) Nursery Rhyme Set
- *Itsy Bitsy Spider*
- *Mary Had a Little Lamb*
- *Jack and Jill*
- *Old Mother Hubbard*
- *Humpty Dumpty*
- *One, Two, Buckle My Shoe*
- *Little Boy Blue*
- *Little Miss Muffet*

___ Set 1 *(level 3,4 & C)*
- *Gingerbread Girl*
- *Keeping Warm*
- *The New Baby*
- *My Mom Likes Blue*
- *Our Van*
- *My Map*
- *My Backpack*
- *Making a Peanut Butter and Jelly Sandwich*

___ Set 2 *(level 3,4,5 & C,D)*
- *Lunch Box*
- *My Snowman*
- *Good Morning*
- *Let's Pretend*
- *Max's Birthday*
- *Together*
- *Going Places*
- *Party Time!*

___ Set 3 *(level 6,7,8 & D,E)*
- *The Zoo Trip*
- *The Three Little Pigs*
- *Lunch Time*
- *Feeding the Birds*
- *Our Favorite Snowman*
- *Growing a Pumpkin*
- *The Soccer Game*
- *Come Over*

___ Set 4 *(level 9,10,11 & F,G)*
- *Notes to Me*
- *Burnt Cookies!*
- *Amost Ready*
- *My Brother's Motorcycle*
- *Max and Mutt*
- *Reading at Home*
- *My Messy Sister*
- *Goldilocks and Baby Bear*

___ Set 5 *(level 12,13,14 & G,H)*
- *The Mystery of the Chocolate Chips*
- *The Birthday Present*
- *Mutt Goes to School*
- *Monkey Tricks*
- *The Smoke Detector*
- *Mugs*
- *Hold On!*
- *The Gingerbread Man*

- - - More on the other side. - - -

I can see a dump truck.

Five, six, pick up sticks

I need a knife to make my sandwich.

I need a plate for my sandwich.

The first little pig built a house of straw.

The second pig built a house of sticks.

Mutt likes to ride in the van but he does not like to go to the vet.

After he got a shot, Mutt did not want to run and play.

"Hi, Grandpa. We learned all about smoke detectors and what to do if there is a fire in the house."
said Rayshawn.
"The fireman visited our school. He brought his truck. We learned—
• If there is a fire, don't hide in the house.
• If there is smoke, crawl out of the house."

The **Caption Book** format encourages beginning readers to interact with the print. Large-sized print is separate from the picture. Print placement establishes a top, left starting position. Ample space between words encourages easy one-to-one matching. Repeated high-frequency words and repeated, predictable language patterns support young children in reading stories while they learn more about the conventions of printed language.

In the **Nursery Rhyme Set**, traditional nursery rhymes are illustrated and have clearly printed text to engage young readers. Teachers can introduce the nursery rhymes through charts and songs. Children can then read and enjoy their own versions at home as they sing, count, read, and recite these old favorites in new multicultural contexts.

Sets 1 and 2 contain eight titles each for Kindergarten and Early First Grade; Teach page has one to three lines of text. The text is supported by pictures and predictable patterns making these sets easy reading to enjoy and practice at home. In Set 2, the character Max is introduced as a baby. In another book, Max's birthday is celebrated. Young readers enjoy becoming acquainted with an ongoing character.

In **Set 3**, the text is supported by the pictures as the vocabulary and language patterns increase in complexity to create wonderful stories for eading and rereading at home. One traditional tale and seven stories, which reflect the interest and experiences of young children, spark interest for reading. Set 3 is suggested for Mid First Grade.

Set 4 books help to ease beginning readers through the transition to longer, more complex story books. There are multiple lines of text on the page as the stories begin to be more complex. The pictures are engaging, while offering moderate support. Familiar family experiences, losing a first tooth, and reading a traditional tale from the point of view of Baby Bear all appeal to the interest of young children. Max eturns in this set with his comical dog, Mutt. Set 4 is suggested for Mid First Grade.

Set 5 books offer easy reading for the end of first/ beginning second grade readers. Full pages of text with less support from the pictures and enriched vocabulary increase the level of text difficulty. Stories offer the fun of a trickster tale, information on fire safety, the excitement of a roller coaster ride, along with a return of our favorite, mischievous dog character, Mutt.

KEEP BOOKS™ with **Math Concepts**

___ (mA CB) Math Concepts Caption Books
(level 2, 3,4,5 & B,C)

- *Making a Mask*
- *The Garage Sale*
- *How Old Are You?*
- *Vegetable Soup*
- *School Times*
- *Sandwich Shapes*
- *What Do I See in the Tree?*
- *Pigs at the Pool*

I see one nest and two birds and three eggs in the tree.

1 + 2 + 3 = ___

___ (mA) Math Concepts Set A *(level 12,13,14 & G,H,I)*

- *"That's Not Fair"*
- *The Contest*
- *Is It Lunch Time?*
- *What a Night*
- *Wait for the Change*
- *The Treasure Hunt*
- *Too Many Pets*
- *Clickety-Clack*

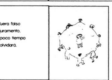

In the **Math Concepts Caption Book** set math concepts are embedded in easy to read stories with Caption Book formats. Large-sized print with ample space between words encourage one-to-one matching. High-frequency words and language patterns are repeated to support young readers in late kindergarten and beginning first grade. The stories provide opportunities for teachers, parents, and students to explore the following math concepts: addition, division, telling time, shapes, money values, time lines/age, measurement, and cardinal/ordinal numbers.

Math Concepts, Set A books are easy reading for the end of first/beginning second grade readers. Through a lively story format children are introduced to math concepts which are part of everyday life. Concepts include: addition, subtraction, counting, making change, telling time, weighing, as well as estimation and making comparisons. Students will enjoy the stories as teachers and parents help them understand the math concepts.

LIBRITOS MÍOS™ Spanish Language **K**EEP BOOKS™

___ (SCB) Spanish Language Caption Book Set
(level 1,2 & A,B)

- *Dinosaurios*
- *¿Qué es lo que veo?*
- *¡ Mírame a mí !*
- *La Granja*
- *Camiones*
- *El Tráfico*
- *Globos*
- *¡ Mírame !*

Yo puedo resbalar.

¡Mírame!

¡Mírame!

Si fuera falso mi juramento, en poco tiempo se olvidara.

___ (SNR) Spanish Language Nursery Rhyme Set

- *Al Juego Chirimbolo*
- *Los Animalitos*
- *Los Pollitos*
- *Tengo, Tengo, Tengo*
- *Cinco Pollitos*
- *Los Maderos de San Juan*
- *Naranja Dulce*
- *Un Elefante Se Balanceaba*

The **Spanish Language Caption Books** are a translation of the English Caption books. Large-sized print is separate from the pictures. Young children enjoy the stories as they learn about the conventions of printed language.

The **Spanish Language Nursery Rhymes** offer Spanish language rhymes, songs, and games for young children to read and enjoy.

KEEP BOOKS™ **Order Form**

Please indicate the quantity for each set ordered

___ Set CB	___ Set 4
___ Set NR	___ Set 5
___ Set 1	___ Set mA CB
___ Set 2	___ Set mA
___ Set 3	___ Set SCB
	___ Set SNR

MasterCard and Visa now accepted!

➡ Send my order of Keep Books™ to this address: ➡

A $100 set will provide 400 books — 50 copies of 8 different titles. Each book has an easy-to-read story, is clearly printed, and is fully illustrated with black-and-white line drawings.

(total number of sets) x $100 each................................._____

Shipping & handling (add 10% effective 1/1/97)..............._____

Total..$ _____

Make check or P.O. payable to The Ohio State University

MasterCard/Visa # _____

Exp. Date _____ Name on Credit Card _____

Name _____

School _____

Address _____

City _____ State _____ Zip _____

Phone_____ P.O./Check No. _____

Our Tax ID Number:
31-6025986

Mail this form to:
OSU, KEEP BOOKS
1929 Kenny Road, Suite 100
Columbus, Ohio 43210

If ordering by credit card, fax the form to: OSU, Keep Books, 614-688-3452

For information about shipping or status of your order, call: (614) 292-2869

For information about Keep Books, call: (614) 292-2909

version date: 3/13/98

The order form must be accompanied by a check, purchase order, or credit card number. PLEASE, no phone orders. All checks or purchase orders must include the amount for shipping and handling, otherwise they will be returned. We do not accept requisitions or purchase order numbers without a copy of the purchase order AND an order form. For residents of **Alaska** and **Hawaii** please add 25% per set for shipping and handling. **International** customers please contact the shipping department for shipping prices before ordering. **Limited Rush Service** is also available; contact the shipping department for prices. **Please keep a copy of your order for future reference.**

All orders (except back orders) are processed and shipped within 2–4 weeks of receipt of the order. If you have a specific date by which you need your Keep Books, we will make every effort to accommodate your deadlines.
I need my Keep Books by: _____

Browsing Box

1

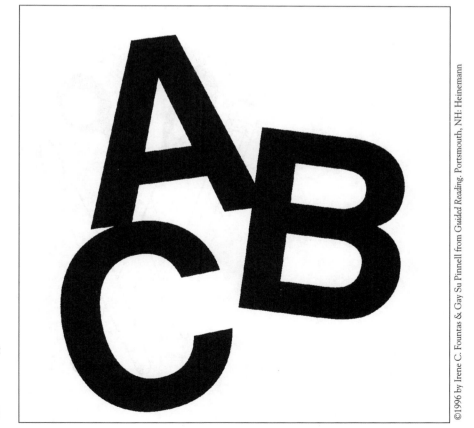

Browsing Box

A B C

2

Listening Center

3

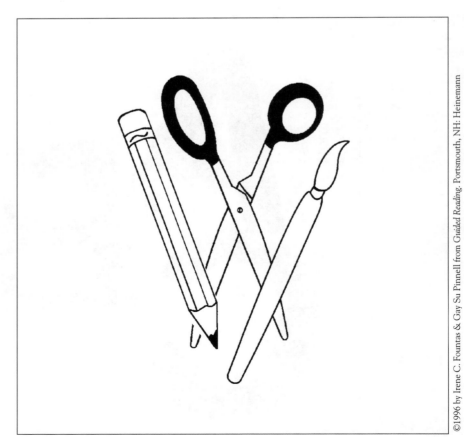

Art

4

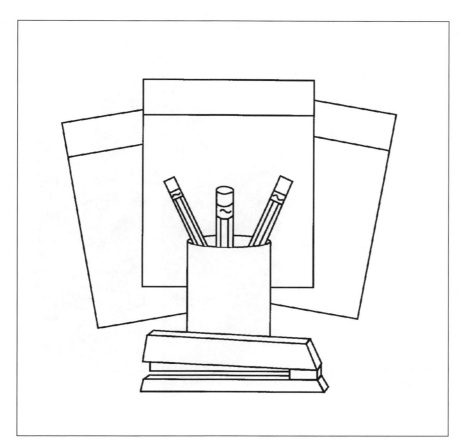

Writing Center

5

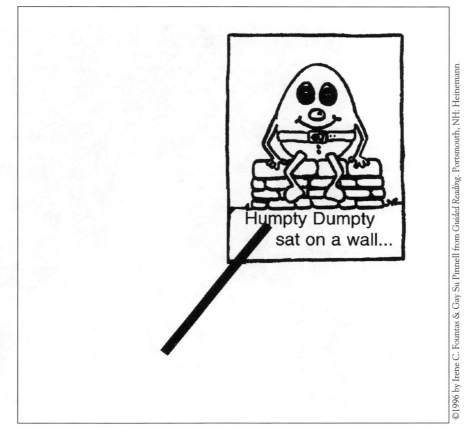

Humpty Dumpty
sat on a wall...

**Read Around
the Room**

6

**Independent
Reading**

7

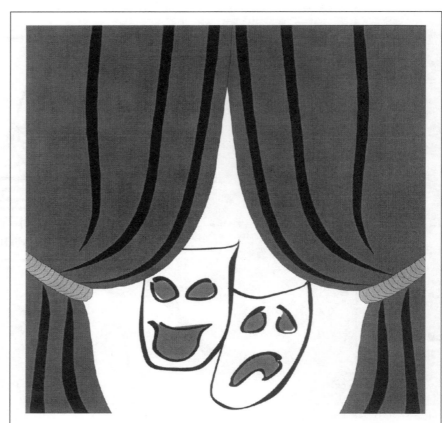

Drama

8

Poem Box

9

Computer

10

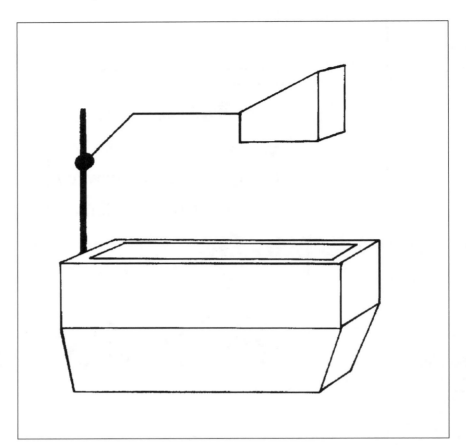

Overhead Projector

11

Buddy Reading

12

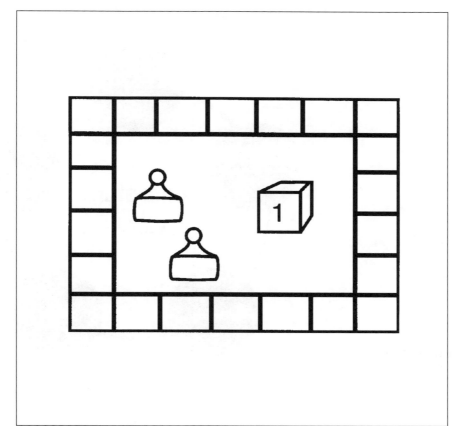

Games

13

Reading Journal

14

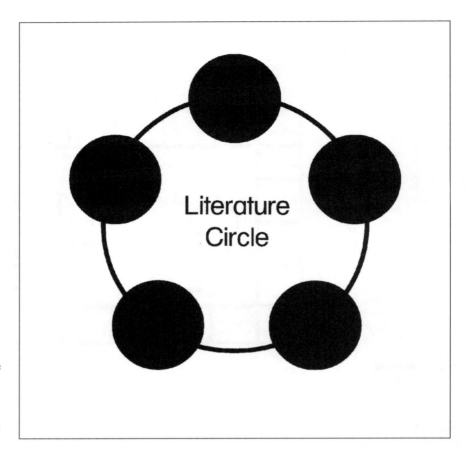

Literature Circle

15

Pocket Chart

Mary had a little lamb.

Its fleece was white as snow.

Everywhere that Mary went

the lamb was sure to go.

16

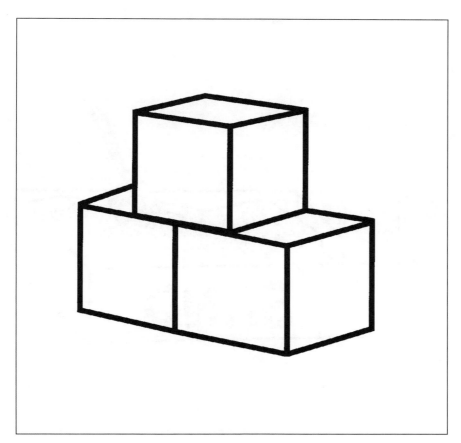

Building

17

Science

18

Sand Table

19

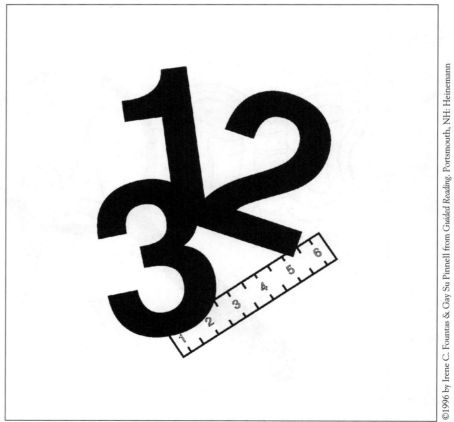

Math

20

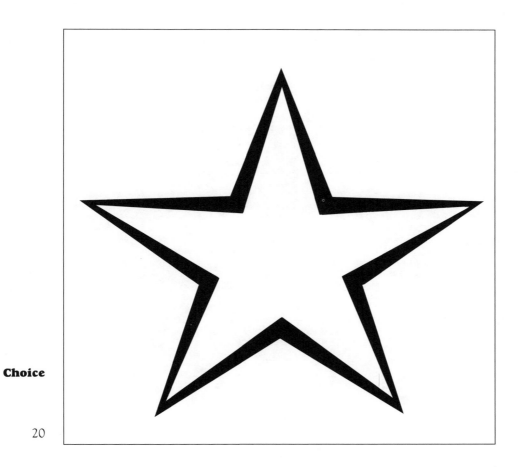

Choice

20

Make Your Own

21

Alphabet

abcd efg hijk lmnop

qrs tuv wx yz

A a apple	**B b** bear	
C c cat	**D d** dog	**E e** elephant	**F f** fish
G g gate	**H h** hat	**I i** igloo	**J j** jack-in-the-box
K k kite	**L l** leaf	**M m** moon	**N n** nest
O o octopus	**P p** pig	**Q q** queen	**R r** ring
S s sun	**T t** turtle	**U u** umbrella	**V v** vacuum
W w window	**X x** x-ray	**Y y** yo-yo	**Z z** zipper

Management of Guided Reading
Ten-Day Plan

Week #1	Guided Reading Groups	Independent Work Groups				
Monday						
Tuesday						
Wednesday						
Thursday						
Friday						
Notes:						

Week #2	Guided Reading Groups					
Monday						
Tuesday						
Wednesday						
Thursday						
Friday						
Notes:						

©1996 by Irene C. Fountas & Gay Su Pinnell from *Guided Reading*. Portsmouth, NH: Heinemann

APPENDIX D: Management of Guided Reading—Ten-Day Plan

Guided Reading Record

Name	Monday	Tuesday	Wednesday	Thursday	Friday

APPENDIX E: Guided Reading Record Version One

©1996 by Irene C. Fountas & Gay Su Pinnell from *Guided Reading*. Portsmouth, NH: Heinemann

Guided Reading Record

Name	Observational Notes

Appendix F: Guiding Reading Record Version Two

Guided Reading Record

Week of _____

Name	Book/Level	Behaviors Observed

©1996 by Irene C. Fountas & Gay Su Pinnell from *Guided Reading*. Portsmouth, NH: Heinemann

APPENDIX G: Guided Reading Observations

Record of Book-Reading Progress

Child's Name: _____

Grade(s): _____ K _____ 1 _____ 2 _____ 3

Title of Book, Accuracy Rate, SC Rate (○ = above 90% ● = below 90%)

Book Level													
S													
R													
Q													
P													
O													
N													
M													
L													
K													
J													
I													
H													
G													
F													
E													
D													
C													
B													
A													
Date													

APPENDIX H: Record of Book-Reading Progress Version One

©1996 by Irene C. Fountas & Gay Su Pinnell from *Guided Reading*. Portsmouth, NH: Heinemann

Record of Book-Reading Progress

Teacher: _____

Grade: _____

School _____

Year: _____

Level	Benchmark Books																									
S																										
R																										
Q																										
P																										
O																										
N																										
M																										
L																										
K																										
J																										
I																										
H																										
G																										
F																										
E																										
D																										
C																										
B																										
A																										
	Children's Names																									

©1996 by Irene C. Fountas & Gay Su Pinnell from *Guided Reading*. Portsmouth, NH: Heinemann

APPENDIX I: Record of Book-Reading Progress Version Two

MAKING A FOLDED LETTER BOOK

1. Fold in half.

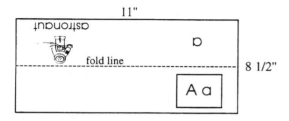

2. Cut paper at fold line.

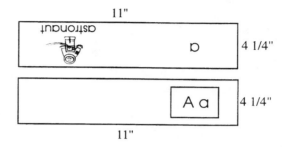

3. Fold both pieces in half, along fold line.

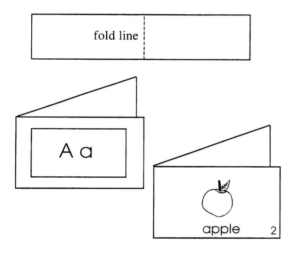

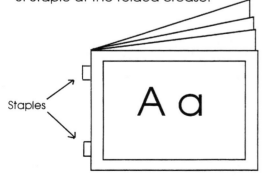

4. Make page numbers follow the correct order.

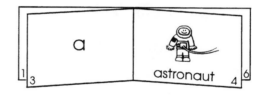

5. Staple at the folded crease.

6. And you have a 6 page letter book.

astronaut

A a

airplane

a

a

apple

bananas

B b

b

b

balloon

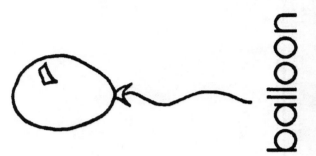

a

bear

cup

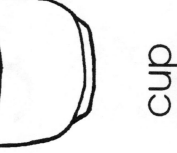

cow

C

C

cat

doll

b

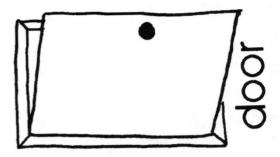

door

p

dog

easel

E e

e

egg

elephant

e

fork

flower

f

fish

f

game

G g

4

3

grapes

G

g

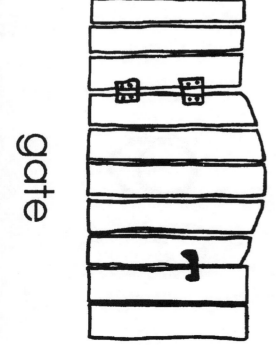

gate

H h

house

h

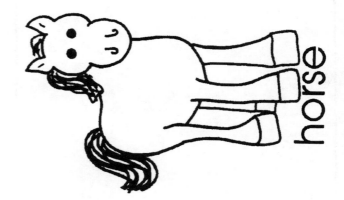

horse

h

h

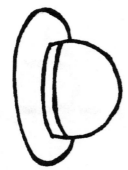

hat

insect

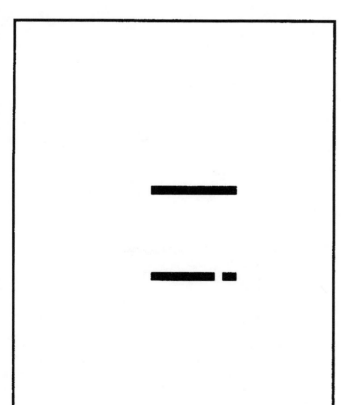

4

3

ice cream

__ -

igloo

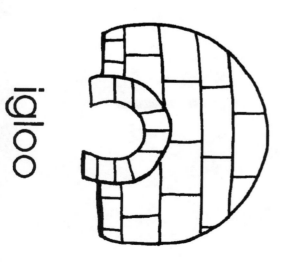

- __

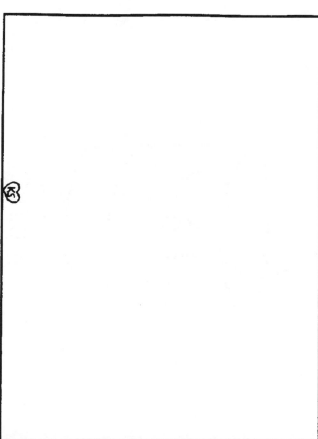

jump rope

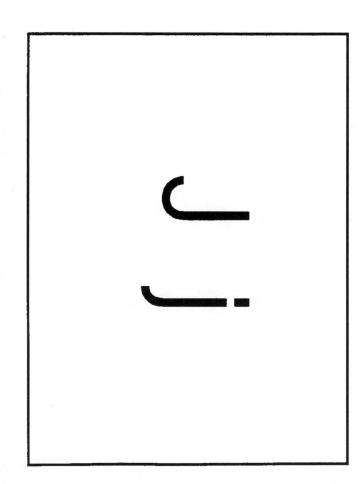

J

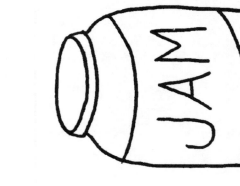

jam

jack-in-the-box

j

king

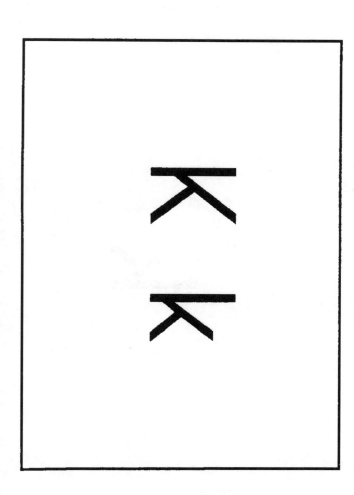

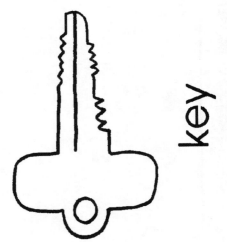

key

K

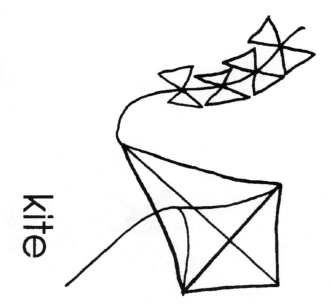

kite

K

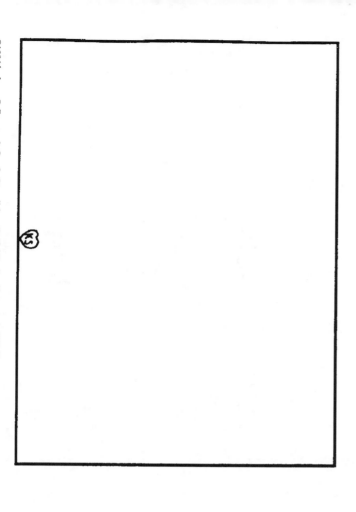

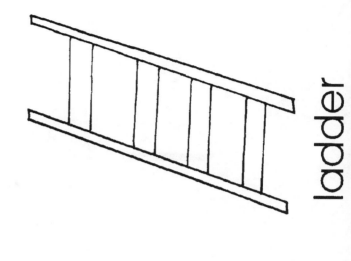

ladder

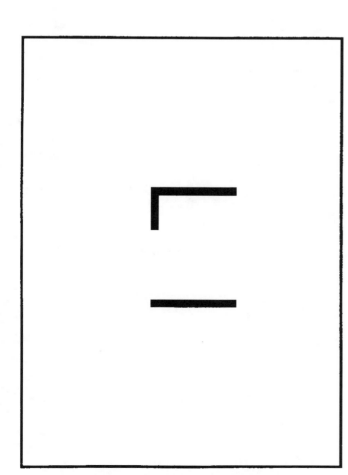

lamp

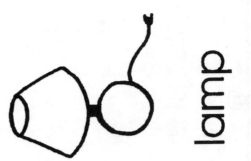

___

leaf

___

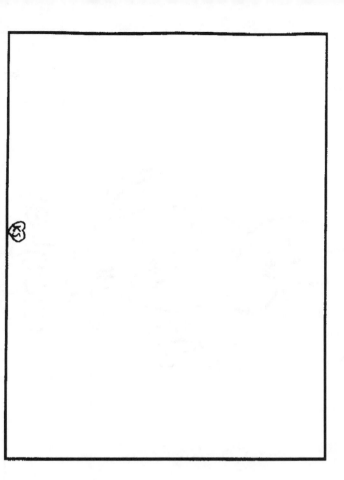

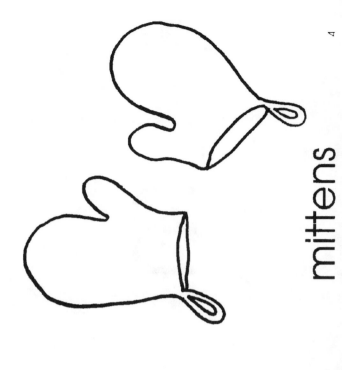

mittens

4

M m

m

3

monkey

M

moon

m

nail

4

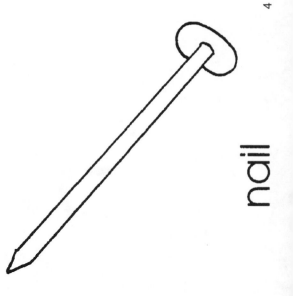

u

3

newspaper

n

n

nest

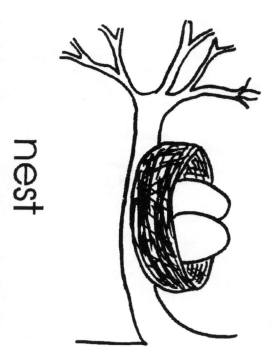

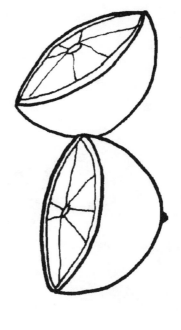

orange

4

3

overalls

○

octopus

○

4

pizza

P p

p

3

pencil

p

P

pig

quarter

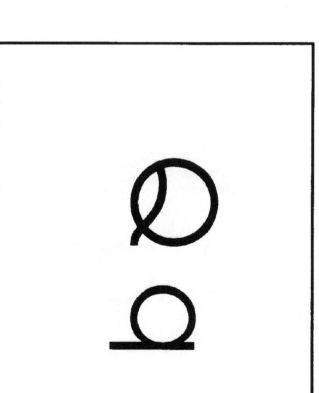

question mark

q

q

queen

radio

R r

ɹ

ruler

r

r

ring

sock

S s

S

snake

S

s

sun

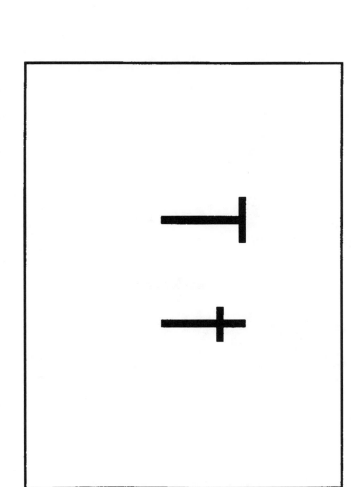

telephone

toothbrush

+

turtle

+

underwear

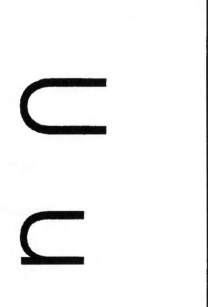

U
u

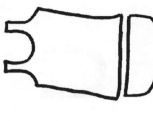

U

U

unicorn

umbrella

u

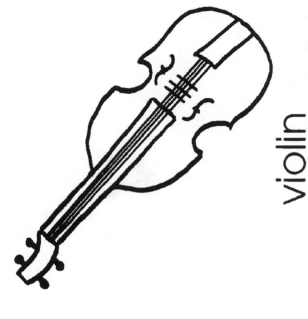

violin

V v

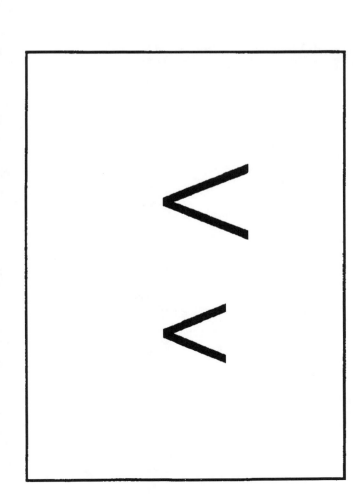

V

volcano

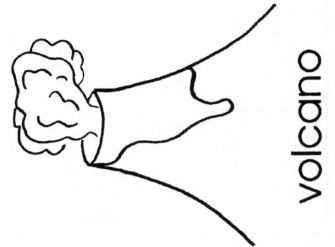

V

v

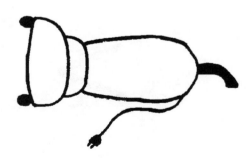

vacuum

W w

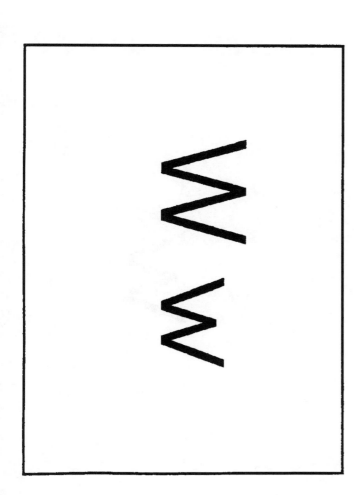

watermelon

watch

W

W

window

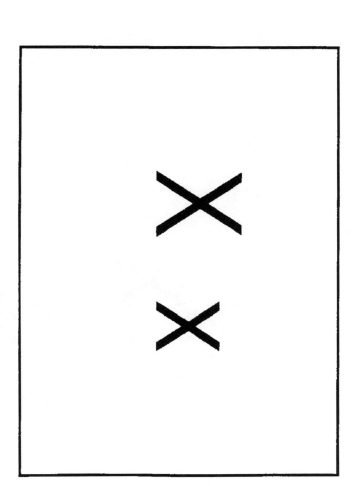

exclamation

exit

X

X

x-ray

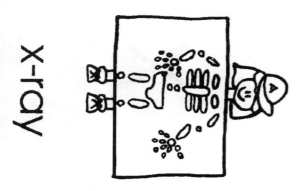

yarn

Y

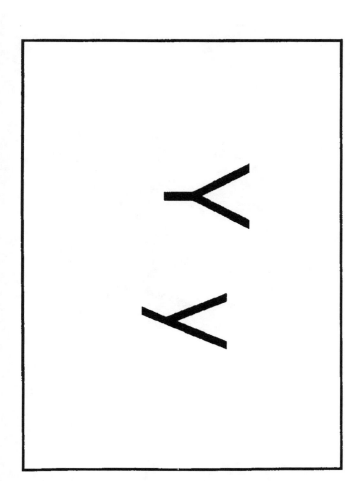

yard

Y

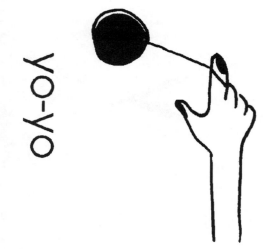

yo-yo

Y

zebra

Z

Z z

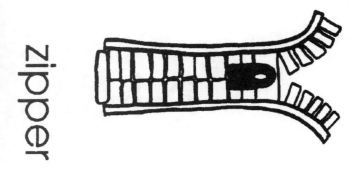

zero

Z

z

zipper

Evaluation Response for Text Gradient

Directions: Since any text gradient is always in the process of construction as it is used with varying groups of children, we expect our list to change every year. We encourage you to try the levels with your students and to provide feedback based on your own experiences. Please suggest changes to existing book levels and suggest new books for the list. Please provide the information requested below.

Name: _____   Grade Level You Teach: _____

Telephone: (   )_____   E-mail Address: _____

Address (street, city, state): _____

Book evaluated:

Book Title: _____

Level: A   B   C   D   E   F   G   H   I   J   K   L   M   N   O   P   Q   R   S

Author: _____

Publisher: _____

This book is:

_____   A book listed on the gradient that I have evaluated by using it with my class.
(Complete SECTION A and make comments in SECTION C.)

_____   A book listed on the gradient that I am recommending as a benchmark for a level.
(Complete SECTION A and make comments in SECTION C.)

_____   A new book that I suggest adding to the collection.
(Complete SECTION B and make comments in SECTION C.)

SECTION A: (For an evaluation of a book currently included in the list)

Is it appropriately placed on the level (explain)? _____

To what level should the book be moved?

A   B   C   D   E   F   G   H   I   J   K   L   M   N   O   P   Q   R   S

Are there points of difficulty that make it harder than it seems? _____

_____

Is the text supportive in ways that might not be noticeable when examining the superficial characteristics? _____

_____

SECTION B: (For the recommendation of a new book)   Indicate recommended level: _____

How does this book support readers at this level? _____

_____

What challenges does it offer? _____

_____

SECTION C: Please place additional comments on the back or on another sheet.

Mail this form to:

Irene Fountas, Lesley College, 29 Everett Street, Cambridge, Massachusetts 02140.
Fax: (617) 349-8490   E-mail: ifountas@mail.lesley.edu

Gay Su Pinnell, The Ohio State University, 200 Ramseyer Hall, 29 W. Woodruff Avenue, Columbus, Ohio 43210.
Fax: (614) 292-4260   E-mail: pinnell.1@osu.edu

©1996 by Irene C. Fountas & Gay Su Pinnell from *Guided Reading*. Portsmouth, NH: Heinemann

Guided Reading Self-Assessment

Teacher _____ Date _____

Grade Level: Kindergarten _____   First Grade _____   Second Grade _____   Third Grade _____

Assessment: General _____ or 1 Lesson (length of time): _____

Directions: Mark the characteristic within each category which most clearly describes your teaching at this time.

Materials: My goal is to have all necessary materials present, organized, and accessible for use during the lesson—particularly the leveled set of books, multiple copies.

| ☐ My books and other materials are at a beginning point in terms of organization. | ☐ I have enough books to practice my teaching but I have not constructed a leveled set yet; I have other materials but they are not yet organized in the guided reading area. | ☐ I have a leveled set of books that I am piloting; I have all other materials—easel, white board, paper, markers, etc.—ready for use. | ☐ A leveled, well organized, and tested collection of books exists and is ready for use; I have an area for guided reading with an easel, white board, paper, markers, and other materials. |

Classroom Management: My goal is to engage all children in independent activities that are related to reading and writing so that I can work without interruption with small groups for 60–90 minutes.

| ☐ I have not yet established a work board and centers for use during reading time; many children need a great deal of attention in order to work independently. | ☐ I have established some centers but I am just beginning to teach children to use them; it is difficult to work with a small group; I do not have a work-board. | ☐ I have established many centers; children can work in them independently. I have not yet organized a guided reading time with a work board. | ☐ My classroom is well managed with a work board and a variety of appropriate activities in centers; almost all children work independently so that I can work without interruption with a small group. |

Groupings: My goal is to form small groups of children who are similar in their development of strategies and in the level of text they can read and to regroup these children through ongoing assessment.

| ☐ I am just beginning to group children and am not sure what measures to use; usually I teach the whole group; I do not know how to use running records. | ☐ I have formed and met with some groups in guided reading and am beginning to observe them more closely. I know how to take running records but not how to use them for grouping and regrouping. | ☐ I have established several groups for reading. I take regular running records and try to interpret the results. I have not yet worked through grouping and regrouping. I need more work in analyzing running records. | ☐ My groups are formed on the basis of systematic observation using running records; groups are formed so that individuals can use strategies effectively; groups are reformed based on assessment. |

Lesson Management: My goal is to manage the lesson well with children demonstrating that they know the routines and all teaching procedures in place, in the appropriate order.

☐ I have not yet implemented any of the steps in guided reading.

☐ I have begun to introduce stories to children and ask them to read it.

☐ I can introduce new books and have children read them but have difficulty in managing the lesson.

☐ My lesson is smoothly managed and includes introduction, reading of the whole text by all children, and teaching after the first reading.

Text Selection: My goal is to select a text that is appropriate for the strategies that children are demonstrating and at the appropriate level for the group.

☐ I am just beginning to understand how to select a text that is right for the group.

☐ I have difficulty selecting a text; often, it is too easy or too hard.

☐ I can select a text that fits most of the group in terms of level but have difficulty relating the text to strategies children need.

☐ I can select texts that are at an appropriate level for most of the group and that support their development of strategies.

Introduction: My goal is to provide access for children to the meaning, language, and print of the story, to support strategic reading, and to leave work that will build the self-extending system.

☐ Introducing texts is difficult; I can introduce words but do not understand how to use the introduction to help children use strategies.

☐ I introduce texts but find it difficult to decide what features to attend to in order to support strategies.

☐ I introduce texts in a way that provides children with control to read it but I have difficulty deciding how to lead strategic problem solving.

☐ My introduction provides children with access but leaves work to do; the introduction supports strategies and places the text within children's control.

Teaching Decisions During First Reading and Afterwards: My goal is to select powerful teaching points that illustrate the reading process and help children learn to solve words while maintaining a focus on meaning.

☐ I am not sure how to make teaching decisions and I am concerned that my teaching points do not connect with what children know; I am not observing a shift in learning.

☐ I am making some good teaching points and am observing shifts but my teaching is uneven. I need to work on decision making and on using running records.

☐ I am generally pleased with my observation during reading but need to work on timing and quick decision making; I am observing progress; sometimes my intervention interferes with reading.

☐ My decisions are well-timed and powerful in illustrating processes and allowing children to use what they know; my teaching points do not interfere with reading; children show evidence of strategic word solving.

©1996 by Irene C. Fountas & Gay Su Pinnell from *Guided Reading*. Portsmouth, NH: Heinemann

Children's Talk: My goal is to engage children in talking about the meaning of the story and about the print.

☐ Children either do not talk about the story or engage in talk completely separate from the story.

☐ Children do talk about the story but not in a way that furthers their understanding; talk is distracting and random at times.

☐ I can engage children in talk about the story; some talk furthers their understanding of the meaning; I would like to sharpen discussion to support strategic reading.

☐ I am able to engage children in talk that furthers their understanding of the meaning of the story and assist them in solving words.

Engagement: My goal is to engage children's attention throughout the lesson.

☐ I am constantly interrupted because my internal management plan isn't working; during guided reading, children's attention is inconsistent.

☐ I can work with a group with a few interruptions but I have difficulty engaging all of the children in the group and focusing their attention on the text.

☐ In general, I can teach a group with very few interruptions; children in the group are attentive, but attention is uneven across the group and from day to day.

☐ During guided reading, children's attention is engaged; almost all members of the group attend; there are almost no interruptions.

Pace: My goal is to lead a fast-paced lesson with children who read fluently and are excited about the new story; another goal is to use all components of guided reading within a 10 to 30 minute period.

☐ My lessons seem to "bog down"; I either have difficulty finishing all components of guided reading or the lessons take much too long.

☐ I am able to use all or most of the components of guided reading but the lesson is slow-paced and I often run out of time in the morning.

☐ I can include all elements—introduction, first reading, and teaching—in the lesson but I would like it to be more fast-paced and exciting for children.

☐ My guided reading lesson is fast-paced and includes all components—children read fluently and I stay within time constraints to support my overall classroom management program.

Comments:

Book list for guided reading

This list was developed using the input of hundreds of early literacy teachers who wanted to use caption books, natural language texts, and children's literature to get children started reading. They wanted an organized list that would help them match readers with an appropriate text that children would enjoy and that would enable the teacher to assist them in developing their problem-solving strategies. The list includes material appropriate for kindergarten through early fourth grade.

The grade level/book level pairings below will vary in relationship to individual classes, schools, and districts. (Please refer to Figure 10–15.) You will find finer gradients in the first-grade levels, when children acquire the earliest reading strategies. Please use the feedback form (Appendix K) to respond to the approximate level as you use these books and offer suggested additions.

The list is presented alphabetically by title and by level. An extensive list of leveled books is available in *Matching Books to Readers* (Fountas & Pinnell 1999a) along with further information for using leveled books. The addresses of distributors are included in Appendix N. Other books may be purchased from a trade book supplier. Usually trade suppliers offer a flat discount to schools.

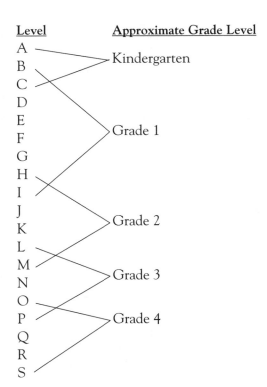

Level	Approximate Grade Level
A	Kindergarten
B	
C	
D	
E	Grade 1
F	
G	
H	
I	
J	Grade 2
K	
L	
M	Grade 3
N	
O	Grade 4
P	
Q	
R	
S	

Guided reading book list organized by title

Title	Level	Author/Series	Publisher/Distributor
1, 2, Kangaroo	C	Reading Corners	Dominie Press
Abracadabra	L	Reading Unlimited	Celebration Press
Accident, The	H	Foundations	Wright Group
Acid Rain	L	Wonder World	Wright Group
Across the Stream	F	Ginsburg, Mirra	Morrow
Adventures of Ali Baba Bernstein	O	Hurwitz, Johanna	Avon Books
Adventures of Ratman	M	Weiss & Freidman	Random House
Adventures of Snail at School	J	Stadler, John	HarperTrophy
Afternoon on the Amazon	L	Osborne, M. Pope	Random House
Airplane, The	B	Sunshine	Wright Group
Albert the Albatross	I	Hoff, Syd	HarperCollins
Aldo Ice Cream	O	Hurwitz, Johanna	Puffin Books
Aldo Peanut Butter	O	Hurwitz, Johanna	Puffin Books
Alexander and the Wind-Up Mouse	L	Lionni, Leo	Scholastic
Alfie's Gift	L	Literacy 2000	Rigby
Ali's Story	D	Sunshine	Wright Group
Alien at the Zoo	E	Sunshine	Wright Group
Aliens Don't Wear Braces	M	Dadey, D. & Jones, M.	Scholastic
Alison Wendlebury	J	Literacy 2000	Rigby
All About Stacy	L	Giff, Patricia Reilly	Dell Publishing
All By Myself	E	Mayer, Mercer	Golden
All Fall Down	C	Wildsmith, Brian	Oxford
All Join In	D	Literacy 2000	Rigby
All Kinds of Food	D	Carousel Readers	Dominie Press
All of Me	B	Literacy 2000	Rigby
All Through the Week with Cat and Dog	C	Learn to Read	Creative Teaching Press
All Tutus Should Be Pink	I	Brownrigg, Sheri	Scholastic
Alligator Shoes	G	Dorros, Arthur	Dutton
Alligators All Around	I	Sendak, Maurice	HarperCollins
Along Comes Jake	D	Sunshine	Wright Group
Amanda's Bear	G	Reading Corners	Dominie Press
Amazing Maze, The	J	Foundations	Wright Group
Amazing Popple Seed, The	G	Read Alongs	Rigby
Amazing Race, The	A	Smart Start	Rigby
Amber Brown Goes Forth	N	Danziger, Paula	Putnam
Amber Brown Is Not a Crayon	N	Danziger, Paula	Scholastic
Amber Brown Wants Extra Credit	N	Danziger, Paula	Putnam
Amelia Bedelia	L	Parish, Peggy	Harper & Row
Amelia Bedelia and the Surprise Shower	L	Parish, Peggy	HarperTrophy
Amelia Bedelia Goes Camping	L	Parish, Peggy	Avon Camelot
Amelia Bedelia Helps Out	L	Parish, Peggy	Avon Camelot
Amelia Bedelia's Family Album	L	Parish, Peggy	Avon Books
Amelia Earhart	P	Parlin, John	Dell Publishing
Amy Loves the Snow	F	Hoban, Julia	Scholastic
Amy Loves the Sun	F	Hoban, Julia	Scholastic
Amy Loves the Wind	F	Hoban, Julia	Scholastic
Anansi's Narrow Waist	I	Little Celebrations	Celebration Press
And Grandpa Sat on Friday	K	Marshall & Tester	SRA/McGraw Hill

Title	Level	Author/Series	Publisher/Distributor
And I Mean It Stanley	J	Bonsall, Crosby	HarperCollins
Angus and the Cat	I	Flack, Marjorie	Viking
Angus Thought He Was Big	G	Giant Step Readers	Educ. Insights
Animal Babies	E	Rookie Reader	Children's Press
Animal Builders	I	Little Celebrations	Celebration Press
Animal Habitats	C	Little Red Readers	Sundance
Animal Homes	B	Little Red Readers	Sundance
Animal Reports	L	Little Red Readers	Sundance
Animal Stretches	C	Little Celebrations	Celebration Press
Animal Tracks	L	Dorros, Arthur	Scholastic
Animal Tricks	H	Wildsmith, Brian	Merrimak
Animals	A	Smart Starts	Rigby
Animals at Night	I	First Start	Troll
Animals at the Zoo	F	First Start	Troll
Animals in the Desert	D	Carousel Readers	Dominie
Animals Went to Bed, The	B	Smart Starts	Rigby
Annie's Pet	J	Brenner, Barbara	Bantam Doubleday Dell
Another Day, Another Challenge	L	Literacy 2000	Rigby
Ants Love Picnics Too	B	Literacy 2000	Rigby
Apple Tree Apple Tree	G	Blocksma, Mary	Children's Press
Applebird	A	Wildsmith, Brian	Oxford
Apples and Pumpkins	I	Rockwell, Anne	Scholastic
Are You a Ladybug?	F	Sunshine	Wright Group
Are You My Mommy?	F	Dijs	Simon & Schuster
Are You My Mother?	I	Eastman, P. D.	Random House
Are You There, Bear?	F	Maris, Ron	Greenwillow
Arguments	K	Read Alongs	Rigby
Armando Asked, "Why?"	I	Ready Set Read	Steck-Vaughn
Armies of Ants	O	Retan, Walter	Scholastic
Around My School	E	Exploring History & Geography	Rigby
Arthur's Christmas Cookies	K	Hoban, Lillian	HarperTrophy
Arthur's Honey Bear	K	Hoban, Lillian	HarperCollins
Arthur's Loose Tooth	K	Hoban, Lillian	HarperCollins
Arthur's Pen Pal	K	Hoban, Lillian	HarperCollins
Arthur's Prize Reader	K	Hoban, Lillian	HarperTrophy
Ashes for Gold	L	Folktales	Mondo
Ask Mr. Bear	J	Flack, Marjorie	Macmillan
Astronauts, The	F	Foundations	Wright Group
At School	B	Sunshine	Wright Group
At the Beach	E	Oxford Reading Tree	Oxford University Press
At the Doctor	J	Story Starter	Wright Group
At the Fair	D	Little Red Readers	Sundance
At the Fair	D	Sunshine	Wright Group
At the Farm	C	Little Red Readers	Sundance
At the Library	C	PM Starters	Rigby
At the Park	D	Little Red Readers	Sundance
At the Playground	C	Little Red Readers	Sundance
At the Pool	C	Foundations	Wright Group
At the Seaside	E	Oxford Reading Tree	Oxford University Press
At the Water Hole	K	Foundations	Wright Group
At the Wildlife Park	B	Little Red Readers	Sundance
At the Zoo	B	Little Readers	Houghton Mifflin
At the Zoo	A	Kloes, Carol	Kaeden Books

Title	Level	Author/Series	Publisher/Distributor
At the Zoo	B	PM Starters	Rigby
At the Zoo	C	Little Red Readers	Sundance
At the Zoo	D	Predictable Storybooks	SRA/McGraw Hill
Auntie Maria and the Cat	D	Sunshine	Wright Group
Awful Mess, The	H	Rockwell, Anne	Four Winds
B-I-N-G-O	C	Tiger Cub	Peguis
Baba Yaga	K	Literacy 2000	Rigby
Babe the Gallant Pig	R	King-Smith, Dick	Random House
Baby Animals	B	Reading Corners	Dominie
Baby Bear Goes Fishing	E	PM Books	Rigby
Baby Bear's Present	F	PM Books	Rigby
Baby Chimp	A	Twig	Wright Group
Baby Elephant Gets Lost	D	Foundations	Wright Group
Baby Elephant's New Bike	G	Foundations	Wright Group
Baby Gets Dressed	A	Sunshine	Wright Group
Baby in the Cart	C	Foundations	Wright Group
Baby Lamb's First Drink	C	PM Books	Rigby
Baby Monkey, The	I	Reading Unlimited	Celebration Press
Baby Says	C	Steptoe, John	Morrow
Baby Sister for Frances, A	K	Hoban, Lillian	Scholastic
Baby, The	E	Burningham, John	Crowell
Baby Writer	J	Hall, N. & Robinson, A.	Nelson/Michaels Assoc.
Baby's Birthday	D	Literacy 2000	Rigby
Bad Day for Benjamin, A	L	Reading Unlimited	Celebration Press
Ball Bounced, The	D	Tafuri, Nancy	Morrow
Ball Game	B	Literacy 2000	Rigby
Ball Game, The	D	Beginning Literacy	Scholastic
Ball Games	B	PM Starters	Rigby
Ballad of Robin Hood, The	M	Literacy 2000	Rigby
Banana Shake	C	Book Bank	Wright Group
Bandages	F	Moskowitz, Ellen	Kaeden Books
Barbecue, The	A	Sunshine	Wright Group
Barney	Q	Literacy 2000	Rigby
Barney's Horse	I	Hoff, Syd	HarperTrophy
Barrel of Gold, A	K	Storybox	Wright Group
Baseball	B	Sunshine	Wright Group
Baseball Fever	O	Hurwitz, Johanna	Wm. Morrow & Co.
Baseball Fun	E	Geddes, Diana	Kaeden Books
Baseball's Best, Five True Stories	P	Gutelle, Andrew	Random House
Baseball's Greatest Pitchers	P	Kramer, S. A.	Random House
Bath for a Beagle	D	First Start	Troll
Bath for Patches, A	E	Carousel Readers	Dominie Press
Bats	M	Literacy 2000	Rigby
Bay Run, The	C	Foundations	Wright Group
Be Quiet	A	Literacy 2000	Rigby
Beach	D	Book Bank	Wright Group
Bean Bag That Mom Made	I	Tadpoles	Rigby
Beans on the Roof	L	Byars, Betsy	Dell Yearling
Bear Goes to Town	K	Browne, Anthony	Doubleday
Bear Lived in a Cave, A	D	Little Red Readers	Sundance
Bear Shadow	J	Asch, Frank	Simon & Schuster
Bear, The	B	Carousel Earlybirds	Dominie Press
Bear's Bargain	J	Asch, Frank	Scholastic

Title	Level	Author/Series	Publisher/Distributor
Bear's Bicycle, The	I	McLeod, Emilie	Little, Brown
Bears in the Night	D	Berenstain, Stan & Jan	Random House
Bears on Hemlock Mountain, The	M	Dalgliesh, Alice	Aladdin
Bears on Wheels	D	Berenstain, Stan & Jan	Random House
Beast in Ms. Rooney's Room	M	Giff, Patricia Reilly	Yearling
Beautiful Pig	J	Read Alongs	Rigby
Beavers Beware!	K	Brenner, Barbara	Bantam
Because a Little Bug Went Ka-Choo	I	Stone, Rosetta	Random House
Beds	C	Interaction	Rigby
Bee, The	C	Storybox	Wright Group
Beekeeper, The	M	Literacy 2000	Rigby
Beep, Beep	F	Gregorich	School Zone
Beezus and Ramona	O	Cleary, Beverly	Avon Books
Ben and the Bear	I	Riddell, Chris	Harper & Row
Ben the Bold	C	Literacy 2000	Rigby
Ben's Banana	C	Foundations	Wright Group
Ben's Dad	E	PM Books	Rigby
Ben's Red Car	B	PM Starters Two	Rigby
Ben's Teddy Bear	D	PM Books	Rigby
Ben's Tooth	H	PM Books	Rigby
Ben's Treasure Hunt	D	PM Books	Rigby
Benny Bakes a Cake	I	Rice, Eve	Greenwillow
Berlioz the Bear	N	Brett, Jan	Scholastic
Bertie the Bear	I	Allen, Pamela	Coward
Best Birthday Present, The	K	Literacy 2000	Rigby
Best Cake, The	F	PM Books	Rigby
Best Friends	D	Little Readers	Houghton Mifflin
Best Nest	J	Eastman, P. D.	Random House
Best Place, The	D	Literacy 2000	Rigby
Best Teacher in the World, The	K	Chardiet & Maccarone	Scholastic
Betsy the Babysitter	F	First Start	Troll
BFG, The	O	Dahl, Roald	Puffin Books
Bicycle, The	C	Storybox	Wright Group
Biff's Aeroplane	E	Oxford Reading Tree	Oxford
Big Al	L	Yoshi, Andrew	Scholastic
Big and Green	D	Wonder World	Wright Group
Big and Little	C	Sunshine	Wright Group
Big and Little	B	Carousel Earlybirds	Dominie Press
Big Balloon Race, The	K	Coerr, Eleanor	HarperTrophy
Big Brown Box	E	Voyages	SRA/McGraw Hill
Big Dog, Little Dog	I	Eastman, P .D.	Random House
Big Fat Worm, The	G	Van Laan, Nancy	Random House
Big Fish Little Fish	K	Folk Tales	Wright Group
Big Friend, Little Friend	E	Greenfield, Eloise	Houghton Mifflin
Big Green Caterpillar, The	J	Literacy 2000	Rigby
Big Hill, The	D	Storybox	Wright Group
Big Kick, The	C	PM Books	Rigby
Big Mama and Grandma Ghana	J	Shelf Medearis, A.	Scholastic
Big or Little?	I	Stinson, Kathy	Dominie Press
Big Red Fire Engine	G	First Start	Troll
Big Sister	B	Visions	Wright Group
Big Sneeze, The	K	Brown, Ruth	Lothrop
Big Sneeze, The	D	Foundations	Wright Group
Big Things	A	PM Starters	Rigby

Title	Level	Author/Series	Publisher/Distributor
Big Toe, The	E	Storybox	Wright Group
Big Toe, The	E	Read-Togethers	Wright Group
Biggest Cake in the World, The	F	Ready to Read	Richard C. Owen/ Celebration Press
Bike Lesson	I	Berenstain, Stan & Jan	Random House
Bikes	F	Foundations	Wright Group
Bill's Baby	E	Tadpoles	Rigby
Billy Goats Gruff	F	Hunia, Fran	Ladybird Books
Bird Talk	C	Little Celebrations	Celebration Press
Birds' Nests	J	Wonder World	Wright Group
Birthday, A	C	New Way	Steck-Vaughn
Birthday Bike for Brimhall, A	K	Delton, Judy	Dell Publishing
Birthday Book	H	Storybox	Wright Group
Birthday Book, The	D	Book Bank	Wright Group
Birthday Cake	D	Literacy 2000	Rigby
Birthday Cake, The	A	Sunshine	Wright Group
Birthday Cake, The	H	Storybox	Wright Group
Birthday Candles	C	Carousel Readers	Dominie Press
Birthday Disaster	Q	Literacy 2000	Rigby
Birthday Party, The	A	Sunshine	Wright Group
Birthdays	K	Purkis, Sallie	Nelson/Michaels Assoc.
Birthdays	I	Sunshine	Wright Group
Black Swan's Breakfast	G	Book Bank	Wright Group
Blackberries	D	PM Books	Rigby
Blackbird's Nest	G	Ready to Read	Richard C. Owen/ Celebration Press
Blackboard Bear	J	Alexander, Martha	Penguin
Blanket, The	E	Burningham, John	Crowell
Blind Men and the Elephant, The	K	Backstein, Karen	Scholastic
Blue Bug Goes to School	D	Poulet, Virginia	Children's Press
Blue Bug's Book of Colors	E	Poulet, Virginia	Children's Press
Blue Day	C	Literacy 2000	Rigby
Blue Jay, The	H	Little Readers	Houghton Mifflin
Blue Lollipops	G	Bridges	Nelson/Michaels Assoc.
Blueberries for Sal	M	McCloskey, Robert	Scholastic
Bo and Peter	C	Beginning Literacy	Scholastic
Boats	G	Rockwell, Anne	Penguin
Boggywooga, The	I	Sunshine	Wright Group
Bogle's Card	H	Sunshine	Wright Group
Bogle's Feet	I	Sunshine	Wright Group
Bonnie on the Beach	H	Little Readers	Houghton Mifflin
Bony-Legs	K	Cole, Joanna	Scholastic
Boo-Hoo	E	Read-Togethers	Wright Group
Boogly, The	E	Literacy 2000	Rigby
Book About Your Skeleton, A	M	Gross, Ruth Belov	Scholastic
Books	B	Sunshine	Wright Group
Books	B	Smart Start	Rigby
Boots	C	Beginning Literacy	Scholastic
Boots and Shoes	E	Cooper, Ann	Kaeden Books
Boots for Toots	C	Ready to Read	Richard C. Owen/ Celebration Press
Boring Old Bed	I	Sunshine	Wright Group
Boris Bad Enough	G	Kraus, Robert	Simon & Schuster
Boss	C	Foundations	Wright Group

Title	Level	Author/Series	Publisher/Distributor
Bossy Bettina	F	Literacy 2000	Rigby
Boxcar Children: Animal Shelter Mystery	O	Warner, Gertrude Chandler	Albert Whitman & Co.
Boxcar Children: Bicycle Mystery	O	Warner, Gertrude Chandler	Albert Whitman & Co.
Boxcar Children: Camp-Out Mystery	O	Warner, Gertrude Chandler	Albert Whitman & Co.
Boxcar Children: Canoe Trip Mystery	O	Warner, Gertrude Chandler	Albert Whitman & Co.
Boxcar Children: Haunted Cabin Mystery	O	Warner, Gertrude Chandler	Albert Whitman & Co.
Boxcar Children: Lighthouse Mystery	O	Warner, Gertrude Chandler	Albert Whitman & Co.
Boxcar Children: Mountain Top Mystery	O	Warner, Gertrude Chandler	Albert Whitman & Co.
Boxcar Children: Mystery at the Dog Show	O	Warner, Gertrude Chandler	Albert Whitman & Co.
Boxcar Children: Mystery at the Fair	O	Warner, Gertrude Chandler	Albert Whitman & Co.
Boxcar Children: Mystery Cruise	O	Warner, Gertrude Chandler	Albert Whitman & Co.
Boxcar Children: Mystery in the Sand	O	Warner, Gertrude Chandler	Albert Whitman & Co.
Boxcar Children: Mystery of the Hidden Beach	O	Warner, Gertrude Chandler	Albert Whitman & Co.
Boxcar Children: Mystery of the Missing Cat	O	Warner, Gertrude Chandler	Albert Whitman & Co.
Boxcar Children: Mystery of the Mixed-Up Zoo	O	Warner, Gertrude Chandler	Albert Whitman & Co.
Boxcar Children: Mystery on Stage	O	Warner, Gertrude Chandler	Albert Whitman & Co.
Boxcar Children: Pizza Mystery	O	Warner, Gertrude Chandler	Albert Whitman & Co.
Boxcar Children: Schoolhouse Mystery	O	Warner, Gertrude Chandler	Albert Whitman & Co.
Boxcar Children: Snowbound Mystery	O	Warner, Gertrude Chandler	Albert Whitman & Co.
Boy and His Donkey, A	K	Literacy 2000	Rigby
Boy and the Lion, The	H	Aesop	Wright Group
Boy Who Cried Wolf, The	H	Sunshine	Wright Group
Boy Who Cried Wolf, The	J	Littledale, Freya	Scholastic
Boy Who Cried Wolf, The	L	Literacy 2000	Rigby
Boy Who Went to the North Wind, The	L	Literacy 2000	Rigby
Brachiosaurus in the River	L	Wesley & the Dinosaurs	Wright Group
Brand New Butterfly, A	L	Literacy 2000	Rigby
Brave Father Mouse	E	PM Books	Rigby
Brave Maddie Egg	M	Standiford, Natalie	Random House
Brave Triceratops	G	PM Books	Rigby
Bravest Dog Ever, The	L	Standiford, Natalie	Random House
Bread	D	Sunshine	Wright Group
Breakfast	C	Foundations	Wright Group
Breakfast in Bed	G	Tadpoles	Rigby
Bremen Town Musicians, The	K	Gross & Kent	Scholastic
Brian's Brilliant Career	Q	Literacy 2000	Rigby
Brigid Beware	L	Leverich, Kathleen	Random House
Brigid Bewitched	L	Leverich, Kathleen	Random House
Brigid the Bad	L	Leverich, Kathleen	Random House
Bringing the Sea Back Home	L	Literacy 2000	Rigby
Brith the Terrible	M	Literacy 2000	Rigby
Brothers	E	Talk About Books	Dominie Press
Brown Bear, Brown Bear	C	Martin, Bill	Henry Holt & Co.
Bubble Gum	B	Carousel Readers	Dominie Press
Bubbles	C	Sunshine	Wright Group
Bubbles	C	Literacy 2000	Rigby

Title	Level	Author/Series	Publisher/Distributor
Bubbling Crocodile	K	Ready to Read	Richard C. Owen/ Celebration Press
Budgie's Dream	J	Story Starter	Wright Group
Buffy	B	Literacy 2000	Rigby
Buffy's Tricks	G	Literacy 2000	Rigby
Bug Watching	B	Twig	Wright Group
Building a House	H	Barton, Byron	Morrow
Building Things	F	Sunshine	Wright Group
Building with Blocks	A	Sunshine	Wright Group
Bumble Bee	D	Ready to Read	Richard C. Owen/ Celebration Press
Bump, Bump, Bump	D	Cat on the Mat	Oxford
Bunnicula	P	Howe, D. & J.	Avon Books
Bunny Hop, The	I	Hello Reader	Scholastic
Bunny Runs Away	K	Chardiet & Maccarone	Scholastic
Bus Ride, The	C	Reading Unlimited	Celebration Press
Bus Ride, The	C	Little Celebrations	Celebration Press
Bus Stop, The	G	Hellen, Nancy	Orchard
Buster McCluster	E	Wonder World	Wright Group
Buster the Balloon	E	Mathtales	Mimosa
Busy Mosquito, The	C	Foundations	Wright Group
But Granny Did	D	Voyages	SRA/McGraw Hill
Butch, the Outdoor Cat	E	Carousel Readers	Dominie Press
Button Soup	K	Orgel, Doris	Bantam Doubleday Dell
Buzz, Buzz, Buzz	H	Barton, Byron	Macmillan
Buzzing Bees	D	Mathtales	Mimosa
Buzzing Flies	C	Sunshine	Wright Group
Buzzzzzz Said the Bee	G	Hello Reader	Scholastic
Cabbage Princess, The	K	Literacy 2000	Rigby
Cake That Mack Ate, The	H	Robart/Kovalski	Little, Brown
Call 911	C	Twig	Wright Group
Cam Jansen and the Mystery at the Monkey House	L	Adler, David A.	Puffin Books
Cam Jansen and the Mystery of Flight 54	L	Adler, David A.	Puffin Books
Cam Jansen and the Mystery of the Babe Ruth Baseball	L	Adler, David A.	Puffin Books
Cam Jansen and the Mystery of the Carnival Pizza	L	Adler, David A.	Puffin Books
Cam Jansen and the Mystery of the Circus Clown	L	Adler, David A.	Puffin Books
Cam Jansen and the Mystery of the Dinosaur Bones	L	Adler, David A.	Puffin Books
Cam Jansen and the Mystery of the Gold Coins	L	Adler, David A.	Puffin Books
Cam Jansen and the Mystery of the Monster Movie	L	Adler, David A.	Puffin Books
Cam Jansen and the Mystery of the Stolen Corn Popper	L	Adler, David A.	Puffin Books
Cam Jansen and the Mystery of the Stolen Diamonds	L	Adler, David A.	Puffin Books
Cam Jansen and the Mystery of the Television Dog	L	Adler, David A.	Puffin Books
Cam Jansen and the Mystery of the U.F.O.	L	Adler, David A.	Puffin Books

Title	Level	Author/Series	Publisher/Distributor
Camping	B	Literacy 2000	Rigby
Camping	E	Sunshine	Wright Group
Camping Outside	F	Book Bank	Wright Group
Camping with Claudine	K	Literacy 2000	Rigby
Can Do, Jenny Archer	M	Conford, Ellen	Random House
Can I Have a Dinosaur?	L	Literacy 2000	Rigby
Can I Have a Lick?	C	Carousel Readers	Dominie Press
Can You See the Eggs?	C	PM Starters	Rigby
Can't You See We're Reading?	D	Hall, N. & Robinson, A.	Nelson/Michaels Assoc.
Canada Geese Quilt, The	R	Kinsey-Warnock, Leslie	Dell Publishing
Candle-Light	G	PM Books	Rigby
Candy Corn Contest, The	L	Giff, Patricia Reilly	Dell Publishing
Caps for Sale	K	Slobodkina, Esphyr	Harper & Row
Captain B's Boat	G	Sunshine	Wright Group
Captain Bumble	L	Storybox	Wright Group
Car Ride, The	A	Little Red Readers	Sundance
Caring	C	Interaction	Rigby
Carla's Breakfast	G	Harper, Leslie	Kaeden Books
Carla's Ribbons	G	Harper, Leslie	Kaeden Books
Carnival, The	F	Oxford Reading Tree	Oxford
Carrot Seed, The	G	Krauss, Ruth	Harper & Row
Carry-Out Food	D	Tadpoles	Rigby
Cars	B	Little Readers	Houghton Mifflin
Cars	F	Rockwell, Anne	Dutton
Case for Jenny Archer, A	M	Conford, Ellen	Random House
Case of the Cool-Itch Kid, The	L	Giff, Patricia Reilly	Dell Publishing
Case of the Elevator Duck, The	M	Brends, P. Berrien	Random House
Case of the Two Masked Robbers, The	K	Hoban, Lillian	HarperTrophy
Cass Becomes a Star	L	Literacy 2000	Rigby
Cassidy's Magic	Q	Literacy 2000	Rigby
Cat and Dog	G	Minarik, E. H.	HarperCollins
Cat and Dog	C	Learn to Read	Creative Teaching Press
Cat and Mouse	B	PM Starters	Rigby
Cat Concert	J	Literacy 2000	Rigby
Cat Goes Fiddle-i-fee	F	Galdone, Paul	Houghton Mifflin
Cat in the Hat	J	Seuss, Dr.	Random House
Cat in the Tree, A	F	Oxford Reading Tree	Oxford
Cat on the Mat	B	Wildsmith, Brian	Oxford
Cat, The	C	Smart Start	Rigby
Cat Who Loved Red, The	D	Salem, L. & Stewart, J.	Seedling
Catch That Frog	E	Reading Unlimited	Celebration Press
Cats	I	Wonder World	Wright Group
Cats and Kittens	F	Reading Unlimited	Celebration Press
Cats and Mice	H	Gelman, Rita	Scholastic
Cave, The	C	Book Bank	Wright Group
Cells	J	Wonder World	Wright Group
Cement Tent	G	First Start	Troll
Centerfield Ballhawk	M	Christopher, Matt	Little, Brown
Chair for My Mother, A	M	Williams, Vera B.	Scholastic
Chalk Box Kid, The	M	Bulla, Clyde Robert	Random House
Chang's Paper Pony	L	Coerr, Eleanor	HarperTrophy
Charlie	L	Literacy 2000	Rigby
Charlie Needs a Cloak	J	de Paola, Tomie	Prentice-Hall
Cherries and Cherry Pits	M	Williams, Vera B.	Houghton Mifflin

Title	Level	Author/Series	Publisher/Distributor
Chester the Wizard	M	Reading Unlimited	Celebration Press
Chick and Duckling, The	D	Ginsburg, Mirra	Macmillan
Chicken Little	L	Traditional Tales	Rigby
Chicken Pox	H	Little Readers	Houghton Mifflin
Chickens	G	Snowball, Diane	Mondo
Chinese Kites	A	Twig	Wright Group
Chocolate Cake	B	Storybox	Wright Group
Choose Me!	H	Reading Corners	Dominie Press
Christmas Tree, The	F	PM Books	Rigby
Cinderella	K	Once Upon a Time	Wright Group
Circus	D	Wonder World	Wright Group
Circus Clown, The	D	Literacy 2000	Rigby
Circus, The	C	Literacy 2000	Rigby
Circus Train, The	A	Little Red Readers	Sundance
City Bus, The	B	Visions	Wright Group
City Lights	B	Visions	Wright Group
City Mouse and Country Mouse	D	Learn to Read	Creative Teaching Press
City Mouse–Country Mouse	J	Aesop	Scholastic
Class Play, The	J	Little Readers	Houghton Mifflin
Claudine's Concert	L	Literacy 2000	Rigby
Clean House for Mole and Mouse, A	H	Ziefert, Harriet	Scholastic
Cleaning Teeth	C	Wonder World	Wright Group
Clever Mr. Brown	K	Storybox	Wright Group
Clever Penguins, The	G	PM Books	Rigby
Click	G	Foundations	Wright Group
Clifford, the Big Red Dog	K	Bridwell, Norman	Scholastic
Clifford the Small Red Puppy	K	Bridwell, Norman	Scholastic
Climbing	B	PM Starters	Rigby
Clock That Couldn't Tell Time	H	Carousel Readers	Dominie Press
Clocks and More Clocks	J	Hutchins, Pat	Scholastic
Closer and Closer	A	Twig	Wright Group
Clothes	F	Talk About Books	Dominie Press
Clothes	O	Wonder World	Wright Group
Clothes	C	Interaction	Rigby
Cloud Book, The	N	de Paola, Tomie	Scholastic
Clouds	M	Literacy 2000	Rigby
Clouds	H	Sunshine	Wright Group
Clouds	B	Voyages	SRA/McGraw Hill
Cloudy with a Chance of Meatballs	M	Barrett, Judi	Atheneum
Clown and Elephant	C	Storybox	Wright Group
Clown Face	A	Twig	Wright Group
Clown, The	B	Urmston, K. & Evans, K.	Kaeden Books
Clown, The	A	Smart Start	Rigby
Clyde Klutter's Room	I	Sunshine	Wright Group
Cock-a-Doodle Do	F	Brandenberg, Franz	Greenwillow
Cold Day, The	F	Oxford Reading Tree	Oxford
Color Wizard, The	J	Brenner, Barbara	Bantam
Colors	D	Foundations	Wright Group
Colors in the City	B	Urmston, K. & Evans, K.	Kaeden Books
Colours	A	Pienkowski, Jan	Penguin
Come and Have Fun	I	Hurd, Edith Thacher	HarperCollins
Come and Play	B	Interaction	Rigby
Come Back, Amelia Bedelia	L	Parish, Peggy	Harper & Row

Title	Level	Author/Series	Publisher/Distributor
Come for a Swim	F	Sunshine	Wright Group
Come On	B	Sunshine	Wright Group
Come on Mom	D	New Way	Steck-Vaughn
Come on, Tim	G	PM Books	Rigby
Come Out and Play Little Mouse	H	Kraus, Robert	Morrow
Come with Me	C	Storybox	Wright Group
Concert Night	K	Literacy 2000	Rigby
Conversation Club, The	L	Stanley, Diane	Aladdin
Cookie's Week	F	Ward, Cindy	Putnam
Cookies	A	Twig	Wright Group
Cooking Pot	F	Sunshine	Wright Group
Cool Off	C	Diaz, Nellie	Mondo
Cooling Off	D	Reading Corners	Dominie Press
Copycat	C	Storybox	Wright Group
Corduroy	K	Freeman, Don	Scholastic
Could It Be?	J	Oppenheim, Joanna	Bantam
Count and See	A	Hoban, Tana	Macmillan
Cow Up a Tree	H	Read Alongs	Rigby
Cows in the Garden	G	PM Books	Rigby
Coyote Plants a Peachtree	I	Books for Young Learners	Richard C. Owen
Crabs	M	Wonder World	Wright Group
Crafty Jackal	L	Folk Tales	Wright Group
Crazy Quilt, The	G	Little Celebrations	Celebration Press
Creepy Caterpillar	E	Little Readers	Houghton Mifflin
Crickets on the Go	D	Little Celebrations	Celebration Press
Crinkum Crankum	M	Ready to Read	Richard C. Owen/ Celebration Press
Critter Race	G	Reese, Bob	Children's Press
Crocodile in the Library	M	Ready to Read	Richard C. Owen/ Celebration Press
Crocodile's Christmas Jandles	M	Ready to Read	Richard C. Owen/ Celebration Press
Crosby Crocodile's Disguise	K	Literacy 2000	Rigby
Cross Country Race, The	H	PM Books	Rigby
Cupid Doesn't Flip Hamburgers	M	Dadey, D. & Jones, M.	Scholastic
Curious Cat	E	Little Celebrations	Celebration Press
Curious George and the Ice Cream	J	Rey, M.	Scholastic
Curse of the Squirrel, The	M	Yep, Laurence	Random House
Custard	E	Wonder World	Wright Group
Dabble Duck	K	Leo Ellis, Anne	HarperTrophy
Dad	B	Little Readers	Houghton Mifflin
Dad	A	PM Starters	Rigby
Dad's Garden	D	Literacy 2000	Rigby
Dad's Headache	F	Sunshine	Wright Group
Dad's New Path	F	Foundations	Wright Group
Dan the Flying Man	C	Read-Togethers	Wright Group
Dancing	C	Visions	Wright Group
Dancing Shoes	B	Literacy 2000	Rigby
Dandelion, The	E	Sunshine	Wright Group
Danger	C	Storybox	Wright Group
Daniel's Basketball Team	E	Carousel Readers	Dominie Press
Daniel's Dog	K	Bogart, Jo Ellen	Scholastic

Title	Level	Author/Series	Publisher/Distributor
Danny and the Dinosaur	J	Hoff, Syd	Scholastic
Danny's Dollars	D	Reading Corners	Dominie Press
Darcy and Gran Don't Like Babies	K	Cutler, Jane	Scholastic
Dark, Dark Tale, A	F	Brown, Ruth	Penguin
Day Buzzy Stopped Being Busy, The	G	First Start	Troll
Day I Had to Play with My Sister, The	G	Bonsall, Crosby	HarperCollins
Day in Town, A	L	Storybox	Wright Group
Day Jimmy's Boa Ate the Wash, The	K	Hakes Noble, T.	Scholastic
Day of the Rain, The	L	Cowley, Joy	Dominie Press
Day of the Snow, The	L	Cowley, Joy	Dominie Press
Day of the Wind, The	L	Cowley, Joy	Dominie Press
Dear Santa	B	Literacy 2000	Rigby
Dear Zoo	F	Campbell, Rod	Macmillan
Debra's Dog	H	Tadpoles	Rigby
Deep in the Woods	E	Carousel Readers	Dominie Press
Deputy Dan Gets His Man	L	Rosembloom, J.	Random House
Desert Dance	G	Little Celebrations	Celebration Press
Desert, The	C	Carousel Readers	Dominie Press
Diana Made Dinner	E	Carousel Readers	Dominie Press
Diary of a Honeybee	L	Literacy 2000	Rigby
Dick Whittington	H	Hunia	Ladybird Books
Did You Carry the Flag Today, Charley?	M	Caudill, Rebecca	Dell Publishing
Did You Say "Fire?"	G	Ready to Read	Richard C. Owen/ Celebration Press
Difficult Day, The	J	Read Alongs	Rigby
Dig, Dig	A	Cat on the Mat/Wood	Oxford
Dinner!	A	Sunshine	Wright Group
Dinosaur Days	L	Milton, Joyce	Random House
Dinosaur in Trouble	G	First Start	Troll
Dinosaur Party	B	Smart Start	Rigby
Dinosaur Reports	L	Sloan, P. & S.	Sundance
Dinosaur Time	K	Parish, Peggy	Harper & Row
Dinosaurs	K	Collins, Michael	Mondo
Dinosaurs	H	Sunshine	Wright Group
Dinosaurs Before Dark	M	Osborne, M. Pope	Random House
Dinosaurs Dinosaurs	G	Barton, Byron	HarperCollins
Dinosaurs on the Motorway	K	Wesley & the Dinosaurs	Wright Group
Diplodocus in the Garden, A	K	Wesley & the Dinosaurs	Wright Group
Dippy Dinner Drippers	I	Sunshine	Wright Group
Dirty Larry	D	Rookie Reader	Children's Press
Do You Like Cats?	K	Oppenheim, Joanne	Bantam
Do-Whacky-Do	H	Read Alongs	Rigby
Dog	B	Ready to Read	Richard C. Owen/ Celebration Press
Dog and Cat	E	Fehner, C.	Children's Press
Dog and Cat	E	Story Basket	Wright Group
Dog Day!	A	Smart Start	Rigby
Dog-Gone Hollywood	L	Weinman Sharmat, M.	Random House
Dog that Pitched a No-Hitter, The	L	Christopher, Matt	Little, Brown
Dog, The	G	Burningham, John	Crowell
Dog Went for Walk	D	Voyages	SRA/McGraw Hill
Dogstar	J	Literacy 2000	Rigby
Dolphins	J	Wonder World	Wright Group

Title	Level	Author/Series	Publisher/Distributor
Dom's Handplant	L	Literacy 2000	Rigby
Don't Be Late	D	Beginning Literacy	Scholastic
Don't Eat Too Much Turkey!	J	Cohen, Miriam	Dell Publishing
Don't Forget the Bacon	M	Hutchins, Pat	Puffin Books
Don't Leave Anything Behind!	C	Literacy 2000	Rigby
Don't Panic	E	Book Bank	Wright Group
Don't Splash Me	A	Windmill-Look & Listen	Wright Group
Don't Throw It Away!	F	Wonder World	Wright Group
Don't Touch!	I	Kline, Suzy	Penguin
Don't Wake the Baby	B	Literacy 2000	Rigby
Don't Worry	J	Literacy 2000	Rigby
Don't You Laugh at Me	E	Sunshine	Wright Group
Donald's Garden	K	Reading Unlimited	Celebration Press
Donkey	M	Literacy 2000	Rigby
Donkey in the Lion's Skin, The	G	Aesop	Wright Group
Donkey's Tale, The	J	Bank Street	Bantam
Doorbell Rang, The	J	Hutchins, Pat	Greenwillow
Double Trouble	M	Literacy 2000	Rigby
Down to Town	A	Sunshine	Wright Group
Dozen Dizzy Dogs, A	G	Bank Street	Bantam
Dr. Green	G	Little Readers	Houghton Mifflin
Dracula Doesn't Drink Lemonade	M	Dadey, Debbie	Scholastic
Dragon	I	Storybox	Wright Group
Dragon Feet	I	Books for Young Learners	Richard C. Owen
Dragon, The	C	Sunshine	Wright Group
Dragon Who Had the Measles, The	J	Literacy 2000	Rigby
Dragonflies	G	Books for Young Learners	Richard C. Owen
Dragon's Birthday, The	L	Literacy 2000	Rigby
Dream in the Wishing Well	H	Allen, R. V.	SRA/McGraw Hill
Dream, The	F	Oxford Reading Tree	Oxford
Dreaming	B	Smart Start	Rigby
Dreams	G	Sunshine	Wright Group
Dreams	E	Book Bank	Wright Group
Dressed Up Sammy	E	Urmston, K. & Evans, K.	Kaeden Books
Dressing Up	A	PM Starters	Rigby
Dressing Up	B	Smart Start	Rigby
Dressing Up	H	Young Writers' World	Nelson/Michaels Assoc.
Dressing Up	A	Jellybeans	Rigby
Dressing Up	C	Literacy 2000	Rigby
Dressing Up	A	Sunshine	Wright Group
Dressing Up Box, The	C	Book Bank	Wright Group
Drinking Gourd	M	Monjo, F. N.	HarperTrophy
Drought Maker, The	M	Literacy 2000	Rigby
Drummer Hoff	J	Emberley, Ed	Prentice-Hall
Drummers	H	Gould, Carol	Kaeden Books
Duck in the Gun, The	M	Literacy 2000	Rigby
Ear Book	E	Perkins, Al	Random House
Eat!	M	Kroll, Steven	Hyperion
Eat Up, Gemma	I	Hayes, S.	Sundance
Eat Your Peas Louise	E	Rookie Reader	Children's Press
Eating	A	Foundations	Wright Group
Eency Weency Spider	I	Bank Street	Bantam
Eeny, Meeny Miney Mouse	G	Giant Step Readers	Educ. Insights

Title	Level	Author/Series	Publisher/Distributor
Effie	K	Allinson, Beverley	Scholastic
Egg	K	Logan, Dick	Cypress
Elaine	J	Stepping Stones	Nelson/Michaels Assoc.
Elephant and Envelope	G	Gregorich	School Zone
Elephant and the Bad Baby, The	J	Hayes, S.	Sundance
Elephant in the House, An	J	Read Alongs	Rigby
Elephant in Trouble	H	First Start	Troll
Elephants	H	Foundations	Wright Group
Elephants Are Coming, The	E	Little Readers	Houghton Mifflin
Elephant's Trunk, An	C	Little Celebrations	Celebration Press
Elves and the Shoemaker	K	New Way	Steck-Vaughn
Elves Don't Wear Hard Hats	M	Dadey, D. & Jones, M.	Scholastic
Emily Arrow Promises to Do Better This Year	M	Giff, Patricia Reilly	Dell Publishing
Emily Eyefinger	M	Ball, Duncan	Aladdin
End, The	C	Tiger Cub	Peguis
Enormous Crocodile, The	N	Dahl, Roald	Puffin Books
Enormous Watermelon, The	H	Tales	Rigby
Errol the Peril	Q	Literacy 2000	Rigby
Every Morning	A	Twig	Wright Group
Everybody Eats Bread	J	Literacy 2000	Rigby
Excuses, Excuses	E	Tadpoles	Rigby
Fables by Aesop	K	Reading Unlimited	Celebration Press
Fabulous Freckles	K	Literacy 2000	Rigby
Face Painting	G	Wonder World	Wright Group
Faces	B	Sunshine	Wright Group
Faces	D	Little Celebrations	Celebration Press
Families	B	Interaction	Rigby
Families Are Different	K	Pellegrini, Nina	Scholastic
Family Photos	F	Literacy 2000	Rigby
Family Soccer	D	Geddes, Diana	Kaeden Books
Fancy Dress Parade, The	H	Stepping Stones	Nelson/Michaels Assoc.
Fantail, Fantail	D	Ready to Read	Richard C. Owen/ Celebration Press
Fantastic Mr. Fox	P	Dahl, Roald	Puffin Books
Farm Concert, The	D	Storybox	Wright Group
Farm Day	D	Little Celebrations	Celebration Press
Farm in Spring, The	D	PM Starters Two	Rigby
Farm, The	B	Sunshine	Wright Group
Farm, The	A	Smart Start	Rigby
Farmer and the Skunk	E	Tiger Cub	Peguis
Farmer Had a Pig, The	G	Tiger Cub	Peguis
Farmer in the Dell	E	Parkinson, Kathy	Whitman
Farmer in the Soup, The	K	Littledale, Freya	Scholastic
Farms	F	Foundations	Wright Group
Fasi Sings/Fasi's Fish	I	Ready to Read	Richard C. Owen/ Celebration Press
Fast and Funny	K	Storybox	Wright Group
Fast Draw Freddie	D	Rookie Reader	Children's Press
Fast Food	D	Foundations	Wright Group
Fast Machines	D	Foundations	Wright Group
Fat Cat	I	Kent, Jack	Scholastic
Fat Cat Tomkin	I	Voyages	SRA/McGraw Hill

Title	Level	Author/Series	Publisher/Distributor
Fat Pig, The	I	Tiger Cub	Peguis
Father Bear Comes Home	I	Minarik, E. H.	HarperCollins
Father Bear Goes Fishing	D	PM Books	Rigby
Feed Me!	I	Bank Street	Bantam
Feet	K	Storybox	Wright Group
Feisty Old Woman Who Lived in the Cozy Cave, The	F	Foundations	Wright Group
Fiddle and the Gun, The	M	Literacy 2000	Rigby
Fight on the Hill, The	J	Read Alongs	Rigby
Find a Caterpillar	E	Book Bank	Wright Group
Fire! Fire!	E	PM Books	Rigby
First Day of School	D	Carousel Readers	Dominie Press
Fishing	C	PM Starters	Rigby
Fishing	D	Yukish, J.	Kaeden Books
Fishing	G	Foundations	Wright Group
Fishy Scales	I	Mathtales	Mimosa
Five Brave Explorers	P	Hudson, Wade	Scholastic
Five Little Monkeys Jumping on the Bed	E	Christelow, Eileen	Houghton Mifflin
Five Little Monsters	D	Learn to Read	Creative Teaching Press
Five Little Speckled Frogs	G	Tiger Cub	Peguis
Five True Dog Stories	M	Davidson, Margaret	Scholastic
Five True Horse Stories	M	Davidson, Margaret	Scholastic
Fix-It	I	McPhail, David	Penguin
Fizz and Splutter	E	Storybox	Wright Group
Flood, The	H	PM Books	Rigby
Floppy the Hero	F	Oxford Reading Tree	Oxford
Floppy's Bath	E	Oxford Reading Tree	Oxford
Flossie & the Fox	O	McKissack, Patricia	Scholastic
Flower of Sheba, The	L	Orgel, Doris	Bantam
Flowers for Mom	E	Carousel Readers	Dominie Press
Flying	E	Crews, Donald	Greenwillow
Flying	C	Storybox	Wright Group
Flying and Floating	B	Little Red Readers	Sundance
Flying Fingers	K	Literacy 2000	Rigby
Flying High	F	Predictable Storybooks	SRA/McGraw Hill
Follow That Fish	K	Oppenheim, Joanne	Bantam
Follow the Leader	B	Windmill-Look & Listen	Wright Group
Food to Eat	B	Little Readers	Houghton Mifflin
Foolish Goose	F	Start to Read	School Zone
Foot Book	E	Seuss, Dr.	Random House
Football	B	Visions	Wright Group
Footprints in the Snow	D	Hello Reader	Scholastic
Forgetful Fred	E	Tadpoles	Rigby
Fortune's Friend	Q	Literacy 2000	Rigby
Four Getters and Arf, The	G	Little Celebrations	Celebration Press
Four Ice Creams	C	PM Starters Two	Rigby
Fox and His Friends	J	Marshall, Edward & James	Scholastic
Fox and the Crow, The	J	Aesop	Wright Group
Fox and the Little Red Hen	L	Traditional Tales	Rigby
Fox on the Box	C	Gregorich	School Zone
Fox, The	C	Books for Young Learners	Richard C. Owen
Fox Who Was Foxed, The	H	PM Books	Rigby
Fraidy Cats	J	Hello Reader	Scholastic
Frankenstein Doesn't Plant Petunias	M	Dadey, Debbie	Scholastic

Title	Level	Author/Series	Publisher/Distributor
Frankenstein Moved onto the 4th Floor	M	Levy, Elizabeth	Harper & Row
Franklin Goes to School	K	Bourgeois & Clark	Scholastic
Freckle Juice	M	Blume, Judy	Dell Yearling
Freddie the Frog	D	First Start	Troll
Freddie's Spaghetti	F	Doyle, R. H.	Random House
Friend for Little White Rabbit	E	PM Books	Rigby
Friendly Snowman	F	First Start	Troll
Friendly Snowman	F	Joyce, William	Scholastic
Friends	B	Little Readers	Houghton Mifflin
Friends	G	Reading Unlimited	Celebration Press
Friends Are Forever	K	Literacy 2000	Rigby
Frightened	B	Storybox	Wright Group
Frog and the Fly	D	Cat on the Mat/Wood	Oxford
Frog and Toad/Friends	K	Lobel, Arnold	Harper & Row
Frog and Toad Together	K	Lobel, Arnold	HarperCollins
Frog Princess, The	K	Literacy 2000	Rigby
Frog Who Thought He Was a Horse, The	L	Literacy 2000	Rigby
Froggy Tale, The	I	Literacy 2000	Rigby
Frogs	A	Twig	Wright Group
Frown, The	K	Read Alongs	Rigby
Fruit Salad	A	Literacy 2000	Rigby
Fun	D	Yannone, Deborah	Kaeden Books
Fun at Camp	H	First Start	Troll
Fun with Hats	B	Malka, Lucy	Mondo
Fun with Mo and Toots	C	Ready to Read	Richard C. Owen/ Celebration Press
Funny Bones	J	Ahlberg, A. & J.	Viking
Funny Man, A	E	Hello Reader	Scholastic
Fur	D	Mark, Jan	Harper & Row
Gail & Me	L	Literacy 2000	Rigby
Gallo and Zorro	J	Literacy 2000	Rigby
Gardening	D	Foundations	Wright Group
Genies Don't Ride Bicycles	M	Dadey, D. & Jones, M.	Scholastic
George and Martha	L	Marshall, James	Houghton Mifflin
George Shrinks	H	Joyce, William	HarperCollins
George's Marvelous Medicine	P	Dahl, Roald	Puffin Books
Get a Grip, Pip!	Q	Literacy 2000	Rigby
Get Lost!	F	Foundations	Wright Group
Get Lost Becka	E	Start to Read	School Zone
Get Set and Go	J	Real Reading	Steck-Vaughn
Getting Dressed	A	Sunshine	Wright Group
Getting Ready for the Ball	C	Literacy 2000	Rigby
Getting the Mail	G	Voyages	SRA/McGraw Hill
Getting There	B	Wonder World	Wright Group
Ghost, The	A	Storybox	Wright Group
Ghosts Don't Eat Potato Chips	M	Dadey, D. & Jones, M.	Scholastic
Giant in the Forest, A	J	Reading Unlimited	Celebration Press
Giant Jam Sandwich, The	K	Vernon Lord, John	Houghton Mifflin
Giant's Boy, The	H	Sunshine	Wright Group
Giant's Breakfast, The	B	Literacy 2000	Rigby
Giant's Cake, The	H	Literacy 2000	Rigby
Giant's Day Out, The	B	Smart Start	Rigby

Title	Level	Author/Series	Publisher/Distributor
Giant's Job, The	H	Stewart, J. & Salem, L.	Seedling
Gifts for Dad	H	Urmston, K. & Evans, K.	Kaeden Books
Ginger	I	Little Readers	Houghton Mifflin
Gingerbread Man, The	I	Traditional Tales	Rigby
Gingerbread Man, The	F	Little Readers	Houghton Mifflin
Gingerbread Man, The	I	Tiger Cub	Peguis
Giraffe and the Pelly and Me, The	P	Dahl, Roald	Puffin Books
Give Me a Hug	B	Sunshine	Wright Group
Glumly	Q	Literacy 2000	Rigby
Go and Hush the Baby	K	Byars, Betsy	Viking
Go Away Dog	I	Nodset, Joan	HarperCollins
Go Back to Sleep	E	Literacy 2000	Rigby
Go Dog Go	E	Eastman, P. D.	Random House
Go, Go, Go	A	Storybox	Wright Group
Go-carts, The	B	PM Starter	Rigby
Gobble, Gobble, Gone	D	Little Celebrations	Celebration Press
Going Fishing	F	Voyages	SRA/McGraw Hill
Going for a Walk	F	DeRegniers, B. S.	Harper & Row
Going Out	D	Foundations	Wright Group
Going Shopping	D	Carousel Readers	Dominie Press
Going to Grandma's	I	Read by Reading	Scholastic
Going to Grandpa's	C	Frankford, Marilyn	Kaeden Books
Going to School	C	Storybox	Wright Group
Going to School	A	Smart Start	Rigby
Going to School	F	Foundations	Wright Group
Going to the Beach	A	Ready to Read	Richard C. Owen/ Celebration Press
Going to the Beach	C	Carousel Readers	Dominie Press
Going to the Hospital	H	Foundations	Wright Group
Going to the Park with Grandaddy	C	Visions	Wright Group
Going Up?	B	Little Celebrations	Celebration Press
Golden Goose, The	M	Literacy 2000	Rigby
Goldilocks and the Three Bears	H	Traditional Tales	Rigby
Goldilocks and the Three Bears	K	Once Upon a Time	Wright Group
Gone Fishing	G	Long, Erlene	Houghton Mifflin
Good as New	L	Douglass, Barbara	Scholastic
Good Bad Cat, The	D	Start to Read	School Zone
Good for You	D	Sunshine	Wright Group
Good News	I	Bank Street	Bantam
Good Night, Little Brother	F	Literacy 2000	Rigby
Good to Eat	B	Twig	Wright Group
Good Work, Amelia Bedelia	L	Parish, Peggy	Avon Camelot
Good-Bye Lucy	D	Sunshine	Wright Group
Goodness Gracious!	I	Literacy 2000	Rigby
Goodnight	D	Voyages	SRA/McGraw Hill
Goodnight, Moon	H	Brown, Margaret Wise	HarperCollins
Goodnight Owl	I	Hutchins, Pat	Macmillan
Goodnight Peter	G	Windmill-Look & Listen	Wright Group
Goose That Laid the Golden Egg, The	G	Aesop	Wright Group
Grandad	L	Literacy 2000	Rigby
Grandma and the Pirate	F	Lloyd, David	Crown
Grandma Mix-Up, The	J	McCully, Emily Arnold	HarperTrophy
Grandma's at the Lake	K	McCully, Emily Arnold	HarperTrophy

Title	Level	Author/Series	Publisher/Distributor
Grandma's Bicycle	G	Read Alongs	Rigby
Grandma's Present	E	Foundations	Wright Group
Grandpa, Grandpa	G	Read-Togethers	Wright Group
Grandpa Snored	F	Literacy 2000	Rigby
Grandpa's Cookies	F	Little Readers	Houghton Mifflin
Granny Bundle's Boring Walk	H	Stepping Stones	Nelson/Michaels Assoc.
Great Big Enormous Turnip	H	Tolstoy/Oxenbury	Watts
Great Big Enormous Turnip, The	H	Reading Unlimited	Celebration Press
Great Day for Up	J	Seuss, Dr.	Random House
Great Enormous Hamburger, The	B	Sunshine	Wright Group
Great-Grandpa	G	Voyages	SRA/McGraw Hill
Great Grumbler and the Wonder	M	Ready to Read	Richard C. Owen/ Celebration Press
Greedy Cat	G	Ready to Read	Richard C. Owen/ Celebration Press
Greedy Cat Is Hungry	D	Ready to Read	Richard C. Owen/ Celebration Press
Greedy Gray Octopus, The	G	Tadpoles	Rigby
Green Bananas	F	Tadpoles	Rigby
Green Eggs and Ham	J	Seuss, Dr.	Random House
Green Eyes	F	Literacy 2000	Rigby
Green Footprints	E	Literacy 2000	Rigby
Green, Green	D	Little Readers	Houghton Mifflin
Gregor the Grumblesome Giant	G	Literacy 2000	Rigby
Gregory, the Terrible Eater	L	Weinman Sharmat, M.	Scholastic
Gregory's Dog	C	Cat on the Mat/Stobbs	Oxford
Gregory's Garden	F	Cat on the Mat/Stobbs	Oxford
Gremlins Don't Chew Bubble Gum	M	Dadey, D. & Jones, M.	Scholastic
Grocery Shopping	D	Yannone, D.	Kaeden Books
Growing	B	Windmill-Look & Listen	Wright Group
Growing Up, Up, Up Book	F	First Start	Troll
Gruff Brothers, The	I	Bank Street	Bantam
Grumpy Elephant	E	Storybox	Wright Group
Guess What Kind of Ball	E	Urmston, K. & Evans, K.	Kaeden Books
Gum on the Drum	E	Gregorich	School Zone
Gumby Shop	I	Read Alongs	Rigby
Ha-Ha Party	J	Sunshine	Wright Group
Hair	B	Foundations	Wright Group
Hair Party, The	J	Literacy 2000	Rigby
Hairy Bear	G	Read-Togethers	Wright Group
Half for You Half for Me	K	Literacy 2000	Rigby
Hand, Hand, Fingers, Thumb	J	Perkins, Al	Random House
Hand Me Downs, The	G	Little Readers	Houghton Mifflin
Hands, Hands, Hands	F	Vaughan, Marcia	Mondo
Hannah	N	Whelan, Gloria	Random House
Hannah	J	Stepping Stones	Nelson/Michaels Assoc.
Hansel and Gretel	G	Hunia	General
Happy Birthday	G	First Start	Troll
Happy Birthday	C	Literacy 2000	Rigby
Happy Birthday, Dear Duck	K	Bunting, Eve	Clarion
Happy Birthday, Martin Luther King	L	Marzollo, Jean	Scholastic
Happy Birthday, Moon	L	Asch, Frank	Simon & Schuster
Happy Birthday, Sam	I	Hutchins, Pat	Greenwillow

Title	Level	Author/Series	Publisher/Distributor
Happy Egg	E	Kraus, Robert	Scholastic
Happy Face, Sad Face	C	Foundations	Wright Group
Happy Faces	H	Reading Unlimited	Celebration Press
Happy Jack	F	First Start	Troll
Hare and the Tortoise, The	K	Literacy 2000	Rigby
Harold and the Purple Crayon	K	Johnson, Crockett	Harper & Row
Harold's Flyaway Kite	G	First Start	Troll
Harry and the Lady Next Door	J	Zion, Gene	HarperTrophy
Harry and Willy and Carrothead	L	Caseley, Judith	Scholastic
Harry Hates Shopping!	K	Armitage, R. & D.	Scholastic
Harry Takes a Bath	F	Ziefert, Harriet	Penguin
Hat Came Back, The	K	Literacy 2000	Rigby
Hats	C	Little Readers	Houghton Mifflin
Hats	F	Talk About Books	Dominie Press
Hattie and the Fox	I	Fox, Mem	Bradbury/Trumpet
Haunted House	E	Storybox	Wright Group
Have You Seen a Javelina?	K	Literacy 2000	Rigby
Have You Seen the Crocodile?	F	West, Colin	Harper & Row
He Bear, She Bear	J	Berenstain, Stan & Jan	Random House
He Who Listens	K	Literacy 2000	Rigby
Hedgehog Bakes a Cake	J	Bank Street	Bantam
Hedgehog is Hungry	C	PM Books	Rigby
Helen Keller	P	Graff, S. & P.	Dell Publishing
Helicopter Over Hawaii	A	Twig	Wright Group
Hello	C	Storybox	Wright Group
Hello, Cat You Need a Hat	I	Gelman, Rita	Scholastic
Hello Creatures!	K	Literacy 2000	Rigby
Hello Goodbye	B	Literacy 2000	Rigby
Help!	H	Giant Step Readers	Educ. Insights
Help!	C	Reading Corners	Dominie Press
Help Me	H	Storybox	Wright Group
Helping You	D	Interaction	Rigby
Hen Can, A	E	Tiger Cub	Peguis
Henny Penny	I	Galdone, Paul	Scholastic
Henry and Beezus	O	Cleary, Beverly	Avon Books
Henry and Mudge and the Forever Sea	J	Rylant, Cynthia	Aladdin
Henry and Mudge in Puddle Trouble	J	Rylant, Cynthia	Aladdin
Henry and Mudge in the Green Time	J	Rylant, Cynthia	Aladdin
Henry and Mudge: The First Book	J	Rylant, Cynthia	Aladdin
Henry and Ribsy	O	Cleary, Beverly	Avon Books
Henry and the Clubhouse	O	Cleary, Beverly	Avon Books
Henry and the Helicopter	D	Literacy 2000	Rigby
Henry and the Paper Route	O	Cleary, Beverly	Avon Books
Henry Huggins	O	Cleary, Beverly	Avon Books
Henry's Busy Day	E	Campbell, Rod	Penguin
Henry's Choice	M	Reading Unlimited	Celebration Press
Here Are My Hands	H	Bobber Book	SRA/McGraw Hill
Here Comes Annette!	E	Voyages	SRA/McGraw Hill
Here Comes Kate!	J	Real Reading	Steck-Vaughn
Here Comes the Bus	F	Ziefert, Harriet	Penguin
Here Comes Winter	G	First Start	Troll
Here Is	B	Carousel Earlybirds	Dominie Press
Here's a House	A	Windmill-Look & Listen	Wright Group
Here's Skipper	B	Salem, L. & Stewart, J.	Seedling

Title	Level	Author/Series	Publisher/Distributor
Herman Henry's Dog	I	Little Readers	Houghton Mifflin
Herman the Helper	E	Kraus, Robert	Simon & Schuster
Herman the Helper Lends a Hand	F	Kraus, Robert	Windmill
Herman's Tooth	H	Foundations	Wright Group
Hermit Crab	E	PM Books	Rigby
Hermit Crab, The	G	Sunshine	Wright Group
Hey There, Bear!	C	Little Celebrations	Celebration Press
Hi, Clouds!	E	Rookie Reader	Children's Press
Hiccups for Elephant	I	Hello Reader	Scholastic
Hide and Seek	B	Literacy 2000	Rigby
Hide and Seek	E	Foundations	Wright Group
Hiding	D	Foundations	Wright Group
Hill of Fire	L	Lewis, T. P.	HarperCollins
Hippopotamus Ate the Teacher, A	J	Thaler, Mike	Avon Books
Hit-Away Kid, The	M	Christopher, Matt	Little, Brown
Hogboggit, The	D	Ready to Read	Richard C. Owen/ Celebration Press
Hoiho's Chicks	D	Ready to Read	Richard C. Owen/ Celebration Press
Hole in Harry's Pocket, The	I	Little Readers	Houghton Mifflin
Hole in the Hedge, The	F	Sunshine	Wright Group
Home for a Puppy	G	First Start	Troll
Home Sweet Home	E	Roffey, Maureen	Bodley
Honey Bees	L	Kahkonen, S.	Steck-Vaughn
Honey for Baby Bear	F	PM Books	Rigby
Honey, My Rabbit	E	Voyages	SRA/McGraw Hill
Honk!	B	Smith, Sue	Mondo
Hooray for Snail	F	Stadler, John	HarperCollins
Hop on Pop	J	Seuss, Dr.	Random House
Horace	D	Storybox	Wright Group
Horrakapotchkin	M	Ready to Read	Richard C. Owen/ Celebration Press
Horrible Big Black Bug, The	D	Tadpoles	Rigby
Horrible Harry and the Ant Invasion	L	Kline, Suzy	Scholastic
Horrible Harry and the Green Slime	L	Kline, Suzy	Puffin Books
Horrible Harry and the Kickball Wedding	L	Kline, Suzy	Puffin Books
Horrible Harry in Room 2B	L	Kline, Suzy	Puffin Books
Horrible Thing with Hairy Feet	H	Read Alongs	Rigby
Horse in Harry's Room	J	Hoff, Syd	HarperCollins
Hot Dogs (Sausages)	C	PM Books	Rigby
Hot Potato and Cold Potato	C	Foundations	Wright Group
Hot Rod Harry	E	Petrie, Kathryn	Children's Press
House	C	Little Celebrations	Celebration Press
House, A	A	PM Starters One	Rigby
House Cleaning	A	Book Bank	Wright Group
House for Little Red	F	Just Beginning	Modern Curriculum
House in the Tree, The	F	PM Books	Rigby
House That Jack Built, The	J	Peppe, Rodney	Delacorte
House-Hunting	G	PM Books	Rigby
Houses	C	Windmill-Look & Listen	Wright Group
Houses	C	Storybox	Wright Group
How a Volcano Is Formed	M	Wonder World	Wright Group
How Do I Put It On?	H	Watanabe, Shigeo	Penguin

Title	Level	Author/Series	Publisher/Distributor
How Do Plants Get Food?	L	Goldish, Meish	Steck-Vaughn
How Do You Make a Bubble?	G	Bank Street	Bantam
How Do You Say Hello to a Ghost?	F	Tiger Cub	Peguis
How Fire Came to Earth	K	Literacy 2000	Rigby
How Grandmother Spider Got the Sun	J	Little Readers	Houghton Mifflin
How Kittens Grow	J	Selsam, Millicent	Scholastic
How Many Bugs in a Box?	D	Carter, David	Simon & Schuster
How Many Legs?	B	Windmill-Look & Listen	Wright Group
How Spider Tricked Snake	K	Real Reading	Steck-Vaughn
How to Eat Fried Worms	M	Rockwell, Thomas	Dell Publishing
How to Make a Card	G	Urmston, K. & Evans, K.	Kaeden Books
How to Make a Mud Pie	H	Little Readers	Houghton Mifflin
How to Make a Mudpie	A	Learn to Read	Creative Teaching Press
How to Ride a Giraffe	I	Little Readers	Houghton Mifflin
How Turtle Raced Beaver	J	Literacy 2000	Rigby
How's the Weather?	B	Learn to Read	Creative Teaching Press
Huberta the Hiking Hippo	L	Literacy 2000	Rigby
Hug Is Warm, A	C	Sunshine	Wright Group
Huggles Breakfast	A	Sunshine	Wright Group
Huggles Can Juggle	A	Sunshine	Wright Group
Huggles Goes Away	A	Sunshine	Wright Group
Huggly, Snuggly Pets	F	Giant Step Readers	Educ. Insights
Humpity-Bump	C	Little Celebrations	Celebration Press
Hundred Hugs, A	I	Sunshine	Wright Group
Hungry Animals	G	Little Readers	Houghton Mifflin
Hungry Bear	C	Smart Start	Rigby
Hungry Giant, The	F	Storybox	Wright Group
Hungry Giant's Soup, The	G	Story Basket	Wright Group
Hungry, Hungry Sharks	L	Cole, Joanna	Random House
Hungry Kitten, The	D	PM Books	Rigby
Hungry Monster	I	Storybox	Wright Group
Hurry Up	D	Voyages	SRA/McGraw Hill
Huzzard Buzzard	F	Reese, Bob	Children's Press
I Am	B	Little Readers	Houghton Mifflin
I Am...	A	Sunshine	Wright Group
I Am a Book Worm	C	Sunshine	Wright Group
I Am Frightened	B	Storybox	Wright Group
I Am Not Afraid	K	Bank Street	Bantam
I Am Thankful	A	Carousel Earlybirds	Dominie Press
I Can	B	Little Readers	Houghton Mifflin
I Can	B	New Way	Steck-Vaughn
I Can Build a House	D	Watanabe, Shigeo	Viking
I Can Dig	C	Can You Do This	SRA/McGraw Hill
I Can Do It Myself	C	Literacy 2000	Rigby
I Can Draw	C	Carousel Earlybirds	Dominie Press
I Can Eat	C	Can You Do This	SRA/McGraw Hill
I Can Fly	A	Sunshine	Wright Group
I Can Fly	F	Carousel Readers	Dominie Press
I Can Hear	A	TOTTS	TOTTS
I Can Jump	C	Sunshine	Wright Group
I Can Make Music	B	Little Red Readers	Sundance
I Can Paint	A	Book Bank	Wright Group
I Can Play	C	Can You Do This	SRA/McGraw Hill

Title	Level	Author/Series	Publisher/Distributor
I Can Read	B	Ready to Read	Richard C. Owen/ Celebration Press
I Can Read	A	Learn to Read	Creative Teaching Press
I Can Read with My Eyes Shut	J	Seuss, Dr.	Random House
I Can Ride	C	Can You Do This	SRA/McGraw Hill
I Can See	A	Carousel Earlybirds	Dominie Press
I Can Spell Dinosaur	F	Predictable Storybooks	SRA/McGraw Hill
I Can Squeak	E	Windmill-Rhyme & Rhythm	Wright Group
I Can Wash	C	Carousel Earlybirds	Dominie Press
I Can Write	A	Learn to Read	Creative Teaching Press
I Can Write, Can You?	B	Stewart, J. & Salem, L.	Seedling
"I Can't" Said the Ant	M	Cameron, Polly	Scholastic
I Can't Sleep	D	Learn to Read	Creative Teaching Press
I Climb	C	This Is the Way	SRA/McGraw Hill
I Could Be	C	Visions	Wright Group
I Crawl	C	This Is the Way	SRA/McGraw Hill
I Dream	K	Sunshine	Wright Group
I Dress Up Like Mama	C	Visions	Wright Group
I Eat Leaves	C	Vandine, JoAnn	Mondo
I Fly	C	This Is the Way	SRA/McGraw Hill
I Get Ready for School	C	Visions	Wright Group
I Get Tired	B	Carousel Earlybirds	Dominie Press
I Go, Go, Go	B	Sunshine	Wright Group
I Have a Pet	B	Reading Corners	Dominie Press
I Have a Question, Grandma	G	Literacy 2000	Rigby
I Jump	C	This Is the Way	SRA/McGraw Hill
I Know a Lady	L	Zolotow, Charlotte	Puffin Books
I Know an Old Lady	H	Readalong Rhythms	Wright Group
I Like	A	Sunshine	Wright Group
I Like	C	Literacy 2000	Rigby
I Like Balloons	A	Reading Corners	Dominie Press
I Like Books	D	Browne, Anthony	Random House
I Like Green	C	Literacy 2000	Rigby
I Like It When...	E	Ready Set Read	Steck-Vaughn
I Like Me	A	Visions	Wright Group
I Like to Eat	A	Reading Corners	Dominie Press
I Like to Paint	A	Reading Corners	Dominie Press
I Like to Play	C	Carousel Readers	Dominie Press
I Like Worms	D	Sunshine	Wright Group
I Love Bugs	C	Lake, Mary Dixon	Mondo
I Love Camping	E	Carousel Readers	Dominie Press
I Love Cats	E	Rookie Reader	Children's Press
I Love Ladybugs	C	Allen, R. V.	SRA/McGraw Hill
I Love Mud and Mud Loves Me	D	Beginning Literacy	Scholastic
I Love Music	C	Carousel Readers	Dominie Press
I Love My Family	B	Sunshine	Wright Group
I Love My Family	B	Foundations	Wright Group
I Love the Beach	M	Literacy 2000	Rigby
I Love to Sneeze	J	Bank Street	Bantam
I Paint	A	Literacy 2000	Rigby
I Read	A	Reading Corners	Dominie Press
I Remember	C	Literacy 2000	Rigby
I Run	C	This Is the Way	SRA/McGraw Hill
I See Colors	B	Learn to Read	Creative Teaching Press

Title	Level	Author/Series	Publisher/Distributor
I Spy	C	Literacy 2000	Rigby
I Swim	C	This Is the Way	SRA/McGraw Hill
I Want a Pet	C	Gregorich	School Zone
I Want Ice Cream	C	Storybox	Wright Group
I Want to Be a Clown	F	Start to Read	School Zone
I Was So Mad	J	Mayer, Mercer	Donovan
I Was Walking Down the Road	H	Barchas, Sarah	Scholastic
I Went Walking	C	Williams, Sue	Harcourt Brace
I Wish I Had a Dinosaur	D	Little Celebrations	Celebration Press
I Wish I Was Sick Too	G	Brandenburg, Franz	Morrow
I Wonder	D	Sunshine	Wright Group
I Wonder	C	Little Celebrations	Celebration Press
I Write	C	Sunshine	Wright Group
I'm a Good Reader	H	Carousel Readers	Dominie Press
I'm Bigger Than You	D	Sunshine	Wright Group
I'm Glad to Say	H	Sunshine	Wright Group
I'm Hungry	C	Visions	Wright Group
I'm King of the Castle	F	Watanabe, Shigeo	Philomel
I'm King of the Mountain	G	Ready to Read	Richard C. Owen/ Celebration Press
I'm Not, I'm Not	C	Windmill-Look & Listen	Wright Group
I'm Sick Today	H	Carousel Readers	Dominie Press
I've Lost My Boot	C	Windmill-Look & Listen	Wright Group
Ice Cream	C	Sunshine	Wright Group
Ice is . . . Whee!	D	Rookie Reader	Children's Press
If I Had an Alligator	H	Mayer, Mercer	Dial
If I Were a Penguin	H	Goeneil, Heidi	Little, Brown
If I Were You	E	Wildsmith, Brian	Oxford
If You Give a Mouse a Cookie	K	Numeroff, L. J.	Scholastic
If You Meet a Dragon	C	Storybox	Wright Group
Imagine That	J	Storybox	Wright Group
In a Dark, Dark Wood	E	Carter, David	S & S Trade
In a Dark, Dark Wood	E	Read-Togethers	Wright Group
In a Town	E	Little Celebrations	Celebration Press
In My Bed	C	Literacy 2000	Rigby
In My Bucket	F	Carousel Readers	Dominie Press
In My Garden	C	Carousel Readers	Dominie Press
In My Pocket	E	Carousel Readers	Dominie Press
In My Room	C	Literacy 2000	Rigby
In the Bathroom	B	Smart Start	Rigby
In the City	C	Pasternac, Susana	Scholastic
In the Clouds	M	Literacy 2000	Rigby
In the Dinosaur's Paw	M	Giff, Patricia Reilly	Dell Publishing
In the Forest	C	Twig	Wright Group
In the Forest	G	Voyages	SRA/McGraw Hill
In the Mirror	B	Storybox	Wright Group
In the Shopping Cart	A	PM Starters One	Rigby
In the Supermarket	A	Smart Start	Rigby
In the Woods	G	Reading Corners	Dominie Press
In Went Goldilocks	C	Literacy 2000	Rigby
Insects That Bother Us	D	Foundations	Wright Group
Inside, Outside, Upside Down	E	Berenstain, Stan & Jan	Random House
Interruptions	F	Scarffe, B. & Snowball, D.	Mondo
Invisible	I	Read Alongs	Rigby

Title	Level	Author/Series	Publisher/Distributor
Iron Horse, The	A	Smart Start	Rigby
Is Anyone Home?	F	Maris, Ron	Greenwillow
Is It Alive?	C	Learn to Read	Creative Teaching Press
Is It Time Yet?	G	Foundations	Wright Group
Is This a Monster?	C	Lovell, Scarlett and Diane	Mondo
Is This You?	F	Krauss, Ruth	Scholastic
Island Baby	M	Keller, Holly	Scholastic
Island Picnic, The	H	PM Books	Rigby
Island, The	D	Wildsmith, Brian	Oxford
It Came to Tea	I	Readalong Rhythms	Wright Group
It Looked Like Spilt Milk	E	Shaw, Charles	Harper & Row
It Takes a Village	N	Cowen-Fletcher, J.	Scholastic
It Takes Time to Grow	H	Sunshine	Wright Group
It's Football Time	C	Geddes, Diana	Kaeden Books
It's Game Day	D	Salem, L. & Stewart, J.	Seedling
It's Halloween	K	Prelutsky, Jack	Scholastic
It's Not Easy Being a Bunny	I	Sadler, Marilyn	Random House
It's Not Fair	F	Tadpoles	Rigby
Itchy Itchy Chicken Pox	F	Hello Reader	Scholastic
Jace, Mace, and the Big Race	H	Gregorich	School Zone
Jack and the Beanstalk	K	Weisner, David	Scholastic
Jack and the Beanstalk	I	Traditional Tales	Rigby
Jack in the Box	I	Storybox	Wright Group
Jack-in-the-Box	B	Literacy 2000	Rigby
Jack-O-Lantern	B	Twig	Wright Group
Jackson's Monster	I	Little Readers	Houghton Mifflin
Jamaica's Find	K	Havill, Juanita	Scholastic
Jamberry	J	Degen, Bruce	Harper & Row
James Is Hiding	A	Windmill-Look & Listen	Wright Group
Jane Goodall and the Wild Chimpanzees	L	Birnbaum, Bette	Steck-Vaughn
Jane's Car	F	PM Books	Rigby
Jason's Bus Ride	G	Ziefert, Harriet	Penguin
Jeb's Barn	G	Little Celebrations	Celebration Press
Jennifer, Too	L	Havill, Juanita	Hyperion
Jesse Owens: Olympic Hero	P	Sabin, Francene	Troll
Jessica's Dress Up	F	Voyages	SRA/McGraw Hill
Jessie's Flower	G	Read Alongs	Rigby
Jigaree, The	E	Storybox	Wright Group
Jillian Jiggs	J	Gilman, Phoebe	Scholastic
Jim Meets the Thing	I	Cohen, Miriam	Dell Publishing
Jim's Dog Muffins	I	Cohen, Miriam	Dell Publishing
Jim's Trumpet	H	Sunshine	Wright Group
Jimmy	D	Foundations	Wright Group
Jimmy Lee Did It	J	Cummings, Pat	Lothrop
Jimmy's Goal	E	Foundations	Wright Group
Job for Jenny Archer, A	M	Conford, Ellen	Little, Brown
Joe and the Mouse	F	Oxford Reading Tree	Oxford
Joe's Father	E	Book Bank	Wright Group
Jog, Frog, Jog	F	Gregorich	School Zone
Johnny Lion's Book	J	Hurd, Edith Thacher	HarperCollins
Johnny Lion's Rubber Boots	F	Hurd, Edith Thacher	Harper & Row
Joke, The	H	Little Readers	Houghton Mifflin
Josefina Story Quilt	L	Coerr, Eleanor	HarperTrophy

Title	Level	Author/Series	Publisher/Distributor
Joshua James Likes Trucks	C	Rookie Reader	Children's Press
Josie Cleans Up	I	Little Readers	Houghton Mifflin
Julia's Lists	D	Little Celebrations	Celebration Press
Julian's Glorious Summer	N	Cameron, Ann	Random House
Jumble Sale, The	E	Oxford Reading Tree	Oxford
Jungle Parade: A Singing Game	D	Little Celebrations	Celebration Press
Junie B. Jones and the Stupid Smelly Bus	M	Park, Barbara	Random House
Junie B. Jones and the Yucky Blucky Fruitcake	M	Park, Barbara	Random House
Just a Mess	I	Mayer, Mercer	Donovan
Just Enough	G	Salem, L. & Stewart, J.	Seedling
Just for Fun	J	Literacy 2000	Rigby
Just for You	G	Mayer, Mercer	Donovan
Just Grandma and Me	I	Mayer, Mercer	Donovan
Just Like Daddy	F	Asch, Frank	Simon & Schuster
Just Like Everyone Else	I	Kuskin, Karla	HarperCollins
Just Like Me	E	Rookie Reader	Children's Press
Just Like Me	F	First Start	Troll
Just Like Me	J	Storybox	Wright Group
Just Look at You	A	Sunshine	Wright Group
Just Me and My Babysitter	H	Mayer, Mercer	Donovan
Just Me and My Dad	H	Mayer, Mercer	Donovan
Just Me and My Puppy	H	Mayer, Mercer	Donovan
Just This Once	H	Sunshine	Wright Group
Just Us Women	J	Caines, Jeannette	Scholastic
Katie Couldn't	F	Rookie Reader	Children's Press
Katie Did It	G	Rookie Reader	Children's Press
Katy and the Big Snow	L	Burton, V. L.	Scholastic
Keep the Lights Burning, Abbie	K	Roop, P. & C.	Scholastic
Keeping Fit	E	Little Celebrations	Celebration Press
Kenny and the Little Kickers	J	Hello Reader	Scholastic
Key to the Treasure	N	Parish, Peggy	Dell Publishing
Kick-a-Lot Shoes	H	Storybox	Wright Group
King Beast's Birthday	L	Literacy 2000	Rigby
King, the Mice and the Cheese	K	Gurney, Nancy	Random House
King's Surprise, The	D	Stewart, J. & Salem, L.	Seedling
Kipper's Birthday	E	Oxford Reading Tree	Oxford
Kiss for Little Bear	J	Minarik, E. H.	Harper & Row
Kitchen Tools	D	Foundations	Wright Group
Kitten Chased a Fly	C	Windmill-Look & Listen	Wright Group
Kittens	C	Literacy 2000	Rigby
Kitty and the Birds	C	PM Books	Rigby
Knit, Knit, Knit, Knit	J	Literacy 2000	Rigby
Knock! Knock!	K	Carter, Jackie	Scholastic
Lady with the Alligator Purse	F	Westcott, Nadine Bernard	Little, Brown
Last Puppy, The	K	Asch, Frank	Simon & Schuster
Late for Soccer (Football)	F	PM Books	Rigby
Late One Night	D	Mader, Jan	Kaeden Books
Later, Rover	G	Ziefert, Harriet	Puffin Books
Laughing Cake, The	G	Reading Corners	Dominie Press
Laura Ingalls Wilder, Pioneer Girl	R	Stine, Megan	Dell Publishing
Lavender the Library Cat	L	Read Alongs	Rigby

Title	Level	Author/Series	Publisher/Distributor
Lazy Lions Lucky Lambs	M	Giff, Patricia Reilly	Dell Publishing
Lazy Mary	D	Read-Togethers	Wright Group
Lazy Pig, The	C	PM Books	Rigby
Leaf Rain	F	Book Bank	Wright Group
Legs	A	Twig	Wright Group
Leo the Late Bloomer	I	Kraus, Robert	Simon & Schuster
Let Me In	I	Storybox	Wright Group
Let's Be Enemies	J	Sendak, Maurice	Harper & Row
Let's Get Moving!	M	Literacy 2000	Rigby
Let's Go	C	Windmill-Look & Listen	Wright Group
Let's Go	A	Reading Corners	Dominie Press
Let's Have a Swim	C	Sunshine	Wright Group
Let's Play Basketball	E	Geddes, Diana	Kaeden Books
Let's Take the Bus	H	Real Reading	Steck-Vaughn
Letter to Amy, A	K	Keats, Ezra Jack	Harper & Row
Letters for Mr. James	H	Sunshine	Wright Group
Library, The	C	Carousel Readers	Dominie Press
Licken Chicken	I	Tiger Cub	Peguis
Lift the Sky Up	H	Little Celebrations	Celebration Press
Light	A	Twig	Wright Group
Lin's Backpack	C	Little Celebrations	Celebration Press
Lion and the Mouse, The	G	PM Books	Rigby
Lion and the Mouse, The	G	Traditional Tales	Rigby
Lion and the Rabbit, The	F	PM Books	Rigby
Lion's Tail, The	F	Reading Unlimited	Celebration Press
Lionel at Large	K	Krensky, Stephen	Puffin Books
Little Bear	J	Minarik, E. H.	HarperCollins
Little Bear's Friend	J	Minarik, E. H.	HarperTrophy
Little Bear's Visit	J	Minarik, E. H.	HarperTrophy
Little Black, a Pony	J	Farley, Walter	Random House
Little Blue and Little Yellow	J	Lionni, Leo	Scholastic
Little Boy and the Balloon Man	E	Tiger Cub	Peguis
Little Brother	A	Sunshine	Wright Group
Little, Brown Jay: A Tale from India, The	L	Claire, Elizabeth	Mondo
Little Bulldozer Man	E	PM Books	Rigby
Little Car	F	Sunshine	Wright Group
Little Danny Dinosaur	G	First Start	Troll
Little Fireman	J	Brown, Margaret Wise	HarperCollins
Little Fish	C	Tiger Cub	Peguis
Little Fish That Got Away	I	Cook, Bernadine	Scholastic
Little Girl and Her Beetle, The	I	Literacy 2000	Rigby
Little Gorilla	J	Bornstein, Ruth	Clarion
Little Kid	H	Literacy 2000	Rigby
Little Knight, The	K	Reading Unlimited	Celebration Press
Little Miss Muffet	F	Literacy 2000	Rigby
Little Monkey Is Stuck	E	Foundations	Wright Group
Little Mouse's Trail Tale	I	Vandine, JoAnn	Mondo
Little Penguin's Tale	L	Wood, Audrey	Scholastic
Little Pig	C	Storybox	Wright Group
Little Red Bus, The	H	PM Books	Rigby
Little Red Hen, The	B	Windmill-Look & Listen	Wright Group
Little Red Hen, The	I	Traditional Tales	Rigby
Little Red Hen, The	J	Galdone, Paul	Viking
Little Seed, A	B	Smart Start	Rigby

Title	Level	Author/Series	Publisher/Distributor
Little Spider, The	L	Literacy 2000	Rigby
Little Swan	M	Geras, Adele	Random House
Little Things	A	PM Starters One	Rigby
Little Tuppen	I	Galdone, Paul	Houghton Mifflin
Little Women	M	Bullseye	Random House
Little Yellow Chicken, The	I	Sunshine	Wright Group
Littles, The	M	Peterson, John	Scholastic
Lizard	E	Foundations	Wright Group
Lizard Loses His Tail	D	PM Books	Rigby
Lizard on a Stick	C	Wonder World	Wright Group
Lizards and Salamanders	M	Reading Unlimited	Celebration Press
Llama Pajamas	N	Clymer, Susan	Scholastic
Locked Out	G	PM Books	Rigby
Lola and Miss Kitty	H	Little Readers	Houghton Mifflin
Lollipop	G	Watson, Wendy	Crowell
Lonely Giant, The	K	Literacy 2000	Rigby
Long, Long Tail, The	B	Sunshine	Wright Group
Look	A	Sunshine	Wright Group
Look Again	C	Montgomery, Charlotte	Mondo
Look at Me	B	PM Starters One	Rigby
Look at Me	F	Literacy 2000	Rigby
Look at This	B	Carousel Earlybirds	Dominie Press
Look for Me	D	Storybox	Wright Group
Look for Me	G	Little Readers	Houghton Mifflin
Look in Mom's Purse	D	Carousel Readers	Dominie Press
Look Out!	B	Literacy 2000	Rigby
Look Out for Your Tail	J	Literacy 2000	Rigby
Look What I Can Do	A	Aruego, Jose	Macmillan
Looking After Grandpa	D	Foundations	Wright Group
Looking Down	C	PM Starters Two	Rigby
Looking for Halloween	C	Urmston, K. & Evans, K.	Kaeden Books
Loose Laces	L	Reading Unlimited	Celebration Press
Loose Tooth, The	H	Breakthrough	Longman/Bow
Lost	A	TOTTS	TOTTS
Lost	C	Storybox	Wright Group
Lost!	B	Smart Start	Rigby
Lost and Found	D	Carousel Readers	Dominie Press
Lost Glove, The	C	Foundations	Wright Group
Lost Sheep, The	I	Little Readers	Houghton Mifflin
Lots of Things	A	Reading Corners	Dominie Press
Lucky Baseball Bat, The	M	Christopher, Matt	Little, Brown
Lucky Feather, The	L	Literacy 2000	Rigby
Lucky Goes to Dog School	E	PM Books	Rigby
Lucky Stone, The	P	Clifton, Lucille	Dell Publishing
Lucky We Have a Station Wagon	F	Foundations	Wright Group
Lucy Meets a Dragon	L	Literacy 2000	Rigby
Lucy's Sore Knee	F	Windmill-Look & Listen	Wright Group
Lump in My Bed, A	D	Book Bank	Wright Group
Lunch	F	Urmston, K. & Evans, K.	Kaeden Books
Lunch Orders	C	Tadpoles	Rigby
Lunch Time	C	Carousel Readers	Dominie Press
Lydia and Her Cat	G	Oxford Reading Tree	Oxford
Lydia and the Ducks	G	Oxford Reading Tree	Oxford
Lydia and the Present	F	Oxford Reading Tree	Oxford

Title	Level	Author/Series	Publisher/Distributor
Madeline	K	Bemelmans, L.	Scholastic
Madeline's Rescue	K	Bemelmans, L.	Scholastic
Magic	A	Twig	Wright Group
Magic All Around	L	Literacy 2000	Rigby
Magic Box, The	K	Brenner, Barbara	Bantam
Magic Finger, The	N	Dahl, Roald	Puffin Books
Magic Fish	L	Littledale, Freya	Scholastic
Magic Food	C	Smart Start	Rigby
Magic Machine	C	Sunshine	Wright Group
Magpie's Baking Day	F	PM Books	Rigby
Mai Li's Surprise	F	Books for Young Learners	Richard C. Owen
Mail Came Today, The	C	Carousel Readers	Dominie Press
Major Jump	B	Sunshine	Wright Group
Make a Wish, Molly	O	Cohen, Barbara	Dell Publishing
Make Way for Ducklings	L	McCloskey, Robert	Puffin Books
Making Friends on Beacon Street	M	Literacy 2000	Rigby
Making Oatmeal	E	Interaction	Rigby
Making Pancakes	D	Carousel Readers	Dominie Press
Making Pictures	B	Foundations	Wright Group
Making Things	D	Foundations	Wright Group
Man Out at First	M	Christopher, Matt	Little, Brown
Manly Ferry Pigeon, The	L	Sunshine	Wright Group
Marcella	L	Literacy 2000	Rigby
Marching Band	B	Urmston, K. & Evans, K.	Kaeden Books
Maria Goes to School	D	Foundations	Wright Group
Mark's Monster	I	Reading Unlimited	Celebration Press
Marmalade's Nap	F	Wheeler, Cindy	Knopf
Marmalade's Snowy Day	F	Wheeler, Cindy	Knopf
Martian Goo	E	Salem, L. & Stewart, J.	Seedling
Martians Don't Take Temperatures	M	Dadey, D. & Jones, M.	Scholastic
Martin and the Teacher's Pets	K	Chardiet & Maccarone	Scholastic
Martin and the Tooth Fairy	K	Chardiet & Maccarone	Scholastic
Martin Luther King, Jr.	N	Greene, Carol	Children's Press
Marvin Redpost: Kidnapped at Birth?	L	Sachar, Louis	Random House
Marvin Redpost: Why Pick on Me?	L	Sachar, Louis	Random House
Mary Wore Her Dress	D	Peek, Merle	Clarion
Math Is Everywhere	F	Sunshine	Wright Group
Matilda	O	Dahl, Roald	Puffin Books
Matthew Likes to Read	J	Ready to Read	Richard C. Owen/ Celebration Press
Matthew's Tantrum	J	Literacy 2000	Rigby
Maui and the Sun	M	Ready to Read	Richard C. Owen/ Celebration Press
Max	J	Isadora, Rachel	Macmillan
Max's Box	B	Little Celebrations	Celebration Press
May I Stay Home Today?	E	Tadpoles	Rigby
Maybe I'll Be	D	Carousel Readers	Dominie Press
Maybe Yes, Maybe No, Maybe Maybe	M	Patron, Susan	Dell Publishing
Me	A	PM Starters	Rigby
Me	C	Reading Corners	Dominie Press
Me Too	K	Mayer, Mercer	Donovan
Meanies	F	Read-Togethers	Wright Group
Meet My Mouse	H	Little Celebrations	Celebration Press
Meg and Mog	J	Nicoll, Helen	Viking

Title	Level	Author/Series	Publisher/Distributor
Melting	F	Bolton, Faye	Mondo
Merry-Go-Round	C	Sunshine	Wright Group
Merry-Go-Round, The	C	PM Books	Rigby
Messy Bessy	I	Rookie Reader	Children's Press
Messy Mark	F	First Start	Troll
Messy Monsters, The	G	Carousel Readers	Dominie Press
Mice	H	Literacy 2000	Rigby
Mick and Max	G	Carousel Readers	Dominie Press
Midge in the Hospital	E	Oxford Reading Tree	Oxford
Mike and Tony: Best Friends	G	Ziefert, Harriet	Penguin
Mike's First Haircut	G	First Start	Troll
Mike's New Bike	F	First Start	Troll
Milton the Early Riser	J	Kraus, Robert	Simon & Schuster
Mine's the Best	G	Bonsall, Crosby	HarperCollins
Misha Disappears	K	Literacy 2000	Rigby
Mishi-Na	I	Sunshine	Wright Group
Miss Mouse Gets Married	K	Folk Tales	Wright Group
Miss Nelson Is Missing	L	Allard, Harry	Houghton Mifflin
Miss Popple's Pets	A	Literacy 2000	Rigby
Missing Necklace, The	H	Reading Unlimited	Celebration Press
Misty's Mischief	H	Campbell, Rod	Viking
Mitten, The	M	Brett, Jan	Scholastic
Moccasins	A	Twig	Wright Group
Model, The	B	Smart Start	Rigby
Mog at the Zoo	L	Nicoll, Helen	Penguin
Mog's Mumps	L	Nicoll, Helen	Penguin
Mollie Whuppie	K	New Way	Steck-Vaughn
Molly's Pilgrim	M	Cohen, Barbara	Dell Publishing
Mom	A	PM Starters	Rigby
Mom Can Fix Anything	D	Learn to Read	Creative Teaching Press
Mom's Birthday	I	Sunshine	Wright Group
Mom's Diet	I	Sunshine	Wright Group
Mom's New Car	D	Foundations	Wright Group
Mommy, Where Are You?	B	Ziefert & Boon	Puffin Books
Moms and Dads	A	PM Starters	Rigby
Monarch Butterfly, The	I	Foundations	Wright Group
Monkey and Fire	J	Literacy 2000	Rigby
Monkey Bridge, The	D	Sunshine	Wright Group
Monkey See, Monkey Do	F	Hello Reader	Scholastic
Monkeys	G	Reading Unlimited	Celebration Press
Monster	I	Read Alongs	Rigby
Monster and the Baby	D	Mueller, Virginia	Whitman
Monster Bus	H	Monster Bus Series	Dominie Press
Monster Can't Sleep	D	Mueller, Virginia	Puffin Books
Monster for Hire	M	Wilson, Trevor	Mondo
Monster from the Sea, The	K	Bank Street	Bantam
Monster Meals	C	Literacy 2000	Rigby
Monster, Monster	C	Reading Corners	Dominie Press
Monster Movie	K	Cole, Joanna	Scholastic
Monster of Mirror Mountain, The	K	Literacy 2000	Rigby
Monster Party	A	Literacy 2000	Rigby
Monster Rabbit Runs Amuck!	M	Giff, Patricia Reilly	Dell Publishing
Monster Sandwich, A	C	Storybox	Wright Group
Monster's Party, The	C	Read-Togethers	Wright Group

Title	Level	Author/Series	Publisher/Distributor
Monsters Don't Scuba Dive	M	Dadey, Debbie	Scholastic
Moon Boy	J	Bank Street	Bantam
Moose Is Loose, A	F	Little Readers	Houghton Mifflin
More and More Clowns	D	Allen, R.V.	SRA/McGraw Hill
More Spaghetti I Say	G	Gelman, Rita	Scholastic
More Stories Julian Tells	N	Cameron, Ann	Random House
More Tales of Amanda Pig	J	Van Leeuwen, Jean	Penguin
More Tales of Oliver Pig	J	Van Leeuwen, Jean	Penguin
Morning Star	J	Literacy 2000	Rigby
Mosquito Buzzed, A	E	Little Readers	Houghton Mifflin
Most Wonderful Doll in the World	O	McGinley, Phyllis	Scholastic
Mother Hen	G	Book Bank	Wright Group
Mother Hippopotamus Goes Shopping	C	Foundations	Wright Group
Mother Hippopotamus's Dry Skin	D	Foundations	Wright Group
Mountain Gorillas	N	Wonder World	Wright Group
Mouse	C	Storybox	Wright Group
Mouse and the Elephant, The	J	Little Readers	Houghton Mifflin
Mouse Soup	J	Lobel, Arnold	HarperCollins
Mouse Tales	J	Lobel, Arnold	Harper & Row
Mouse Who Wanted to Marry, The	J	Bank Street	Bantam
Mouse's Baby Blanket	D	Brown, Beverly Swerdlow	Seedling
Moving	B	Little Red Readers	Sundance
Moving Day	E	Sunshine	Wright Group
Moving In	D	Foundations	Wright Group
Moving to America	E	Carousel Readers	Dominie Press
Mr. Clutterbus	H	Voyages	SRA/McGraw Hill
Mr. Cricket Finds a Friend	G	Carousel Readers	Dominie Press
Mr. Cricket's New Home	F	Carousel Readers	Dominie Press
Mr. Fixit	H	Sunshine	Wright Group
Mr. Grump	D	Sunshine	Wright Group
Mr. Gumpy's Motor Car	K	Burningham, John	HarperCollins
Mr. Gumpy's Outing	L	Burningham, John	Holt
Mr. Noisy	D	Learn to Read	Creative Teaching Press
Mr. Pepperpot's Pet	K	Literacy 2000	Rigby
Mr. Putter and Tabby Bake the Cake	J	Rylant, Cynthia	Harcourt Brace
Mr. Putter and Tabby Pick and Pears	J	Rylant, Cynthia	Harcourt Brace
Mr. Putter and Tabby Pour the Tea	J	Rylant, Cynthia	Harcourt Brace
Mr. Putter and Tabby Walk the Dog	J	Rylant, Cynthia	Harcourt Brace
Mr. Sun and Mr. Sea	I	Little Celebrations	Celebration Press
Mr. Whisper	H	Sunshine	Wright Group
Mr. Wumple's Travels	I	Read Alongs	Rigby
Mrs. Bold	F	Literacy 2000	Rigby
Mrs. Brice's Mice	J	Hoff, Syd	HarperTrophy
Mrs. Bubble's Baby	M	Ready to Read	Richard C. Owen/ Celebration Press
Mrs. Grindy's Shoes	I	Sunshine	Wright Group
Mrs. Huggins and Her Hen Hannah	K	Dabcovich, Lydia	Dutton
Mrs. Muddle's Mud-Puddle	I	Sunshine	Wright Group
Mrs. Murphy's Bears	I	Little Readers	Houghton Mifflin
Mrs. Sato's Hen	E	Little Celebrations	Celebration Press
Mrs. Spider's Beautiful Web	H	PM Books	Rigby
Mrs. Wishy-Washy	E	Storybox	Wright Group
Much Ado About Aldo	O	Hurwitz, Johanna	Puffin Books
Mud	D	Lewison, Wendy	Random House

Title	Level	Author/Series	Publisher/Distributor
Mud Pie	C	Literacy 2000	Rigby
Muffy and Fluffy	F	First Start	Troll
Muggie Maggie	O	Cleary, Beverly	Avon Camelot
Mumps	D	PM Books	Rigby
Munching Mark	G	Tadpoles	Rigby
Mushrooms for Dinner	G	PM Books	Rigby
My Accident	C	PM Starters Two	Rigby
My Best Friend	I	Hutchins, Pat	Greenwillow
My Best Friend	C	Little Celebrations	Celebration Press
My Big Box	D	Voyages	SRA/McGraw Hill
My Big Wheel	C	Visions	Wright Group
My Bike	D	Ready to Read	Richard C. Owen/ Celebration Press
My Birthday Party	A	Little Readers	Houghton Mifflin
My Birthday Party	C	Visions	Wright Group
My Boat	G	Sunshine	Wright Group
My Book	A	Maris, Ron	Viking
My Box	A	Literacy 2000	Rigby
My Brother, the Brat	E	Hello Reader	Scholastic
My Brown Bear Barney	H	Butler, Dorothy	Morrow
My Cat	H	Taylor, Judy	Macmillan
My Circus Family	C	Lake, Mary Dixon	Mondo
My Class	A	Stewart, J. & Salem, L.	Seedling
My Clothes	C	Carousel Earlybirds	Dominie Press
My Dad	F	Talk About Books	Dominie Press
My Dad Cooks	C	Carousel Readers	Dominie Press
My Dad Lost His Job	E	Carousel Readers	Dominie Press
My Dog	G	Taylor, Judy	Macmillan
My Dog Willy	C	Little Readers	Houghton Mifflin
My Doll	E	Yukish, Joe	Kaeden Books
My Dream	C	Wildsmith, Brian	Oxford
My Family	A	Sunshine	Wright Group
My Father	J	Mayer, Laura	Scholastic
My Father's Dragon	M	Stiles Gannett, Ruth	Random House
My Friend	B	Sunshine	Wright Group
My Friend Alan	D	Carousel Readers	Dominie Press
My Friend at School	C	Visions	Wright Group
My Friend Goes Left	F	Gregorich	School Zone
My Friends	D	Little Celebrations	Celebration Press
My Garden	B	Beginning Literacy	Scholastic
My Grandpa	F	Mitchell, Greg	Mondo
My Holiday Diary	F	Hall, N. & Robinson, A.	Nelson/Michaels Assoc.
My Home	B	Sunshine	Wright Group
My Home	C	Storybox	Wright Group
My Home	A	Literacy 2000	Rigby
My Home	C	Sunshine	Wright Group
My House	A	Carousel Earlybirds	Dominie Press
My Kitchen	F	Rockwell, Harlow	Morrow
My Little Brother	C	Windmill-Look & Listen	Wright Group
My Little Dog	C	PM Starters Two	Rigby
My Messy Room	D	Hello Reader	Scholastic
My Mom	F	Talk About Books	Dominie Press
My New Boy	F	Step into Reading	Random House
My New House	C	Reading Corners	Dominie Press

Title	Level	Author/Series	Publisher/Distributor
My New Pet	F	Little Readers	Houghton Mifflin
My Pet	D	Salem, L. & Stewart, J.	Seedling
My Pet Bobby	E	Little Readers	Houghton Mifflin
My Picture	C	Carousel Readers	Dominie Press
My Planet	A	Smart Start	Rigby
My Puppy	B	Sunshine	Wright Group
My Puppy	C	Little Celebrations	Celebration Press
My Room	A	Carousel Earlybirds	Dominie Press
My School	B	Little Readers	Houghton Mifflin
My Secret Hiding Place	G	First Start	Troll
My Secret Place	G	Wonder World	Wright Group
My Shadow	C	Sunshine	Wright Group
My Shadow	C	Foundations	Wright Group
My Shadow	A	Book Bank	Wright Group
My Skateboard	D	Carousel Readers	Dominie Press
My Sloppy Tiger	I	Sunshine	Wright Group
My Sloppy Tiger Goes to School	J	Sunshine	Wright Group
My Story	A	Wonder World	Wright Group
My Tiger Cat	E	Frankford, Marilyn	Kaeden Books
My Tower	A	Windmill-Look & Listen	Wright Group
My Treasure Garden	J	Book Bank	Wright Group
My Two Homes	E	Carousel Readers	Dominie Press
My Very Hungry Pet	F	Reading Corners	Dominie Press
My Wonderful Chair	F	Windmill-Look & Listen	Wright Group
Mystery of Pony Hollow, The	N	Hall, Lynn	Random House
Mystery of the Phantom Pony, The	N	Hall, Lynn	Random House
Mystery of the Pirate Ghost, The	L	Hayes, Geoffrey	Random House
Mystery Seeds	L	Reading Unlimited	Celebration Press
Nana's in the Plum Tree	M	Ready to Read	Richard C. Owen
Nate the Great	K	Sharmat, M. Weinman	Dell Publishing
Nate the Great and the Boring Beach Bag	K	Sharmat, M. Weinman	Dell Publishing
Nate the Great and the Fishy Prize	K	Sharmat, M. Weinman	Dell Publishing
Nate the Great and the Halloween Hunt	K	Sharmat, M. Weinman	Dell Publishing
Nate the Great and the Lost List	K	Sharmat, M. Weinman	Dell Publishing
Nate the Great and the Missing Key	K	Sharmat, M. Weinman	Dell Publishing
Nate the Great and the Mushy Valentine	K	Sharmat, M. Weinman	Dell Publishing
Nate the Great and the Musical Note	K	Sharmat, M. Weinman	Dell Publishing
Nate the Great and the Phony Clue	K	Sharmat, M. Weinman	Dell Publishing
Nate the Great and the Pillowcase	K	Sharmat, M. Weinman	Dell Publishing
Nate the Great and the Snowy Trail	K	Sharmat, M. Weinman	Dell Publishing
Nate the Great and the Sticky Case	K	Sharmat, M. Weinman	Dell Publishing
Nate the Great and the Stolen Base	K	Sharmat, M. Weinman	Dell Publishing
Nate the Great Goes Down in the Dumps	K	Sharmat, M. Weinman	Dell Publishing
Nate the Great Goes Undercover	K	Sharmat, M. Weinman	Dell Publishing
Nate the Great Stalks Stupidweed	K	Sharmat, M. Weinman	Dell Publishing
Nathan & Nicholas Alexander	K	Delacre, Lulu	Scholastic
Nature's Celebration	M	Literacy 2000	Rigby
Naughty Ann, The	G	PM Books	Rigby
Naughty Kitten!	A	Smart Start	Rigby
Naughty Patch	D	Foundations	Wright Group

Title	Level	Author/Series	Publisher/Distributor
Nests	E	Literacy 2000	Rigby
Never Be	D	Salem, L. & Stewart, J.	Seedling
Never Snap at a Bubble	G	Giant Step Readers	Educ. Insights
New Baby, The	E	PM Books	Rigby
New Building, The	H	Sunshine	Wright Group
New Cat, The	B	Ready to Read	Richard C. Owen
New House for Mole and Mouse, A	G	Ziefert, Harriet	Penguin
New Nest, The	E	Foundations	Wright Group
Next Spring an Oriole	N	Whelan, Gloria	Random House
Next Time I Will	K	Bank Street	Bantam
Nice New Neighbors	K	Brandenberg, Franz	Scholastic
Nick's Glasses	E	Ready to Read	Richard C. Owen/ Celebration Press
Nicky Upstairs and Downstairs	G	Ziefert, Harriet	Penguin
Night in the Desert	D	Carousel Readers	Dominie Press
Night the Lights Went Out, The	H	Little Readers	Houghton Mifflin
Night Train, The	E	Storybox	Wright Group
Night Walk	F	Books for Young Learners	Richard C. Owen
Nighttime	C	Storybox	Wright Group
Nine Men Chase a Hen	G	Gregorich	School Zone
No Ball Games Here	H	Ziefert, Harriet	Penguin
No Jumping on the Bed!	L	Arnold, Tedd	Scholastic
No Luck	F	Stewart, J. & Salem, L.	Seedling
No No	D	Storybox	Wright Group
No One Is Going to Nashville	O	Jukes, Mavis	Bullseye Books
No Room for a Dog	N	Kane Nichols, Joan	Avon Books
Nobody Knew My Name	G	Foundations	Wright Group
Nobody Listens to Andrew	I	Guilfoile, Elizabeth	Modern Curriculum
Noise	G	Sunshine	Wright Group
Noisy Breakfast	D	Blonder, Ellen	Scholastic
Noisy Nora	I	Wells, Rosemary	Scholastic
Nose Book	E	Perkins, Al	Random House
Not Me, Said the Monkey	G	West, Colin	Harper & Row
Not Now! Said the Cow	J	Bank Street	Bantam
Not Yet	D	Reading Links	Steck-Vaughn
Notes from Mom	F	Salem, L. & Stewart, J.	Seedling
Notes to Dad	F	Stewart, J. & Salem, L.	Seedling
Nothing in the Mailbox	F	Books for Young Learners	Richard C. Owen
Now I Am Five	I	Sunshine	Wright Group
Now I Ride	D	Carousel Readers	Dominie Press
Now Listen, Stanley	K	Literacy 2000	Rigby
Now We Can Go	C	Jonas, Ann	Greenwillow
Nowhere and Nothing	I	Sunshine	Wright Group
Number One	J	Ready to Read	Richard C. Owen/ Celebration Press
Oatmeal	F	Wonder World	Wright Group
Obadiah	G	Read-Togethers	Wright Group
Obstacle Course, The	H	Foundations	Wright Group
Octopus Goes to School	C	Bordelon, Carolyn	Seedling
Octopuses and Squids	N	Wonder World	Wright Group
Oh Dear	F	Campbell, Rod	Macmillan
Oh, Jump in the Sack	E	Storybox	Wright Group
Oh, No!	G	Little Celebrations	Celebration Press

Title	Level	Author/Series	Publisher/Distributor
Oh, No, Sherman	E	Erickson, Betty	Seedling
Oh, What a Daughter!	L	Literacy 2000	Rigby
Old and New	C	Interaction	Rigby
Old Car, The	F	Voyages	SRA/McGraw Hill
Old Grizzly	H	Sunshine	Wright Group
Old Hat, New Hat	H	Berenstain, Stan & Jan	Random House
Old Mother Hubbard	H	Literacy 2000	Rigby
Old Oak Tree, The	F	Little Celebrations	Celebration Press
Old Red Rocking Chair, The	M	Root, Phyllis	Scholastic
Old Teeth, New Teeth	F	Wonder World	Wright Group
Old Tuatara	C	Ready to Read	Richard C. Owen/ Celebration Press
Old Woman and the Pig, The	I	Tiger Cub	Peguis
Oliver	H	Kraus, Robert	Simon & Schuster
On a Chair	C	Storybox	Wright Group
On a Cold, Cold Day	C	Tadpoles	Rigby
On Friday the Giant	K	The Giant	Wright Group
On Monday the Giant	K	The Giant	Wright Group
On Safari	A	Smart Start	Rigby
On Sunday the Giant	K	The Giant	Wright Group
On the Beach	B	Smart Start	Rigby
On the Farm	C	Literacy 2000	Rigby
On the Go	C	Learn to Read	Creative Teaching Press
On the School Bus	F	Little Readers	Houghton Mifflin
On Thursday the Giant	K	The Giant	Wright Group
On Top of Spaghetti	G	Little Celebrations	Celebration Press
On Tuesday the Giant	K	The Giant	Wright Group
On Vacation	D	Little Red Readers	Sundance
On Wednesday the Giant	K	The Giant	Wright Group
Once When I Was Shipwrecked	L	Literacy 2000	Rigby
One Bear All Alone	H	Bucknall, Caroline	Dial
One Bird Sat on the Fence	C	Wonder World	Wright Group
One Cold Wet Night	D	Read-Togethers	Wright Group
One Day in the Tropical Rain Forest	P	Craighead George, Jean	HarperTrophy
One Day in the Woods	P	Craighead George, Jean	HarperTrophy
One Eyed Jake	M	Hutchins, Pat	Morrow
One Hunter	A	Hutchins, Pat	Greenwillow
One in the Middle is a Green Kangaroo, The	M	Blume, Judy	Dell Yearling
One Monday Morning	G	Shulevitz, Uri	Scribner
One, One is the Sun	B	Storybox	Wright Group
One Pig, Two Pigs	B	Tiger Cub	Peguis
One Sock, Two Socks	H	Reading Corners	Dominie Press
One Stormy Night	F	Story Basket	Wright Group
One Sun in the Sky	E	Windmill-Look & Listen	Wright Group
One Thousand Currant Buns	H	Sunshine	Wright Group
Only an Octopus	H	Literacy 2000	Rigby
Oogly Gum Chasing Game, The	K	Literacy 2000	Rigby
Oops!	D	Mayer, Mercer	Penguin
Otto the Cat	J	Herman, Gail	Grosset & Dunlap
Ouch!	A	Literacy 2000	Rigby
Our Baby	B	Literacy 2000	Rigby
Our Cat	E	Foundations	Wright Group
Our Dog Sam	C	Literacy 2000	Rigby

Title	Level	Author/Series	Publisher/Distributor
Our Garage	F	Urmston, K. & Evans, K.	Kaeden Books
Our Grandad	C	Sunshine	Wright Group
Our Granny	C	Sunshine	Wright Group
Our House Had a Mouse	E	Worthington, Denise	Seedling
Our Pumpkin	B	Learn to Read	Creative Teaching Press
Our Street	C	Sunshine	Wright Group
Our Teacher, Miss Pool	D	Ready to Read	Richard C. Owen/ Celebration Press
Out in the Weather	B	PM Starters Two	Rigby
Out the Door	E	Rookie Reader	Children's Press
Over in the Meadow	G	Little Readers	Houghton Mifflin
Over in the Meadow	L	Galdone, Paul	Simon & Schuster
Over the Bridge	B	Little Red Readers	Sundance
Owl and the Pussy Cat	L	Lear, Edward	Scholastic
Owl at Home	J	Lobel, Arnold	HarperCollins
Packing	B	Foundations	Wright Group
Packing My Bag	B	PM Starters Two	Rigby
Painters	A	Twig	Wright Group
Painting	C	Storybox	Wright Group
Pancake, The	K	Lobel, Anita	Dell Publishing
Pancakes	G	Foundations	Wright Group
Pancakes, Crackers and Pizza	C	Rookie Reader	Children's Press
Panda's Surprise	H	Little Readers	Houghton Mifflin
Pandora's Box	Q	Literacy 2000	Rigby
Paper Bag Trail	E	Beginning Literacy	Scholastic
Pardon? Said the Giraffe	F	West, Colin	Harper & Row
Party, A	A	Storybox	Wright Group
Paru Has a Bath	J	Ready to Read	Richard C. Owen/ Celebration Press
Pat, Pat, Pat	B	Book Bank	Wright Group
Pat's New Puppy	E	Reading Unlimited	Celebration Press
Patches	M	Szymanski, Lois	Avon Camelot
Paul	F	Ready to Read	Richard C. Owen/ Celebration Press
Paul and Lucy	J	Stepping Stones	Nelson/Michaels Assoc.
Paul the Pitcher	D	Rookie Reader	Children's Press
Peaches the Pig	E	Little Readers	Houghton Mifflin
Peanut Butter and Jelly	E	Little Readers	Houghton Mifflin
Pee Wee Scouts: Cookies and Crutches	L	Delton, Judy	Dell Publishing
Pee Wees on First	L	Delton, Judy	Dell Publishing
Pee Wees on Parade	L	Delton, Judy	Dell Publishing
Pee Wees on Skis	L	Delton, Judy	Dell Publishing
Pencil, The	B	PM Starters Two	Rigby
People on the Beach	F	Carousel Readers	Dominie Press
Pepper's Adventure	H	PM Books	Rigby
Perfect the Pig	L	Jeschke, Susan	Scholastic
Pet for You	J	Story Starter	Wright Group
Pet Parade	C	Literacy 2000	Rigby
Pet That I Want, The	E	Hello Reader	Scholastic
Pete Little	G	PM Books	Rigby
Pete the Parakeet	F	First Start	Troll
Pete's New Shoes	G	Literacy 2000	Rigby

Title	Level	Author/Series	Publisher/Distributor
Pete's Story	L	Literacy 2000	Rigby
Peter and the North Wind	K	Littledale, Freya	Scholastic
Peter's Chair	J	Keats, Ezra Jack	HarperTrophy
Peter's Move	H	Little Readers	Houghton Mifflin
Peter's Painting	F	Moss, Sally	Mondo
Pets	J	Ready to Read	Richard C. Owen/ Celebration Press
Pets	A	PM Starters	Rigby
Pets	F	Literacy 2000	Rigby
Photo Book, The	C	PM Books	Rigby
Pick a Pet	C	Little Celebrations	Celebration Press
Picking Apples and Pumpkins	L	Hutchins, A. & R.	Scholastic
Pickle Puss	L	Giff, Patricia Reilly	Dell Publishing
Picnic	A	Book Bank	Wright Group
Picnic Tea	I	Bridges	Nelson/Michaels Assoc.
Picnic, The	G	Wonder World	Wright Group
Picture for Harold's Room, A	H	Johnson, Crockett	HarperCollins
Pied Piper of Hamelin, The	K	Hautzig, Deborah	Random House
Pig William's Midnight Walk	H	Book Bank	Wright Group
Piggle	K	Bonsall, Crosby	HarperCollins
Pigs Peek	C	Books for Young Learners	Richard C. Owen
Pinky and Rex	L	Howe, James	Avon Books
Pinky and Rex and the Mean Old Witch	L	Howe, James	Avon Books
Pinky and Rex and the Spelling Bee	L	Howe, James	Avon Books
Pioneer Bear	L	Sandin, Joan	Random House
Pioneer Cat	N	William H. Hooks	Random House
Pip and the Little Monkey	F	Oxford Reading Tree	Oxford
Pip at the Zoo	F	Oxford Reading Tree	Oxford
Pitty Pitty Pat	C	Little Celebrations	Celebration Press
Pizza for Dinner	H	Literacy 2000	Rigby
Pizza Party!	F	Hello Reader	Scholastic
Places	C	Little Red Readers	Sundance
Play Ball	A	Twig	Wright Group
Play Ball, Amelia Bedelia	L	Parish, Peggy	Scholastic
Play Ball, Kate	D	Giant First Step	Troll
Playhouse for Monster	C	Mueller, Virginia	Whitman
Playing	A	PM Starters One	Rigby
Plop	C	Storybox	Wright Group
Pocket for Corduroy, A	K	Freeman, Don	Scholastic
Polka Dots!	F	Little Celebrations	Celebration Press
Pony Pals: A Pony for Keeps	O	Betancourt, Jeanne	Scholastic
Pony Pals: A Pony in Trouble	O	Betancourt, Jeanne	Scholastic
Pony Pals: Give Me Back My Pony	O	Betancourt, Jeanne	Scholastic
Pony Pals: I Want a Pony	O	Betancourt, Jeanne	Scholastic
Pony Pals: Pony to the Rescue	O	Betancourt, Jeanne	Scholastic
Pony Pals: The Wild Pony	O	Betancourt, Jeanne	Scholastic
Pookie and Joe	K	Literacy 2000	Rigby
Pooped Troop, The	L	Delton, Judy	Dell Publishing
Poor Old Polly	F	Read-Togethers	Wright Group
Poor Sore Paw, The	I	Sunshine	Wright Group
Popcorn Book, The	K	Reading Unlimited	Celebration Press
Popcorn Shop, The	J	Low, Alice	Scholastic
Porcupine's Pajama Party	J	Harshman, Terry Webb	HarperTrophy

Title	Level	Author/Series	Publisher/Distributor
Postcard Pest, The	M	Giff, Patricia Reilly	Dell Publishing
Pot of Gold, The	I	Reading Unlimited	Celebration Press
Potatoes, Potatoes	H	Wonder World	Wright Group
Potter in Fiji, A	P	Wonder World	Wright Group
Powder Puff Puzzle, The	L	Giff, Patricia, Reilly	Dell Publishing
Praying Mantis, The	D	Ready to Read	Richard C. Owen/ Celebration Press
Present from Aunt Skidoo, The	M	Literacy 2000	Rigby
Present, The	E	Literacy 2000	Rigby
Pretty Good Magic	J	Dubowski, Cathy	Random House
Princess, the Mud Pies, and the Dragon, The	I	Little Readers	Houghton Mifflin
Prize for Purry, A	K	Literacy 2000	Rigby
Pterodactyl at the Airport	K	Wesley & the Dinosaurs	Wright Group
Pukeko Morning	G	Ready to Read	Richard C. Owen/ Celebration Press
Pumpkin House, The	J	Literacy 2000	Rigby
Pumpkin That Kim Carved, The	H	Little Readers	Houghton Mifflin
Pumpkin, The	E	Storybox	Wright Group
Puppet Show	F	First Start	Troll
Puppy Who Wanted a Boy, The	L	Thayer, Jane	Scholastic
Purple Is Part of a Rainbow	E	Rookie Reader	Children's Press
Put Me in the Zoo	H	Lopshire, Robert	Random House
Puzzle, The	B	Smart Start	Rigby
Quack, Quack, Quack	I	Sunshine	Wright Group
"Quack" Said the Billy Goat	H	Causley, Charles	Harper & Row
Queen's Parrot, The: A Play	J	Literacy 2000	Rigby
Quilt Story, The	L	Johnston & de Paola	Scholastic
Quilt, The	I	Jonas, Ann	Morrow
Rabbit Stew	L	Literacy 2000	Rigby
Rabbit, The	H	Burningham, John	Crowell
Rabbit's Birthday Kite	J	Bank Street	Bantam
Rabbits	M	Literacy 2000	Rigby
Race, The	B	Windmill-Look & Listen	Wright Group
Race, The	F	Little Readers	Houghton Mifflin
Race, The	C	Sunshine	Wright Group
Race, The	E	Little Celebrations	Celebration Press
Rain	C	Kalan, Robert	Greenwillow
Rain	B	Reading Corners	Dominie Press
Rain Puddle	J	Holl, Adelaide	Morrow
Rain, Rain	G	Ready to Read	Richard C. Owen/ Celebration Press
Rain, The	G	Foundations	Wright Group
Rainbow of My Own	I	Freeman, Don	Penguin
Raindrops	C	Beginning Literacy	Scholastic
Ralph S. Mouse	O	Cleary, Beverly	Avon Books
Ramona and Her Father	O	Cleary, Beverly	Avon Books
Ramona and Her Mother	O	Cleary, Beverly	Avon Books
Ramona Forever	O	Cleary, Beverly	Avon Books
Ramona Quimby, Age 8	O	Cleary, Beverly	Avon Books
Ramona the Brave	O	Cleary, Beverly	Avon Books
Ramona the Pest	O	Cleary, Beverly	Avon Books
Rap Party, The	F	Foundations	Wright Group

Title	Level	Author/Series	Publisher/Distributor
Rapid Robert Roadrunner	H	Reese, Bob	Children's Press
Rapunzel	L	Literacy 2000	Rigby
Ratty Tatty	H	Sunshine	Wright Group
Reading Is Everywhere	D	Sunshine	Wright Group
Ready Set Go	G	First Start	Troll
Ready Steady Jump	D	Ready to Read	Richard C. Owen/ Celebration Press
Rebus Bears, The	I	Bank Street	Bantam
Red and Blue Mittens	M	Reading Unlimited	Celebration Press
Red Is Best	I	Stinson, Kathy	Annick/Toronto
Red Ribbon Rosie	M	Marzollo, Jean	Random House
Red Rose, The	E	Read-Togethers	Wright Group
Red Socks and Yellow Socks	G	Sunshine	Wright Group
Reflections	I	Jonas, Ann	Morrow
Rescue, The	L	Ready to Read	Richard C. Owen/ Celebration Press
Return of Rinaldo, the Sly Fox	M	Scheffler, Ursel	North-South Books
Rex's Dance	E	Little Readers	Houghton Mifflin
Ribsy	O	Cleary, Beverly	Avon Books
Riddle Book	F	Reading Unlimited	Celebration Press
Ride in the Country, A	D	Carousel Readers	Dominie Press
Riding	C	Foundations	Wright Group
Rip Roaring Russell	M	Hurwitz, Johanna	Puffin Books
Rise and Shine, Mariko-chan	K	Tomioka, Chiyoko	Scholastic
River, The	D	Foundations	Wright Group
Road Work Ahead	I	Little Readers	Houghton Mifflin
Robber, The	B	Smart Start	Rigby
Robert, The Rose Horse	I	Heilbroner, Joan	Random House
Robot, The	A	Smart Start	Rigby
Rock Pools, The	B	PM Starters Two	Rigby
Rockets	C	Little Celebrations	Celebration Press
Rocks	D	Voyages	SRA/McGraw Hill
Roll Over!	C	Peek, Merle	Clarion
Roll Over	F	Gerstein, Mordicai	Crown
Roller Blades, The	F	Foundations	Wright Group
Roller Coaster Ride, The	G	Carousel Readers	Dominie Press
Roller Skates!	J	Hello Reader	Scholastic
Roly-Poly	I	Storybox	Wright Group
Rooster and the Weather Vane	H	First Start	Troll
Rose	F	Wheeler, Cindy	Knopf
Rosie at the Zoo	H	Ready to Read	Richard C. Owen/ Celebration Press
Rosie's Button Box	F	Bridges	Nelson/Michaels Assoc.
Rosie's House	K	Literacy 2000	Rigby
Rosie's Party	E	Little Readers	Houghton Mifflin
Rosie's Pool	G	Little Readers	Houghton Mifflin
Rosie's Story	L	Gogoll, Martine	Mondo
Rosie's Walk	F	Hutchins, Pat	Macmillan
Round and Round	C	Storybox	Wright Group
Row, Row, Row Your Boat	J	Bank Street	Bantam
Royal Baby-Sitters	J	Sunshine	Wright Group
Royal Family, The	A	Stewart, J. & Salem, L.	Seedling
Ruby the Copycat	K	Rathman, Peggy	Scholastic
Rum, Tum, Tum	E	Storybox	Wright Group

Title	Level	Author/Series	Publisher/Distributor
Rumpelstiltskin	M	Once Upon a Time	Wright Group
Run	B	Sunshine	Wright Group
Run! Run!	C	Vandine, JoAnn	Mondo
Runaway Ralph	O	Cleary, Beverly	Avon Books
Running	C	Foundations	Wright Group
Rupert and the Griffin	Q	Hurwitz, Johanna	Puffin Books
Russel Rides Again	M	Hurwitz, Johanna	Puffin Books
Russell Sprouts	M	Hurwitz, Johanna	Puffin Books
Sadie and the Snowman	L	Morgan, Allen	Scholastic
Safe Place, The	H	Ready to Read	Richard C. Owen/ Celebration Press
Safety	C	Interaction	Rigby
Salad Feast, A	D	Little Readers	Houghton Mifflin
Sally and the Daisy	C	PM Books	Rigby
Sally and the Elephant	C	Wonder World	Wright Group
Sally's Beans	D	PM Books	Rigby
Sally's Friends	F	PM Books	Rigby
Sally's New Shoes	B	PM Starters Two	Rigby
Sally's Red Bucket	E	PM Books	Rigby
Sam and the Firefly	J	Eastman, P. D.	Random House
Sam the Scarecrow	F	First Start	Troll
Sam Who Never Forgets	K	Rice, Eve	Morrow
Sam's Glasses	M	Literacy 2000	Rigby
Sam's Mask	E	Ready to Read	Richard C. Owen/ Celebration Press
Sam's Solution	K	Literacy 2000	Rigby
Sammy at the Farm	C	Urmston, K. & Evans, K.	Kaeden Books
Sammy's Supper	I	Reading Unlimited	Celebration Press
Samuel's Sprout	F	Little Celebrations	Celebration Press
Sand	E	Giant Step Readers	Educ. Insights
Sand	B	Voyages	SRA/McGraw Hill
Sand Picnic, The	E	New Way	Steck-Vaughn
Sandwich, The	C	Carousel Earlybirds	Dominie Press
Sandwiches	D	New Way	Steck-Vaughn
Sandy's Suitcase	K	Edwards, Elsy	SRA/McGraw Hill
Sarah Snail	E	Voyages	SRA/McGraw Hill
Saturday Morning	G	Ready to Read	Richard C. Owen/ Celebration Press
Say "Cheese"	L	Giff, Patricia, Reilly	Dell Publishing
Say Goodnight	G	Gregorich	School Zone
Say It, Sign It	G	Beginning Literacy	Scholastic
Scare-Kid	K	Literacy 2000	Rigby
Scarecrow	C	Literacy 2000	Rigby
Scaredy Cat	C	Learn to Read	Creative Teaching Press
Scaredy Cat Runs Away	D	Learn to Read	Creative Teaching Press
Scary Larry	G	Rookie Reader	Children's Press
Scat Said the Cat	D	Sunshine	Wright Group
School Bus	D	Crews, Donald	Morrow
School, The	E	Burningham, John	Crowell
School's Out	N	Hurwitz, Johanna	Scholastic
Schoolyard Mystery, The	L	Levy, Elizabeth	Scholastic
Scratch My Back	D	Foundations	Wright Group
Scrumptious Sundae	B	Literacy 2000	Rigby

Title	Level	Author/Series	Publisher/Distributor
Seagull Is Clever	E	PM Books	Rigby
Second Grade—Friends Again!	M	Cohen, Miriam	Scholastic
Second Grade Star	Q	Alberts, Nancy	Scholastic
Secret at the Polk Street School, The	M	Giff, Patricia Reilly	Dell Publishing
Secret Friend, The	E	Little Celebrations	Celebration Press
Secret of Spooky House	J	Sunshine	Wright Group
See You Tomorrow, Charles	J	Cohen, Miriam	Dell Publishing
Seed, The	D	Sunshine	Wright Group
Seed, The	A	Wonder World	Wright Group
Seesaw, The	C	Voyages	SRA/McGraw Hill
Selfish Giant, The	L	Literacy 2000	Rigby
Sense	D	Voyages	SRA/McGraw Hill
Seven Little Monsters	H	Sendak, Maurice	HarperCollins
Shadows	D	Literacy 2000	Rigby
Shape Walk	C	Little Celebrations	Celebration Press
Shapes	D	Carousel Readers	Dominie Press
Sharing	C	Literacy 2000	Rigby
Sharing Danny's Dad	G	Little Celebrations	Celebration Press
Sharing Time	D	Carousel Readers	Dominie Press
Shark in a Sack	C	Sunshine	Wright Group
Shark in School	N	Giff, Patricia Reilly	Dell Publishing
Sharks	L	Wonder World	Wright Group
She'll Be Coming Around the Mountain	J	Bank Street	Bantam
Sheep in a Jeep	G	Shaw, Nancy	Houghton Mifflin
Sheila Rae, the Brave	K	Henkes, Kevin	Scholastic
SHHH	F	Henkes, Kevin	Morrow
Shhhh!	G	Kline, Suzy	Whitman
Shine Sun	F	Rookie Reader	Children's Press
Shintaro's Umbrellas	I	Books for Young Learners	Richard C. Owen
Shoe Grabber, The	I	Read Alongs	Rigby
Shoes	F	Talk About Books	Dominie Press
Shoes	D	Book Bank	Wright Group
Shoo!	C	Sunshine	Wright Group
Shopping	D	Literacy 2000	Rigby
Shopping	C	Little Red Readers	Sundance
Shopping	A	Sunshine	Wright Group
Shopping	C	Interaction	Rigby
Shopping at the Mall	G	Urmston, K. & Evans, K.	Kaeden Books
Shopping at the Supermarket	B	Foundations	Wright Group
Shopping Mall, The	B	PM Starters One	Rigby
Shopping with a Crocodile	M	Ready to Read	Richard C. Owen/ Celebration Press
Shortest Kid in the World, The	K	Bliss, Corinne Demas	Random House
Shorty	M	Literacy 2000	Rigby
Show and Tell	G	First Start	Troll
Show-and-Tell Frog, The	J	Bank Street	Bantam
Show Time at the Polk Street School	M	Giff, Patricia Reilly	Dell Publishing
Sidetrack Sam	K	Literacy 2000	Rigby
Sidewalk Story	N	Mathis, Sharon Bell	Puffin Books
Sideways Stories from Wayside School	O	Sachar, Louis	Avon Books
Signs	B	Literacy 2000	Rigby
Signs	C	Little Celebrations	Celebration Press
Silent World, A	L	Literacy 2000	Rigby

Title	Level	Author/Series	Publisher/Distributor
Silly Old Possum	C	Storybox	Wright Group
Simply Sam	E	Voyages	SRA/McGraw Hill
Sing a Song	E	Read-Togethers	Wright Group
Sing to the Moon	K	Storybox	Wright Group
Sisters	E	Talk About Books	Dominie Press
Skating on Thin Ice	G	First Start	Troll
Skeleton on the Bus, The	J	Literacy 2000	Rigby
Skeletons Don't Play Tubas	M	Dadey, D. & Jones, M.	Scholastic
Skier, The	B	PM Starter	Rigby
SkyFire	J	Asch, Frank	Scholastic
SkyScraper, The	K	Little Red Readers	Sundance
Sleeping Out	D	Storybox	Wright Group
Slim, Shorty and the Mules	L	Reading Unlimited	Celebration Press
Sloppy Tiger and the Party	I	Sunshine	Wright Group
Sloppy Tiger Bedtime	I	Sunshine	Wright Group
Slug and Snails	H	Wonder World	Wright Group
Sly Fox and Red Hen	F	Hunia, Fran	Ladybird Books
Sly Fox and the Little Red Hen	F	Southgate	Ladybird Books
Small World, A	H	Sunshine	Wright Group
Smallest Cow in the World, The	K	Paterson, Katherine	HarperTrophy
Smallest Tree, The	K	Literacy 2000	Rigby
Smarty Pants	E	Read-Togethers	Wright Group
Smile	D	Read Alongs	Rigby
Smile, Baby	F	Little Readers	Houghton Mifflin
Snaggle Doodles	M	Giff, Patricia Reilly	Dell Publishing
Snail Saves the Day	G	Stadler, John	HarperCollins
Snails	E	Foundations	Wright Group
Snake Slithers, A	H	Reading Unlimited	Celebration Press
Snakes	A	Twig	Wright Group
Snap	B	Sunshine	Wright Group
Snow	H	Young Writers' World	Nelson/Michaels Assoc.
Snow Goes to Town	L	Literacy 2000	Rigby
Snow Joe	D	Rookie Reader	Children's Press
Snow, The	G	Burningham, John	Crowell
Snow Walk	D	Reading Corners	Dominie Press
Snowflakes	D	Urmston, K. & Evans, K.	Kaeden Books
Snowman	A	Smart Start	Rigby
Snowshoe Thompson	K	Smiler Levinson, N.	HarperTrophy
Snowy Day, The	J	Keats, Ezra Jack	Scholastic
Soap Soup and Other Verses	K	Kuskin, Karla	HarperTrophy
Soccer Game!	F	Hello Readers	Scholastic
Soccer Sam	M	Marzollo, Jean	Random House
Socks	O	Cleary, Beverly	Avon Books
Socks	A	Smart Start	Rigby
Some Dogs Don't	B	Tiger Cub	Peguis
Some People	D	Reading Corners	Dominie Press
Something New	D	Little Celebrations	Celebration Press
Something Soft for Danny Bear	M	Literacy 2000	Rigby
Something to Share	D	Carousel Readers	Dominie Press
Sometimes	A	Wonder World	Wright Group
Sometimes I'm Silly	C	Visions	Wright Group
Sometimes Things Change	G	Eastman, P. D.	Children's Press
Sophie's Chicken	H	Tadpoles	Rigby
Soup Can Telephone	I	Wonder World	Wright Group

Title	Level	Author/Series	Publisher/Distributor
Souvenirs	K	Literacy 2000	Rigby
Space	H	Sunshine	Wright Group
Space Ark, The	B	Sunshine	Wright Group
Space Journey	A	Sunshine	Wright Group
Space Race	J	Sunshine	Wright Group
Spaghetti Party, The	K	Bank Street	Bantam
Spaghetti, Spaghetti	G	Book Bank	Wright Group
Special Friend, A	F	Carousel Readers	Dominie Press
Special Things	G	Literacy 2000	Rigby
Spectacular Stone Soup	M	Giff, Patricia Reilly	Yearling
Speed Boat, The	D	Sunshine	Wright Group
Spider and the King, The	L	Literacy 2000	Rigby
Spider Can't Fly	G	Book Bank	Wright Group
Spider Man	M	Literacy 2000	Rigby
Spider, Spider	D	Sunshine	Wright Group
Spiders, Spiders Everywhere!	D	Learn to Read	Creative Teaching Press
Spinning Top	I	Wonder World	Wright Group
Splash	C	Foundations	Wright Group
Splish Splash	B	Windmill-Look & Listen	Wright Group
Splish Splash	D	Little Celebrations	Celebration Press
Splosh	C	Storybox	Wright Group
Spooky Pet	B	Smart Start	Rigby
Spot's Birthday	I	Hill, Eric	Putnam
Spot's First Walk	G	Hill, Eric	Putnam
Spots	E	Oxford Reading Tree	Oxford
Spots	E	Literacy 2000	Rigby
Spots	A	Smart Start	Rigby
Spots	B	Visions	Wright Group
Spots, Feathers and Curly Tails	C	Tafuri, Nancy	Morrow
Spy on Third Base, The	M	Christopher, Matt	Little, Brown
Squanto and the First Thanksgiving	L	Celsi, Teresa	Steck-Vaughn
Squire Takes a Wife, A	J	Ready Set Read	Steck-Vaughn
Ssh, Don't Wake the Baby	F	Voyages	SRA/McGraw Hill
Stables Are for Horses	I	Windmill-Rhyme & Rhythm	Wright Group
Stacy Says Good-Bye	M	Giff, Patricia Reilly	Dell Publishing
Stan the Hot Dog Man	K	Kessler, E. & L.	HarperTrophy
Star	M	Simon, Jo Ann	Random House
Staying with Grandma Norma	F	Salem L. & Stewart, J.	Seedling
Sticky Stanley	F	First Start	Troll
Stone Soup	J	McGovern, Ann	Scholastic
Stone Works	K	Wonder World	Wright Group
Stop	C	Storybox	Wright Group
Stop!	B	PM Starters	Rigby
Stop!	C	Wonder World	Wright Group
Stop That Rabbit	G	First Start	Troll
Stories Julian Tells, The	N	Cameron, Ann	Random House
Storm, The	B	Sunshine	Wright Group
Storm, The	D	Foundations	Wright Group
Storm, The	C	Storybox	Wright Group
Story of Chicken Licken	I	Ormerod, Jan	Lothrop
Story of Harriet Tubman, Conductor of the Underground Railroad	P	McMullan, Kate	Dell Publishing
Story of Jackie Robinson, Bravest Man in Baseball	P	Davidson, Margaret	Dell Publishing

Title	Level	Author/Series	Publisher/Distributor
Story of Walt Disney, Maker of Magical Worlds	P	Selden, Bernice	Dell Publishing
Strange Meetings	Q	Literacy 2000	Rigby
Strawberry Jam	E	Oxford Reading Tree	Oxford
Stripes	A	Twig	Wright Group
Strongest Animal, The	F	Books for Young Learners	Richard C. Owen
Sue Likes Blue	G	Gregorich	School Zone
Sunflower That Went Flop, The	L	Storybox	Wright Group
Sunny-Side Up	M	Giff, Patricia Reilly	Dell Publishing
Sunrise	C	Literacy 2000	Rigby
Sunshine Street	H	Sunshine	Wright Group
Sunshine, the Black Cat	G	Carousel Readers	Dominie Press
Super-Duper Sunflower Seeds, The	I	Book Bank	Wright Group
Super Parrot	J	Real Reading	Steck-Vaughn
Superkids	H	Sunshine	Wright Group
Surprise for Mom	E	Urmston, K. & Evans, K.	Kaeden Books
Surprise Party	K	Hutchins, Pat	Macmillan
Surprise Party, The	J	Proger, Annabelle	Random House
Susie Goes Shopping	F	First Start	Troll
Swat It!	D	Bauer, Roger	Kaeden Books
Sword in the Stone, The	J	Hello Reader	Scholastic
T-Shirt Triplets, The	L	Literacy 2000	Rigby
T-Shirts	F	Ready to Read	Richard C. Owen/ Celebration Press
Tabby in the Tree	F	PM Books	Rigby
Tails	D	Vaughan, Marcia	Mondo
Tails	B	Book Bank	Wright Group
Tails Can Tell	I	Wonder World	Wright Group
Take a Bow, Jody	D	Eaton, Audry and Jane	Seedling
Taking Care of Rosie	E	Salem, L. & Stewart, J.	Seedling
Taking Jason to Grandma's	F	Book Bank	Wright Group
Taking Our Photo	E	Voyages	SRA/McGraw Hill
Tale of Peter Rabbit, The	L	Potter, Beatrix	Scholastic
Tale of Veruschka Babuschka, The	M	Literacy 2000	Rigby
Talking Yam, The	I	Little Readers	Houghton Mifflin
Tarantulas Are Spiders	F	Platnick, Norman	Mondo
Teacher's Pet	O	Hurwitz, Johanna	Scholastic
Teddy Bear, Teddy Bear	E	Tiger Cub	Peguis
Teddy Bears	I	Purkis, Sallie	Nelson/Michaels Assoc.
Teddy Bears Cure a Cold	K	Gretz, Susanna	Scholastic
Tee Ball	C	Little Celebrations	Celebration Press
Teeny Tiny	I	Bennett, Jill	Putnam
Teeny Tiny Tina	C	Literacy 2000	Rigby
Teeny Tiny Woman, The	J	Seuling, Barbara	Scholastic
Television Drama	Q	Literacy 2000	Rigby
Ten Apples Up on Top	J	LaSieg, Theo	Random House
Ten Bears in My Bed	G	Mack, Stan	Pantheon
Ten Little Bears	G	Reading Unlimited	Celebration Press
Ten Little Garden Snails	H	PM Books	Rigby
Ten Sleepy Sheep	G	Keller, Holly	Morrow
Ten Traveling Tigers	H	Little Readers	Houghton Mifflin
Tents	I	Reading Unlimited	Celebration Press

Title	Level	Author/Series	Publisher/Distributor
Terrible Fright	K	Storybox	Wright Group
Terrible Tiger	G	Sunshine	Wright Group
Terrible Twos	E	Tadpoles	Rigby
Tess and Paddy	J	Sunshine	Wright Group
Thank You	J	Ready to Read	Richard C. Owen/ Celebration Press
Thank You, Nicky!	F	Ziefert, Harriet	Penguin
Thanksgiving	F	Urmston, K. & Evans, K.	Kaeden Books
That Dog	E	Foundations	Wright Group
That Fat Hat	K	Barkan, Joanne	Scholastic
That's a Laugh: Four Funny Fables	M	Literacy 2000	Rigby
That's Dangerous	D	Voyages	SRA/McGraw Hill
That's Not All	G	Start to Read	School Zone
That's Really Weird!	K	Read Alongs	Rigby
There Is a Carrot in My Ear and Other Noodle Tales	J	Schwartz, Alvin	HarperTrophy
There's a Hippopotamus Under My Bed	J	Thaler, Mike	Avon Books
There's a Nightmare in My Closet	I	Mayer, Mercer	Penguin
There's an Alligator Under My Bed	J	Mayer, Mercer	Penguin
There's Something in My Attic	J	Mayer, Mercer	Penguin
Thing in the Log, The	H	Reading Unlimited	Celebration Press
Things I Like	D	Browne, Anthony	Random House
Things I Like to Do	C	Carousel Earlybirds	Dominie Press
Things on Wheels	C	Little Red Readers	Sundance
Things People Do for Fun	E	Foundations	Wright Group
Things That Go: A Traveling Alphabet	L	Bank Street	Bantam
This Game	B	Carousel Earlybirds	Dominie Press
This Hat	D	Little Celebrations	Celebration Press
This Is the Bear	I	Hayes, S. & Craig, H.	Harper & Row
This Is the House That Bjorn...	I	Tiger Cub	Peguis
This Is The Place for Me	I	Cole, Joanna	Scholastic
This Is the Plate	D	Little Celebrations	Celebration Press
This Is the Seed	I	Little Celebrations	Celebration Press
Three Bears, The	K	Galdone, Paul	Scholastic
Three Bears, The	I	Tiger Cub	Peguis
Three Billy Goats Gruff	K	Stevens, Janet	Harcourt Brace
Three Billy Boats Gruff	I	Traditional Tales	Rigby
Three Billy Goats Gruff, The	G	Little Readers	Houghton Mifflin
Three Billy Goats Gruff, The	I	Brown, Marcia	Harcourt Brace
Three Billy Goats Gruff, The	G	New Way	Steck-Vaughn
Three Blind Mice Mystery, The	L	Krensky, Stephen	Dell Publishing
Three Cheers for Hippo	G	Stadler, John	HarperCollins
Three Kittens	G	Ginsburg, Mirra	Crown
Three Little Ducks	E	Read-Togethers	Wright Group
Three Little Pigs	G	Little Readers	Houghton Mifflin
Three Little Pigs	L	Galdone, Paul	Houghton Mifflin
Three Little Pigs	I	Traditional Tales	Rigby
Three Little Pigs	L	Once Upon a Time	Wright Group
Three Little Pigs, The	H	Reading Unlimited	Celebration Press
Three Little Pigs, The	L	Marshall, James	Scholastic
Three Little Pigs, The	I	Reading Corners	Dominie Press
Three Little Witches	G	First Start	Troll

Title	Level	Author/Series	Publisher/Distributor
Three Magicians, The	K	Literacy 2000	Rigby
Three Muddy Monkeys	F	Foundations	Wright Group
Three Sillies, The	L	Literacy 2000	Rigby
Three Silly Monkeys	D	Foundations	Wright Group
Three Smart Pals	L	Rocklin, Joanne	Scholastic
Through Grandpa's Eyes	L	MacLachlan, P.	HarperTrophy
Tickle-Bugs, The	J	Literacy 2000	Rigby
Tidy Titch	I	Hutchins, Pat	Morrow
Tiger Is a Scaredy Cat	F	Step into Reading	Random House
Tiger, Tiger	C	PM Books	Rigby
Tim's Painting	A	Literacy 2000	Rigby
Time for Bed	B	Smart Start	Rigby
Time for Dinner	B	PM Starters One	Rigby
Time for Dinner	A	Smart Start	Rigby
Time for Sale	Q	Literacy 2000	Rigby
Timmy	E	Literacy 2000	Rigby
Tiny Woman's Coat	H	Sunshine	Wright Group
Tires	E	Foundations	Wright Group
Titanic, The	N	Donnelly, Judy	Random House
Titch	G	Hutchins, Pat	Penguin
To JJ From CC	Q	Literacy 2000	Rigby
To Market, to Market	I	Read-Togethers	Wright Group
To New York	D	Storybox	Wright Group
To School	A	Sunshine	Wright Group
To the Beach	D	Urmston, K. & Evans, K.	Kaeden Books
To Town	F	Read-Togethers	Wright Group
Toby Tomato	D	Little Celebrations	Celebration Press
Together	C	Sunshine	Wright Group
Tom Edison's Bright Idea	M	Keller, Jack	Steck-Vaughn
Tom Is Brave	D	PM Books	Rigby
Tom the TV Cat	J	Heilbroner, Joan	Random House
Tomatoes and Bricks	E	Windmill-Rhyme & Rhythm	Wright Group
Tommy's Treasure	I	Literacy 2000	Rigby
Tommy's Tummy Ache	C	Literacy 2000	Rigby
Tongues Are for Tasting, Licking, Tricking	L	Literacy 2000	Rigby
Too Big for Me	D	Storybox	Wright Group
Too Fast	A	Reading Corners	Dominie Press
Too Many Babas	K	Croll, Carolyn	HarperTrophy
Too Many Balloons	D	Rookie Reader	Children's Press
Too Many Mice	J	Bank Street	Bantam
Too Many Rabbits	J	Parish, Peggy	Dell Publishing
Too Much Noise	J	McGovern, Ann	Scholastic
Too Much Noise	H	Literacy 2000	Rigby
Tool Box	H	Rockwell, Anne	Macmillan
Toot, Toot	C	Wildsmith, Brian	Oxford
Tooth Race, The	I	Little Readers	Houghton Mifflin
Totara Tree, The	M	Book Bank	Wright Group
Town Mouse and Country Mouse, The	I	Aesop	Wright Group
Toy Box	A	Literacy 2000	Rigby
Toys	E	Talk About Books	Dominie Press
Toys	D	Tiger Cub	Peguis
Toys	B	Foundations	Wright Group

Title	Level	Author/Series	Publisher/Distributor
Traffic Jam	E	Harper, Leslie	Kaeden Books
Train Ride, The	C	Literacy 2000	Rigby
Train, The	C	Visions	Wright Group
Transportation Museum, The	C	Little Red Readers	Sundance
Trash	H	Sunshine	Wright Group
Treasure Hunt	A	Smart Start	Rigby
Treasure Hunting	M	Literacy 2000	Rigby
Tree House Fun	G	First Start	Troll
Tree House, The	B	Sunshine	Wright Group
Tree Stump, The	B	Little Celebrations	Celebration Press
Tree, The	F	Sunshine	Wright Group
Tree, the Trunk and the Tuba, The	Q	Literacy 2000	Rigby
Trees	A	Twig	Wright Group
Trees	J	Literacy 2000	Rigby
Trees Belong to Everyone	L	Literacy 2000	Rigby
Trek, The	I	Jonas, Ann	Greenwillow
Triceratops on the Farm	L	Wesley & the Dinosaurs	Wright Group
Tricking Tracy	F	Tadpoles	Rigby
Trip to the Park, The	F	Foundations	Wright Group
Triplet Trouble and the Field Day Disaster	L	Dadey, D. & Jones, M.	Scholastic
Triplet Trouble and the Red Heart Race	L	Dadey, D. & Jones, M.	Scholastic
Triplet Trouble and the Runaway Reindeer	L	Dadey, D. & Jones, M.	Scholastic
Triplet Trouble and the Talent Show Mess	L	Dadey, D. & Jones, M.	Scholastic
Trolley Ride	C	Tadpoles	Rigby
Trouble in the Ark	J	Rose, Gerald	Oxford
Trouble in the Sandbox	F	Foundations	Wright Group
Trucks	I	Rockwell, Anne	Penguin
Trucks	E	Foundations	Wright Group
Trucks	C	Literacy 2000	Rigby
Try It!	D	Reading Corners	Dominie Press
Try to Be a Brave Girl, Sarah	F	Windmill-Look & Listen	Wright Group
Tug of War	I	Folk Tales	Wright Group
Turtle Flies South	K	Literacy 2000	Rigby
Turtle Nest	H	Books for Young Learners	Richard C. Owen
Turtle, The	D	Foundations	Wright Group
TweedledeDee Tumbleweed	G	Reese, Bob	Children's Press
Twits, The	P	Dahl, Roald	Puffin Books
Two	E	Carousel Readers	Dominie Press
Two Bear Cubs	H	Jonas, Ann	Morrow
Two Feet	F	Giant Step Readers	Educ. Insights
Two Foolish Cats	K	Literacy 2000	Rigby
Two Little Dogs	E	Storybox	Wright Group
Two Little Mice, The	I	Literacy 2000	Rigby
Two Points	B	Kennedy, J. & Eaton, A.	Seedling
Tyler Toad and Thunder	M	Crowe, Robert	Dutton
Tyler's Train	C	Little Celebrations	Celebration Press
Tyrannosaurus the Terrible	L	Wesley & the Dinosaurs	Wright Group
Ugly Duckling, The	K	Traditional Tales	Rigby
Uh-Oh! Said the Crow	J	Bank Street	Bantam
Uncle Buncle's House	C	Sunshine	Wright Group

Title	Level	Author/Series	Publisher/Distributor
Uncle Elephant	J	Lobel, Arnold	HarperCollins
Uncle Timi's Sleep	G	Ready to Read	Richard C. Owen/ Celebration Press
Under the Bed	A	Smart Start	Rigby
Underground	C	Twig	Wright Group
Underwater	A	Twig	Wright Group
Underwater Journey	F	Sunshine	Wright Group
Up in a Tree	C	Sunshine	Wright Group
Up Went the Goat	C	Gregorich	School Zone
Vacations	B	Smart Start	Rigby
Vagabond Crabs	J	Literacy 2000	Rigby
Vampires Don't Wear Polka Dots	M	Dadey, D. & Jones, M.	Scholastic
Very Busy Spider, The	I	Carle, Eric	Philomel
Very Hungry Caterpillar, The	J	Carle, Eric	Putnam
Very Thin Cat of Alloway Road, The	L	Literacy 2000	Rigby
Vicky the High Jumper	K	Literacy 2000	Rigby
Victor and the Kite	F	Oxford Reading Tree	Oxford
Victor and the Martian	H	Oxford Reading Tree	Oxford
Victor and the Sail Kart	H	Oxford Reading Tree	Oxford
Victor Makes a TV	H	Reading Unlimited	Celebration Press
Victor the Champion	G	Oxford Reading Tree	Oxford
Victor the Hero	H	Oxford Reading Tree	Oxford
Visit to the Library, A	E	Foundations	Wright Group
Visiting Grandma and Grandpa	G	Carousel Readers	Dominie Press
Visiting the Vet	H	Foundations	Wright Group
Wagon, The	H	Reading Unlimited	Celebration Press
Wait Skates	G	Rookie Reader	Children's Press
Waiting for the Rain	J	Foundations	Wright Group
Wake Me in Spring	J	Preller, James	Scholastic
Wake Up, Baby!	J	Bank Street	Bantam
Wake Up, Dad	C	PM Books	Rigby
Wake Up, Emily, It's Mother's Day	M	Giff, Patricia Reilly	Yearling
Wake Up, Mom!	C	Sunshine	Wright Group
Wake Up, Wake Up!	D	Wildsmith, B. & R.	Scholastic
Walk	G	Reading Unlimited	Celebration Press
Walk with Grandpa	L	Read Alongs	Rigby
Walking to School	C	Voyages	SRA/McGraw Hill
Walking, Walking	C	Twig	Wright Group
Wash Day	B	Voyages	SRA/McGraw Hill
Washing	F	Foundations	Wright Group
Watch Out!	C	Literacy 2000	Rigby
Watching the Whales	L	Foundations	Wright Group
Watching TV	D	Foundations	Wright Group
Water	B	Literacy 2000	Rigby
Water	H	Wonder World	Wright Group
Water	C	Carousel Readers	Dominie Press
Water Boatman, The	F	Ready to Read	Richard C. Owen/ Celebration Press
Waving Sheep, The	H	PM Books	Rigby
Wax Man, The	I	Beginning Literacy	Scholastic
Way I Go to School, The	B	PM Starters One	Rigby
Wayside School Is Falling Down	Q	Sachar, Louis	Avon Books

Title	Level	Author/Series	Publisher/Distributor
We Are Best Friends	H	Aliki	Morrow
We Can Run	C	PM Starters Two	Rigby
We Go Out	A	PM Starters One	Rigby
We Go to School	B	Carousel Earlybirds	Dominie Press
We Like	C	Foundations	Wright Group
We Like Fish	D	PM Starters Two	Rigby
We Make Pizza	C	Carousel Readers	Dominie Press
We Scream for Ice Cream	K	Chardiet & Maccarone	Scholastic
We Went to the Zoo	B	Little Red Readers	Sundance
We're in Big Trouble, Black Board Bear	I	Alexander, Martha	Dial
Weather	A	Smart Start	Rigby
Well Fed Bear, The	E	Literacy 2000	Rigby
Well I Never	K	Storybox	Wright Group
Werewolves Don't Go to Summer Camp	M	Dadey, D. & Jones, M.	Scholastic
Wet Grass	H	Storybox	Wright Group
Whales	O	Wonder World	Wright Group
Whales	G	Foundations	Wright Group
Whale—The Gentle Giants	L	Milton, Joyce	Random House
What a Dog	F	First Start	Troll
What a Funny Thing to Do	K	Hall, N. & Robinson, A.	Nelson/Michaels Assoc.
What a Mess	C	Storybox	Wright Group
What a Mess!	A	Smart Start	Rigby
What a School	F	Salem, L. & Stewart, J.	Seedling
What a Tale!	C	Wildsmith, Brian	Oxford
What Am I?	F	Just Beginning	Modern Curriculum
What Am I?	G	Sunshine	Wright Group
What Are Purple Elephants Good For?	H	Reading Corners	Dominie Press
What Are You?	A	Literacy 2000	Rigby
What Are You Going to Buy?	F	Read Alongs	Rigby
What Can I Read?	A	Carousel Earlybirds	Dominie Press
What Can We Do Today?	G	Carousel Readers	Dominie Press
What Can You Be?	C	Tiger Cub	Peguis
What Can You Do?	C	Tiger Cub	Peguis
What Can You Hear?	D	Tiger Cub	Peguis
What Can You See?	C	Literacy 2000	Rigby
What Can You See?	B	Tiger Cub	Peguis
What Cat Is That?	J	Real Reading	Steck-Vaughn
What Comes First?	C	Swanson-Natsues, Lyn	Mondo
What Comes Out at Night?	B	Little Red Readers	Sundance
What Did Ben Want?	A	Smart Start	Rigby
What Did Kim Catch?	C	Literacy 2000	Rigby
What Did They Want?	C	Smart Start	Rigby
What Do You Do?	E	Tiger Cub	Peguis
What Do You Have?	C	Tiger Cub	Peguis
What Do You See?	B	Carousel Readers	Dominie Press
What Else?	I	Sunshine	Wright Group
What Fell Out?	D	Carousel Readers	Dominie Press
What Game Shall We Play?	H	Hutchins, Pat	Sundance
What Goes in the Bathtub?	C	Literacy 2000	Rigby
What Has Spots?	B	Literacy 2000	Rigby
What I Like at School	C	Little Red Readers	Sundance
What I Would Do	I	Read Alongs	Rigby
What Is a Huggles?	B	Sunshine	Wright Group

Title	Level	Author/Series	Publisher/Distributor
What Is a Reptile?	M	Now I Know	Troll
What Is Blue?	C	Carousel Earlybirds	Dominie Press
What Is Green?	B	Carousel Readers	Dominie Press
What Is It Called?	D	Reading Unlimited	Celebration Press
What Is Red?	B	Literacy 2000	Rigby
What Is Red?	B	Carousel Earlybirds	Dominie Press
What Is This?	A	Tiger Cub	Peguis
What Kind of Babysitter Is This?	L	Johnson, Dolores	Scholastic
What Made Teddalik Laugh	M	Folk Tales	Wright Group
What Next, Baby Bear?	L	Murphy, Jill	Dial
What Shall I Wear?	E	Book Bank	Wright Group
What Would the Zoo Do?	D	Salem, Lynn	Seedling
What Would You Like?	D	Sunshine	Wright Group
What You See Is What You Get	I	McLenighan, V.	Modern Curriculum
What's Cooking, Jenny Archer?	M	Conford, Ellen	Little, Brown
What's for Dinner?	E	Salem, L. & Stewart, J.	Seedling
What's for Lunch?	B	Storybox	Wright Group
What's in This Egg?	A	Sunshine	Wright Group
What's Inside?	K	Wonder World	Wright Group
What's Inside?	G	Foundations	Wright Group
What's on Your T-Shirt?	C	Carousel Readers	Dominie Press
What's That?	B	Sunshine	Wright Group
What's That?	C	Carousel Earlybirds	Dominie Press
What's the Time Mr. Wolf?	C	Windmill-Look & Listen	Wright Group
What's Under the Ocean?	H	Now I Know	Troll
Wheels	C	Sunshine	Wright Group
Wheels on the Bus	F	Ziefert, Harriet	Random House
When Dad Went to Daycare	H	Sunshine	Wright Group
When Goldilocks Went to the House of the Bears	E	Tiger Cub	Peguis
When Goldilocks Went to the House of the Bears	F	Rendall, Jenny	Mondo
When I Get Bigger	K	Mayer, Mercer	Donovan
When I Look Up	B	Foundations	Wright Group
When I Play	C	Literacy 2000	Rigby
When I Was Sick	F	Literacy 2000	Rigby
When It Rains	C	Foundations	Wright Group
When It Rains	F	Frankford, Marilyn	Kaeden Books
When Itchy Witchy Sneezes	C	Sunshine	Wright Group
When Lana Was Absent	F	Tadpoles	Rigby
When the Circus Comes to Town	A	Little Red Readers	Sundance
When the Giants Came to Town	L	Leonard, Marcia	Scholastic
When the King Rides By	J	Mahy, Margaret	Mondo
When Will We Be Sisters?	K	Kroll, Virginia	Scholastic
When You Were a Baby	G	Jonas, Ann	Morrow
Where Are My Socks?	D	Ready to Read	Richard C. Owen/ Celebration Press
Where Are the Babies?	B	PM Starters Two	Rigby
Where Are the Car Keys?	B	Windmill-Look & Listen	Wright Group
Where Are the Sunhats?	D	PM Books	Rigby
Where Are They Going?	C	Storybox	Wright Group
Where Are You Going?	D	Learn to Read	Creative Teaching Press
Where Are You Going, Aja Rose?	D	Sunshine	Wright Group
Where Are You Going, Little Mouse?	H	Kraus, Robert	Greenwillow

Title	Level	Author/Series	Publisher/Distributor
Where Can It Be?	E	Jonas, Ann	Morrow
Where Can Kitty Sleep?	B	Windmill-Look & Listen	Wright Group
Where Can Pussy Sleep?	B	Windmill-Look & Listen	Wright Group
Where Can We Put an Elephant?	B	Windmill-Look & Listen	Wright Group
Where Do Monsters Live?	C	Learn to Read	Creative Teaching Press
Where Do You Live?	C	Tiger Cub	Peguis
Where Does the Teacher Sleep?	C	Gibson, Kathleen	Seedling
Where I Live	B	Carousel Earlybirds	Dominie Press
Where Is Daniel?	E	Carousel Readers	Dominie Press
Where Is It?	D	Rookie Reader	Children's Press
Where Is It?	F	Tiger Cub	Peguis
Where Is Miss Pool?	D	Ready to Read	Richard C. Owen/ Celebration Press
Where Is My Caterpillar?	H	Wonder World	Wright Group
Where Is My Grandma?	C	Foundations	Wright Group
Where Is My Pet?	A	Literacy 2000	Rigby
Where Is Nancy?	E	Literacy 2000	Rigby
Where Is Teddy's Head?	A	Windmill-Look & Listen	Wright Group
Where Is the Bear?	K	Nims, Bonnie	Whitman
Where Is the Milk?	D	Foundations	Wright Group
Where Is the School Bus?	D	Carousel Readers	Dominie Press
Where the Wild Things Are	J	Sendak, Maurice	Harper & Row
Where Will You Sleep Tonight?	C	Foundations	Wright Group
Where's Al?	D	Barton, Byron	Houghton Mifflin
Where's Baby Tom?	D	Book Bank	Wright Group
Where's Bear?	C	Windmill-Look & Listen	Wright Group
Where's Cupcake?	D	Little Readers	Houghton Mifflin
Where's Little Mole?	C	Little Celebrations	Celebration Press
Where's Lulu?	I	Bank Street	Bantam
Where's My Daddy?	F	Watanabe, Shigeo	Putnam
Where's Spot?	E	Hill, Eric	Putnam
Where's the Egg Cup?	B	Windmill-Look & Listen	Wright Group
Where's Tim?	C	Sunshine	Wright Group
Where's Your Tooth?	C	Learn to Read	Creative Teaching Press
Whipping Boy	O	Fleischman, Sid	Troll
Whiskers	A	Wonder World	Wright Group
Whistle for Willie	L	Keats, Ezra Jack	Penguin
White Horse, The	K	Literacy 2000	Rigby
White Wednesday	H	Literacy 2000	Rigby
Who Am I?	E	Hello Reader	Scholastic
Who Ate the Broccoli?	E	Little Readers	Houghton Mifflin
Who Cried for Pie?	D	First Start	Troll
Who Fed the Chickens?	C	Little Celebrations	Celebration Press
Who Goes Out on Halloween?	G	Bank Street	Bantam
Who Is Who?	D	Rookie Reader	Children's Press
Who Likes Ice Cream?	A	Literacy 2000	Rigby
Who Likes the Cold?	A	Twig	Wright Group
Who Lives Here?	C	Learn to Read	Creative Teaching Press
Who Lives Here?	C	Storybox	Wright Group
Who Lives in this Hole?	C	Twig	Wright Group
Who Made These Tracks?	B	Literacy 2000	Rigby
Who Pushed Humpty?	K	Literacy 2000	Rigby
Who Sank the Boat?	K	Allen, Pamela	Coward
Who Spilled the Beans?	E	Story Basket	Wright Group

Title	Level	Author/Series	Publisher/Distributor
Who Took the Farmer's Hat	I	Nodset, Joan	Scholastic
Who Wants One?	I	Serfozo, Mary	Macmillan
Who Wants to Live in My House?	D	Book Bank	Wright Group
Who Wears This Hat?	B	Windmill-Look & Listen	Wright Group
Who Will Be My Mother?	E	Read-Togethers	Wright Group
Who Will Help?	D	Learn to Read	Creative Teaching Press
Who Will Help?	B	Carousel Readers	Dominie Press
Who's Afraid?	I	Reading Unlimited	Celebration Press
Who's Afraid of the Big, Bad Bully?	K	Slater, Teddy	Scholastic
Who's Behind the Door at My House	G	Salmon, Michael	Steck-Vaughn
Who's Behind the Door at My School	G	Salmon, Michael	Steck-Vaughn
Who's Coming for a Ride?	B	Literacy 2000	Rigby
Who's Going to Lick the Bowl?	C	Storybox	Wright Group
Who's Hiding?	D	Learn to Read	Creative Teaching Press
Whose Birthday Is It Today?	C	Book Bank	Wright Group
Whose Eggs Are These?	E	Sunshine	Wright Group
Whose Forest Is It?	C	Learn to Read	Creative Teaching Press
Whose Mouse Are You?	H	Kraus, Robert	Macmillan
Why Can't I Fly?	G	Gelman, Rita	Scholastic
Why The Sea Is Salty	L	Literacy 2000	Rigby
Wibble Wobble Albatross	H	Ready to Read	Richard C. Owen/ Celebration Press
Wicked Pirates, The	I	Sunshine	Wright Group
Wiggle, Jiggly, Joggly, Tooth	E	Little Celebrations	Celebration Press
Wild Wet Wellington Wind	I	Ready to Read	Richard C. Owen/ Celebration Press
Wild, Wooly Child, The	J	Read Alongs	Rigby
William, Where Are You?	F	Gerstein, Mordicai	Crown
William's Skateboard	G	Windmill-Look & Listen	Wright Group
Willie the Slowpoke	G	First Start	Troll
Willie's Wonderful Pet	I	Hello Reader	Scholastic
Willy the Helper	D	Little Readers	Houghton Mifflin
Willy's Hats	E	Stewart, J. & Salem, L.	Seedling
Wind	E	Ready to Read	Richard C. Owen/ Celebration Press
Wind and Sun	G	Literacy 2000	Rigby
Wind and the Sun	J	Story Starter	Wright Group
Wind and the Sun, The	J	New Way	Steck-Vaughn
Wind Blew, The	L	Hutchins, Pat	Puffin Books
Wind Blows Strong	E	Sunshine	Wright Group
Wind Power	J	Ready to Read	Richard C. Owen/ Celebration Press
Wind Surfing	D	Sunshine	Wright Group
Wing High, Gooftah	Q	Literacy 2000	Rigby
Winter Sleeps	F	Reading Corners	Dominie Press
Wishy-Washy Day	E	Story Basket	Wright Group
Witch's Haircut, The	G	Windmill-Look & Listen	Wright Group
Witches Don't Do Backflips	M	Dadey, D. & Jones, M.	Scholastic
Wolf's First Deer	M	Book Bank	Wright Group
Women at Work	G	Foundations	Wright Group
Wood	B	Twig	Wright Group
Woof!	C	Literacy 2000	Rigby
Woolly Sally	I	Ready to Read	Richard C. Owen/ Celebration Press

Title	Level	Author/Series	Publisher/Distributor
Woosh	E	Read-Togethers	Wright Group
Words	M	Ready to Read	Richard C. Owen/ Celebration Press
Wordsong	K	Bobber Books	SRA/McGraw Hill
World's Greatest Juggler, The	E	Little Readers	Houghton Mifflin
Worms	D	Literacy 2000	Rigby
Worms for Breakfast	I	Little Readers	Houghton Mifflin
Would You Like to Fly?	C	Twig	Wright Group
Writer's Work, A	N	Wonder World	Wright Group
Wrong Way Around Magic	O	Chew, Ruth	Scholastic
Wrong-Way Rabbit, The	J	Hello Reader	Scholastic
Yard Sale, The	I	Little Readers	Houghton Mifflin
Yellow	B	Literacy 2000	Rigby
Yellow Overalls	L	Literacy 2000	Rigby
Yes Ma'am	H	Read-Togethers	Wright Group
Yoo Hoo, Moon!	I	Bank Street	Bantam
You	C	Carousel Earlybirds	Dominie Press
You Are Much Too Small	J	Bank Street	Bantam
You Can't Catch Me	J	Oppenheim, Joanne	Houghton Mifflin
You Can't Eat Your Chicken Pox, Amber Brown	N	Danziger, Paula	Scholastic
You Look Funny	G	First Start	Troll
You Might Fall	H	Young Writers' World	Nelson/Michaels Assoc.
You'll Soon Grow into Them Titch	H	Hutchins, Pat	Morrow
You're So Clever	H	Voyages	SRA/McGraw Hill
Young Jackie Robinson: Baseball Hero	L	First Start Biography	Troll
Young Wolf's First Hunt	M	Shefelman, Janice	Random House
Yuk Soup	B	Sunshine	Wright Group
Yum and Yuk	I	Storybox	Wright Group
Yummy, Tum, Tee	C	Little Celebrations	Celebration Press
Yummy, Yummy	F	Grey, Judith	Troll
Zack's Alligator	K	Mozelle, Shirley	HarperTrophy
Zithers	H	Little Celebrations	Celebration Press
Zoe at the Fancy Dress Ball	J	Literacy 2000	Rigby
Zoo	A	Literacy 2000	Rigby
Zoo	B	Wonder World	Wright Group
Zoo Babies	F	Little Celebrations	Celebration Press
Zoo Food	C	Reading Corners	Dominie Press
Zoo in Willy's Bed, The	E	Sturnman Gorman, Kate	Seedling
Zoo Party, A	H	Book Bank	Wright Group
Zoo, The	C	Carousel Readers	Dominie Press
Zunid	J	Stepping Stones	Nelson/Michaels Assoc.

Guided reading book list organized by level

Title	Level	Author/Series	Publisher/Distributor
Amazing Race, The	A	Smart Start	Rigby
Animals	A	Smart Start	Rigby
Applebird	A	Wildsmith, Brian	Oxford
At the Zoo	A	Kloes, Carol	Kaeden Books
Baby Chimp	A	Twig	Wright Group
Baby Gets Dressed	A	Sunshine	Wright Group
Barbecue, The	A	Sunshine	Wright Group
Be Quiet	A	Literacy 2000	Rigby
Big Things	A	PM Starters	Rigby
Birthday Cake, The	A	Sunshine	Wright Group
Birthday Party, The	A	Sunshine	Wright Group
Building with Blocks	A	Sunshine	Wright Group
Car Ride, The	A	Little Red Readers	Sundance
Chinese Kites	A	Twig	Wright Group
Circus Train, The	A	Little Red Readers	Sundance
Closer and Closer	A	Twig	Wright Group
Clown Face	A	Twig	Wright Group
Clown, The	A	Smart Start	Rigby
Colours	A	Pienkowski, Jan	Penguin
Cookies	A	Twig	Wright Group
Count and See	A	Hoban, Tana	Macmillan
Dad	A	PM Starters	Rigby
Dig, Dig	A	Cat on the Mat/Wood	Oxford
Dinner!	A	Sunshine	Wright Group
Dog Day!	A	Smart Start	Rigby
Don't Splash Me	A	Windmill-Look & Listen	Wright Group
Down to Town	A	Sunshine	Wright Group
Dressing Up	A	PM Starters One	Rigby
Dressing Up	A	Jellybeans	Rigby
Dressing Up	A	Sunshine	Wright Group
Eating	A	Foundations	Wright Group
Every Morning	A	Twig	Wright Group
Farm, The	A	Smart Start	Rigby
Frogs	A	Twig	Wright Group
Fruit Salad	A	Literacy 2000	Rigby
Getting Dressed	A	Sunshine	Wright Group
Ghost	A	Storybox	Wright Group
Go, Go, Go	A	Storybox	Wright Group
Going to School	A	Smart Start	Rigby
Going to the Beach	A	Ready to Read	Richard C. Owen/ Celebration Press
Helicopter Over Hawaii	A	Twig	Wright Group
Here's a House	A	Windmill-Look & Listen	Wright Group
House, A	A	PM Starters	Rigby
House Cleaning	A	Book Bank	Wright Group
How to Make a Mudpie	A	Learn to Read	Creative Teaching Press
Huggles Breakfast	A	Sunshine	Wright Group
Huggles Can Juggle	A	Sunshine	Wright Group
Huggles Goes Away	A	Sunshine	Wright Group
I Am . . .	A	Sunshine	Wright Group

Title	Level	Author/Series	Publisher/Distributor
I Am Thankful	A	Carousel Earlybirds	Dominie Press
I Can Fly	A	Sunshine	Wright Group
I Can Hear	A	TOTTS	TOTTS
I Can Paint	A	Book Bank	Wright Group
I Can Read	A	Learn to Read	Creative Teaching Press
I Can See	A	Carousel Earlybirds	Dominie Press
I Can Write	A	Learn to Read	Creative Teaching Press
I Like	A	Sunshine	Wright Group
I Like Balloons	A	Reading Corners	Dominie Press
I Like Me	A	Visions	Wright Group
I Like to Eat	A	Reading Corners	Dominie Press
I Like to Paint	A	Reading Corners	Dominie Press
I Paint	A	Literacy 2000	Rigby
I Read	A	Reading Corners	Dominie Press
In the Shopping Cart	A	PM Starters	Rigby
In the Supermarket	A	Smart Start	Rigby
Iron Horse, The	A	Smart Start	Rigby
James Is Hiding	A	Windmill-Look & Listen	Wright Group
Just Look at You	A	Sunshine	Wright Group
Legs	A	Twig	Wright Group
Let's Go	A	Reading Corners	Dominie Press
Light	A	Twig	Wright Group
Little Brother	A	Sunshine	Wright Group
Little Things	A	PM Starters	Rigby
Look	A	Sunshine	Wright Group
Look What I Can Do	A	Aruego, Jose	Macmillan
Lost	A	TOTTS	TOTTS
Lots of Things	A	Reading Corners	Dominie Press
Magic	A	Twig	Wright Group
Me	A	PM Starters	Rigby
Miss Popple's Pets	A	Literacy 2000	Rigby
Moccasins	A	Twig	Wright Group
Mom	A	PM Starters	Rigby
Moms and Dads	A	PM Starters	Rigby
Monster Party	A	Literacy 2000	Rigby
My Birthday Party	A	Little Readers	Houghton Mifflin
My Book	A	Maris, Ron	Viking
My Box	A	Literacy 2000	Rigby
My Class	A	Stewart, J. & Salem, L.	Seedling
My Family	A	Sunshine	Wright Group
My Home	A	Literacy 2000	Rigby
My House	A	Carousel Earlybirds	Dominie Press
My Planet	A	Smart Start	Rigby
My Room	A	Carousel Earlybirds	Dominie Press
My Shadow	A	Book Bank	Wright Group
My Story	A	Wonder World	Wright Group
My Tower	A	Windmill-Look & Listen	Wright Group
Naughty Kitten!	A	Smart Start	Rigby
On Safari	A	Smart Start	Rigby
One Hunter	A	Hutchins, Pat	Greenwillow
Ouch!	A	Literacy 2000	Rigby
Painters	A	Twig	Wright Group
Party, The	A	Storybox	Wright Group
Pets	A	PM Starters	Rigby

Title	Level	Author/Series	Publisher/Distributor
Picnic	A	Book Bank	Wright Group
Play Ball	A	Twig	Wright Group
Playing	A	PM Starters	Rigby
Robot, The	A	Smart Start	Rigby
Royal Family, The	A	Stewart, J. & Salem, L.	Seedling
Seed, The	A	Wonder World	Wright Group
Shopping	A	Sunshine	Wright Group
Snakes	A	Twig	Wright Group
Snowman	A	Smart Start	Rigby
Socks	A	Smart Start	Rigby
Sometimes	A	WonderWorld	Wright Group
Space Journey	A	Sunshine	Wright Group
Spots	A	Smart Start	Rigby
Stripes	A	Twig	Wright Group
Tim's Painting	A	Literacy 2000	Rigby
Time for Dinner	A	Smart Start	Rigby
To School	A	Sunshine	Wright Group
Too Fast	A	Reading Corners	Dominie Press
Toy Box	A	Literacy 2000	Rigby
Treasure Hunt	A	Smart Start	Rigby
Trees	A	Twig	Wright Group
Under the Bed	A	Smart Start	Rigby
Underwater	A	Twig	Wright Group
We Go Out	A	PM Starters	Rigby
Weather	A	Smart Start	Rigby
What a Mess!	A	Smart Start	Rigby
What Are You?	A	Literacy 2000	Rigby
What Can I Read?	A	Carousel Earlybirds	Dominie Press
What Did Ben Want?	A	Smart Start	Rigby
What Is This?	A	Tiger Cub	Peguis
What's in This Egg?	A	Sunshine	Wright Group
When the Circus Comes to Town	A	Little Red Readers	Sundance
Where Is My Pet?	A	Literacy 2000	Rigby
Where Is Teddy's Head?	A	Windmill-Look & Listen	Wright Group
Whiskers	A	Wonder World	Wright Group
Who Likes Ice Cream?	A	Literacy 2000	Rigby
Who Likes the Cold?	A	Twig	Wright Group
Zoo	A	Literacy 2000	Rigby
Airplane, The	B	Sunshine	Wright Group
All of Me	B	Literacy 2000	Rigby
Animal Homes	B	Little Red Readers	Sundance
Animals Went to Bed, The	B	Smart Start	Rigby
Ants Love Picnics Too	B	Literacy 2000	Rigby
At School	B	Sunshine	Wright Group
At the Wildlife Park	B	Little Red Readers	Sundance
At the Zoo	B	Little Readers	Houghton Mifflin
At the Zoo	B	PM Starters	Rigby
Baby Animals	B	Reading Corners	Dominie Press
Ball Game	B	Literacy 2000	Rigby
Ball Games	B	PM Starters	Rigby
Baseball	B	Sunshine	Wright Group
Bear, The	B	Carousel Earlybirds	Dominie Press
Ben's Red Car	B	PM Starters	Rigby

Title	Level	Author/Series	Publisher/Distributor
Big and Little	B	Carousel Earlybirds	Dominie Press
Big Sister	B	Visions	Wright Group
Books	B	Sunshine	Wright Group
Books	B	Smart Start	Rigby
Bubble Gum	B	Carousel Books	Dominie Press
Buffy	B	Literacy 2000	Rigby
Bug Watching	B	Twig	Wright Group
Camping	B	Literacy 2000	Rigby
Cars	B	Little Readers	Houghton Mifflin
Cat and Mouse	B	PM Starters	Rigby
Cat on the Mat	B	Wildsmith, Brian	Oxford
Chocolate Cake	B	Storybox	Wright Group
City Bus, The	B	Visions	Wright Group
City Lights	B	Visions	Wright Group
Climbing	B	PM Starters	Rigby
Clouds	B	Voyages	SRA/McGraw Hill
Clown, The	B	Urmston, K. & Evans, K.	Kaeden Books
Colors in the City	B	Urmston, K. & Evans, K.	Kaeden Books
Come and Play	B	Interaction	Rigby
Come On	B	Sunshine	Wright Group
Dad	B	Little Readers	Houghton Mifflin
Dancing Shoes	B	Literacy 2000	Rigby
Dear Santa	B	Literacy 2000	Rigby
Dinosaur Party	B	Smart Start	Rigby
Dog	B	Ready to Read	Richard C. Owen
Don't Wake the Baby	B	Literacy 2000	Rigby
Dreaming	B	Smart Start	Rigby
Dressing Up	B	Smart Start	Rigby
Faces	B	Sunshine	Wright Group
Families	B	Interaction	Rigby
Farm, The	B	Sunshine	Wright Group
Flying and Floating	B	Little Red Readers	Sundance
Follow the Leader	B	Windmill-Look & Listen	Wright Group
Food to Eat	B	Little Readers	Houghton Mifflin
Football	B	Visions	Wright Group
Friends	B	Little Readers	Houghton Mifflin
Frightened	B	Storybox	Wright Group
Fun with Hats	B	Malka, Lucy	Mondo
Getting There	B	Wonder World	Wright Group
Giant's Breakfast	B	Literacy 2000	Rigby
Giant's Day Out, The	B	Smart Start	Rigby
Give Me a Hug	B	Sunshine	Wright Group
Go-carts, The	B	PM Starters	Rigby
Going Up?	B	Little Celebrations	Celebration Press
Good to Eat	B	Twig	Wright Group
Great Enormous Hamburger	B	Sunshine	Wright Group
Growing	B	Windmill-Look & Listen	Wright Group
Hair	B	Foundations	Wright Group
Hello Goodbye	B	Literacy 2000	Rigby
Here Is	B	Carousel Earlybirds	Dominie Press
Here's Skipper	B	Salem, L. & Stewart, J.	Seedling
Hide and Seek	B	Literacy 2000	Rigby
Honk!	B	Smith, Sue	Mondo
How Many Legs?	B	Windmill-Look & Listen	Wright Group

Title	Level	Author/Series	Publisher/Distributor
How's the Weather?	B	Learn to Read	Creative Teaching Press
I Am	B	Little Readers	Houghton Mifflin
I Am Frightened	B	Storybox	Wright Group
I Can	B	Little Readers	Houghton Mifflin
I Can	B	New Way	Steck-Vaughn
I Can Make Music	B	Little Red Readers	Sundance
I Can Read	B	Ready to Read	Richard C. Owen/ Celebration Press
I Can Write, Can You?	B	Stwart, J. & Salem, L.	Seedling
I Get Tired	B	Carousel Earlybirds	Dominie Press
I Go, Go, Go	B	Sunshine	Wright Group
I Have a Pet	B	Reading Corners	Dominie Press
I Love My Family	B	Sunshine	Wright Group
I Love My Family	B	Foundations	Wright Group
I See Colors	B	Learn to Read	Creative Teaching Press
In the Bathroom	B	Smart Start	Rigby
In the Mirror	B	Storybox	Wright Group
Jack-in-the-Box	B	Literacy 2000	Rigby
Jack-O-Lantern	B	Twig	Wright Group
Little Red Hen	B	Windmill-Look & Listen	Wright Group
Little Seed, A	B	Smart Start	Rigby
Long, Long Tail	B	Sunshine	Wright Group
Look at Me	B	PM Starters	Rigby
Look at This	B	Carousel Earlybirds	Dominie Press
Look Out!	B	Literacy 2000	Rigby
Lost!	B	Foundations	Rigby
Major Jump	B	Sunshine	Wright Group
Making Pictures	B	Foundations	Wright Group
Marching Band	B	Urmston, K. & Evans, K.	Kaeden Books
Max's Box	B	Little Celebrations	Celebration Press
Model, The	B	Smart Start	Rigby
Mommy, Where Are You?	B	Ziefert & Boon	Puffin Books
Moving	B	Little Red Readers	Sundance
My Friend	B	Sunshine	Wright Group
My Garden	B	Beginning Literacy	Scholastic
My Home	B	Sunshine	Wright Group
My Puppy	B	Sunshine	Wright Group
My School	B	Little Readers	Houghton Mifflin
New Cat, The	B	Ready to Read	Richard C. Owen/ Celebration Press
On the Beach	B	Smart Start	Rigby
One, One Is the Sun	B	Storybox	Wright Group
One Pit, Two Pigs	B	Tiger Cub	Peguis
Our Baby	B	Literacy 2000	Rigby
Our Pumpkin	B	Learn to Read	Creative Teaching Press
Out in the Weather	B	PM Starters	Rigby
Over the Bridge	B	Little Red Readers	Sundance
Packing	B	Foundations	Wright Group
Packing My Bag	B	PM Starters	Rigby
Pat, Pat, Pat	B	Book Bank	Wright Group
Pencil, The	B	PM Starters	Rigby
Puzzle, The	B	Smart Start	Rigby
Race, The	B	Windmill-Look & Listen	Wright Group
Rain	B	Reading Corners	Dominie Press

Title	Level	Author/Series	Publisher/Distributor
Robber, The	B	Smart Start	Rigby
Rock Pools, The	B	PM Starters	Rigby
Run	B	Sunshine	Wright Group
Sally's New Shoes	B	PM Starters	Rigby
Sand	B	Voyages	SRA/McGraw Hill
Scrumptious Sundae	B	Literacy 2000	Rigby
Shopping at the Supermarket	B	Foundations	Wright Group
Shopping Mall, The	B	PM Starters	Rigby
Signs	B	Literacy 2000	Rigby
Skier, The	B	PM Starter	Rigby
Snap	B	Sunshine	Wright Group
Some Dogs Don't	B	Tiger Cub	Peguis
Space Ark, The	B	Sunshine	Wright Group
Splish Splash	B	Windmill-Look & Listen	Wright Group
Spooky Pet	B	Smart Start	Rigby
Spots	B	Visions	Wright Group
Stop!	B	PM Starters	Rigby
Storm, The	B	Sunshine	Wright Group
Tails	B	Book Bank	Wright Group
This Game	B	Carousel Earlybirds	Dominie Press
Time for Bed	B	Smart Start	Rigby
Time of Dinner	B	PM Starters	Rigby
Toys	B	Foundations	Wright Group
Tree House, The	B	Sunshine	Wright Group
Tree Stump, The	B	Little Celebrations	Celebration Press
Two Points	B	Kennedy, J. & Eaton, A.	Seedling
Vacations	B	Smart Start	Rigby
Wash Day	B	Voyages	SRA/McGraw Hill
Water	B	Literacy 2000	Rigby
Way I Go to School, The	B	PM Starters	Rigby
We Go to School	B	Carousel Earlybirds	Dominie Press
We Went to the Zoo	B	Little Red Readers	Sundance
What Can You See?	B	Tiger Cub	Peguis
What Comes Out at Night?	B	Little Red Readers	Sundance
What Do You See?	B	Carousel Readers	Dominie Press
What Has Spots?	B	Literacy 2000	Rigby
What Is a Huggles?	B	Sunshine	Wright Group
What Is Green?	B	Carousel Readers	Dominie Press
What Is Red?	B	Literacy 2000	Rigby
What Is Red?	B	Carousel Earlybirds	Dominie Press
What's for Lunch?	B	Storybox	Wright Group
What's That?	B	Sunshine	Wright Group
When I Look Up	B	Foundations	Wright Group
Where Are the Babies?	B	PM Starters	Rigby
Where Are the Car Keys?	B	Windmill-Look & Listen	Wright Group
Where Can Kitty Sleep?	B	Windmill-Look & Listen	Wright Group
Where Can Pussy Sleep?	B	Windmill-Look & Listen	Wright Group
Where Can We Put an Elephant?	B	Windmill-Look & Listen	Wright Group
Where I Live	B	Carousel Earlybirds	Dominie Press
Where's the Egg Cup?	B	Windmill-Look & Listen	Wright Group
Who Made These Tracks?	B	Literacy 2000	Rigby
Who Wears This Hat?	B	Windmill-Look & Listen	Wright Group
Who Will Help?	B	Carousel Readers	Dominie Press
Who's Coming for a Ride?	B	Literacy 2000	Rigby

Title	Level	Author/Series	Publisher/Distributor
Wood	B	Twig	Wright Group
Yellow	B	Literacy 2000	Rigby
Yuk Soup	B	Sunshine	Wright Group
Zoo	B	Wonder World	Wright Group
1, 2, Kangaroo	C	Reading Corners	Dominie Press
All Fall Down	C	Wildsmith, Brian	Oxford
All Through the Week with Cat and Dog	C	Learn to Read	Creative Teaching Press
Animal Habitats	C	Little Red Readers	Sundance
Animal Stretches	C	Little Celebrations	Celebration Press
At the Farm	C	Little Red Readers	Sundance
At the Library	C	PM Starters	Rigby
At the Playground	C	Little Red Readers	Sundance
At the Pool	C	Foundations	Wright Group
At the Zoo	C	Little Red Readers	Sundance
B-I-N-G-O	C	Tiger Cub	Peguis
Baby in the Cart	C	Foundations	Wright Group
Baby Lamb's First Drink	C	PM Books	Rigby
Baby Says	C	Steptoe, John	Morrow
Banana Shake	C	Book Bank	Wright Group
Bay Run, The	C	Foundations	Wright Group
Beds	C	Interaction	Rigby
Bee, The	C	Storybox	Wright Group
Ben the Bold	C	Literacy 2000	Rigby
Ben's Banana	C	Foundations	Wright Group
Bicycle, The	C	Storybox	Wright Group
Big and Little	C	Sunshine	Wright Group
Big Kick, The	C	PM Books	Rigby
Bird Talk	C	Little Celebrations	Celebration Press
Birthday, A	C	New Way	Steck-Vaughn
Birthday Candles	C	Carousel Readers	Dominie Press
Blue Day	C	Literacy 2000	Rigby
Bo and Peter	C	Beginning Literacy	Scholastic
Boots	C	Beginning Literacy	Scholastic
Boots for Toots	C	Ready to Read	Richard C. Owen/ Celebration Press
Boss	C	Foundations	Wright Group
Breakfast	C	Foundations	Wright Group
Brown Bear, Brown Bear	C	Martin, Bill	Henry Holt & Co.
Bubbles	C	Sunshine	Wright Group
Bubbles	C	Literacy 2000	Rigby
Bus Ride, The	C	Reading Unlimited	Celebration Press
Bus Ride, The	C	Little Celebrations	Celebration Press
Busy Mosquito, The	C	Foundations	Wright Group
Buzzing Flies	C	Sunshine	Wright Group
Call 911	C	Twig	Wright Group
Can I Have a Lick?	C	Carousel Readers	Dominie Press
Can You See the Eggs?	C	PM Starters	Rigby
Caring	C	Interaction	Rigby
Cat, The	C	Smart Start	Rigby
Cat and Dog	C	Learn to Read	Creative Teaching Press
Cave	C	Book Bank	Wright Group
Circus, The	C	Literacy 2000	Rigby

Title	Level	Author/Series	Publisher/Distributor
Cleaning Teeth	C	Wonder World	Wright Group
Clothes	C	Interaction	Rigby
Clown and Elephant	C	Storybox	Wright Group
Come with Me	C	Storybox	Wright Group
Cool Off	C	Diaz, Nellie	Mondo
Copycat	C	Storybox	Wright Group
Dan the Flying Man	C	Read-Togethers	Wright Group
Dancing	C	Visions	Wright Group
Danger	C	Storybox	Wright Group
Desert, The	C	Carousel Readers	Dominie Press
Don't Leave Anything Behind!	C	Literacy 2000	Rigby
Dragon, The	C	Sunshine	Wright Group
Dressing Up	C	Literacy 2000	Rigby
Dressing Up Box, The	C	Book Bank	Wright Group
Elephant's Trunk, An	C	Little Celebrations	Celebration Press
End, The	C	Tiger Cub	Peguis
Fishing	C	PM Starters	Rigby
Flying	C	Storybox	Wright Group
Four Ice Creams	C	PM Starters	Rigby
Fox on the Box	C	Gregorich	School Zone
Fox, The	C	Books for Young Learners	Richard C. Owen
Fun with Mo and Toots	C	Ready to Read	Richard C. Owen/ Celebration Press
Getting Ready for the Ball	C	Literacy 2000	Rigby
Going to Grandpa's	C	Frankford, Marilyn	Kaeden Books
Going to School	C	Storybox	Wright Group
Going to the Beach	C	Carousel Readers	Dominie Press
Going to the Park with Grandaddy	C	Visions	Wright Group
Gregory's Dog	C	Cat on the Mat/Stobbs	Oxford
Happy Birthday	C	Literacy 2000	Rigby
Happy Face, Sad Face	C	Foundations	Wright Group
Hats	C	Little Readers	Houghton Mifflin
Hedgehog Is Hungry	C	PM Books	Rigby
Hello	C	Storybox	Wright Group
Help!	C	Reading Corners	Dominie Press
Hey There, Bear!	C	Little Celebrations	Celebration Press
Hot Dogs (Sausages)	C	PM Books	Rigby
Hot Potato and Cold Potato	C	Foundations	Wright Group
House	C	Little Celebrations	Celebration Press
Houses	C	Windmill-Look & Listen	Wright Group
Houses	C	Storybox	Wright Group
Hug Is Warm, A	C	Sunshine	Wright Group
Humpity-Bump	C	Little Celebrations	Celebration Press
Hungry Bear	C	Smart Start	Rigby
I Am a Book Worm	C	Sunshine	Wright Group
I Can Dig	C	Can You Do This	SRA/McGraw Hill
I Can Do It Myself	C	Literacy 2000	Rigby
I Can Draw	C	Carousel Earlybirds	Dominie Press
I Can Eat	C	Can You Do This	SRA/McGraw Hill
I Can Jump	C	Sunshine	Wright Group
I Can Play	C	Can You Do This	SRA/McGraw Hill
I Can Ride	C	Can You Do This	SRA/McGraw Hill
I Can Wash	C	Carousel Earlybirds	Dominie Press
I Climb	C	This Is the Way	SRA/McGraw Hill

Title	Level	Author/Series	Publisher/Distributor
I Could Be	C	Visions	Wright Group
I Crawl	C	This Is the Way	SRA/McGraw Hill
I Dress Up Like Mama	C	Visions	Wright Group
I Eat Leaves	C	Vandine, JoAnn	Mondo
I Fly	C	This Is the Way	SRA/McGraw Hill
I Get Ready for School	C	Visions	Wright Group
I Jump	C	This Is the Way	SRA/McGraw Hill
I Like	C	Literacy 2000	Rigby
I Like Green	C	Literacy 2000	Rigby
I Like to Play	C	Carousel Readers	Dominie Press
I Love Bugs	C	Lake, Mary Dixon	Mondo
I Love Ladybugs	C	Allen, R. V.	SRA/McGraw Hill
I Love Music	C	Carousel Readers	Dominie Press
I Remember	C	Literacy 2000	Rigby
I Run	C	This Is the Way	SRA/McGraw Hill
I Spy	C	Literacy 2000	Rigby
I Swim	C	This Is the Way	SRA/McGraw Hill
I Want a Pet	C	Gregorich	School Zone
I Want Ice Cream	C	Storybox	Wright Group
I Went Walking	C	Williams, Sue	Harcourt Brace
I Wonder	C	Little Celebrations	Celebration Press
I Write	C	Sunshine	Wright Group
I'm Hungry	C	Visions	Wright Group
I'm Not, I'm Not	C	Windmill-Look & Listen	Wright Group
I've Lost My Boot	C	Windmill-Look & Listen	Wright Group
Ice Cream	C	Sunshine	Wright Group
If You Meet a Dragon	C	Storybox	Wright Group
In My Bed	C	Literacy 2000	Rigby
In My Garden	C	Carousel Readers	Dominie Press
In My Room	C	Literacy 2000	Rigby
In the City	C	Pasternac, Susana	Scholastic
In the Forest	C	Twig	Wright Group
In Went Goldilocks	C	Literacy 2000	Rigby
Is It Alive?	C	Learn to Read	Creative Teaching Press
Is This a Monster?	C	Lovell, Scarlett and Diane	Mondo
It's Football Time	C	Geddes, Diana	Kaeden Books
Joshua James Likes Trucks	C	Rookie Reader	Children's Press
Kitten Chased a Fly	C	Windmill-Look & Listen	Wright Group
Kittens	C	Literacy 2000	Rigby
Kitty and the Birds	C	PM Books	Rigby
Lazy Pig, The	C	PM Books	Rigby
Let's Go	C	Windmill-Look & Listen	Wright Group
Let's Have a Swim	C	Sunshine	Wright Group
Library, The	C	Carousel Readers	Dominie Press
Lin's Backpack	C	Little Celebrations	Celebration Press
Little Fish	C	Tiger Cub	Peguis
Little Pig	C	Storybox	Wright Group
Lizard on a Stick	C	Wonder World	Wright Group
Look Again	C	Montgomery, Charlotte	Mondo
Looking Down	C	PM Starters	Rigby
Looking for Halloween	C	Urmston, K. & Evans, K.	Kaeden Books
Lost	C	Storybox	Wright Group
Lost Glove, The	C	Foundations	Wright Group
Lunch Orders	C	Tadpoles	Rigby

Title	Level	Author/Series	Publisher/Distributor
Lunch Time	C	Carousel Readers	Dominie Press
Magic Food	C	Smart Start	Rigby
Magic Machine	C	Sunshine	Wright Group
Mail Came Today, The	C	Carousel Readers	Dominie Press
Me	C	Reading Corners	Dominie Press
Merry-Go-Round	C	Sunshine	Wright Group
Merry-Go-Round, The	C	PM Books	Rigby
Monster Meals	C	Literacy 2000	Rigby
Monster, Monster	C	Reading Corners	Dominie Press
Monster Sandwich, A	C	Storybox	Wright Group
Monster's Party, The	C	Read-Togethers	Wright Group
Mother Hippopotamus Goes Shopping	C	Foundations	Wright Group
Mouse	C	Storybox	Wright Group
Mud Pie	C	Literacy 2000	Rigby
My Accident	C	PM Starters	Rigby
My Best Friend	C	Little Celebrations	Celebration Press
My Big Wheel	C	Visions	Wright Group
My Birthday Party	C	Visions	Wright Group
My Circus Family	C	Lake, Mary Dixon	Mondo
My Clothes	C	Carousel Earlybirds	Dominie Press
My Dad Cooks	C	Carousel Readers	Dominie Press
My Dog Willy	C	Little Readers	Houghton Mifflin
My Dream	C	Wildsmith, Brian	Oxford
My Friend at School	C	Visions	Wright Group
My Home	C	Storybox	Wright Group
My Home	C	Sunshine	Wright Group
My Little Brother	C	Windmill-Look & Listen	Wright Group
My Little Dog	C	PM Starters	Rigby
My New House	C	Reading Corners	Dominie Press
My Picture	C	Carousel Readers	Dominie Press
My Puppy	C	Little Celebrations	Celebration Press
My Shadow	C	Foundations	Wright Group
My Shadow	C	Sunshine	Wright Group
Nighttime	C	Storybox	Wright Group
Now We Can Go	C	Jonas, Ann	Greenwillow
Octopus Goes to School	C	Bordelon, Carolyn	Seedling
Old and New	C	Interaction	Rigby
Old Tuatara	C	Ready to Read	Richard C. Owen/ Celebration Press
On a Chair	C	Storybox	Wright Group
On a Cold, Cold Day	C	Tadpoles	Rigby
On the Go	C	Learn to Read	Creative Teaching Press
One Bird Sat on the Fence	C	Wonder World	Wright Group
Our Grandad	C	Sunshine	Wright Group
Our Granny	C	Sunshine	Wright Group
Our Street	C	Sunshine	Wright Group
Painting	C	Storybox	Wright Group
Pancakes, Crackers and Pizza	C	Rookie Reader	Children's Press
Pet Parade	C	Literacy 2000	Rigby
Photo Book, The	C	PM Books	Rigby
Pick a Pet	C	Little Celebrations	Celebration Press
Pigs Peek	C	Books for Young Learners	Richard C. Owen
Pitty Pitty Pat	C	Little Celebrations	Celebration Press
Places	C	Little Red Readers	Sundance

Title	Level	Author/Series	Publisher/Distributor
Playhouse for Monster	C	Mueller, Virginia	Whitman
Plop	C	Storybox	Wright Group
Race, The	C	Sunshine	Wright Group
Rain	C	Kalan, Robert	Greenwillow
Raindrops	C	Beginning Literacy	Scholastic
Riding	C	Foundations	Wright Group
Rockets	C	Little Celebrations	Celebration Press
Roll Over!	C	Peek, Merle	Clarion
Round and Round	C	Storybox	Wright Group
Run! Run!	C	Vandine, JoAnn	Mondo
Running	C	Foundations	Wright Group
Safety	C	Interaction	Rigby
Sally and the Daisy	C	PM Books	Rigby
Sally and the Elephant	C	Wonder World	Wright Group
Sammy at the Farm	C	Urmston, K. & Evans, K.	Kaeden Books
Sandwich, The	C	Carousel Earlybirds	Dominie Press
Scarecrow	C	Literacy 2000	Rigby
Scaredy Cat	C	Learn to Read	Creative Teaching Press
Seesaw, The	C	Voyages	SRA/McGraw Hill
Shape Walk	C	Little Celebrations	Celebration Press
Sharing	C	Literacy 2000	Rigby
Shark in a Sack	C	Sunshine	Wright Group
Shoo!	C	Sunshine	Wright Group
Shopping	C	Little Red Readers	Sundance
Shopping	C	Interaction	Rigby
Signs	C	Little Celebrations	Celebration Press
Silly Old Possum	C	Storybox	Wright Group
Sometimes I'm Silly	C	Visions	Wright Group
Speed Boat, The	C	Sunshine	Wright Group
Splash	C	Foundations	Wright Group
Splosh	C	Storybox	Wright Group
Spots, Feathers and Curly Tails	C	Tafuri, Nancy	Morrow
Stop	C	Storybox	Wright Group
Stop!	C	Wonder World	Wright Group
Storm, The	C	Storybox	Wright Group
Sunrise	C	Literacy 2000	Rigby
Tee Ball	C	Little Celebrations	Celebration Press
Teeny Tiny Tina	C	Literacy 2000	Rigby
Things I Like to Do	C	Carousel Earlybirds	Dominie Press
Things on Wheels	C	Little Red Readers	Sundance
Tiger, Tiger	C	PM Books	Rigby
Together	C	Sunshine	Wright Group
Tommy's Tummy Ache	C	Literacy 2000	Rigby
Toot, Toot	C	Wildsmith, Brian	Oxford
Train Ride, The	C	Literacy 2000	Rigby
Train, The	C	Visions	Wright Group
Transportation Museum, The	C	Little Red Readers	Sundance
Trolley Ride	C	Tadpoles	Rigby
Trucks	C	Literacy 2000	Rigby
Tyler's Train	C	Little Celebrations	Celebration Press
Uncle Buncle's House	C	Sunshine	Wright Group
Underground	C	Twig	Wright Group
Up in a Tree	C	Sunshine	Wright Group
Up Went the Goat	C	Gregorich	School Zone

Title	Level	Author/Series	Publisher/Distributor
Wake Up, Dad!	C	PM Books	Rigby
Wake Up, Mom!	C	Sunshine	Wright Group
Walking to School	C	Voyages	SRA/McGraw Hill
Walking, Walking	C	Twig	Wright Group
Watch Out!	C	Literacy 2000	Rigby
Water	C	Carousel Readers	Dominie Press
We Can Run	C	PM Starters	Rigby
We Like	C	Foundations	Wright Group
We Make Pizza	C	Carousel Readers	Dominie Press
What a Mess	C	Storybox	Wright Group
What a Tale!	C	Wildsmith, Brian	Oxford
What Can You Be?	C	Tiger Cub	Peguis
What Can You Do?	C	Tiger Cub	Peguis
What Can You See?	C	Literacy 2000	Rigby
What Comes First?	C	Swanson-Natsues, Lyn	Mondo
What Did Kim Catch?	C	Literacy 2000	Rigby
What Did They Want?	C	Smart Start	Rigby
What Do You Have?	C	Tiger Cub	Peguis
What Goes in the Bathtub?	C	Literacy 2000	Rigby
What I Like at School	C	Little Red Readers	Sundance
What Is Blue?	C	Carousel Earlybirds	Dominie Press
What's on Your T-Shirt?	C	Carousel Readers	Dominie Press
What's That?	C	Carousel Earlybirds	Dominie Press
What's the Time Mr. Wolf?	C	Windmill-Look & Listen	Wright Group
Wheels	C	Sunshine	Wright Group
When I Play	C	Literacy 2000	Rigby
When It Rains	C	Foundations	Wright Group
When Itchy Witchy Sneezes	C	Sunshine	Wright Group
Where Are They Going?	C	Storybox	Wright Group
Where Do Monsters Live?	C	Learn to Read	Creative Teaching Press
Where Do You Live?	C	Tiger Cub	Peguis
Where Does the Teacher Sleep?	C	Gibson, Kathleen	Seedling
Where Is My Grandma?	C	Foundations	Wright Group
Where Will You Sleep Tonight?	C	Foundations	Wright Group
Where's Bear?	C	Windmill-Look & Listen	Wright Group
Where's Little Mole?	C	Little Celebrations	Celebration Press
Where's Tim?	C	Sunshine	Wright Group
Where's Your Tooth?	C	Learn to Read	Creative Teaching Press
Who Fed the Chickens?	C	Little Celebrations	Celebration Press
Who Lives Here?	C	Learn to Read	Creative Teaching Press
Who Lives Here?	C	Storybox	Wright Group
Who Lives in this Hole?	C	Twig	Wright Group
Who's Going to Lick the Bowl?	C	Storybox	Wright Group
Whose Birthday Is It Today?	C	Book Bank	Wright Group
Whose Forest Is It?	C	Learn to Read	Creative Teaching Press
Woof!	C	Literacy 2000	Rigby
Would You Like to Fly?	C	Twig	Wright Group
You	C	Carousel Earlybirds	Dominie Press
Yummy, Tum, Tee	C	Little Celebrations	Celebration Press
Zoo Food	C	Reading Corners	Dominie Press
Zoo, The	C	Carousel Readers	Dominie Press
Ali's Story	D	Sunshine	Wright Group
All Join In	D	Literacy 2000	Rigby

Title	Level	Author/Series	Publisher/Distributor
All Kinds of Food	D	Carousel Readers	Dominie Press
Along Comes Jake	D	Sunshine	Wright Group
Animals in the Desert	D	Carousel Readers	Dominie Press
At the Fair	D	Little Red Readers	Sundance
At the Fair	D	Sunshine	Wright Group
At the Park	D	Little Red Readers	Sundance
At the Seaside	D	Oxford Reading Tree	Oxford
At the Zoo	D	Predictable Storybooks	SRA/McGraw Hill
Auntie Maria and the Cat	D	Sunshine	Wright Group
Baby Elephant Gets Lost	D	Foundations	Wright Group
Baby's Birthday	D	Literacy 2000	Rigby
Ball Bounced, The	D	Tafuri, Nancy	Morrow
Ball Game, The	D	Beginning Literacy	Scholastic
Bath for a Beagle	D	First Start	Troll
Beach	D	Book Bank	Wright Group
Bear Lived in a Cave	D	Little Red Readers	Sundance
Bears in the Night	D	Berenstain, Stan & Jan	Random House
Bears on Wheels	D	Berenstain, Stan & Jan	Random House
Ben's Teddy Bear	D	PM Books	Rigby
Ben's Treasure Hunt	D	PM Books	Rigby
Best Friends	D	Little Readers	Houghton Mifflin
Best Place, The	D	Literacy 2000	Rigby
Big and Green	D	Wonder World	Wright Group
Big Hill, The	D	Storybox	Wright Group
Big Sneeze, The	D	Foundations	Wright Group
Birthday Book	D	Book Bank	Wright Group
Birthday Cake	D	Literacy 2000	Rigby
Blackberries	D	PM Books	Rigby
Blue Bug Goes to School	D	Poulet, Virginia	Children's Press
Bread	D	Sunshine	Wright Group
Bumble Bee	D	Ready to Read	Richard C. Owen/ Celebration Press
Bump, Bump, Bump	D	Cat on the Mat/Wood	Oxford
But Granny Did	D	Voyages	SRA/McGraw Hill
Buzzing Bees	D	Mathtales	Mimosa
Can't You See We're Reading	D	Hall, N. & Robinson, A.	Nelson/Michaels Assoc.
Carry-Out Food	D	Tadpoles	Rigby
Cat Who Loved Red, The	D	Salem, L. & Stewart, J.	Seedling
Chick and Duckling, The	D	Ginsburg, Mirra	Macmillan
Circus	D	Wonder World	Wright Group
Circus Clown, The	D	Literacy 2000	Rigby
City Mouse and the Country Mouse	D	Learn to Read	Creative Teaching Press
Colors	D	Foundations	Wright Group
Come on Mom	D	New Way	Steck-Vaughn
Cooling Off	D	Reading Corners	Dominie Press
Crickets on the Go	D	Little Celebrations	Celebration Press
Dad's Garden	D	Literacy 2000	Rigby
Danny's Dollars	D	Reading Corners	Dominie Press
Dirty Larry	D	Rookie Reader	Children's Press
Dog Went for Walk	D	Voyages	SRA/McGraw Hill
Don't Be Late	D	Beginning Literacy	Scholastic
Faces	D	Little Celebrations	Celebration Press
Fantail, Fantail	D	Ready to Read	Richard C. Owen/ Celebration Press

Title	Level	Author/Series	Publisher/Distributor
Family Soccer	D	Geddes, Diana	Kaeden Books
Farm Concert	D	Storybox	Wright Group
Farm Day	D	Little Celebrations	Celebration Press
Farm in Spring, The	D	PM Starters Two	Rigby
Fast Draw Freddie	D	Rookie Reader	Children's Press
Fast Food	D	Foundations	Wright Group
Fast Machines	D	Foundations	Wright Group
Father Bear Goes Fishing	D	PM Books	Rigby
Feet	D	Storybox	Wright Group
First Day of School	D	Carousel Readers	Dominie Press
Fishing	D	Yukish, J.	Kaeden Books
Five Little Monsters	D	Learn to Read	Creative Teaching Press
Footprints in the Snow	D	Hello Reader	Scholastic
Freddie the Frog	D	First Start	Troll
Frog and the Fly	D	Cat on the Mat/Wood	Oxford
Fun	D	Yannone, Deborah	Kaeden Books
Fur	D	Mark, Jan	Harper & Row
Gardening	D	Foundations	Wright Group
Gobble, Gobble, Gone	D	Little Celebrations	Celebration Press
Going Out	D	Foundations	Wright Group
Going Shopping	D	Carousel Readers	Dominie Press
Good Bad Cat, The	D	Start to Read	School Zone
Good for You	D	Sunshine	Wright Group
Good-Bye Lucy	D	Sunshine	Wright Group
Goodnight	D	Voyages	SRA/McGraw Hill
Greedy Cat Is Hungry	D	Ready to Read	Richard C. Owen/ Celebration Press
Green, Green	D	Little Readers	Houghton Mifflin
Grocery Shopping	D	Yannone, D.	Kaeden Books
Helping You	D	Interaction	Rigby
Henry and the Helicopter	D	Literacy 2000	Rigby
Hiding	D	Foundations	Wright Group
Hogboggit, The	D	Ready to Read	Richard C. Owen/ Celebration Press
Hoiho's Chicks	D	Ready to Read	Richard C. Owen/ Celebration Press
Horace	D	Storybox	Wright Group
Horrible Big Black Bug, The	D	Tadpoles	Rigby
How Many Bugs in a Box?	D	Carter, David	Simon & Schuster
Hungry Kitten, The	D	PM Books	Rigby
Hurry Up	D	Voyages	SRA/McGraw Hill
I Can Build a House	D	Watanabe, Shigeo	Viking
I Can't Sleep	D	Learn to Read	Creative Teaching Press
I Like Books	D	Browne, Anthony	Random House
I Like Worms	D	Sunshine	Wright Group
I Love Mud and Mud Loves Me	D	Beginning Literacy	Scholastic
I Wish I Had a Dinosaur	D	Little Celebrations	Celebration Press
Ice Is . . . Whee!	D	Rookie Reader	Children's Press
I'm Bigger Than You	D	Sunshine	Wright Group
Insects That Bother Us	D	Foundations	Wright Group
Island, The	D	Wildsmith, Brian	Oxford
It's Game Day	D	Salem, L. & Stewart, J.	Seedling
Jimmy	D	Foundations	Wright Group
Julia's Lists	D	Little Celebrations	Celebration Press

Title	Level	Author/Series	Publisher/Distributor
Jungle Parade: A Singing Game	D	Little Celebrations	Celebration Press
King's Surprise, The	D	Stewart, J. & Salem, L.	Seedling
Kitchen Tools	D	Foundations	Wright Group
Late One Night	D	Mader, Jan	Kaeden Books
Lazy Mary	D	Read-Togethers	Wright Group
Lizard Loses His Tail	D	PM Books	Rigby
Look for Me	D	Storybox	Wright Group
Look in Mom's Purse	D	Carousel Readers	Dominie Press
Looking After Grandpa	D	Foundations	Wright Group
Lost and Found	D	Carousel Readers	Dominie Press
Lump in My Bed	D	Book Bank	Wright Group
Making Pancakes	D	Carousel Readers	Dominie Press
Making Things	D	Foundations	Wright Group
Maria Goes to School	D	Foundations	Wright Group
Mary Wore Her Dress	D	Peek, Merle	Clarion
Maybe I'll Be	D	Carousel Readers	Dominie Press
Mom Can Fix Anything	D	Learn to Read	Creative Teaching Press
Mom's New Car	D	Foundations	Wright Group
Monkey Bridge, The	D	Sunshine	Wright Group
Monster and the Baby	D	Mueller, Virginia	Whitman
Monster Can't Sleep	D	Mueller, Virginia	Puffin Books
More and More Clowns	D	Allen, R. V.	SRA/McGraw Hill
Mother Hoppopotamus's Dry Skin	D	Foundations	Wright Group
Mouse's Baby Blanket	D	Brown, Beverly Swerdlow	Seedling
Moving In	D	Foundations	Wright Group
Mr. Grump	D	Sunshine	Wright Group
Mr. Noisy	D	Learn to Read	Creative Teaching Press
Mud	D	Lewison, Wendy	Random House
Mumps	D	PM Books	Rigby
My Big Box	D	Voyages	SRA/McGraw Hill
My Bike	D	Ready to Read	Richard C. Owen/ Celebration Press
My Friend Alan	D	Carousel Readers	Dominie Press
My Friends	D	Little Celebrations	Celebration Press
My Messy Room	D	Hello Reader	Scholastic
My Pet	D	Salem, L. & Stewart, J.	Seedling
My Skateboard	D	Carousel Readers	Dominie Press
Naughty Patch	D	Foundations	Wright Group
Never Be	D	Salem, L. & Stewart, J.	Seedling
Night in the Desert	D	Carousel Readers	Dominie Press
No No	D	Storybox	Wright Group
Noisy Breakfast	D	Blonder, Ellen	Scholastic
Not Yet	D	Reading Links	Steck-Vaughn
Now I Ride	D	Carousel Readers	Dominie Press
On the Farm	D	Literacy 2000	Rigby
On Vacation	D	Little Red Readers	Sundance
One Cold Wet Night	D	Read-Togethers	Wright Group
Oops!	D	Mayer, Mercer	Penguin
Our Dog Sam	D	Literacy 2000	Rigby
Our Teacher, Miss Pool	D	Ready to Read	Richard C. Owen/ Celebration Press
Paul the Pitcher	D	Rookie Reader	Children's Press
Play Ball, Kate	D	Giant First Step	Troll

Title	Level	Author/Series	Publisher/Distributor
Praying Mantis, The	D	Ready to Read	Richard C. Owen/ Celebration Press
Reading Is Everywhere	D	Sunshine	Wright Group
Ready Steady Jump	D	Ready to Read	Richard C. Owen/ Celebration Press
Ride in the Country, A	D	Carousel Readers	Dominie Press
River, The	D	Foundations	Wright Group
Rocks	D	Voyages	SRA/McGraw Hill
Salad Feast	D	Little Readers	Houghton Mifflin
Sally's Beans	D	PM Books	Rigby
Sandwiches	D	New Way	Steck-Vaughn
Scaredy Cat Runs Away	D	Learn to Read	Creative Teaching Press
Scat Said the Cat	D	Sunshine	Wright Group
School Bus	D	Crews, Donald	Morrow
Scratch My Back	D	Foundations	Wright Group
Seed, The	D	Sunshine	Wright Group
Sense	D	Voyages	SRA/McGraw Hill
Shadows	D	Literacy 2000	Rigby
Shapes	D	Carousel Readers	Dominie Press
Sharing Time	D	Carousel Readers	Dominie Press
Shoes	D	Book Bank	Wright Group
Shopping	D	Literacy 2000	Rigby
Sleeping Out	D	Storybox	Wright Group
Smile	D	Read Alongs	Rigby
Snow Joe	D	Rookie Reader	Children's Press
Snow Walk	D	Reading Corners	Dominie Press
Snowflakes	D	Urmston, K. & Evans, K.	Kaeden Books
Some People	D	Reading Corners	Dominie Press
Something New	D	Little Celebrations	Celebration Press
Something to Share	D	Carousel Readers	Dominie Press
Spider, Spider	D	Sunshine	Wright Group
Spiders, Spiders Everywhere!	D	Learn to Read	Creative Teaching Press
Splish Splash	D	Little Celebrations	Celebration Press
Storm, The	D	Foundations	Wright Group
Susie Goes Shopping	D	Bauer, Roger	Kaeden Books
Swat It!	D	Bauer, Roger	Kaeden Books
Tails	D	Vaughan, Marcia	Mondo
Take a Bow, Jody	D	Eaton, Audry and Jane	Seedling
That's Dangerous	D	Voyages	SRA/McGraw Hill
Things I Like	D	Browne, Anthony	Random House
This Hat	D	Little Celebrations	Celebration Press
This Is the Plate	D	Little Celebrations	Celebration Press
Three Silly Monkeys	D	Foundations	Wright Group
To New York	D	Storybox	Wright Group
To the Beach	D	Urmston, K. & Evans, K.	Kaeden Books
Toby Tomato	D	Little Celebrations	Celebration Press
Tom Is Brave	D	PM Books	Rigby
Too Big for Me	D	Storybox	Wright Group
Too Many Balloons	D	Rookie Reader	Children's Press
Toys	D	Tiger Cub	Peguis
Try It!	D	Reading Corners	Dominie Press
Turtle, The	D	Foundations	Wright Group
Wake Up, Wake Up!	D	Wildsmith, B. & R.	Scholastic
Watching TV	D	Foundations	Wright Group

Title	Level	Author/Series	Publisher/Distributor
We Like Fish	D	PM Starters	Rigby
What Can You Hear?	D	Tiger Cub	Peguis
What Fell Out?	D	Carousel Readers	Dominie Press
What Is It Called?	D	Reading Unlimited	Celebration Press
What Would the Zoo Do?	D	Salem, Lynn	Seedling
What Would You Like?	D	Sunshine	Wright Group
Where Are My Socks?	D	Ready to Read	Richard C. Owen/ Celebration Press
Where Are the Sunhats?	D	PM Books	Rigby
Where Are You Going?	D	Learn to Read	Creative Teaching Press
Where Are You Going, Aja Rose?	D	Sunshine	Wright Group
Where Is It?	D	Rookie Reader	Children's Press
Where Is Miss Pool?	D	Ready to Read	Richard C. Owen/ Celebration Press
Where Is the Milk?	D	Foundations	Wright Group
Where Is the School Bus?	D	Carousel Readers	Dominie Press
Where's Al?	D	Barton, Byron	Houghton Mifflin
Where's Baby Tom?	D	Book Bank	Wright Group
Where's Cupcake?	D	Little Readers	Houghton Mifflin
Who Cried for Pie?	D	First Start	Troll
Who Is Who?	D	Rookie Reader	Children's Press
Who Wants to Live in My House?	D	Book Bank	Wright Group
Who Will Help?	D	Learn to Read	Creative Teaching Press
Who's Hiding?	D	Learn to Read	Creative Teaching Press
Willy the Helper	D	Little Readers	Houghton Mifflin
Wind Surfing	D	Sunshine	Wright Group
Worms	D	Literacy 2000	Rigby
Alien at the Zoo	E	Sunshine	Wright Group
All By Myself	E	Mayer, Mercer	Golden
Animal Babies	E	Rookie Reader	Children's Press
Around My School	E	Exploring History	Rigby
At the Beach	E	Oxford Reading Tree	Oxford University Press
At the Seaside	E	Oxford Reading Tree	Oxford
Baby, The	E	Burningham, John	Crowell
Baby Bear Goes Fishing	E	PM Books	Rigby
Baseball Fun	E	Geddes, Diana	Kaeden Books
Bath for Patches, A	E	Carousel Readers	Dominie Press
Ben's Dad	E	PM Books	Rigby
Biff's Aeroplane	E	Oxford Reading Tree	Oxford
Big Brown Box	E	Voyages	SRA/McGraw Hill
Big Friend, Little Friend	E	Greenfield, Eloise	Houghton Mifflin
Big Toe, The	E	Storybox	Wright Group
Big Toe, The	E	Read-Togethers	Wright Group
Bill's Baby	E	Tadpoles	Rigby
Blanket, The	E	Burningham, John	Crowell
Blue Bug's Book of Colors	E	Poulet, Virginia	Children's Press
Boo-Hoo	E	Read-Togethers	Wright Group
Boogly, The	E	Literacy 2000	Rigby
Boots and Shoes	E	Cooper, Ann	Kaeden Books
Brave Father Mouse	E	PM Books	Rigby
Brothers	E	Talk About Books	Dominie Press
Buster McCluster	E	Wonder World	Wright Group
Buster the Balloon	E	Mathtales	Mimosa

Title	Level	Author/Series	Publisher/Distributor
Butch, the Outdoor Cat	E	Carousel Readers	Dominie Press
Camping	E	Sunshine	Wright Group
Catch That Frog	E	Reading Unlimited	Celebration Press
Creepy Caterpillar	E	Little Readers	Houghton Mifflin
Curious Cat	E	Little Celebrations	Celebration Press
Custard	E	Wonder World	Wright Group
Dandelion, The	E	Sunshine	Wright Group
Daniel's Basketball Team	E	Carousel Readers	Dominie Press
Deep in the Woods	E	Carousel Readers	Dominie Press
Diana Made Dinner	E	Carousel Readers	Dominie Press
Dog and Cat	E	Fehner, C.	Children's Press
Dog and Cat	E	Story Basket	Wright Group
Don't Panic	E	Book Bank	Wright Group
Don't Throw It Away!	E	Wonder World	Wright Group
Don't You Laugh at Me	E	Sunshine	Wright Group
Dreams	E	Book Bank	Wright Group
Dressed Up Sammy	E	Urmston, K. & Evans, K.	Kaeden Books
Ear Book	E	Perkins, Al	Random House
Eat Your Peas Louise	E	Rookie Reader	Children's Press
Elephants Are Coming, The	E	Little Readers	Houghton Mifflin
Excuses, Excuses	E	Tadpoles	Rigby
Farmer and the Skunk	E	Tiger Cub	Peguis
Farmer in the Dell	E	Parkinson, Kathy	Whitman
Find a Caterpillar	E	Book Bank	Wright Group
Fire! Fire!	E	PM Books	Rigby
Five Little Monkeys Jumping on the Bed	E	Christelow, Eileen	Houghton Mifflin
Fizz and Splutter	E	Storybox	Wright Group
Floppy's Bath	E	Oxford Reading Tree	Oxford
Flowers for Mom	E	Carousel Readers	Dominie Press
Flying	E	Crews, Donald	Greenwillow
Foot Book	E	Seuss, Dr.	Random House
Forgetful Fred	E	Tadpoles	Rigby
Friend for Little White Rabbit	E	PM Books	Rigby
Funny Man, A	E	Hello Reader	Scholastic
Get Lost Becka	E	Start to Read	School Zone
Go Back to Sleep	E	Literacy 2000	Rigby
Go Dog Go	E	Eastman, P. D.	Random House
Grandma's Present	E	Foundations	Wright Group
Green Footprints	E	Literacy 2000	Rigby
Grumpy Elephant	E	Storybox	Wright Group
Guess What Kind of Ball	E	Urmston, K. & Evans, K.	Kaeden Books
Gum on the Drum	E	Gregorich	School Zone
Hands, Hands, Hands	E	Vaughan, Marcia	Mondo
Happy Egg	E	Kraus, Robert	Scholastic
Haunted House	E	Storybox	Wright Group
Hen Can, A	E	Tiger Cub	Peguis
Henry's Busy Day	E	Campbell, Rod	Penguin
Here Comes Annette!	E	Voyages	SRA/McGraw Hill
Herman the Helper	E	Kraus, Robert	Simon & Schuster
Hermit Crab	E	PM Books	Rigby
Hi, Clouds!	E	Rookie Reader	Children's Press
Hide and Seek	E	Foundations	Wright Group
Home Sweet Home	E	Roffey, Maureen	Bodley
Honey, My Rabbit	E	Voyages	SRA/McGraw Hill

Title	Level	Author/Series	Publisher/Distributor
Hot Rod Harry	E	Petrie, Kathryn	Children's Press
I Can Squeak	E	Windmill-Rhyme & Rhythm	Wright Group
I Like it When . . .	E	Ready Set Read	Steck-Vaughn
I Love Camping	E	Carousel Readers	Dominie Press
I Love Cats	E	Rookie Reader	Children's Press
If I Were You	E	Wildsmith, Brian	Oxford
In a Dark, Dark Wood	E	Carter, David	S & S Trade
In a Dark, Dark Wood	E	Read-Togethers	Wright Group
In a Town	E	Little Celebrations	Celebration Press
In My Pocket	E	Carousel Readers	Dominie Press
Inside, Outside, Upside Down	E	Berenstain, Stan & Jan	Random House
It Looked Like Spilt Milk	E	Shaw, Charles	Harper & Row
Jigaree, The	E	Storybox	Wright Group
Jimmy's Goal	E	Foundations	Wright Group
Joe's Father	E	Book Bank	Wright Group
Jumble Sale, The	E	Oxford Reading Tree	Oxford
Just Like Me	E	Rookie Reader	Children's Press
Keeping Fit	E	Little Celebrations	Celebration Press
Kipper's Birthday	E	Oxford Reading Tree	Oxford
Let's Play Basketball	E	Geddes, Diana	Kaeden Books
Little Boy and the Balloon Man	E	Tiger Cub	Peguis
Little Bulldozer	E	PM Books	Rigby
Lizard	E	Foundations	Wright Group
Lucky Goes to Dog School	E	PM Books	Rigby
Making Oatmeal	E	Interaction	Rigby
Martian Goo	E	Salem, L. & Stewart, J.	Seedling
May I Stay Home Today?	E	Tadpoles	Rigby
Midge in the Hospital	E	Oxford Reading Tree	Oxford
Mosquito Buzzed, A	E	Little Readers	Houghton Mifflin
Moving Day	E	Sunshine	Wright Group
Moving to America	E	Carousel Readers	Dominie Press
Mrs. Sato's Hen	E	Little Celebrations	Celebration Press
Mrs. Wishy Washy	E	Storybox	Wright Group
My Brother, The Brat	E	Hello Reader	Scholastic
My Dad Lost His Job	E	Carousel Readers	Dominie Press
My Doll	E	Yukish, Joe	Kaeden Books
My Pet Bobby	E	Little Readers	Houghton Mifflin
My Tiger Cat	E	Frankford, Marilyn	Kaeden Books
My Two Homes	E	Carousel Readers	Dominie Press
Nests	E	Literacy 2000	Rigby
New Baby, The	E	PM Books	Rigby
New Nest, The	E	Foundations	Wright Group
Nick's Glasses	E	Ready to Read	Richard C. Owen
Night Train, The	E	Storybox	Wright Group
Nose Book	E	Perkins, Al	Random House
Oh, Jump in the Sack	E	Storybox	Wright Group
Oh, No, Sherman	E	Erickson, Betty	Seedling
One Sun in the Sky	E	Windmill-Rhyme & Rhythm	Wright Group
Our Cat	E	Foundations	Wright Group
Our House Had a Mouse	E	Worthington, Denise	Seedling
Out the Door	E	Rookie Reader	Children's Press
Paper Bag Trail	E	Beginning Literacy	Scholastic
Pat's New Puppy	E	Reading Unlimited	Celebration Press
Peaches the Pig	E	Little Readers	Houghton Mifflin

Title	Level	Author/Series	Publisher/Distributor
Peanut Butter and Jelly	E	Little Readers	Houghton Mifflin
People on the Beach	E	Carousel Readers	Dominie Press
Pet That I Want, The	E	Hello Reader	Scholastic
Present, The	E	Literacy 2000	Rigby
Pumpkin, The	E	Storybox	Wright Group
Purple Is Part of a Rainbow	E	Rookie Reader	Children's Press
Race, The	E	Little Celebrations	Celebration Press
Red Rose, The	E	Read-Togethers	Wright Group
Rex's Dance	E	Little Readers	Houghton Mifflin
Rosie's Party	E	Little Readers	Houghton Mifflin
Rum, Tum, Tum	E	Storybox	Wright Group
Sally's Red Bucket	E	PM Books	Rigby
Sam's Mask	E	Ready to Read	Richard C. Owen/ Celebration Press
Sand	E	Giant Step Readers	Educ. Insights
Sand Picnic, The	E	New Way	Steck-Vaughn
Sarah Snail	E	Voyages	SRA/McGraw Hill
School, The	E	Burningham, John	Crowell
Seagull Is Clever	E	PM Books	Rigby
Secret Friend, The	E	Little Celebrations	Celebration Press
Simply Sam	E	Voyages	SRA/McGraw Hill
Sing a Song	E	Read-Togethers	Wright Group
Sisters	E	Talk About Books	Dominie Press
Smarty Pants	E	Read-Togethers	Wright Group
Snails	E	Foundations	Wright Group
Spots	E	Oxford Reading Tree	Oxford
Spots	E	Literacy 2000	Rigby
Stables Are for Horses	E	Windmill-Rhyme & Rhythm	Wright Group
Strawberry Jam	E	Oxford Reading Tree	Oxford
Surprise for Mom	E	Urmston, K. & Evans, K.	Kaeden Books
Taking Care of Rosie	E	Salem, L. & Steward, J.	Seedling
Taking Our Photo	E	Voyages	SRA/McGraw Hill
Teddy Bear, Teddy Bear	E	Tiger Cub	Peguis
Terrible Twos	E	Tadpoles	Rigby
That Dog	E	Foundations	Wright Group
Things People Do for Fun	E	Foundations	Wright Group
Three Little Ducks	E	Read-Togethers	Wright Group
Timmy	E	Literacy 2000	Rigby
Tires	E	Foundations	Wright Group
Tomatoes and Bricks	E	Windmill-Rhyme & Rhythm	Wright Group
Toys	E	Talk About Books	Dominie Press
Traffic Jam	E	Harper, Leslie	Kaeden Books
Trucks	E	Foundations	Wright Group
Two	E	Carousel Readers	Dominie Press
Two Little Dogs	E	Storybox	Wright Group
Visit to the Library, A	E	Foundations	Wright Group
Well Fed Bear, The	E	Literacy 2000	Rigby
What Do You Do?	E	Tiger Cub	Peguis
What Shall I Wear?	E	Book Bank	Wright Group
What's for Dinner?	E	Salem, L. & Stewart, J.	Seedling
When Goldilocks Went to the House of the Bears	E	Tiger Cub	Peguis
Where Can It Be?	E	Jonas, Ann	Morrow
Where Is Daniel?	E	Carousel Readers	Dominie Press

Title	Level	Author/Series	Publisher/Distributor
Where Is Nancy?	E	Literacy 2000	Rigby
Where's Spot?	E	Hill, Eric	Putnam
Who Am I?	E	Hello Reader	Scholastic
Who Ate the Broccoli	E	Little Readers	Houghton Mifflin
Who Spilled the Beans?	E	Story Basket	Wright Group
Who Will Be My Mother?	E	Read-Togethers	Wright Group
Whose Eggs Are These?	E	Sunshine	Wright Group
Wiggly, Jiggly, Joggly, Tooth	E	Little Celebrations	Celebration Press
Willy's Hats	E	Stewart, J. & Salem, L.	Seedling
Wind	E	Ready to Read	Richard C. Owen/ Celebration Press
Wind Blows Strong	E	Sunshine	Wright Group
Wishy-Washy Day	E	Story Basket	Wright Group
Woosh	E	Read-Togethers	Wright Group
World's Greatest Juggler, The	E	Little Readers	Houghton Mifflin
Zoo in Willy's Bed, The	E	Gorman, Kate Sturnman	Seedling
Across the Stream	F	Ginsburg, Mirra	Morrow
Amy Loves the Snow	F	Hoban, Julia	Scholastic
Amy Loves the Sun	F	Hoban, Julia	Scholastic
Amy Loves the Wind	F	Hoban, Julia	Scholastic
Animals at the Zoo	F	First Start	Troll
Are You a Ladybug?	F	Sunshine	Wright Group
Are You My Mommy?	F	Dijs	Simon & Schuster
Are You There, Bear?	F	Maris, Ron	Greenwillow
Astronauts, The	F	Foundations	Wright Group
Baby Bear's Present	F	PM Books	Rigby
Bandages	F	Moskowitz, Ellen	Kaeden Books
Beep, Beep	F	Gregorich	School Zone
Best Cake, The	F	PM Books	Rigby
Betsy the Babysitter	F	First Start	Troll
Biggest Cake in the World, The	F	Ready to Read	Richard C. Owen
Bikes	F	Foundations	Wright Group
Billy Goats Gruff	F	Hunia, Fran	General
Bossy Bettina	F	Literacy 2000	Rigby
Building Things	F	Sunshine	Wright Group
Camping Outside	F	Book Bank	Wright Group
Carnival, The	F	Oxford Reading Tree	Oxford
Cars	F	Rockwell, Anne	Dutton
Cat Goes Fiddle-i-fee	F	Galdone, Paul	Houghton Mifflin
Cat in the Tree, A	F	Oxford Reading Tree	Oxford
Cats and Kittens	F	Reading Unlimited	Celebration Press
Christmas Tree, The	F	PM Books	Rigby
Clothes	F	Talk About Books	Dominie Press
Cock-A-Doodle Do	F	Brandenberg, Franz	Greenwillow
Cold Day, The	F	Oxford Reading Tree	Oxford
Come for a Swim	F	Sunshine	Wright Group
Cookie's Week	F	Ward, Cindy	Putnam
Cooking Pot	F	Sunshine	Wright Group
Dad's Headache	F	Sunshine	Wright Group
Dad's New Path	F	Foundations	Wright Group
Dark, Dark Tale	E	Brown, Ruth	Penguin
Dear Zoo	F	Campbell, Rod	Macmillan
Dream, The	F	Oxford Reading Tree	Oxford

Title	Level	Author/Series	Publisher/Distributor
Family Photos	F	Literacy 2000	Rigby
Farms	F	Foundations	Wright Group
Feisty Old Woman Who Lived in the Cozy Cave, The	F	Foundations	Wright Group
Floppy the Hero	F	Oxford Reading Tree	Oxford
Flying High	F	Predictable Storybooks	SRA/McGraw Hill
Foolish Goose	F	Start to Read	School Zone
Freddie's Spaghetti	F	Doyle, R. H.	Random House
Friendly Snowman	F	First Start	Troll
Friendly Snowman	F	Joyce, William	Scholastic
Get Lost!	F	Foundations	Wright Group
Gingerbread Man, The	F	Little Readers	Houghton Mifflin
Going Fishing	F	Voyages	SRA/McGraw Hill
Going for a Walk	F	DeRegniers, B. S.	Harper & Row
Going to School	F	Foundations	Wright Group
Good Night, Little Brother	F	Literacy 2000	Rigby
Grandma and the Pirate	F	Lloyd, David	Crown
Grandpa Snored	F	Literacy 2000	Rigby
Grandpa's Cookies	F	Little Readers	Houghton Mifflin
Green Bananas	F	Tadpoles	Rigby
Green Eyes	F	Literacy 2000	Rigby
Gregory's Garden	F	Cat on the Mat/Stobbs	Oxford
Growing Up, Up, Up Book	F	First Start	Troll
Happy Jack	F	First Start	Troll
Harry Takes a Bath	F	Ziefert, Harriet	Penguin
Hats	F	Talk About Books	Dominie Press
Have You Seen the Crocodile?	F	West, Colin	Harper & Row
Here Comes the Bus	F	Ziefert, Harriet	Penguin
Herman the Helper Lends a Hand	F	Kraus, Robert	Windmill
Hole in the Hedge, The	F	Sunshine	Wright Group
Honey for Baby Bear	F	PM Books	Rigby
Hooray for Snail	F	Stadler, John	HarperCollins
House for Little Red	F	Just Beginning	Modern Curriculum
House in the Tree, The	F	PM Books	Rigby
How Do You Say Hello to a Ghost?	F	Tiger Cub	Peguis
Huggly, Snuggly Pets	F	Giant Step Readers	Educ. Insights
Hungry Giant, The	F	Storybox	Wright Group
Huzzard Buzzard	F	Reese, Bob	Children's Press
I Can Fly	F	Carousel Readers	Dominie Press
I Can Spell Dinosaur	F	Predictable Storybooks	SRA/McGraw Hill
I Want to Be a Clown	F	Start to Read	School Zone
I Wonder	F	Sunshine	Wright Group
I'm King of the Castle	F	Watanabe, Shigeo	Philomel
In My Bucket	F	Carousel Readers	Dominie Press
Interruptions	F	Scarffe, B. & Snowball, D.	Mondo
Is Anyone Home?	F	Maris, Ron	Greenwillow
Is This You?	F	Krauss, Ruth	Scholastic
It's Not Fair	F	Tadpoles	Rigby
Itchy Itchy Chicken Pox	F	Hello Reader	Scholastic
Jane's Car	F	PM Books	Rigby
Jessica's Dress Up	F	Voyages	SRA/McGraw Hill
Joe and the Mouse	F	Oxford Reading Tree	Oxford
Jog, Frog, Jog	F	Gregorich	School Zone

Title	Level	Author/Series	Publisher/Distributor
Johnny Lion's Rubber Boots	F	Hurd, Edith Thacher	Harper & Row
Just Like Daddy	F	Asch, Frank	Simon & Schuster
Just Like Me	F	First Start	Troll
Katie Couldn't	F	Rookie Reader	Children's Press
Lady with the Alligator Purse	F	Westcott, Nadine Bernard	Little, Brown
Late for Soccer (Football)	F	PM Books	Rigby
Leaf Rain	F	Book Bank	Wright Group
Lion and the Rabbit, The	F	PM Books	Rigby
Lion's Tail, The	F	Reading Unlimited	Celebration Press
Little Car	F	Sunshine	Wright Group
Little Miss Muffet	F	Literacy 2000	Rigby
Look at Me	F	Literacy 2000	Rigby
Lucky We Have a Station Wagon	F	Foundations	Wright Group
Lucy's Sore Knee	F	Windmill-Look & Listen	Wright Group
Lunch	F	Urmston, K. & Evans, K.	Kaeden Books
Lydia and the Present	F	Oxford Reading Tree	Oxford
Magpie's Baking Day	F	PM Books	Rigby
Mai Li's Surprise	F	Books for Young Learners	Richard C. Owen
Marmalade's Nap	F	Wheeler, Cindy	Knopf
Marmalade's Snowy Day	F	Wheeler, Cindy	Knopf
Math Is Everywhere	F	Sunshine	Wright Group
Meanies	F	Read-Togethers	Wright Group
Melting	F	Bolton, Faye	Mondo
Messy Mark	F	First Start	Troll
Monkey See, Monkey Do	F	Hello Reader	Scholastic
Monster Bus	F	Monster Bus Series	Dominie Press
Moose Is Loose, A	F	Little Readers	Houghton Mifflin
Mr. Cricket's New Home	F	Carousel Readers	Dominie Press
Mrs. Bold	F	Literacy 2000	Rigby
Muffy and Fluffy	F	First Start	Troll
My Dad	F	Talk About Books	Dominie Press
My Friend Goes Left	F	Gregorich	School Zone
My Grandpa	F	Mitchell, Greg	Mondo
My Holiday Diary	F	Hall, N. & Robinson, A.	Nelson/Michaels Assoc.
My Kitchen	F	Rockwell, Harlow	Morrow
My Mom	F	Talk About Books	Dominie Press
My New Boy	F	Step into Reading	Random House
My New Pet	F	Little Readers	Houghton Mifflin
My Very Hungry Pet	F	Reading Corners	Dominie Press
My Wonderful Chair	F	Windmill-Look & Listen	Wright Group
Night Walk	F	Books for Young Learners	Richard C. Owen
No Luck	F	Stewart, J. & Salem, L.	Seedling
Notes from Mom	F	Stewart, J. & Salem, L.	Seedling
Notes to Dad	F	Stewart, J. & Salem, L.	Seedling
Nothing in the Mailbox	F	Books for Young Learners	Richard C. Owen
Oatmeal	F	Wonder World	Wright Group
Oh Dear	F	Campbell, Rod	Macmillan
Old Car, The	F	Voyages	SRA/McGraw Hill
Old Oak Tree, The	F	Little Celebrations	Celebration Press
Old Teeth, New Teeth	F	Wonder World	Wright Group
On the School Bus	F	Little Readers	Houghton Mifflin
One Stormy Night	F	Story Basket	Wright Group
Our Garage	F	Urmston, K. & Evans, K.	Kaeden Books

Title	Level	Author/Series	Publisher/Distributor
Pardon? Said the Giraffe	F	West, Colin	Harper & Row
Paul	F	Ready to Read	Richard C. Owen Celebration Press
Pete the Parakeet	F	First Start	Troll
Peter's Painting	F	Moss, Sally	Mondo
Pets	F	Literacy 2000	Rigby
Pip and the Little Monkey	F	Oxford Reading Tree	Oxford
Pip at the Zoo	F	Oxford Reading Tree	Oxford
Pizza Party!	F	Hello Reader	Scholastic
Polka Dots!	F	Little Celebrations	Celebration Press
Poor Old Polly	F	Read-Togethers	Wright Group
Puppet Show	F	First Start	Troll
Race, The	F	Little Readers	Houghton Mifflin
Rap Party, The	F	Foundations	Wright Group
Riddle Book	F	Reading Unlimited	Celebration Press
Roll Over	F	Gerstein, Mordicai	Crown
Roller Blades, The	F	Foundations	Wright Group
Rose	F	Wheeler, Cindy	Knopf
Rosie's Button Box	F	Bridges	Nelson/Michaels Assoc.
Rosie's Walk	F	Hutchins, Pat	Macmillan
Sally's Friends	F	PM Books	Rigby
Sam the Scarecrow	F	First Start	Troll
Samuel's Sprout	F	Little Celebrations	Celebration Press
SHHH	F	Henkes, Kevin	Morrow
Shine Sun	F	Rookie Reader	Children's Press
Shoes	F	Talk About Books	Dominie Press
Sly Fox and Red Hen	F	Hunia, Fran	Ladybird Books
Sly Fox and the Little Red Hen	F	Southgate	Ladybird Books
Smile, Baby	F	Little Readers	Houghton Mifflin
Soccer Game!	F	Hello Readers	Scholastic
Special Friend, A	F	Carousel Readers	Dominie Press
Ssh, Don't Wake the Baby	F	Voyages	SRA/McGraw Hill
Staying with Grandma Norma	F	Salem, L. & Stewart, J.	Seedling
Sticky Stanley	F	First Start	Troll
Strongest Animal, The	F	Books for Young Learners	Richard C. Owen
Susie Goes Shopping	F	First Start	Troll
T-Shirts	F	Ready to Read	Richard C. Owen/ Celebration Press
Tabby in the Tree	F	PM Books	Rigby
Taking Jason to Grandma's	F	Book Bank	Wright Group
Tarantulas Are Spiders	F	Platnick, Norman	Mondo
Thank You, Nicky!	F	Ziefert, Harriet	Penguin
Thanksgiving	F	Urmston, K. & Evans, K.	Kaeden Books
Three Muddy Monkeys	F	Foundations	Wright Group
Tiger is a Scaredy Cat	F	Step into Reading	Random House
To Town	F	Read-Togethers	Wright Group
Tree, The	F	Sunshine	Wright Group
Tricking Tracy	F	Tadpoles	Rigby
Trip to the Park, The	F	Foundations	Wright Group
Trouble in the Sandbox	F	Foundations	Wright Group
Try to Be a Brave Girl, Sarah	F	Windmill-Look & Listen	Wright Group
Two Feet	F	Giant Step Readers	Educ. Insights
Underwater Journey	F	Sunshine	Wright Group
Victor and the Kite	F	Oxford Reading Tree	Oxford

Title	Level	Author/Series	Publisher/Distributor
Washing	F	Foundations	Wright Group
Water Boatman, The	F	Ready to Read	Richard C. Owen/ Celebration Press
What a Dog	F	First Start	Troll
What a School	F	Salem, L. & Stewart, J.	Seedling
What Am I?	F	Just Beginning	Modern Curriculum
What Are You Going to Buy?	F	Read Alongs	Rigby
Wheels on the Bus	F	Ziefert, Harriet	Random House
When Goldilocks Went to the House of the Bears	F	Rendall, Jenny	Mondo
When I Was Sick	F	Literacy 2000	Rigby
When It Rains	F	Frankford, Marilyn	Kaeden Books
When Lana Was Absent	F	Tadpoles	Rigby
Where Is It?	F	Tiger Cub	Peguis
Where's My Daddy?	F	Watanabe, Shigeo	Putnam
William, Where Are You?	F	Gerstein, Mordicai	Crown
Winter Sleeps	F	Reading Corners	Dominie Press
Yummy, Yummy	F	Grey, Judith	Troll
Zoo Babies	F	Little Celebrations	Celebration Press
Alligator Shoes	G	Dorros, Arthur	Dutton
Amanda's Bear	G	Reading Corners	Dominie Press
Amazing Popple Seed, The	G	Read Alongs	Rigby
Angus Thought He Was Big	G	Giant Step Readers	Educ. Insights
Apple Tree Apple Tree	G	Blocksma, Mary	Children's Press
Baby Elephant's New Bike	G	Foundations	Wright Group
Big Fat Worm, The	G	Van Laan, Nancy	Random House
Big Red Fire Engine	G	First Start	Troll
Black Swan's Breakfast	G	Book Bank	Wright Group
Blackbird's Nest	G	Ready to Read	Richard C. Owen/ Celebration Press
Blue Lollipops	G	Stepping Stones	Nelson/Michaels Assoc.
Boats	G	Rockwell, Anne	Penguin
Boris Bad Enough	G	Kraus, Robert	Simon & Schuster
Brave Triceratops	G	PM Books	Rigby
Breakfast in Bed	G	Tadpoles	Rigby
Buffy's Tricks	G	Literacy 2000	Rigby
Bus Stop, The	G	Hellen, Nancy	Orchard
Buzzzzzz Said the Bee	G	Hello Reader	Scholastic
Candle-Light	G	PM Books	Rigby
Captain B's Boat	G	Sunshine	Wright Group
Carla's Breakfast	G	Harper, Leslie	Kaeden Books
Carla's Ribbons	G	Harper, Leslie	Kaeden Books
Carrot Seed, The	G	Krauss, Ruth	Harper & Row
Cat and Dog	G	Minarik, E. H.	HarperCollins
Cement Tent	G	First Start	Troll
Chickens	G	Snowball, Diane	Mondo
Clever Penguins, The	G	PM Books	Rigby
Click	G	Foundations	Wright Group
Come On, Tim	G	PM Books	Rigby
Cows in the Garden	G	PM Books	Rigby
Crazy Quilt, The	G	Little Celebrations	Celebration Press
Critter Race	G	Reese, Bob	Children's Press
Day Buzzy Stopped Being Busy	G	First Start	Troll

Title	Level	Author/Series	Publisher/Distributor
Day I Had to Play with My Sister	G	Bonsall, Crosby	HarperCollins
Desert Dance	G	Little Celebrations	Celebration Press
Did You Say "Fire?"	G	Ready to Read	Richard C. Owen/ Celebration Press
Dinosaur in Trouble	G	First Start	Troll
Dinosaurs Dinosaurs	G	Barton, Byron	HarperCollins
Dog, The	G	Burningham, John	Crowell
Donkey in the Lion's Skin, The	G	Aesop	Wright Group
Dozen Dizzy Dogs, A	G	Bank Street	Bantam
Dr. Green	G	Little Readers	Houghton Mifflin
Dragonflies	G	Books for Young Learners	Richard C. Owen
Dreams	G	Sunshine	Wright Group
Eeny, Meeny Miney Mouse	G	Giant Step Readers	Educ. Insights
Elephant and Envelope	G	Gregorich	School Zone
Face Painting	G	Wonder World	Wright Group
Farmer Had a Pig, The	G	Tiger Cub	Peguis
Fishing	G	Foundations	Wright Group
Five Little Speckled Frogs	G	Tiger Cub	Peguis
Four Getters and Arf, The	G	Little Celebrations	Celebration Press
Friends	G	Reading Unlimited	Celebration Press
Getting the Mail	G	Voyages	SRA/McGraw Hill
Gone Fishing	G	Long, Erlene	Houghton Mifflin
Goodnight Peter	G	Windmill-Look & Listen	Wright Group
Goose That Laid the Golden Egg, The	G	Aesop	Wright Group
Grandma's Bicycle	G	Read Alongs	Rigby
Grandpa, Grandpa	G	Read-Togethers	Wright Group
Great-Grandpa	G	Voyages	SRA/McGraw Hill
Greedy Cat	G	Ready to Read	Richard C. Owen/ Celebration Press
Greedy Gray Octopus, The	G	Tadpoles	Rigby
Hairy Bear	G	Read-Togethers	Wright Group
Hand Me Downs, The	G	Little Readers	Houghton Mifflin
Hansel and Gretel	G	Hunia, Fran	Ladybird Books
Happy Birthday	G	First Start	Troll
Harold's Flyaway Kite	G	First Start	Troll
Here Comes Winter	G	First Start	Troll
Hermit Crab, The	G	Sunshine	Wright Group
Home for a Puppy	G	First Start	Troll
House-Hunting	G	PM Books	Rigby
How Do You Make a Bubble?	G	Bank Street	Bantam
How to Make a Card	G	Urmston, K. & Evans, K.	Kaeden Books
Hungry Animals	G	Little Readers	Houghton Mifflin
Hungry Giant's Soup, The	G	Story Basket	Wright Group
I Have a Question, Grandma	G	Literacy 2000	Rigby
I Wish I Was Sick Too	G	Brandenburg, Franz	Morrow
I'm King of the Mountain	G	Ready to Read	Richard C. Owen/ Celebration Press
In the Forest	G	Voyages	SRA/McGraw Hill
In the Woods	G	Reading Corners	Dominie Press
Is It Time Yet?	G	Foundations	Wright Group
Jason's Bus Ride	G	Ziefert, Harriet	Penguin
Jeb's Barn	G	Little Celebrations	Celebration Press
Jessie's Flower	G	Read Alongs	Rigby

Title	Level	Author/Series	Publisher/Distributor
Just Enough	G	Salem, L. & Stewart, J.	Seedling
Just for You	G	Mayer, Mercer	Donovan
Katie Did It	G	Rookie Reader	Children's Press
Later, Rover	G	Ziefert, Harriet	Puffin Books
Laughing Cake, The	G	Reading Corners	Dominie Press
Lion and the Mouse, The	G	PM Books	Rigby
Lion and the Mouse, The	G	Traditional Tales	Rigby
Little Danny Dinosaur	G	First Start	Troll
Little Monkey Is Stuck	G	Foundations	Wright Group
Locked Out	G	PM Books	Rigby
Lollipop	G	Watson, Wendy	Crowell
Look for Me	G	Little Readers	Houghton Mifflin
Lydia and Her Cat	G	Oxford Reading Tree	Oxford
Lydia and the Ducks	G	Oxford Reading Tree	Oxford
Messy Monsters, The	G	Carousel Readers	Dominie Press
Mick and Max	G	Carousel Readers	Dominie Press
Mike and Tony: Best Friends	G	Ziefert, Harriet	Penguin
Mike's First Haircut	G	First Start	Troll
Mine's the Best	G	Bonsall, Crosby	HarperCollins
Monkeys	G	Reading Unlimited	Celebration Press
More Spaghetti I Say	G	Gelman, Rita	Scholastic
Mother Hen	G	Book Bank	Wright Group
Mr. Cricket Finds a Friend	G	Carousel Readers	Dominie Press
Munching Mark	G	Tadpoles	Rigby
Mushrooms for Dinner	G	PM Books	Rigby
My Boat	G	Sunshine	Wright Group
My Dog	G	Taylor, Judy	Macmillan
My Secret Hiding Place	G	First Start	Troll
My Secret Place	G	Wonder World	Wright Group
Naughty Ann, The	G	PM Books	Rigby
Never Snap at a Bubble	G	Giant Step Readers	Educ. Insights
New House for Mole and Mouse, A	G	Ziefert, Harriet	Penguin
Nicky Upstairs and Downstairs	G	Ziefert, Harriet	Penguin
Nine Men Chase a Hen	G	Gregorich	School Zone
Nobody Knew My Name	G	Foundations	Wright Group
Noise	G	Sunshine	Wright Group
Not Me, Said the Monkey	G	West, Colin	Harper & Row
Obadiah	G	Read-Togethers	Wright Group
Oh, No!	G	Little Celebrations	Celebration Press
On Top of Spaghetti	G	Little Celebrations	Celebration Press
One Monday Morning	G	Shulevitz, Uri	Scribner
Over in the Meadow	G	Little Readers	Houghton Mifflin
Pancakes	G	Foundations	Wright Group
Pete Little	G	PM Books	Rigby
Pete's New Shoes	G	Literacy 2000	Rigby
Picnic, The	G	Wonder World	Wright Group
Pukeko Morning	G	Ready to Read	Richard C. Owen/ Celebration Press
Rain, Rain	G	Ready to Read	Richard C. Owen/ Celebration Press
Rain, The	G	Foundations	Wright Group
Ready Set Go	G	First Start	Troll
Red Socks and Yellow Socks	G	Sunshine	Wright Group
Roller Coaster Ride, The	G	Carousel Readers	Dominie Press

Title	Level	Author/Series	Publisher/Distributor
Rosie's Pool	G	Little Readers	Houghton Mifflin
Saturday Morning	G	Ready to Read	Richard C. Owen/ Celebration Press
Say Goodnight	G	Gregorich	School Zone
Say It, Sign It	G	Beginning Literacy	Scholastic
Scary Larry	G	Rookie Reader	Children's Press
Sharing Danny's Dad	G	Little Celebrations	Celebration Press
Sheep in a Jeep	G	Shaw, Nancy	Houghton Mifflin
Shhhh!	G	Kline, Suzy	Whitman
Shopping at the Mall	G	Urmston, K. & Evans, K.	Kaeden Books
Show and Tell	G	First Start	Troll
Skating on Thin Ice	G	First Start	Troll
Snail Saves the Day	G	Stadler, John	HarperCollins
Snow, The	G	Burningham, John	Crowell
Sometimes Things Change	G	Eastman, P. D.	Children's Press
Spaghetti, Spaghetti	G	Book Bank	Wright Group
Special Things	G	Literacy 2000	Rigby
Spider Can't Fly	G	Book Bank	Wright Group
Spot's First Walk	G	Hill, Eric	Putnam
Stop That Rabbit	G	First Start	Troll
Sue Likes Blue	G	Gregorich	School Zone
Sunshine, the Black Cat	G	Carousel Readers	Dominie Press
Ten Bears in My Bed	G	Mack, Stan	Pantheon
Ten Little Bears	G	Reading Unlimited	Celebration Press
Ten Sleepy Sheep	G	Keller, Holly	Morrow
Terrible Tiger	G	Sunshine	Wright Group
That's Not All	G	Start to Read	School Zone
Three Billy Goats Gruff, The	G	Little Readers	Houghton Mifflin
Three Billy Goats Gruff, The	G	New Way	Steck-Vaughn
Three Cheers for Hippo	G	Stadler, John	HarperCollins
Three Kittens	G	Ginsburg, Mirra	Crown
Three Little Pigs	G	Little Readers	Houghton Mifflin
Three Little Witches	G	First Start	Troll
Titch	G	Hutchins, Pat	Penguin
Tree House Fun	G	First Start	Troll
TweedledeDee Tumbleweed	G	Reese, Bob	Children's Press
Uncle Timi's Sleep	G	Ready to Read	Richard C. Owen/ Celebration Press
Victor the Champion	G	Oxford Reading Tree	Oxford
Visiting Grandma and Grandpa	G	Carousel Readers	Dominie Press
Wait Skates	G	Rookie Reader	Children's Press
Walk	G	Reading Unlimited	Celebration Press
Whales	G	Foundations	Wright Group
What Am I?	G	Sunshine	Wright Group
What Can We Do Today?	G	Carousel Readers	Dominie Press
What's Inside?	G	Foundations	Wright Group
When You Were a Baby	G	Jonas, Ann	Morrow
Who Goes Out on Halloween?	G	Bank Street	Bantam
Who's Behind the Door at My House	G	Salmon, Michael	Steck-Vaughn
Who's Behind the Door at My School	G	Salmon, Michael	Steck-Vaughn
Why Can't I Fly	G	Gelman, Rita	Scholastic
William's Skateboard	G	Windmill-Look & Listen	Wright Group
Willie the Slowpoke	G	First Start	Troll
Wind and Sun	G	Literacy 2000	Rigby

Title	Level	Author/Series	Publisher/Distributor
Witch's Haircut, The	G	Windmill-Look & Listen	Wright Group
Women at Work	G	Foundations	Wright Group
You Look Funny	G	First Start	Troll
Accident, The	H	Foundations	Wright Group
Animal Tricks	H	Wildsmith, Brian	Merrimak
Awful Mess, The	H	Rockwell, Anne	Four Winds
Ben's Tooth	H	PM Books	Rigby
Birthday Book	H	Storybox	Wright Group
Birthday Cake	H	Storybox	Wright Group
Blue Jay	H	Little Readers	Houghton Mifflin
Bogle's Card	H	Sunshine	Wright Group
Bonnie on the Beach	H	Little Readers	Houghton Mifflin
Boy and the Lion, The	H	Aesop	Wright Group
Boy Who Cried Wolf	H	Sunshine	Wright Group
Building a House	H	Barton, Byron	Morrow
Buzz, Buzz, Buzz	H	Barton, Byron	Macmillan
Cake That Mack Ate, The	H	Robart/Kovalski	Little, Brown
Cats and Mice	H	Gelman, Rita	Scholastic
Chicken Pox	H	Little Readers	Houghton Mifflin
Choose Me!	H	Reading Corners	Dominie Press
Clean House for Mole and Mouse	H	Ziefert, Harriet	Scholastic
Clock That Couldn't Tell Time	H	Carousel Readers	Dominie Press
Clouds	H	Sunshine	Wright Group
Come Out and Play Little Mouse	H	Kraus, Robert	Morrow
Cow Up a Tree	H	Read Alongs	Rigby
Cross Country Race, The	H	PM Books	Rigby
Debra's Dog	H	Tadpoles	Rigby
Dick Whittington	H	Hunia, Fran	Ladybird Books
Dinosaurs	H	Sunshine	Wright Group
Do-Whacky-Do	H	Read Alongs	Rigby
Dream in the Wishing Well	H	Allen, R. V.	SRA/McGraw Hill
Dressing Up	H	Stepping Stones	Nelson/Michaels Assoc.
Drummers	H	Gould, Carol	Kaeden Books
Elephant in Trouble	H	First Start	Troll
Elephants	H	Foundations	Wright Group
Enormous Watermelon, The	H	Tales	Rigby
Fancy Dress Parade, The	H	Stepping Stones	Nelson/Michaels Assoc.
Flood, The	H	PM Books	Rigby
Fox Who Was Foxed, The	H	PM Books	Rigby
Fun at Camp	H	First Start	Troll
George Shrinks	H	Joyce, William	HarperCollins
Giant's Boy, The	H	Sunshine	Wright Group
Giant's Cake, The	H	Literacy 2000	Rigby
Giant's Job, The	H	Stewart, J. & Salem, L.	Seedling
Gifts for Dad	H	Urmston, K. & Evans, K.	Kaeden Books
Going to the Hospital	H	Foundations	Wright Group
Goldilocks and the Three Bears	H	Traditional Tales	Rigby
Goodnight, Moon	H	Brown, Margaret Wise	HarperCollins
Granny Bundle's Boring Walk	H	Stepping Stones	Nelson/Michaels Assoc.
Great Big Enormous Turnip	H	Tolstoy/Oxenbury	Watts
Great Big Enormous Turnip, The	H	Reading Unlimited	Celebration Press
Happy Faces	H	Reading Unlimited	Celebration Press
Help!	H	Giant Step Readers	Educ. Insights

Title	Level	Author/Series	Publisher/Distributor
Help Me	H	Storybox	Wright Group
Here Are My Hands	H	Bobber Book	SRA/McGraw Hill
Herman's Tooth	H	Foundations	Wright Group
Horrible Thing with Hairy Feet	H	Read Alongs	Rigby
How Do I Put It On?	H	Watanabe, Shigeo	Penguin
How to Make a Mud Pie	H	Little Readers	Houghton Mifflin
I Know an Old Lady	H	Readalong Rhythms	Wright Group
I Was Walking Down the Road	H	Barchas, Sarah	Scholastic
I'm a Good Reader	H	Carousel Readers	Dominie Press
I'm Glad to Say	H	Sunshine	Wright Group
I'm Sick Today	H	Carousel Readers	Dominie Press
If I Had an Alligator	H	Mayer, Mercer	Dial
If I Were a Penguin	H	Goeneil, Heidi	Little, Brown
Island Picnic, The	H	PM Books	Rigby
It Takes Time to Grow	H	Sunshine	Wright Group
Jace, Mace, and the Big Race	H	Gregorich	School Zone
Jim's Trumpet	H	Sunshine	Wright Group
Joke, The	H	Little Readers	Houghton Mifflin
Just Me and My Babysitter	H	Mayer, Mercer	Donovan
Just Me and My Dad	H	Mayer, Mercer	Donovan
Just Me and My Puppy	H	Mayer, Mercer	Donovan
Just This Once	H	Sunshine	Wright Group
Kick-a-lot Shoes	H	Storybox	Wright Group
Let's Take the Bus	H	Real Reading	Steck-Vaughn
Letters for Mr. James	H	Sunshine	Wright Group
Lift the Sky Up	H	Little Celebrations	Celebration Press
Little Kid	H	Literacy 2000	Rigby
Little Red Bus, The	H	PM Books	Rigby
Lola and Miss Kitty	H	Little Readers	Houghton Mifflin
Loose Tooth, The	H	Breakthrough	Longman/Bow
Meet My Mouse	H	Little Celebrations	Celebration Press
Mice	H	Literacy 2000	Rigby
Mike's New Bike	H	First Start	Troll
Missing Necklace, The	H	Reading Unlimited	Celebration Press
Misty's Mischief	H	Campbell, Rod	Viking
Mr. Clutterbus	H	Voyages	SRA/McGraw Hill
Mr. Fixit	H	Sunshine	Wright Group
Mr. Whisper	H	Sunshine	Wright Group
Mrs. Spider's Beautiful Web	H	PM Books	Rigby
My Brown Bear Barney	H	Butler, Dorothy	Morrow
My Cat	H	Taylor, Judy	Macmillan
New Building, The	H	Sunshine	Wright Group
Night the Lights Went Out, The	H	Little Readers	Houghton Mifflin
No Ball Games Here	H	Ziefert, Harriet	Penguin
Obstacle Course, The	H	Foundations	Wright Group
Old Grizzly	H	Sunshine	Wright Group
Old Hat, New Hat	H	Berenstain, Stan & Jan	Random House
Old Mother Hubbard	H	Literacy 2000	Rigby
Oliver	H	Kraus, Robert	Simon & Schuster
One Bear All Alone	H	Bucknall, Caroline	Dial
One Sock, Two Socks	H	Reading Corners	Dominie Press
One Thousand Currant Buns	H	Sunshine	Wright Group
Only an Octopus	H	Literacy 2000	Rigby
Panda's Surprise	H	Little Readers	Houghton Mifflin

Title	Level	Author/Series	Publisher/Distributor
Pepper's Adventure	H	PM Books	Rigby
Peter's Move	H	Little Readers	Houghton Mifflin
Picture for Harold's Room	H	Johnson, Crockett	HarperCollins
Pig William's Midnight Walk	H	Book Bank	Wright Group
Pizza for Dinner	H	Literacy 2000	Rigby
Potatoes, Potatoes	H	Wonder World	Wright Group
Pumpkin That Kim Carved, The	H	Little Readers	Houghton Mifflin
Put Me in the Zoo	H	Lopshire, Robert	Random House
"Quack" Said the Billy Goat	H	Causley, Charles	Harper & Row
Rabbit, The	H	Burningham, John	Crowell
Rapid Robert Roadrunner	H	Reese, Bob	Children's Press
Ratty Tatty	H	Sunshine	Wright Group
Rooster and the Weather Vane	H	First Start	Troll
Rosie at the Zoo	H	Ready to Read	Richard C. Owen/ Celebration Press
Safe Place, The	H	Ready to Read	Richard C. Owen/ Celebration Press
Seven Little Monsters	H	Sendak, Maurice	HarperCollins
Slug and Snails	H	Wonder World	Wright Group
Small World, A	H	Sunshine	Wright Group
Snake Slithers, A	H	Reading Unlimited	Celebration Press
Snow	H	Stepping Stones	Nelson/Michaels Assoc.
Sophie's Chicken	H	Tadpoles	Rigby
Space	H	Sunshine	Wright Group
Sunshine Street	H	Sunshine	Wright Group
Superkids	H	Sunshine	Wright Group
Ten Little Garden Snails	H	PM Books	Rigby
Ten Traveling Tigers	H	Little Readers	Houghton Mifflin
Thing in the Log, The	H	Reading Unlimited	Celebration Press
Three Little Pigs, The	H	Reading Unlimited	Celebration Press
Tiny Woman's Coat	H	Sunshine	Wright Group
Too Much Noise	H	Literacy 2000	Rigby
Tool Box	H	Rockwell, Anne	Macmillan
Trash	H	Sunshine	Wright Group
Turtle Nest	H	Books for Young Learners	Richard C. Owen
Two Bear Cubs	H	Jonas, Ann	Morrow
Victor and the Martian	H	Oxford Reading Tree	Oxford
Victor and the Sail Kart	H	Oxford Reading Tree	Oxford
Victor Makes a TV	H	Reading Unlimited	Celebration Press
Victor the Hero	H	Oxford Reading Tree	Oxford
Visiting the Vet	H	Foundations	Wright Group
Wagon, The	H	Reading Unlimited	Celebration Press
Water	H	Wonder World	Wright Group
Waving Sheep, The	H	PM Books	Rigby
We Are Best Friends	H	Aliki	Morrow
Wet Grass	H	Storybox	Wright Group
What Are Purple Elephants Good For?	H	Reading Corners	Dominie Press
What Game Shall We Play?	H	Hutchins, Pat	Sundance
What's Under the Ocean?	H	Now I Know	Troll
When Dad Went to Daycare	H	Sunshine	Wright Group
Where Are You Going, Little Mouse?	H	Kraus, Robert	Greenwillow
Where Is My Caterpillar?	H	Wonder World	Wright Group
White Wednesday	H	Literacy 2000	Rigby
Whose Mouse Are You?	H	Kraus, Robert	Macmillan

Title	Level	Author/Series	Publisher/Distributor
Wibble Wobble Albatross	H	Ready to Read	Richard C. Owen/ Celebration Press
Yes Ma'am	H	Read-Togethers	Wright Group
You Might Fall	H	Stepping Stones	Nelson/Michaels Assoc.
You'll Soon Grow into Them Titch	H	Hutchins, Pat	Morrow
You're So Clever	H	Voyages	SRA/McGraw Hill
Zithers	H	Little Celebrations	Celebration Press
Zoo Party, A	H	Book Bank	Wright Group
Albert the Albatross	I	Hoff, Syd	HarperCollins
All Tutus Should Be Pink	I	Hello Reader	Scholastic
Alligators All Around	I	Sendak, Maurice	HarperCollins
Anansi's Narrow Waist	I	Little Celebrations	Celebration Press
Angus and the Cat	I	Flack, Marjorie	Viking
Animal Builders	I	Little Celebrations	Celebration Press
Animals at Night	I	First Start	Troll
Apples and Pumpkins	I	Rockwell, Anne	Scholastic
Are You My Mother?	I	Eastman, P. D.	Random House
Armando Asked, "Why?"	I	Ready Set Read	Steck-Vaughn
Baby Monkey, The	I	Reading Unlimited	Celebration Press
Barney's Horse	I	Syd Hoff	HarperTrophy
Bean Bag That Mom Made	I	Tadpoles	Rigby
Bear's Bicycle, The	I	McLeod, Emilie	Little, Brown
Because a Little Bug Went Ka-Choo	I	Stone, Rosetta	Random House
Ben and the Bear	I	Riddell, Chris	Harper & Row
Benny Bakes a Cake	I	Rice, Eve	Greenwillow
Bertie the Bear	I	Allen, Pamela	Coward
Big Dog, Little Dog	I	Eastman, P. D.	Random House
Big or Little?	I	Stinson, Kathy	Dominie Press
Bike Lesson	I	Berenstain, Stan & Jan	Random House
Birthdays	I	Sunshine	Wright Group
Boggywooga, The	I	Sunshine	Wright Group
Bogle's Feet	I	Sunshine	Wright Group
Boring Old Bed	I	Sunshine	Wright Group
Bunny Hop, The	I	Hello Reader	Scholastic
Cats	I	Wonder World	Wright Group
Clyde Klutter's Room	I	Sunshine	Wright Group
Come and Have Fun	I	Hurd, Edith Thacher	HarperCollins
Coyote Plants a Peachtree	I	Books for Young Learners	Richard C. Owen
Dippy Dinner Drippers	I	Sunshine	Wright Group
Don't Touch!	I	Kline, Suzy	Penguin
Dragon	I	Storybox	Wright Group
Dragon Feet	I	Books for Young Learners	Richard C. Owen
Eat Up, Gemma	I	Hayes, S.	Sundance
Eency Weency Spider	I	Bank Street	Bantam
Fasi Sings/Fasi's Fish	I	Ready to Read	Richard C. Owen/ Celebration Press
Fat Cat	I	Kent, Jack	Scholastic
Fat Cat Tomkin	I	Voyages	SRA/McGraw Hill
Fat Pig, The	I	Tiger Cub	Peguis
Father Bear Comes Home	I	Minarik, E. H.	HarperCollins
Feed Me!	I	Bank Street	General
Fishy Scales	I	Mathtales	Mimosa
Fix-It	I	McPhail, David	Penguin

Title	Level	Author/Series	Publisher/Distributor
Froggy Tale, The	I	Literacy 2000	Rigby
Ginger	I	Little Readers	Houghton Mifflin
Gingerbread Man, The	I	Tiger Cub	Peguis
Gingerbread Man, The	I	Traditional Tales	Rigby
Go Away Dog	I	Nodset, Joan	HarperCollins
Going to Grandma's	I	Read by Reading	Scholastic
Good News	I	Bank Street	Bantam
Goodness Gracious!	I	Literacy 2000	Rigby
Goodnight Owl	I	Hutchins, Pat	Macmillan
Gregor the Grumblesome Giant	I	Literacy 2000	Rigby
Gruff Brothers, The	I	Bank Street	Bantam
Gumby Shop	I	Read Alongs	Rigby
Hannah	I	Stepping Stones	Nelson/Michaels Assoc.
Happy Birthday, Sam	I	Hutchins, Pat	Greenwillow
Hattie and the Fox	I	Fox, Mem	Bradbury
Hello, Cat You Need a Hat	I	Gelman, Rita	Scholastic
Henny Penny	I	Galdone, Paul	Scholastic
Herman Henry's Dog	I	Little Readers	Houghton Mifflin
Hiccups for Elephant	I	Hello Reader	Scholastic
Hole in Harry's Pocket, The	I	Little Readers	Houghton Mifflin
How to Ride a Giraffe	I	Little Readers	Houghton Mifflin
Hundred Hugs, A	I	Sunshine	Wright Group
Hungry Monster	I	Storybox	Wright Group
Invisible	I	Read Alongs	Rigby
It Came to Tea	I	Readalong Rhythms	Wright Group
It's Not Easy Being a Bunny	I	Sadler, Marilyn	Random House
Jack and the Beanstalk	I	Traditional Tales	Rigby
Jack in the Box	I	Storybox	Wright Group
Jackson's Monster	I	Little Readers	Houghton Mifflin
Jim Meets the Thing	I	Cohen, Miriam	Dell Publishing
Jim's Dog Muffins	I	Cohen, Miriam	Dell Publishing
Josie Cleans Up	I	Little Readers	Houghton Mifflin
Just a Mess	I	Mayer, Mercer	Donovan
Just Grandma and Me	I	Mayer, Mercer	Donovan
Just Like Everyone Else	I	Kuskin, Karla	HarperCollins
Leo the Late Bloomer	I	Kraus, Robert	Simon & Schuster
Let Me In	I	Storybox	Wright Group
Licken Chicken	I	Tiger Cub	Peguis
Little Fish That Got Away	I	Cook, Bernadine	Scholastic
Little Girl and Her Beetle, The	I	Literacy 2000	Rigby
Little Mouse's Trail Tale	I	Vandine, JoAnn	Mondo
Little Red Hen	I	Traditional Tales	Rigby
Little Tuppen	I	Galdone, Paul	Houghton Mifflin
Little Yellow Chicken, The	I	Sunshine	Wright Group
Lost Sheep, The	I	Little Readers	Houghton Mifflin
Mark's Monster	I	Reading Unlimited	Celebration Press
Messy Bessy	I	Rookie Reader	Children's Press
Mishi-Na	I	Sunshine	Wright Group
Mom's Birthday	I	Sunshine	Wright Group
Mom's Diet	I	Sunshine	Wright Group
Monarch Butterfly, The	I	Foundations	Wright Group
Monster	I	Read Alongs	Rigby
Mr. Sun and Mr. Sea	I	Little Celebrations	Celebration Press
Mr. Wumple's Travels	I	Read Alongs	Rigby

©1996 by Irene C. Fountas & Gay Su Pinnell from *Guided Reading*. Portsmouth, NH: Heinemann. May not be reproduced without written permission of the publisher.

Title	Level	Author/Series	Publisher/Distributor
Mrs. Brice's Mice	I	Hoff, Syd	HarperTrophy
Mrs. Brindy's Shoes	I	Sunshine	Wright Group
Mrs. Muddle's Mud-Puddle	I	Sunshine	Wright Group
Mrs. Murphy's Bears	I	Little Readers	Houghton Mifflin
My Best Friend	I	Hutchins, Pat	Greenwillow
My Sloppy Tiger	I	Sunshine	Wright Group
Nobody Listens to Andrew	I	Guilfoile, Elizabeth	Modern Curriculum
Noisy Nora	I	Wells, Rosemary	Scholastic
Now I Am Five	I	Sunshine	Wright Group
Nowhere and Nothing	I	Sunshine	Wright Group
Old Woman and the Pig, The	I	Tiger Cub	Peguis
Picnic Tea	I	Stepping Stones	Nelson/Michaels Assoc.
Poor Sore Paw, The	I	Sunshine	Wright Group
Pot of Gold, The	I	Reading Unlimited	Celebration Press
Princess, the Mud Pies, and the Dragon, The	I	Little Readers	Houghton Mifflin
Quack, Quack, Quack	I	Sunshine	Wright Group
Quilt, The	I	Jonas, Ann	Morrow
Rainbow of My Own	I	Freeman, Don	Penguin
Rebus Bears, The	I	Bank Street	Bantam
Red Is Best	I	Stinson, Kathy	Annick/Toronto
Reflections	I	Jonas, Ann	Morrow
Road Work Ahead	I	Little Readers	Houghton Mifflin
Robert, the Rose Horse	I	Heilbroner, Joan	Random House
Roly-Poly	I	Storybox	Wright Group
Sammy's Supper	I	Reading Unlimited	Celebration Press
Shintaro's Umbrellas	I	Books for Young Learners	Richard C. Owen
Shoe Grabber, The	I	Read Alongs	Rigby
Sloppy Tiger and the Party	I	Sunshine	Wright Group
Sloppy Tiger Bedtime	I	Sunshine	Wright Group
Soup Can Telephone	I	Wonder World	Wright Group
Spinning Top	I	Wonder World	Wright Group
Spot's Birthday	I	Hill, Eric	Putnam
Stables Are for Horses	I	Windmill-Rhyme & Rhythm	Wright Group
Story of Chicken Licken	I	Ormerod, Jan	Lothrop
Super-Duper Sunflower Seeds, The	I	Book Bank	Wright Group
Tails Can Tell	I	Wonder World	Wright Group
Talking Yam, The	I	Little Readers	Houghton Mifflin
Teddy Bears	I	Purkis, Sallie	Nelson/Michaels Assoc.
Teeny Tiny	I	Bennett, Jill	Putnam
Tents	I	Reading Unlimited	Celebration Press
There's a Nightmare in My Closet	I	Mayer, Mercer	Penguin
This Is the Bear	I	Hayes, S. & Craig, H.	Harper & Row
This Is the House That Bjorn . . .	I	Tiger Cub	Peguis
This Is the Place for Me	I	Cole, Joanna	Scholastic
This Is the Seed	I	Little Celebrations	Celebration Press
Three Bears, The	I	Tiger Cub	Peguis
Three Billy Goats Gruff	I	Traditional Tales	Rigby
Three Billy Goats Gruff, The	I	Brown, Marcia	Harcourt Brace
Three Little Pigs	I	Traditional Tales	Rigby
Three Little Pigs, The	I	Reading Corners	Dominie Press
Tidy Titch	I	Hutchins, Pat	Morrow
To Market, to Market	I	Read-Togethers	Wright Group

Title	Level	Author/Series	Publisher/Distributor
Tommy's Treasure	I	Literacy 2000	Rigby
Tooth Race, The	I	Little Readers	Houghton Mifflin
Town Mouse and Country Mouse, The	I	Aesop	Wright Group
Trek, The	I	Jonas, Ann	Greenwillow
Trucks	I	Rockwell, Anne	Penguin
Tug of War	I	Folk Tales	Wright Group
Two Little Mice, The	I	Literacy 2000	Rigby
Very Busy Spider, The	I	Carle, Eric	Philomel
Wax Man, The	I	Beginning Literacy	Scholastic
We're in Big Trouble, Black Board Bear	I	Alexander, Martha	Dial
What Else?	I	Sunshine	Wright Group
What I Would Do	I	Read Alongs	Rigby
What You See Is What You Get	I	McLenighan, V.	Modern Curriculum
Where's Lulu?	I	Bank Street	Bantam
Who Took the Farmer's Hat	I	Nodset, Joan	Scholastic
Who Wants One?	I	Serfozo, Mary	Macmillan
Who's Afraid?	I	Reading Unlimited	Celebration Press
Wicked Pirates, The	I	Sunshine	Wright Group
Wild Wet Wellington Wind	I	Ready to Read	Richard C. Owen/ Celebration Press
Willie's Wonderful Pet	I	Hello Reader	Scholastic
Woolly Sally	I	Ready to Read	Richard C. Owen/ Celebration Press
Worms for Breakfast	I	Little Readers	Houghton Mifflin
Yard Sale, The	I	Little Readers	Houghton Mifflin
Yoo Hoo, Moon!	I	Bank Street	Bantam
Yum and Yuk	I	Storybox	Wright Group
Adventures of Snail at School	J	Stadler, John	HarperTrophy
Alison Wendlebury	J	Literacy 2000	Rigby
Amazing Maze, The	J	Foundations	Wright Group
And I Mean it Stanley	J	Bonsall, Crosby	HarperCollins
Annie's Pet	J	Bank Street	Bantam Doubleday Dell
Ask Mr. Bear	J	Flack, Marjorie	Macmillan
At the Doctor	J	Story Starter	Wright Group
Baby Writer	J	Hall, N. & Robinson, A.	Nelson/Michaels Assoc.
Barney's Horse	J	Hoff, Syd	HarperTrophy
Bear Shadow	J	Asch, Frank	Simon & Schuster
Bear's Bargain	J	Asch, Frank	Scholastic
Beautiful Pig	J	Read Alongs	Rigby
Best Nest	J	Eastman, P. D.	Random House
Big Green Caterpillar, The	J	Literacy 2000	Rigby
Big Mama and Grandma Ghana	J	Shelf Medearis, A.	Scholastic
Birds' Nest	J	Wonder World	Wright Group
Blackboard Bear	J	Alexander, Martha	Penguin
Boy Who Cried Wolf, The	J	Littledale, Freya	Scholastic
Budgie's Dream	J	Story Starter	Wright Group
Cat Concert	J	Literacy 2000	Rigby
Cat in the Hat	J	Seuss, Dr.	Random House
Cells	J	Wonder World	Wright Group
Charlie Needs a Cloak	J	de Paola, Tomie	Prentice-Hall
City Mouse-Country Mouse	J	Aesop	Scholastic
Class Play, The	J	Little Readers	Houghton Mifflin
Clocks and More Clocks	J	Hutchins, Pat	Scholastic

Title	Level	Author/Series	Publisher/Distributor
Color Wizard, The	J	Bank Street	Bantam
Could It Be?	J	Bank Street	Bantam
Curious George and the Ice Cream	J	Rey, M.	Scholastic
Danny and the Dinosaur	J	Hoff, Syd	Scholastic
Difficult Day, The	J	Read Alongs	Rigby
Dogstar	J	Literacy 2000	Rigby
Dolphins	J	Wonder World	Wright Group
Don't Eat Too Much Turkey!	J	Cohen, Miriam	Dell Publishing
Don't Worry	J	Literacy 2000	Rigby
Donkey's Tale, The	J	Bank Street	Bantam
Doorbell Rang, The	J	Hutchins, Pat	Greenwillow
Dragon Who Had the Measles, The	J	Literacy 2000	Rigby
Drummer Hoff	J	Emberley, Ed	Prentice-Hall
Elaine	J	Stepping Stones	Nelson/Michaels Assoc.
Elephant and the Bad Baby, The	J	Hayes, S.	Sundance
Elephant in the House, An	J	Read Alongs	Rigby
Everybody Eats Bread	J	Literacy 2000	Rigby
Fight on the Hill, The	J	Read Alongs	Rigby
Fox and His Friends	J	Marshall, Edward & James	Scholastic
Fox and the Crow, The	J	Aesop	Wright Group
Fraidy Cats	J	Hello Reader	Scholastic
Funny Bones	J	Ahlberg, A. & J.	Viking
Gallo and Zorro	J	Literacy 2000	Rigby
Get Set and Go	J	Real Reading	Steck-Vaughn
Giant in the Forest, A	J	Reading Unlimited	Celebration Press
Grandma Mix-Up, The	J	McCully, Emily Arnold	HarperTrophy
Great Day for Up	J	Seuss, Dr.	Random House
Green Eggs and Ham	J	Seuss, Dr.	Random House
Ha-Ha Party	J	Sunshine	Wright Group
Hair Party, The	J	Literacy 2000	Rigby
Half for You Half for Me	J	Literacy 2000	Rigby
Hand, Hand, Fingers, Thumb	J	Perkins, Al	Random House
Harry and the Lady Next Door	J	Zion, Gene	HarperTrophy
He Bear, She Bear	J	Berenstain, Stan & Jan	Random House
Hedgehog Bakes a Cake	J	Bank Street	Bantam
Henry and Mudge and the Forever Sea	J	Rylant, Cynthia	Aladdin
Henry and Mudge in Puddle Trouble	J	Rylant, Cynthia	Aladdin
Henry and Mudge in the Green Time	J	Rylant, Cynthia	Aladdin
Henry and Mudge: The First Book	J	Rylant, Cynthia	Aladdin
Here Comes Kate!	J	Real Reading	Steck-Vaughn
Hippopotamus Ate the Teacher, A	J	Thaler, Mike	Avon Books
Hop on Pop	J	Seuss, Dr.	Random House
Horse in Harry's Room	J	Hoff, Syd	HarperCollins
House That Jack Built, The	J	Peppe, Rodney	Delacorte
How Grandmother Spider Got the Sun	J	Little Readers	Houghton Mifflin
How Kittens Grow	J	Selsam, Millicent	Scholastic
How Turtle Raced Beaver	J	Literacy 2000	Rigby
I Can Read with My Eyes Shut	J	Seuss, Dr.	Random House
I Love to Sneeze	J	Bank Street	Bantam
I Was So Mad	J	Mayer, Mercer	Donovan
Imagine That	J	Storybox	Wright Group
Jamberry	J	Degen, Bruce	Harper & Row
Jillian Jiggs	J	Gilman, Phoebe	Scholastic
Jimmy Lee Did It	J	Cummings, Pat	Lothrop

Title	Level	Author/Series	Publisher/Distributor
Johnny Lion's Book	J	Hurd, Edith Thacher	HarperCollins
Just for Fun	J	Literacy 2000	Rigby
Just Like Me	J	Storybox	Wright Group
Just Us Women	J	Caines, Jeannette	Scholastic
Kenny and the Little Kickers	J	Hello Reader	Scholastic
Kiss for Little Bear	J	Minarik, E. H.	Harper & Row
Knit, Knit, Knit, Knit	J	Literacy 2000	Rigby
Let's Be Enemies	J	Sendak, Maurice	Harper & Row
Little Bear	J	Minarik, E. H.	HarperCollins
Little Bear's Friend	J	Minarik, E. H.	HarperTrophy
Little Bear's Visit	J	Minarik, E. H.	HarperTrophy
Little Black, a Pony	J	Farley, Walter	Random House
Little Blue and Little Yellow	J	Lionni, Leo	Scholastic
Little Fireman	J	Brown, Margaret Wise	HarperCollins
Little Gorilla	J	Bornstein, Ruth	Clarion
Little Red Hen, The	J	Galdone, Paul	Viking
Look Out for Your Tail	J	Literacy 2000	Rigby
Matthew Likes to Read	J	Ready to Read	Richard C. Owen/ Celebration Press
Matthew's Tantrum	J	Literacy 2000	Rigby
Max	J	Isadora, Rachel	Macmillan
Meg and Mog	J	Nicoll, Helen	Viking
Milton the Early Riser	J	Kraus, Robert	Simon & Schuster
Monkey and Fire	J	Literacy 2000	Rigby
Moon Boy	J	Bank Street	Bantam
Morning Star	J	Literacy 2000	Rigby
Mouse and the Elephant, The	J	Little Readers	Houghton Mifflin
Mouse Soup	J	Lobel, Arnold	HarperCollins
Mouse Tales	J	Lobel, Arnold	Harper & Row
Mouse Who Wanted to Marry, The	J	Bank Street	Bantam
Mr. Putter and Tabby Bake the Cake	J	Rylant, Cynthia	Harcourt Brace
Mr. Putter and Tabby Pick and Pears	J	Rylant, Cynthia	Harcourt Brace
Mr. Putter and Tabby Pour the Tea	J	Rylant, Cynthia	Harcourt Brace
Mr. Putter and Tabby Walk the Dog	J	Rylant, Cynthia	Harcourt Brace
My Father	J	Mayer, Laura	Scholastic
My Sloppy Tiger Goes to School	J	Sunshine	Wright Group
My Treasure Garden	J	Book Bank	Wright Group
Not Now! Said the Cow	J	Bank Street	Bantam
Number One	J	Ready to Read	Richard C. Owen/ Celebration Press
Otto the Cat	J	Herman, Gail	Grosset & Dunlap
Owl at Home	J	Lobel, Arnold	HarperCollins
Paru Has a Bath	J	Ready to Read	Richard C. Owen/ Celebration Press
Paul and Lucy	J	Stepping Stones	Nelson/Michaels Assoc.
Pet for You	J	Story Starter	Wright Group
Peter's Chair	J	Keats, Ezra Jack	HarperTrophy
Pets	J	Ready to Read	Richard C. Owen/ Celebration Press
Popcorn Shop, The	J	Low, Alice	Scholastic
Porcupine's Pajama Party	J	Harshman, Terry Webb	HarperTrophy
Pretty Good Magic	J	Dubowski, Cathy	Random House
Pumpkin House, The	J	Literacy 2000	Rigby
Queen's Parrot, The: A Play	J	Literacy 2000	Rigby

Title	Level	Author/Series	Publisher/Distributor
Rabbit's Birthday Kite	J	Bank Street	Bantam
Rain Puddle	J	Holl, Adelaide	Morrow
Roller Skates!	J	Hello Reader	Scholastic
Row, Row, Row Your Boat	J	Bank Street	Bantam
Royal Baby-Sitters	J	Sunshine	Wright Group
Sam and the Firefly	J	Eastman, P. D.	Random House
Secret of Spooky House	J	Sunshine	Wright Group
See You Tomorrow, Charles	J	Cohen, Miriam	Dell Publishing
She'll Be Coming Around the Mountain	J	Bank Street	Bantam
Show-and-Tell Frog, The	J	Bank Street	Bantam
Skeleton on the Bus, The	J	Literacy 2000	Rigby
SkyFire	J	Asch, Frank	Scholastic
Snowy Day, The	J	Keats, Ezra Jack	Scholastic
Space Race	J	Sunshine	Wright Group
Squire Takes a Wife, A	J	Ready Set Read	Steck-Vaughn
Stone Soup	J	McGovern, Ann	Scholastic
Super Parrot	J	Real Reading	Steck-Vaughn
Surprise Party, The	J	Proger, Annabelle	Random House
Sword in the Stone, The	J	Hello Reader	Scholastic
Teeny Tiny Woman, The	J	Seuling, Barbara	Scholastic
Ten Apples Up on Top	J	LaSieg, Theo	Random House
Tess and Paddy	J	Sunshine	Wright Group
Thank You	J	Ready to Read	Richard C. Owen/ Celebration Press
There Is a Carrot in My Ear and Other Noodle Tales	J	Schwartz, Alvin	HarperTrophy
There's a Hippopotamus Under My Bed	J	Thaler, Mike	Avon Books
There's an Alligator Under My Bed	J	Mayer, Mercer	Penguin
There's Something in My Attic	J	Mayer, Mercer	Penguin
Tickle-Bugs, The	J	Literacy 2000	Rigby
Tom the TV Cat	J	Heilbroner, Joan	Random House
Too Many Mice	J	Bank Street	Bantam
Too Many Rabbits	J	Parish, Peggy	Dell Publishing
Too Much Noise	J	McGovern, Ann	Scholastic
Trees	J	Literacy 2000	Rigby
Trouble in the Ark	J	Rose, Gerald	Oxford
Uh-Oh! Said the Crow	J	Bank Street	Bantam
Uncle Elephant	J	Lobel, Arnold	HarperCollins
Vagabond Crabs	J	Literacy 2000	Rigby
Very Hungry Caterpillar, The	J	Carle, Eric	Putnam
Waiting for the Rain	J	Foundations	Wright Group
Wake Me in Spring	J	Preller, James	Scholastic
Wake Up, Baby!	J	Bank Street	Bantam
What Cat Is That?	J	Real Reading	Steck-Vaughn
When the King Rides By	J	Mahy, Margaret	Mondo
Where the Wild Things Are	J	Sendak, Maurice	Harper & Row
Wild, Wooly Child, The	J	Read Alongs	Rigby
Wind and the Sun	J	Story Starter	Wright Group
Wind and the Sun, The	J	New Way	Steck-Vaughn
Wind Power	J	Ready to Read	Richard C. Owen/ Celebration Press
Wrong-Way Rabbit, The	J	Hello Reader	Scholastic
You Are Much Too Small	J	Bank Street	Bantam

Title	Level	Author/Series	Publisher/Distributor
You Can't Catch Me	J	Oppenheim, Joanne	Houghton Mifflin
Zoe at the Fancy Dress Ball	J	Literacy 2000	Rigby
Zunid	J	Stepping Stones	Nelson/Michaels Assoc.
And Grandpa Sat on Friday	K	Marshall & Tester	SRA/McGraw Hill
Arguments	K	Read Alongs	Rigby
Arthur's Christmas Cookies	K	Read Alongs	Rigby
Arthur's Christmas Cookies	K	Hoban, Lillian	HarperTrophy
Arthur's Honey Bear	K	Hoban, Lillian	HarperCollins
Arthur's Loose Tooth	K	Hoban, Lillian	HarperCollins
Arthur's Pen Pal	K	Hoban, Lillian	HarperCollins
Arthur's Prize Reader	K	Hoban, Lillian	HarperTrophy
At the Water Hole	K	Foundations	Wright Group
Baba Yaga	K	Literacy 2000	Rigby
Baby Sister for Frances, A	K	Hoban, Russell	Scholastic
Barrel of Gold	K	Storybox	Wright Group
Bear Goes to Town	K	Browne, Anthony	Doubleday
Beavers Beware!	K	Bank Street	Bantam
Best Birthday Present, The	K	Literacy 2000	Rigby
Best Teacher in the World, The	K	Chardiet & Maccarone	Scholastic
Big Balloon Race, The	K	Coerr, Eleanor	HarperTrophy
Big Fish Little Fish	K	Folk Tales	Wright Group
Big Sneeze, The	K	Brown, Ruth	Lothrop
Birthday Bike for Brimhall, A	K	Delton, Judy	Dell Publishing
Birthdays	K	Purkis, Sallie	Nelson/Michaels Assoc.
Blind Men and the Elephant, The	K	Backstein, Karen	Scholastic
Bony-Legs	K	Cole, Joanna	Scholastic
Boy and His Donkey, A	K	Literacy 2000	Rigby
Bremen Town Musicians, The	K	Gross & Kent	Scholastic
Bubbling Crocodile	K	Ready to Read	Richard C. Owen/ Celebration Press
Bunny Runs Away	K	Chardiet & Maccarone	Scholastic
Button Soup	K	Bank Street	Bantam Doubleday Dell
Cabbage Princess, The	K	Literacy 2000	Rigby
Camping with Claudine	K	Literacy 2000	Rigby
Caps for Sale	K	Slobodkina, Esphyr	Harper & Row
Case of the Two Masked Robbers, The	K	Hoban, Lillian	HarperTrophy
Cinderella	K	Once Upon a Time	Wright Group
Clever Mr. Brown	K	Storybox	Wright Group
Clifford, the Big Red Dog	K	Bridwell, Norman	Scholastic
Clifford, the Small Red Puppy	K	Bridwell, Norman	Scholastic
Concert Night	K	Literacy 2000	Rigby
Corduroy	K	Freeman, Don	Scholastic
Crosby Crocodile's Disguise	K	Literacy 2000	Rigby
Dabble Duck	K	Leo Ellis, Anne	HarperTrophy
Daniel's Dog	K	Bogart, Jo Ellen	Scholastic
Darcy and Gran Don't Like Babies	K	Cutler, Jane	Scholastic
Day Jimmy's Boa Ate the Wash, The	K	Hakes Noble, T.	Scholastic
Dinosaur Time	K	Parish, Peggy	Harper & Row
Dinosaurs	K	Collins, Michael	Mondo
Dinosaurs on the Motorway	K	Wesley & the Dinosaurs	Wright Group
Diplodocus in the Garden, A	K	Wesley & the Dinosaurs	Wright Group
Do You Like Cats?	K	Bank Street	Bantam
Donald's Garden	K	Reading Unlimited	Celebration Press

Title	Level	Author/Series	Publisher/Distributor
Effie	K	Allinson, Beverley	Scholastic
Egg	K	Logan, Dick	Cypress
Elves and the Shoemaker	K	New Way	Steck Vaughn
Fables by Aesop	K	Reading Unlimited	Celebration Press
Fabulous Freckles	K	Literacy 2000	Rigby
Families Are Different	K	Pellegrini, Nina	Scholastic
Farmer in the Soup, The	K	Littledale, Freya	Scholastic
Fast and Funny	K	Storybox	Wright Group
Flying Fingers	K	Literacy 2000	Rigby
Follow That Fish	K	Oppenheim, Joanne	Bantam
Franklin Goes to School	K	Bourgeois & Clark	Scholastic
Friends Are Forever	K	Literacy 2000	Rigby
Frog and Toad/Friends	K	Lobel, Arnold	Harper & Row
Frog and Toad Together	K	Lobel, Arnold	HarperCollins
Frog Princess, The	K	Literacy 2000	Rigby
Frown, The	K	Read Alongs	Rigby
Giant Jam Sandwich, The	K	Vernon Lord, John	Houghton Mifflin
Go and Hush the Baby	K	Byars, Betsy	Viking
Goldilocks and the Three Bears	K	Once Upon a Time	Wright Group
Grandma's at the Lake	K	McCully, Emily Arnold	HarperTrophy
Happy Birthday, Dear Duck	K	Bunting, Eve	Clarion
Hare and the Tortoise, The	K	Literacy 2000	Rigby
Harold and the Purple Crayon	K	Johnson, Crockett	Harper & Row
Harry Hates Shopping!	K	Armitage, R. & D.	Scholastic
Hat Came Back, The	K	Literacy 2000	Rigby
Have You Seen a Javelina?	K	Literacy 2000	Rigby
He Who Listens	K	Literacy 2000	Rigby
Hello Creatures!	K	Literacy 2000	Rigby
How Fire Came to Earth	K	Literacy 2000	Rigby
How Spider Tricked Snake	K	Real Reading	Steck-Vaughn
I Am Not Afraid!	K	Bank Street	Bantam
I Dream	K	Sunshine	Wright Group
If You Give a Mouse a Cookie	K	Numeroff, L. J.	Scholastic
It's Halloween	K	Prelutsky, Jack	Scholastic
Jack and the Beanstalk	K	Wiesner, David	Scholastic
Jamaica's Find	K	Havill, Juanita	Scholastic
Keep the Lights Burning, Abbie	K	Roop, P. & C.	Scholastic
King, the Mice and the Cheese	K	Gurney, Nancy	Random House
Knock! Knock!	K	Carter, Jackie	Scholastic
Last Puppy, The	K	Asch, Frank	Simon & Schuster
Letter to Amy, A	K	Keats, Ezra Jack	Harper & Row
Lionel at Large	K	Krensky, Stephen	Puffin Books
Little, Brown Jay: A Tale from India, The	K	Claire, Elizabeth	Mondo
Little Knight, The	K	Reading Unlimited	Celebration Press
Little Penguin's Tale	K	Wood, Audrey	Scholastic
Lonely Giant, The	K	Literacy 2000	Rigby
Madeline	K	Bemelmans, L.	Scholastic
Madeline's Rescue	K	Bemelmans, L.	Scholastic
Magic Box, The	K	Brenner, Barbara	Bantam
Martin and the Teacher's Pets	K	Chardiet & Maccarone	Scholastic
Martin and the Tooth Fairy	K	Chardiet & Maccarone	Scholastic
Me Too	K	Mayer, Mercer	Donovan
Misha Disappears	K	Literacy 2000	Rigby

Title	Level	Author/Series	Publisher/Distributor
Miss Mouse Gets Married	K	Folk Tales	Wright Group
Mollie Whuppie	K	New Way	Steck-Vaughn
Monster from the Sea, The	K	Bank Street	Bantam
Monster Movie	K	Cole, Joanna	Scholastic
Monster of Mirror Mountain, The	K	Literacy 2000	Rigby
More Tales of Amanda Pig	K	Van Leeuwen, Jean	Penguin
More Tales of Oliver Pig	K	Van Leeuwen, Jean	Penguin
Mr. Gumpy's Motor Car	K	Burningham, John	HarperCollins
Mr. Pepperpot's Pet	K	Literacy 2000	Rigby
Mrs. Huggins and Her Hen Hannah	K	Dabcovich, Lydia	Dutton
Nate the Great	K	Sharmat, M. Weinman	Dell Publishing
Nate the Great and the Boring Beach Bag	K	Sharmat, M. Weinman	Dell Publishing
Nate the Great and the Fishy Prize	K	Sharmat, M. Weinman	Dell Publishing
Nate the Great and the Halloween Hunt	K	Sharmat, M. Weinman	Dell Publishing
Nate the Great and the Lost List	K	Sharmat, M. Weinman	Dell Publishing
Nate the Great and the Missing Key	K	Sharmat, M. Weinman	Dell Publishing
Nate the Great and the Mushy Valentine	K	Sharmat, M. Weinman	Dell Publishing
Nate the Great and the Musical Note	K	Sharmat, M. Weinman	Dell Publishing
Nate the Great and the Phony Clue	K	Sharmat, M. Weinman	Dell Publishing
Nate the Great and the Pillowcase	K	Sharmat, M. Weinman	Dell Publishing
Nate the Great and the Snowy Trail	K	Sharmat, M. Weinman	Dell Publishing
Nate the Great and the Sticky Case	K	Sharmat, M. Weinman	Dell Publishing
Nate the Great and the Stolen Base	K	Sharmat, M. Weinman	Dell Publishing
Nate the Great Goes Down in the Dumps	K	Sharmat, M. Weinman	Dell Publishing
Nate the Great Goes Undercover	K	Sharmat, M. Weinman	Dell Publishing
Nate the Great Stalks Stupidweed	K	Sharmat, M. Weinman	Dell Publishing
Nathan & Nicholas Alexander	K	Delacre, Lulu	Scholastic
Next Time I Will	K	Bank Street	Bantam
Nice New Neighbors	K	Brandenberg, Franz	Scholastic
Now Listen, Stanley	K	Literacy 2000	Rigby
On Friday the Giant	K	The Giant	Wright Group
On Monday the Giant	K	The Giant	Wright Group
On Sunday the Giant	K	The Giant	Wright Group
On Thursday the Giant	K	The Giant	Wright Group
On Tuesday the Giant	K	The Giant	Wright Group
On Wednesday the Giant	K	The Giant	Wright Group
Oogly Gum Chasing Game, The	K	Literacy 2000	Rigby
Pancake, The	K	Lobel, Anita	Dell Publishing
Peter and the North Wind	K	Littledale, Freya	Scholastic
Pied Piper of Hamelin, The	K	Hautzig, Deobrah	Random House
Piggle	K	Bonsall, Crosby	HarperCollins
Pocket for Corduroy, A	K	Freeman, Don	Scholastic
Pookie and Joe	K	Literacy 2000	Rigby
Popcorn Book, The	K	Reading Unlimited	Celebration Press
Prize for Purry, A	K	Literacy 2000	Rigby
Pterodactyl at the Airport	K	Wesley & the Dinosaurs	Wright Group
Rise and Shine, Mariko-chan	K	Tomioka, Chiyoko	Scholastic
Rosie's House	K	Literacy 2000	Rigby

Title	Level	Author/Series	Publisher/Distributor
Ruby the Copycat	K	Rathman, Peggy	Scholastic
Sam Who Never Forgets	K	Rice, Eve	Morrow
Sam's Solution	K	Literacy 2000	Rigby
Sandy's Suitcase	K	Edwards, Elsy	SRA/McGraw Hill
Scare-Kid	K	Literacy 2000	Rigby
Sheila Rae, the Brave	K	Henkes, Kevin	Scholastic
Shortest Kid in the World, The	K	Bliss, Corinne Demas	Random House
Sidetrack Sam	K	Literacy 2000	Rigby
Sing to the Moon	K	Storybox	Wright Group
SkyScraper, The	K	Little Red Readers	Sundance
Smallest Cow in the World, The	K	Paterson, Katherine	HarperTrophy
Smallest Tree, The	K	Literacy 2000	Rigby
Snowshoe Thompson	K	Smiler Levinson, N.	HarperTrophy
Soap Soup and Other Verses	K	Kuskin, Karla	HarperTrophy
Souvenirs	K	Literacy 2000	Rigby
Spaghetti Party, The	K	Bank Street	Bantam
Stan the Hot Dog Man	K	Kessler, E. & L.	HarperTrophy
Stone Works	K	Wonder World	Wright Group
Surprise Party	K	Hutchins, Pat	Macmillan
Teddy Bears Cure a Cold	K	Gretz, Susanna	Scholastic
Terrible Fright	K	Storybox	Wright Group
That Fat Hat	K	Barkan, Joanne	Scholastic
That's Really Weird!	K	Read Alongs	Rigby
Three Bears, The	K	Galdone, Paul	Scholastic
Three Billy Goats Gruff	K	Stevens, Janet	Harcourt Brace
Three Magicians, The	K	Literacy 2000	Rigby
Too Many Babas	K	Croll, Carolyn	HarperTrophy
Turtle Flies South	K	Literacy 2000	Rigby
Two Foolish Cats, The	K	Literacy 2000	Rigby
Ugly Duckling, The	K	Traditional Tales	Rigby
Vicky the High Jumper	K	Literacy 2000	Rigby
We Scream for Ice Cream	K	Chardiet & Maccarone	Scholastic
Well I Never	K	Storybox	Wright Group
What a Funny Thing to Do	K	Hall, N. & Robinson, A.	Nelson/Michaels Assoc.
What's Inside?	K	Wonder World	Wright Group
When I Get Bigger	K	Mayer, Mercer	Donovan
When Will We Be Sisters?	K	Kroll, Virginia	Scholastic
Where Is the Bear?	K	Nims, Bonnie	Whitman
White Horse, The	K	Literacy 2000	Rigby
Who Pushed Humpty?	K	Literacy 2000	Rigby
Who Sank the Boat?	K	Allen, Pamela	Coward
Who's Afraid of the Big, Bad Bully?	K	Slater, Teddy	Scholastic
Wordsong	K	Bobber Books	SRA/McGraw Hill
Zack's Alligator	K	Mozelle, Shirley	HarperTrophy
Abracadabra	L	Reading Unlimited	Celebration Press
Acid Rain	L	Wonder World	Wright Group
Afternoon on the Amazon	L	Osborne, M. Pope	Random House
Alexander and the Wind-Up Mouse	L	Lionni, Leo	Scholastic
Alfie's Gift	L	Literacy 2000	Rigby
All About Stacy	L	Giff, Patricia Reilly	Dell Publishing
Amelia Bedelia	L	Parish, Peggy	Harper & Row
Amelia Bedelia and the Surprise Shower	L	Parish, Peggy	HarperTrophy

Title	Level	Author/Series	Publisher/Distributor
Amelia Bedelia Goes Camping	L	Parish, Peggy	Avon Camelot
Amelia Bedelia Helps Out	L	Parish, Peggy	Avon Camelot
Amelia Bedelia's Family Album	L	Parish, Peggy	Avon Books
Animal Reports	L	Sloan, P. & S.	Sundance
Animal Tracks	L	Dorros, Arthur	Scholastic
Another Day, Another Challenge	L	Literacy 2000	Rigby
Ashes for Gold	L	Folktales	Mondo
Bad Day for Benjamin	L	Reading Unlimited	Celebration Press
Beans on the Roof	L	Byars, Betsy	Dell Yearling
Big Al	L	Clements Yoshi, A.	Scholastic
Boy Who Cried Wolf, The	L	Literacy 2000	Rigby
Boy Who Went to the North Wind, The	L	Literacy 2000	Rigby
Brachiosaurus in the River	L	Wesley & the Dinosaurs	Wright Group
Brand New Butterfly	L	Literacy 2000	Rigby
Bravest Dog Ever, The	L	Standiford, Natalie	Random House
Brigid Beware	L	Leverich, Kathleen	Random House
Brigid Bewitched	L	Leverich, Kathleen	Random House
Brigid the Bad	L	Leverich, Kathleen	Random House
Bringing the Sea Back Home	L	Literacy 2000	Rigby
Cam Jansen and the Mystery at the Monkey House	L	Adler, David A.	Puffin Books
Cam Jansen and the Mystery of Flight 54	L	Adler, David A.	Puffin Books
Cam Jansen and the Mystery of the Babe Ruth Baseball	L	Adler, David A.	Puffin Books
Cam Jansen and the Mystery of the Carnival Pizza	L	Adler, David A.	Puffin Books
Cam Jansen and the Mystery of the Circus Clown	L	Adler, David A.	Puffin Books
Cam Jansen and the Mystery of the Dinosaur Bones	L	Adler, David A.	Puffin Books
Cam Jansen and the Mystery of the Gold Coins	L	Adler, David A.	Puffin Books
Cam Jansen and the Mystery of the Monster Movie	L	Adler, David A.	Puffin Books
Cam Jansen and the Mystery of the Stolen Corn Popper	L	Adler, David A.	Puffin Books
Cam Jansen and the Mystery of the Stolen Diamonds	L	Adler, David A.	Puffin Books
Cam Jansen and the Mystery of the Television Dog	L	Adler, David A.	Puffin Books
Cam Jansen and the Mystery of the U.F.O.	L	Adler, David A.	Puffin Books
Can I Have a Dinosaur?	L	Literacy 2000	Rigby
Candy Corn Contest, The	L	Giff, Patricia Reilly	Dell Publishing
Captain Bumble	L	Storybox	Wright Group
Case of the Cool-Itch Kid, The	L	Giff, Patricia Reilly	Dell Publishing
Cass Becomes a Star	L	Literacy 2000	Rigby
Chang's Paper Pony	L	Coerr, Eleanor	HarperTrophy
Charlie	L	Literacy 2000	Rigby
Chicken Little	L	Traditional Tales	Rigby
Claudine's Concert	L	Literacy 2000	Rigby
Come Back, Amelia Bedelia	L	Parish, Peggy	Harper & Row

Title	Level	Author/Series	Publisher/Distributor
Conversation Club, The	L	Stanley, Diane	Aladdin
Crafty Jackal	L	Folk Tales	Wright Group
Day in Town	L	Storybox	Wright Group
Day of the Rain, The	L	Cowley, Joy	Dominie Press
Day of the Snow, The	L	Cowley, Joy	Dominie Press
Day of the Wind, The	L	Cowley, Joy	Dominie Press
Deputy Dan Gets His Man	L	Rosembloom, J.	Random House
Diary of a Honeybee	L	Literacy 2000	Rigby
Dinosaur Days	L	Milton, Joyce	Random House
Dinosaur Reports	L	Sloan, P. & S.	Sundance
Dog that Pitched a No-Hitter, The	L	Christopher, Matt	Little, Brown
Dog-Gone Hollywood	L	Sharmat, M. Weinman	Random House
Dom's Handplant	L	Literacy 2000	Rigby
Dragon's Birthday, The	L	Literacy 2000	Rigby
Flower of Sheba, The	L	Orgel, Doris	Bantam
Fox and the Little Red Hen	L	Traditional Tales	Rigby
Frog Who Thought He Was a Horse, The	L	Literacy 2000	Rigby
Gail & Me	L	Literacy 2000	Rigby
George and Martha	L	Marshall, James	Houghton Mifflin
Good as New	L	Douglass, Barbara	Scholastic
Good Work, Amelia Bedelia	L	Parish, Peggy	Avon Camelot
Grandad	L	Literacy 2000	Rigby
Gregory, the Terrible Eater	L	Sharmat, M. Weinman	Scholastic
Happy Birthday, Martin Luther King	L	Marzollo, Jean	Scholastic
Happy Birthday, Moon	L	Asch, Frank	Simon & Schuster
Harry and Willy and Carrothead	L	Caseley, Judith	Scholastic
Hill of Fire	L	Lewis, T. P.	HarperCollins
Honey Bees	L	Kahkonen, S.	Steck-Vaughn
Horrible Harry and the Art Invasion	L	Kline, Suzy	Scholastic
Horrible Harry and the Green Slime	L	Kline, Suzy	Puffin Books
Horrible Harry and the Kickball Wedding	L	Kline, Suzy	Puffin Books
Horrible Harry in Room 2B	L	Kline, Suzy	Puffin Books
How Do Plants Get Food?	L	Goldish, Meish	Steck-Vaughn
Huberta the Hiking Hippo	L	Literacy 2000	Rigby
Hungry, Hungry Sharks	L	Cole, Joanna	Random House
I Know a Lady	L	Zolotow, Charlotte	Puffin Books
Jane Goodall and the Wild Chimpanzees	L	Birnbaum, Bette	Steck-Vaughn
Jennifer, Too	L	Havill, Juanita	Hyperion
Josefina Story Quilt, The	L	Coerr, Eleanor	HarperTrophy
Katy and the Big Snow	L	Burton, V. L.	Scholastic
King Beast's Birthday	L	Literacy 2000	Rigby
Lavender the Library Cat	L	Read Alongs	Rigby
Little Spider, The	L	Literacy 2000	Rigby
Littles, The	L	Peterson, John	Scholastic
Loose Laces	L	Reading Unlimited	Celebration Press
Lucky Feather, The	L	Literacy 2000	Rigby
Lucy Meets a Dragon	L	Literacy 2000	Rigby
Magic All Around	L	Literacy 2000	Rigby
Magic Fish	L	Littledale, Freya	Scholastic
Make Way for Ducklings	L	McCloskey, Robert	Puffin Books
Manly Ferry Pigeon	L	Sunshine	Wright Group

Title	Level	Author/Series	Publisher/Distributor
Marcella	L	Literacy 2000	Rigby
Marvin Redpost: Kidnapped at Birth?	L	Sachar, Louis	Random House
Marvin Redpost: Why Pick on Me?	L	Sachar, Louis	Random House
Miss Nelson Is Missing	L	Allard, Harry	Houghton Mifflin
Mog at the Zoo	L	Nicoll, Helen	Penguin
Mog's Mumps	L	Nicoll, Helen	Penguin
Mr. Gumpy's Outing	L	Burningham, John	Holt
Mystery of the Pirate Ghost, The	L	Hayes, Geoffrey	Random House
Mystery Seeds	L	Reading Unlimited	Celebration Press
No Jumping on the Bed!	L	Arnold, Tedd	Scholastic
Oh, What a Daughter!	L	Literacy 2000	Rigby
Once When I Was Shipwrecked	L	Literacy 2000	Rigby
Over in the Meadow	L	Galdone, Paul	Simon & Schuster
Owl and the Pussy Cat	L	Lear, Edward	Scholastic
Pee Wee Scouts: Cookies and Crutches	L	Delton, Judy	Dell Publishing
Pee Wees on First	L	Delton, Judy	Dell Publishing
Pee Wees on Parade	L	Delton, Judy	Dell Publishing
Pee Wees on Skis	L	Delton, Judy	Dell Publishing
Perfect the Pig	L	Jeschke, Susan	Scholastic
Pete's Story	L	Literacy 2000	Rigby
Picking Apples and Pumpkins	L	Hutchings, A. & R.	Scholastic
Pickle Puss	L	Giff, Patricia Reilly	Dell Publishing
Pinky and Rex	L	Howe, James	Avon Books
Pinky and Rex and the Mean Old Witch	L	Howe, James	Avon Books
Pinky and Rex and the Spelling Bee	L	Howe, James	Avon Books
Pioneer Bear	L	Sandin, Joan	Random House
Play Ball, Amelia Bedelia	L	Parish, Peggy	Scholastic
Pooped Troop, The	L	Delton, Judy	Dell Publishing
Powder Puff Puzzle, The	L	Giff, Patricia Reilly	Dell Publishing
Puppy Who Wanted a Boy, The	L	Thayer, Jane	Scholastic
Quilt Story, The	L	Johnston & de Paola	Scholastic
Rabbit Stew	L	Literacy 2000	Rigby
Rapunzel	L	Literacy 2000	Rigby
Rescue, The	L	Ready to Read	Richard C. Owen/ Celebration Press
Rosie's Story	L	Gogoll, Martine	Mondo
Sadie and the Snowman	L	Morgan, Allen	Scholastic
Say "Cheese"	L	Giff, Patricia Reilly	Dell Publishing
Schoolyard Mystery, The	L	Levy, Elizabeth	Scholastic
Selfish Giant, The	L	Literacy 2000	Rigby
Sharks	L	Wonder World	Wright Group
Silent World, A	L	Literacy 2000	Rigby
Slim, Shorty and the Mules	L	Reading Unlimited	Celebration Press
Snow Goes to Town	L	Literacy 2000	Rigby
Something Soft for Danny Bear	L	Literacy 2000	Rigby
Spider and the King, The	L	Literacy 2000	Rigby
Squanto and the First Thanksgiving	L	Celsi, Teresa	Steck-Vaughn
Sunflower That Went Flop	L	Storybox	Wright Group
T-Shirt Triplets, The	L	Literacy 2000	Rigby
Tale of Peter Rabbit, The	L	Potter, Beatrix	Scholastic
Things That Go: A Traveling Alphabet	L	Bank Street	Bantam
Three Blind Mice Mystery, The	L	Krensky, Stephen	Dell Publishing
Three Little Pigs	L	Galdone, Paul	Houghton Mifflin

Title	Level	Author/Series	Publisher/Distributor
Three Little Pigs	L	Once Upon a Time	Wright Group
Three Little Pigs, The	L	Marshall, James	Scholastic
Three Sillies, The	L	Literacy 2000	Rigby
Three Smart Pals	L	Rocklin, Joanne	Scholastic
Through Grandpa's Eyes	L	MacLachlan, P.	HarperTrophy
Tongues Are for Tasting, Licking, Tricking	L	Literacy 2000	Rigby
Trees Belong to Everyone	L	Literacy 2000	Rigby
Triceratops on the Farm	L	Wesley & the Dinosaurs	Wright Group
Triplet Trouble and the Field Day Disaster	L	Dadey, D. & Jones, M.	Scholastic
Triplet Trouble and the Red Heart Race	L	Dadey, D. & Jones, M.	Scholastic
Triplet Trouble and the Runaway Reindeer	L	Dadey, D. & Jones, M.	Scholastic
Triplet Trouble and the Talent Show Mess	L	Dadey, D. & Jones, M.	Scholastic
Tyrannosaurus the Terrible	L	Wesley & the Dinosaurs	Wright Group
Very Thin Cat of Alloway Road, The	L	Literacy 2000	Rigby
Walk with Grandpa	L	Read Alongs	Rigby
Watching the Whales	L	Foundations	Wright Group
Whales—The Gentle Giants	L	Milton, Joyce	Random House
What Kind of Babysitter Is This?	L	Johnson, Dolores	Scholastic
What Next, Baby Bear?	L	Murphy, Jill	Dial
When the Giants Came to Town	L	Leonard, Marcia	Scholastic
Whistle for Willie	L	Keats, Ezra Jack	Penguin
Why the Sea Is Salty	L	Literacy 2000	Rigby
Wind Blew, The	L	Hutchins, Pat	Puffin Books
Yellow Overalls	L	Literacy 2000	Rigby
Young Jackie Robinson: Baseball Hero	L	First Start Biography	Troll
Adventures of Ratman	M	Weiss & Friedman	Random House
Aliens Don't Wear Braces	M	Dadey, D. & Jones, M.	Scholastic
Ballad of Robin Hood, The	M	Literacy 2000	Rigby
Bats	M	Literacy 2000	Rigby
Bears on Hemlock Mountain	M	Dalgliesh, Alice	Aladdin
Beast in Ms. Rooney's Room	M	Giff, Patricia Reilly	Yearling
Beekeeper, The	M	Literacy 2000	Rigby
Blueberries for Sal	M	McCloskey, Robert	Scholastic
Book About Your Skeleton, A	M	Belov Gross, Ruth	Scholastic
Brave Maddie Egg	M	Standiford, Natalie	Random House
Brith the Terrible	M	Literacy 2000	Rigby
Can Do, Jenny Archer	M	Conford, Ellen	Random House
Case for Jenny Archer, A	M	Conford, Ellen	Random House
Case of the Elevator Duck, The	M	Berrien Berends, P.	Random House
Centerfield Ballhawk	M	Christopher, Matt	Little, Brown
Chair for My Mother, A	M	Williams, Vera B.	Scholastic
Chalk Box Kid, The	M	Bulla, Clyde Robert	Random House
Cherries and Cherry Pits	M	Williams, Vera B.	Houghton Mifflin
Chester the Wizard	M	Reading Unlimited	Celebration Press
Clouds	M	Literacy 2000	Rigby
Cloudy with a Chance of Meatballs	M	Barrett, Judi	Atheneum
Crabs	M	Wonder World	Wright Group
Crinkum Crankum	M	Ready to Read	Richard C. Owen/ Celebration Press

Title	Level	Author/Series	Publisher/Distributor
Crocodile in the Library	M	Ready to Read	Richard C. Owen/ Celebration Press
Crocodile's Christmas Jandles	M	Ready to Read	Richard C. Owen/ Celebration Press
Cupid Doesn't Flip Hamburgers	M	Dadey, D. & Jones, M.	Scholastic
Curse of the Squirrel, The	M	Yep, Laurence	Random House
Did You Carry the Flag Today, Charley?	M	Caudill, Rebecca	Dell Publishing
Dinosaurs Before Dark	M	Pope Osborne, M.	Random House
Donkey	M	Literacy 2000	Rigby
Don't Forget the Bacon	M	Hutchins, Pat	Puffin Books
Double Trouble	M	Literacy 2000	Rigby
Dracula Doesn't Drink Lemonade	M	Dadey, Debbie	Scholastic
Drinking Gourd	M	Monjo, F. N.	HarperTrophy
Drought Maker, The	M	Literacy 2000	Rigby
Duck in the Gun, The	M	Literacy 2000	Rigby
Eat!	M	Kroll, Steven	Hyperion
Elves Don't Wear Hard Hats	M	Dadey, D. & Jones, M.	Scholastic
Emily Arrow Promises to Do Better This Year	M	Giff, Patricia Reilly	Dell Publishing
Emily Eyefinger	M	Ball, Duncan	Aladdin
Fiddle and the Gun, The	M	Literacy 2000	Rigby
Five True Dog Stories	M	Davidson, Margaret	Scholastic
Five True Horse Stories	M	Davidson, Margaret	Scholastic
Frankenstein Doesn't Plant Petunias	M	Dadey, Debbie	Scholastic
Frankenstein Moved on to the 4th Floor	M	Levy, Elizabeth	Harper & Row
Freckle Juice	M	Blume, Judy	Dell Yearling
Genies Don't Ride Bicycles	M	Dadey, D. & Jones, M.	Scholastic
Ghosts Don't Eat Potato Chips	M	Dadey, D. & Jones, M.	Scholastic
Golden Goose, The	M	Literacy 2000	Rigby
Great Grumbler and the Wonder	M	Ready to Read	Richard C. Owen
Gremlins Don't Chew Bubble Gum	M	Dadey, D. & Jones, M.	Scholastic
Henry's Choice	M	Reading Unlimited	Celebration Press
Hit-Away Kid, The	M	Christopher, Matt	Little, Brown
Horrakapotchkin	M	Ready to Read	Richard C. Owen
How a Volcano Is Formed	M	Wonder World	Wright Group
How to Eat Fried Worms	M	Rockwell, Thomas	Dell Publishing
"I Can't" said the Ant	M	Cameron, Polly	Scholastic
I Love the Beach	M	Literacy 2000	Rigby
In the Clouds	M	Literacy 2000	Rigby
In the Dinosaur's Paw	M	Giff, Patricia Reilly	Dell Publishing
Island Baby	M	Keller, Holly	Scholastic
Job for Jenny Archer, A	M	Conford, Ellen	Little, Brown
Junie B. Jones and the Stupid Smelly Bus	M	Park, Barbara	Random House
Junie B. Jones and the Yucky Blucky Fruitcake	M	Park, Barbara	Random House
Lazy Lions Lucky Lambs	M	Giff, Patricia Reilly	Dell Publishing
Let's Get Moving!	M	Literacy 2000	Rigby
Little Swan	M	Geras, Adele	Random House
Little Women	M	Bullseye	Random House
Lizards and Salamanders	M	Reading Unlimited	Celebration Press
Lucky Baseball Bat, The	M	Christopher, Matt	Little, Brown

Title	Level	Author/Series	Publisher/Distributor
Making Friends on Beacon Street	M	Literacy 2000	Rigby
Man Out at First	M	Christopher, Matt	Little, Brown
Martians Don't Take Temperatures	M	Dadey, D. & Jones, M.	Scholastic
Maui and the Sun	M	Ready to Read	Richard C. Owen/ Celebration Press
Maybe Yes, Maybe No, Maybe Maybe	M	Patron, Susan	Dell Publishing
Mitten, The	M	Brett, Jan	Scholastic
Molly's Pilgrim	M	Cohen, Barbara	Dell Publishing
Monster for Hire	M	Wilson, Trevor	Mondo
Monster Rabbit Runs Amuck!	M	Giff, Patricia Reilly	Dell Publishing
Monsters Don't Scuba Dive	M	Dadey, Debbie	Scholastic
Mrs. Bubble's Baby	M	Ready to Read	Richard C. Owen/ Celebration Press
My Father's Dragon	M	Stiles, Ruth Gannett	Random House
Nana's in the Plum Tree	M	Ready to Read	Richard C. Owen/ Celebration Press
Nature's Celebration	M	Literacy 2000	Rigby
Old Red Rocking Chair, The	M	Root, Phyllis	Scholastic
One Eyed Jake	M	Hutchins, Pat	Morrow
One in the Middle Is a Green Kangaroo, The	M	Blume, Judy	Dell Yearling
Patches	M	Szymanski, Lois	Avon Camelot
Postcard Pest, The	M	Giff, Patricia Reilly	Dell Publishing
Present from Aunt Skidoo, The	M	Literacy 2000	Rigby
Rabbits	M	Literacy 2000	Rigby
Red and Blue Mittens	M	Reading Unlimited	Celebration Press
Red Ribbon Rosie	M	Marzollo, Jean	Random House
Return of Rinaldo, the Sly Fox	M	Scheffler, Ursel	North-South Books
Rip Roaring Russell	M	Hurwitz, Johanna	Puffin Books
Rumpelstiltskin	M	Once Upon a Time	Wright Group
Rupert and the Griffin	M	Hurwitz, Johanna	Puffin Books
Russell Rides Again	M	Hurwitz, Johanna	Puffin Books
Russell Sprouts	M	Hurwitz, Johanna	Puffin Books
Sam's Glasses	M	Literacy 2000	Rigby
Second Grade—Friends Again!	M	Cohen, Miriam	Scholastic
Secret at the Polk Street School, The	M	Giff, Patricia Reilly	Dell Publishing
Shopping with a Crocodile	M	Ready to Read	Richard C. Owen/ Celebration Press
Shorty	M	Literacy 2000	Rigby
Show Time at the Polk Street School	M	Giff, Patricia Reilly	Dell Publishing
Skeletons Don't Play Tubas	M	Dadey, D. & Jones, M.	Scholastic
Snaggle Doodles	M	Giff, Patricia Reilly	Dell Publishing
Soccer Sam	M	Marzollo, Jean	Random House
Spectacular Stone Soup	M	Giff, Patricia Reilly	Yearling
Spider Man	M	Literacy 2000	Rigby
Spy on Third Base, The	M	Christopher, Matt	Little, Brown
Stacy Says Good-Bye	M	Giff, Patricia Reilly	Dell Publishing
Star	M	Simon, Jo Ann	Random House
Sunny-Side Up	M	Giff, Patricia Reilly	Dell Publishing
Tale of Veruschka Babuschka, The	M	Literacy 2000	Rigby
That's a Laugh: Four Funny Fables	M	Literacy 2000	Rigby
Tom Edison's Bright Idea	M	Keller, Jack	Steck-Vaughn
Totara Tree, The	M	Book Bank	Wright Group
Treasure Hunting	M	Literacy 2000	Rigby

Title	Level	Author/Series	Publisher/Distributor
Tyler Toad and Thunder	M	Crowe, Robert	Dutton
Vampires Don't Wear Polka Dots	M	Dadey, D. & Jones, M.	Scholastic
Wake Up, Emily, It's Mother's Day	M	Giff, Patricia Reilly	Yearling
Werewolves Don't Go To Summer Camp	M	Dadey, D. & Jones, M.	Scholastic
What Is a Reptile?	M	Now I Know	Troll
What Made Teddalik Laugh	M	Folk Tales	Wright Group
What's Cooking, Jenny Archer?	M	Conford, Ellen	Little, Brown
Witches Don't Do Backflips	M	Dadey, D. & Jones, M.	Scholastic
Wolf's First Deer	M	Book Bank	Wright Group
Words	M	Ready to Read	Richard C. Owen/ Celebration Press
Young Wolf's First Hunt	M	Shefelman, Janice	Random House
Amber Brown Goes Forth	N	Danziger, Paula	Putnam
Amber Brown Is Not a Crayon	N	Danziger, Paula	Scholastic
Amber Brown Wants Extra Credit	N	Danziger, Paula	Putnam
Berlioz the Bear	N	Brett, Jan	Scholastic
Cloud Book, The	N	de Paola, Tomie	Scholastic
Enormous Crocodile, The	N	Dahl, Roald	Puffin Books
Hannah	N	Whelan, Gloria	Random House
It Takes a Village	N	Cowen-Fletcher, J.	Scholastic
Julian's Glorious Summer	N	Cameron, Ann	Random House
Key to the Treasure	N	Parish, Peggy	Dell Publishing
Llama Pajamas	N	Clymer, Susan	Scholastic
Magic Finger, The	N	Dahl, Roald	Puffin Books
Martin Luther King, Jr.	N	Greene, Carol	Children's Press
More Stories Julian Tells	N	Cameron, Ann	Random House
Mountain Gorillas	N	Wonder World	Wright Group
Mystery of Pony Hollow, The	N	Hall, Lynn	Random House
Mystery of the Phantom Pony, The	N	Hall, Lynn	Random House
Next Spring an Oriole	N	Whelan, Gloria	Random House
No Room for a Dog	N	Kane Nichols, Joan	Avon Books
Octopuses and Squids	N	Wonder World	Wright Group
Pioneer Cat	N	William H. Hooks	Random House
School's Out	N	Hurwitz, Johanna	Scholastic
Shark in School	N	Giff, Patricia Reilly	Dell Publishing
Sidewalk Story	N	Mathis, Sharon Bell	Puffin Books
Stories Julian Tells	N	Cameron, Ann	Random House
Titanic, The	N	Donnelly, Judy	Random House
Writer's Work, A	N	Wonder World	Wright Group
You Can't Eat Your Chicken Pox, Amber Brown	N	Danziger, Paula	Scholastic
Adventures of Ali Baby Bernstein	O	Hurwitz, Johanna	Avon Books
Aldo Ice Cream	O	Hurwitz, Johanna	Puffin Books
Aldo Peanut Butter	O	Hurwitz, Johanna	Puffin Books
Armies of Ants	O	Retan, Walter	Scholastic
Baseball Fever	O	Hurwitz, Johanna	Wm. Morrow & Co.
Beezus and Ramona	O	Cleary, Beverly	Avon Books
BFG, The	O	Dahl, Roald	Puffin Books
Boxcar Children: Mystery of the Mixed-Up Zoo	O	Warner, Gertrude Chandler	Albert Whitman

Title	Level	Author/Series	Publisher/Distributor
Boxcar Children: Animal Shelter Mystery	O	Warner, Gertrude Chandler	Albert Whitman
Boxcar Children: Bicycle Mystery	O	Warner, Gertrude Chandler	Albert Whitman
Boxcar Children: Camp-Out Mystery	O	Warner, Gertrude Chandler	Albert Whitman
Boxcar Children: Canoe Trip Mystery	O	Warner, Gertrude Chandler	Albert Whitman
Boxcar Children: Haunted Cabin Mystery	O	Warner, Gertrude Chandler	Albert Whitman
Boxcar Children: Lighthouse Mystery	O	Warner, Gertrude Chandler	Albert Whitman
Boxcar Children: Mountain Top Mystery	O	Warner, Gertrude Chandler	Albert Whitman
Boxcar Children: Mystery at the Dog Show	O	Warner, Gertrude Chandler	Albert Whitman
Boxcar Children: Mystery at the Fair	O	Warner, Gertrude Chandler	Albert Whitman
Boxcar Children: Mystery Cruise	O	Warner, Gertrude Chandler	Albert Whitman
Boxcar Children: Mystery in the Sand	O	Warner, Gertrude Chandler	Albert Whitman
Boxcar Children: Mystery of the Hidden Beach	O	Warner, Gertrude Chandler	Albert Whitman
Boxcar Children: Mystery of the Missing Cat	O	Warner, Gertrude Chandler	Albert Whitman
Boxcar Children: Mystery on Stage	O	Warner, Gertrude Chandler	Albert Whitman
Boxcar Children: Pizza Mystery	O	Warner, Gertrude Chandler	Albert Whitman
Boxcar Children: Schoolhouse Mystery	O	Warner, Gertrude Chandler	Albert Whitman
Boxcar Children: Snowbound Mystery	O	Warner, Gertrude Chandler	Albert Whitman
Clothes	O	Wonder World	Wright Group
Flossie & the Fox	O	McKissack, Patricia	Scholastic
Henry and Beezus	O	Cleary, Beverly	Avon Books
Henry and Ribsy	O	Cleary, Beverly	Avon Books
Henry and the Clubhouse	O	Cleary, Beverly	Avon Books
Henry and the Paper Route	O	Cleary, Beverly	Avon Books
Henry Huggins	O	Cleary, Beverly	Avon Books
Make a Wish, Molly	O	Cohen, Barbara	Dell Publishing
Matilda	O	Dahl, Roald	Puffin Books
Most Wonderful Doll in the World	O	McGinley, Phyllis	Scholastic
Much Ado About Aldo	O	Hurwitz, Johanna	Puffin Books
Muggie Maggie	O	Cleary, Beverly	Avon Camelot
No One Is Going to Nashville	O	Jukes, Mavis	Bullseye Books
Pandora's Box	O	Literacy 2000	Rigby
Pony Pals: A Pony for Keeps	O	Betancourt, Jeanne	Scholastic
Pony Pals: A Pony in Trouble	O	Betancourt, Jeanne	Scholastic
Pony Pals: Give Me Back My Pony	O	Betancourt, Jeanne	Scholastic
Pony Pals: I Want a Pony	O	Betancourt, Jeanne	Scholastic
Pony Pals: Pony to the Rescue	O	Betancourt, Jeanne	Scholastic
Pony Pals: The Wild Pony	O	Betancourt, Jeanne	Scholastic
Ralph S. Mouse	O	Cleary, Beverly	Avon Books
Ramona and Her Father	O	Cleary, Beverly	Avon Books
Ramona and Her Mother	O	Cleary, Beverly	Avon Books
Ramona Forever	O	Cleary, Beverly	Avon Books
Ramona Quimby, Age 8	O	Cleary, Beverly	Avon Books
Ramona the Brave	O	Cleary, Beverly	Avon Books
Ramona the Pest	O	Cleary, Beverly	Avon Books
Ribsy	O	Cleary, Beverly	Avon Books
Runaway Ralph	O	Cleary, Beverly	Avon Books
Sideways Stories from Wayside School	O	Sachar, Louis	Avon Books
Socks	O	Cleary, Beverly	Avon Books

Title	Level	Author/Series	Publisher/Distributor
Teacher's Pet	O	Hurwitz, Johanna	Scholastic
Whales	O	Wonder World	Wright Group
Whipping Boy	O	Fleischman, Sid	Troll
Wrong Way Around Magic	O	Chew, Ruth	Scholastic
Amelia Earhart	P	Parlin, John	Dell Publishing
Baseball's Best, Five True Stories	P	Gutelle, Andrew	Random House
Baseball's Greatest Pitchers	P	Kramer, S. A.	Random House
Bunnicula	P	Howe, D. & J.	Avon Books
Fantastic Mr. Fox	P	Dahl, Roald	Puffin Books
Five Brave Explorers	P	Hudson, Wade	Scholastic
George's Marvelous Medicine	P	Dahl, Roald	Puffin Books
Giraffe and the Pelly and Me, The	P	Dahl, Roald	Puffin Books
Helen Keller	P	Graff, S. & P.	Dell Publishing
Jesse Owens: Olympic Hero	P	Sabin, Francene	Troll
Lucky Stone, The	P	Clifton, Lucille	Dell Publishing
One Day in the Tropical Rain Forest	P	Craighead George, Jean	HarperTrophy
One Day in the Woods	P	Craighead George, Jean	HarperTrophy
Potter in Fiji, A	P	Wonder World	Wright Group
Story of Harriet Tubman, Conductor of the Underground Railroad	P	McMullan, Kate	Dell Publishing
Story of Jackie Robinson, Bravest Man in Baseball	P	Davidson, Margaret	Dell Publishing
Story of Walt Disney, Maker of Magical Worlds	P	Selden, Bernice	Dell Publishing
Twits, The	P	Dahl, Roald	Puffin Books
Barney	Q	Literacy 2000	Rigby
Birthday Disaster	Q	Literacy 2000	Rigby
Brian's Brilliant Career	Q	Literacy 2000	Rigby
Cassidy's Magic	Q	Literacy 2000	Rigby
Errol the Peril	Q	Literacy 2000	Rigby
Fortune's Friend	Q	Literacy 2000	Rigby
Get a Grip, Pip!	Q	Literacy 2000	Rigby
Glumly	Q	Literacy 2000	Rigby
Rupert and the Griffin	Q	Literacy 2000	Rigby
Second Grade Star	Q	Alberts, Nancy	Scholastic
Strange Meetings	Q	Literacy 2000	Rigby
Television Drama	Q	Literacy 2000	Rigby
Time for Sale	Q	Literacy 2000	Rigby
To JJ From CC	Q	Literacy 2000	Rigby
Tree, the Trunk and the Tuba, The	Q	Literacy 2000	Rigby
Wayside School Is Falling Down	Q	Sachar, Louis	Avon Books
Wing High, Gooftah	Q	Literacy 2000	Rigby
Babe the Gallant Pig	R	King-Smith, Dick	Random House
Canada Geese Quilt. The	R	Kinsey-Warnock, Leslie	Dell Publishing
Laura Ingalls Wilder, Pioneer Girl	R	Stine, Megan	Dell Publishing

Publishers/Distributors

Some companies publish their own titles, while others distribute series books from a variety of sources. Ordering information on series books is available from the following sources:

Benchmark Education
629 Fifth Avenue
Pelham, NY 10803
Phone 1-877-236-2465
Fax 1-914-738-5063
Benchmark@aol.com

Capstone Press
151 Good Counsel Drive
P.O. Box 669
Mankato, MN 56002-0669
Phone 1-800-747-4992
Fax 1-888-262-0705

Celebration Press
10 Bank Street, 8th Floor
White Plains, NY 10602
Phone 1-800-552-2259
Fax 1-800-333-3328
www.celebrationpress.com

Creative Teaching Press
10701 Holder Street
Cypress, CA 90603
Phone 1-800-444-4287
Fax 1-800-229-9929
www.creativeteaching.com

Dominie Press, Inc.
1949 Kellogg Avenue
Carlsbad, CA 92008
Phone 1-800-232-4570
Fax 1-760-431-8777
www.dominie.com
info@dominie.com

Education Insights
19560 S. Ranch Way
Dominguez Hills, CA 90220
Phone 1-800-933-3277
Fax 1-800-995-0506
www.edin.com

Grolier Press
90 Sherman Turnpike
Danbury, CT 06816
Phone 1-800-621-1115
Fax 1-203-797-3197
http://publishing.grolier.com

Hampton Brown
P.O. Box 369
Marina, CA 93933
Phone 1-800-333-3510
Fax 1-831-384-8940

Houghton Mifflin
1900 South Batavia Avenue
Geneva, IL 60134
Phone 1-800-334-3284
Fax 1-800-733-2098
www.edutlace.com

Kaeden Books
P.O. Box 16190
Rocky River, OH 44116
Phone 1-800-890-READ
Fax 1-440-356-5081

Michaels Associates
409 Beatty Road, Suite 100
Monroeville, PA 15146
Phone: 1-800-869-1467
Fax: 1-412-374-9363

Modern Curriculum Press
4350 Equity Drive
P.O. Box 2649
Columbus, OH 43216
Phone 1-800-321-3106
Fax 1-800-393-3156
www.msschool.com

Mondo Publishing
One Plaza Road
Greenvale, NY 11548
Phone 1-888-88-MONDO
Fax 1-516-484-7813
mondopub@aol.com

Newbridge Educational Publishing
333 East 38th Street
New York, NY 10016-2745
Phone 1-800-867-0307
Fax 1-978-486-8759

Outside the Box, Inc.
2455 Teller Road
Thousand Oaks, CA 91320
Phone 1-800-808-4199
Fax 1-805-499-0871
www.sagepub.com/otb

Oxford University Press
Box 1550
Woodstock, IL 60098
Phone 1-888-551-5454
Fax 1-815-344-1551
oxford@mc.net

Peguis Publishing Ltd.
100–318 McDermot Road
Winnipeg, Manitoba
Canada R3A OA2
Phone 1-800-667-9673
Fax 1-204-947-0080
books@peguis.com
www.peguis.com

Pioneer Valley Educational Press
P.O. Box 9375
North Amherst, MA 01059
Phone: 1-413-367-9817
Fax 1-413-548-4914

Richard C. Owen Publishers
P.O. Box 585
Katonah, NY 10536
Phone 1-800-336-5588
Fax 1-914-232-3977
www.rcowen.com

Rigby
P.O. Box 797
Crystal Lake, IL 60039-0797
Phone 1-800-822-8661
Fax 1-800-427-4429
www.rigby.com

Sadlier-Oxford
9 Pine Street, 2nd Floor
New York, NY 10005-1002
Phone: 1-800-221-5175
Fax: 1-212-312-6080
www.sadlier-oxford.com

Scholastic Inc.
P.O. Box 7502
Jefferson City, MO 65102-9968
Phone 1-800-724-6527
Fax 1-800-223-4011
www.scholastic.com

School Zone Publishing
1819 Industrial Drive
P.O. Box 777
Grand Haven, MI 49417
Phone 1-800-253-0564
Fax 1-616-846-6181
www.schoolzone.com

Scott Foresman
1900 East Lake Avenue
Glenview, IL 60025
Phone 1-800-554-4411
Fax 1-800-841-8939
www.sf.aw.com

Shortland Publications
50 South Steele Street, Suite 755
Denver, CO 80209-9927
Phone 1-800-775-9995
Fax 1-800-775-9597

Seedling Publications
4079 Overlook Drive East
Columbus, OH 43214
Phone 1-614-451-2412
Fax 1-614-267-4205
www.seedlingpub.com
sales@seedlingpub.com

SRA/McGraw Hill
220 East Danieldale Road
DeSoto, TX 75115-2490
Phone 1-888-772-4543
Fax 1-972-228-1982
www.sra4kids.com

Steck Vaughn
P.O. Box 690789
Orlando, FL 32819-0789
Phone 1-800-531-5015
Fax 1-800-699-9459
www.steck.vaughn.com

Sundance
P.O. Box 1326
Littleton, MA 01460
Phone 1-800-343-3204
Fax 1-800-456-2419
www.sundancepub.com

Tott Publications
Debbie Tauber
4197 Weller Drive
Bellbrook, OH 45305
Phone 1-937-427-7638

Troll Publications
100 Corporate Drive
Matwah, NJ 07430
Phone 1-800-526-5289
Fax 1-800-979-8765
www.troll.com

University of Maine
Center for Early Literacy
5766 Shibles Hall
Orono, ME 04469-5766
Phone 1-207-581-2418
Fax 1-207-581-2438

Wright Group
19201 120th Avenue NE
Bothell, WA 98011-9512
Phone 1-800-523-2371
Fax 1-800-543-7323
www.wrightgroup.com

Trade Book Publishers

Books published by these companies can be ordered through paperback suppliers, many of which offer a flat paperback discount to schools.

Aladdin
Albert Whitman & Co.
Alfred A. Knopf
Atheneum
Avon Books
Avon Camelot
Bantam Doubleday Dell
Bantam Skylark
Barron's Educational
Beach Tree Books
Blue Sky Press
Bodley
Boyds Mills Press
Bradbury/Trumpet
Bullseye Books
Candlewick Press
Carolrhoda Books
Checkerboard
Children's Press
Clarion
Creative Edge
Crowell
Crown
Cypress
Delacorte
Dell Yearling
Dial
Donovan
Dutton
Farrar, Straus & Giroux
Four Winds
Golden
Greenwillow
Grosset & Dunlop

Gulf Publishing
Harcourt Brace
Harper & Row
HarperCollins
HarperTrophy
Hearst
Henry Holt & Co.
Holiday House
Houghton Mifflin
Hyperion
Ladybird Books
Little, Brown & Co.
Longman/Bow
Lothrop
Macmillan
North/South Books
Orchard
Pantheon
Penguin Group
Philomel
Pocket Books
Prentice-Hall
Puffin Books
Putnam
Random House
Scribner
Seal Books
Secret Passage Press
Simon & Schuster
Tom Doherty
Viking
Whitman
Wm. Morrow & Co.
Yearling

References

Adams, M. 1990. *Beginning to Read: Thinking and Learning About Print.* Cambridge, MA: MIT Press.

Allington, R. L. 1983. "The Reading Instruction Provided Readers of Differing Ability." *Elementary School Journal* 83:548–59.

Allington, R. L., and A. McGill-Franzen. 1989. "Different Programs, Indifferent Instruction." In *Beyond Separate Education: Quality Education for All,* edited by D. K. Lipsky and A. Gartner. Baltimore, MD: Paul H. Brookes.

Allington, R. L., and P. M. Cunningham. 1996. *Schools That Work: Where All Children Read and Write.* New York: HarperCollins.

Anderson, R. C., and W. E. Nagy. 1992. "The Vocabulary Conundrum." *American Educator* 16(4):14–18, 44–47.

Anthony, R. J., T. D. Johnson, N. I. Mickelson, and A. Preece. 1991. *Evaluating Literacy: A Perspective for Change.* Portsmouth, NH: Heinemann.

Askew, B. J. 1991. *Analysis of the Comprehending Process Within the Setting of Reading Recovery Lessons: New Insights.* The National Reading Conference.

Atwell, N. 1987. *In the Middle: Writing, Reading, and Learning with Adolescents.* Portsmouth, NH: Heinemann.

Barrs, M. 1989. *Primary Language Record.* Portsmouth, NH: Heinemann.

Beaver, J., et al. 1997. *Developmental Primary Assessment.* Upper Arlington, OH: Upper Arlington Public Schools.

Beck, I., M. G. McKeown, and R. C. Omanson. 1987. "The Effects and Uses of Diverse Vocabulary Instructional Techniques." In *The Nature of Vocabulary Acquisition,* edited by M. G. McKeown and M. E. Curtis. Hillsdale, NJ: Erlbaum.

Bissex, G. 1980. *GNYS at Work: A Child Learns to Write and Read.* Cambridge, MA: Harvard University Press.

Booth, D. 1994. *Classroom Voices: Language-Based Learning in the Elementary School.* Ontario, Canada: Harcourt Brace & Co.

Britton, J. 1983. "Writing and the Story World." In *Explorations in the Development of Writing: Theory, Research and Practice*, edited by B. Kroll and G. Wells. Chichester, England: John Wiley.

Bruner, J. S. 1974. "Organization of Early Skilled Action." In *The Integration of a Child into a Social World*, edited by M. P. M. Richard. London: Cambridge University Press.

Button, K., M. Johnson, & P. Furgerson. 1996. "Interactive Writing in a Primary Classroom." *The Reading Teacher* 49(6):446–454.

Calkins, L. M. 1983. *Lessons from a Child: On the Teaching and Learning of Writing*. Portsmouth, NH: Heinemann.

———. 1986. *The Art of Teaching Writing*. Portsmouth, NH: Heinemann.

Clark, M. M. 1976. *Young Fluent Readers: What Can They Teach Us?* London: Heinemann.

Clay, M. M. 1975. *What Did I Write?* Portsmouth, NH: Heinemann.

———. 1979. *Reading: The Patterning of Complex Behavior*. Auckland, NZ: Heinemann.

———. 1991a. *Becoming Literate: The Construction of Inner Control*. Portsmouth, NH: Heinemann.

———. 1991b. "Introducing a New Storybook to Young Readers." *The Reading Teacher* 45:264–73.

———. 1993a. *An Observation Survey of Early Literacy Achievement*. Portsmouth, NH: Heinemann.

———. 1993b. *Reading Recovery: A Guidebook for Teachers in Training*. Portsmouth, NH: Heinemann.

Cochran-Smith, M. 1984. *The Making of a Reader*. Norwood, NJ: Ablex.

Cohen, D. 1968. "The Effects of Literature on Vocabulary and Reading Achievement." *Elementary English* 45:209–13, 217.

Cunningham, P. M. 1995. *Phonics They Use*. New York: HarperCollins.

Dale, E. 1965. "Vocabulary Measurement: Techniques and Major Findings." *Elementary English* 42(8):895–901, 948.

Department of Education. 1985. *Reading in Junior Classes*. Wellington, NZ: Department of Education.

Durkin, D. 1966. *Children Who Read Early*. New York: Teachers College Press.

Dyson, A. H. 1982. "Reading, Writing and Language: Young Children Solve the Written Language Puzzle." *Language Arts* 59:829–39.

Eder, D. 1983. "Ability Grouping and Students' Academic Self-Concepts: A Case Study." *Elementary School Journal* 84:149–61.

Escamilla, K., A. M. Andrade, A. G. M. Basurto, and O. A. Ruiz. 1996. *Instrumento de Observacion de los Logros de la Lecto-Escritura Inicial*. Spanish Reconstruction of *An Observation Survey: A Bilingual Text*. Portsmouth, NH: Heinemann.

Ferreiro, E., and A. Teberosky. 1982. *Literacy Before Schooling*. Portsmouth, NH: Heinemann.

Filby, N., B. Barnett, and S. Bossart. 1982. *Grouping Practices and Their Consequences*. San Francisco, CA: Far West Laboratory for Educational Research and Development.

Fountas, I. C., and G. S. Pinnell. 1999a. *Matching Books to Readers: A Leveled Book List for Guided Reading, K–3*. Portsmouth, NH: Heinemann.

———, eds. 1999b. *Voices on Word Matters: Learning About Phonics and Spelling in the Literacy Classroom*. Portsmouth, NH: Heinemann.

Giacobbe, M. E. 1981. "Who Says Children Can't Write the First Week?" In *Donald Graves in Australia*, edited by R. D. Walshe. Rozelle, New South Wales: Primary English Teaching Association.

Good, T., and S. Marshall. 1984. "Do Students Learn More in Heterogeneous or Homogeneous Groups?" In *The Social Context of Instruction*, edited by P. L. Peterson, L. C. Wilkinson, and M. Hallinan. New York: Academic Press.

Goodman, K. S. 1982. *Language and Literacy: The Selected Works of Kenneth S. Goodman.* Boston: Routledge & Kegan Paul.

———. 1996. *Reading Strategies: Focus on Comprehension.* Katonah, NY: Richard C. Owen.

Goodman, Y. 1984. "The Development of Initial Literacy." In *Awakening to Literacy*, edited by H. Goelman, A. Oberg, and F. Smith. Portsmouth, NH: Heinemann.

Graves, D. 1983. *Writing: Teachers and Children at Work.* Portsmouth, NH: Heinemann.

———. 1994. *A Fresh Look at Writing.* Portsmouth, NH: Heinemann.

Graves, D., and J. Hansen. 1983. "The Author's Chair." *Language Arts* 60:176–83.

Green, J. L., and J. O. Harker. 1982. "Reading to Children: A Communicative Process." In *Reader Meets Author/Bridging the Gap: A Psycholinguistic and Sociolinguistic Perspective*, edited by J. A. Langer and M. T. Smith-Burke, 196–221. Newark, DE: International Reading Association.

Griffin, P., P. Smith, and L. Burrill. 1995. *The American Literacy Profile Scales: A Framework for Authentic Assessment.* Portsmouth, NH: Heinemann.

Guidelines and Standards for the North American Reading Recovery Council. 1993. Columbus, OH: The North American Reading Recovery Council.

Hall, D. P., C. Prevatte, and P. M. Cunningham. 1995. "Eliminating Ability Grouping and Reducing Failure in the Primary Grades." In *No Quick Fix: Rethinking Literacy Programs in America's Elementary Schools*, edited by R. L. Allington and S. A. Walmsley. New York: Teachers College Press.

Harste, J. E., V. A. Woodward, and C. L. Burke. 1984. *Language Stories and Literacy Lessons.* Portsmouth, NH: Heinemann.

Hiebert, E. H. 1983. "An Examination of Ability Grouping for Reading Instruction." *Reading Research Quarterly* 18:231–55.

———. 1988. "The Role of Literacy Experiences in Early Childhood Programs." *Elementary School Journal* 89:161–71.

HMSO. 1993. *Reading Recovery in New Zealand: A Report from the Office of Her Majesty's Chief Inspector of Schools.* London, England: HMSO.

Holdaway, D. 1979. *The Foundations of Literacy.* Sydney, Australia: Ashton Scholastic.

Huck, C. 1994. "The Use and Abuse of Children's Literature." In *Children's Literature in the Classroom: Extending Charlotte's Web*, edited by J. Hickman, B. Cullinan, and S. Hepler, 1–15. Norwich, MA: Christopher-Gordon.

Huck, C., S. Hepler, and J. Hickman. 1993. *Children's Literature in the Elementary School.* Madison, WI: Brown & Benchmark.

Johnson, D., R. Johnson, D. Nelson, and L. Skon. 1981. "Effects Of Cooperative, Competitive and Individualistic Goal Structures on Achievement: A Meta-Analysis." *Psychological Bulletin* 89:47–62.

Johnston, P. 1992. *Constructive Evaluation of Literate Activity.* White Plains, NY: Longman.

Jones, N. K. 1990. "Getting Started: Creating a Literate Classroom Environment." In *What Matters? A Primer for Teaching Reading*, edited by D. Stephens. Portsmouth, NH: Heinemann.

King, M. L. 1980. "Learning How to Mean in Written Language." *Theory into Practice* 19:163–69.

Lyons, C. A., G. S. Pinnell, and D. E. DeFord. 1993. *Partners in Learning: Teachers and Children in Reading Recovery.* New York: Teachers College Press.

Martinez, M., and N. Roser. 1985. "Read It Again: The Value of Repeated Readings During Storytime." *Reading Teacher* 38:782–86.

Massachusetts Reading Association Studies and Research Committee. 1991. "Grouping Students for Literacy Learning: What Works." *Massachusetts Primer.* Plymouth, MA: Massachusetts Reading Association.

McCarrier, A., G. S. Pinnell, and I. C. Fountas. 2000. *Interactive Writing: How Language and Literacy Come Together, K–2.* Portsmouth, NH: Heinemann.

McCarrier, A. M., and I. Patacca. 1994. "Children's Literature: The Focal Point of an Early Literacy Learning Program." In *Extending Charlotte's Web,* edited by B. Cullinan and J. Hickman. Norwood, MA: Christopher-Gordon.

McCarrier, A. M., J. Henry, and K. Bartley. 1995. "Meeting the Instructional Needs of Students Through Flexible Grouping of Children During Guided Reading Lessons: A Look at One Teacher's Decision Making." Paper presented at the National Reading Conference, New Orleans, LA.

McDermott, R. P. 1977. "Social Relations as Contexts for Learning in School." *Harvard Educational Review* 47:198–213, 503–4.

McKenzie, M. G. 1986. *Journeys into Literacy.* Huddersfield, England: Schofield & Sims.

———. 1989. *Extending Literacy: Part One.* Huddersfield, England: Schofield & Sims.

Meek, M. 1988. *How Texts Teach What Readers Learn.* Great Britain: The Thimble Press.

Morrow, L. M. 1988. "Young Children's Responses to One-to-One Story Readings in School Settings." *Reading Research Quarterly* 23:89–107.

Nagy, W. 1985. *Vocabulary Instruction: Implications of the New Research (No. CS 008 263).* ERIC Document Reproduction Service No. ED 266 405.

National Assessment of Educational Progress, with G. S. Pinnell, et al. 1993. "Comparing Instructional Models for the Literacy Education of High-Risk First Graders." *Reading Research Quarterly* 29:8–39.

Ninio, A. 1980. "Picture-Book Reading in Mother-Infant Dyads Belonging to Two Subgroups in Israel." *Child Development* 51:587–90.

Oxley, P., et al. 1991. *Reading and Writing—Where It All Begins: Helping Your Children at Home.* Columbus, OH: Literacy Connection.

Pappas, C. C., and E. Brown. 1987. "Learning to Read by Reading: Learning How to Extend the Functional Potential of Language." *Research in the Teaching of English* 21:160–84.

Pinnell, G. S., M. D. Fried, and R. M. Estice. 1991. "Reading Recovery: Learning How to Make a Difference." In *Bridges to Literacy: Learning from Reading Recovery,* edited by D. E. Deford, C. A. Lyons, and G. S. Pinnell, 11–35. Portsmouth, NH: Heinemann.

Pinnell, G. S., and A. McCarrier. 1994. "Interactive Writing: A Transition Tool for Assisting Children in Learning to Read and Write." In *Getting Reading Right from the Start: Effective Early Literacy Interventions,* edited by E. Hiebert and B. Taylor. Needham Heights, MA: Allyn & Bacon.

Pinnell, G. S., J. J. Pikluski, K. K. Wixson, J. R. Campbell, P. B. Gough, and A. S. Beatty. 1995. *Listening to Children Read Aloud: Data from*

NAEP's *Integrated Reading Performance Record (IRPR) at Grade 4.* Report No. 23-FR-04, prepared by the Educational Testing Service. Washington, DC: Office of Educational Research And Improvement, U.S. Department of Education.

Pinnell, G. S., and I. Fountas. 1998. *Word Matters: Teaching Phonics and Spelling in the Reading/Writing Classroom.* Portsmouth, NH: Heinemann.

————. 2002. *Leveled Books for Readers, Grade 3–6.* Portsmouth, NH: Heinemann.

Read, C. 1970. "Children's Perceptions of the Sounds of English." Doctoral dissertation, Harvard University, Cambridge, MA.

————. 1975. *Children's Categorization of Speech Sounds in English.* Urbana, IL: National Council of Teachers of English.

Rhodes, L. K., ed. 1993. *Literacy Assessment: A Handbook of Instruments.* Portsmouth, NH: Heinemann.

Rhodes, L. K., and N. Shanklin. 1993. *Windows into Literacy: Assessing Learners K–8.* Portsmouth, NH: Heinemann.

Rogoff, B. 1990. *Apprenticeship in Thinking: Cognitive Development in Social Context.* New York: Oxford University Press.

Routman, R. 1991. *Invitations: Changing as Teachers and Learner K–12.* Portsmouth, NH: Heinemann.

Rowe, D. W. 1987. "Literacy Learning as an Intertextual Process." *National Reading Conference Yearbook* 36:101–12.

Schickendanz, J. 1978. "'Please Read That Story Again!' Exploring Relationships Between Story Reading and Learning to Read." *Young Children* 33:48–55.

————. 1986. *More Than ABC's: The Early Stages of Reading and Writing.* Washington, D.C.: National Association for the Education of Young Children.

Slavin, R. 1983a. *Cooperative Learning.* New York: Longman.

————. 1983b. "When Does Cooperative Learning Increase Student Achievement?" *Psychological Bulletin* 94:429–45.

————. 1987. "Ability Grouping and Student Achievement in Elementary School: A Best Evidence Synthesis." *Review of Educational Research* 57:293–336.

Smith, F. 1994. *Understanding Reading.* Hillsdale, NJ: Erlbaum.

Smith, J., and W. Elley. 1994. *Learning to Read in New Zealand.* Katonah, NY: Richard C. Owen.

Snow, C. E. 1983. "Literacy and Language: Relationships During the Preschool Years." *Harvard Educational Review* 53(2):165–89.

Sorenson, A. B., and M. T. Hallinan. 1986. "Effects of Ability Grouping on Growth in Academic Achievement." *American Educational Research Journal* 23:519–42.

Sulzby, E. 1985. "Children's Emergent Reading of Favorite Storybooks: A Developmental Study." *Reading Research Quarterly* 20:458–81.

Taylor, D. 1993. *From the Child's Point of View.* Portsmouth, NH: Heinemann.

Teale, W. H., and E. Sulzby, eds. 1986. *Emergent Literacy: Writing and Reading.* Norwood, NJ: Ablex.

Tharp, R., and R. Gallimore. 1988. *Rousing Minds to Life: Teaching, Learning and School in Social Context.* Cambridge, England: Cambridge University Press.

Tierney, R. J. 1990. "Redefining Reading Comprehension." *Educational Leadership* 37–42.

Wells, C. G. 1985. "Preschool Literacy-Related Activities and Success in School." In *Literacy, Language, and Learning: The Nature and*

Consequences of Literacy, edited by D. Olson, N. Torrance, and A. Hildyard, 229–55. Cambridge, England: Cambridge University Press.

Wong, S. D., L. A. Groth, and J. D. O'Flahavan. 1994. *Characterizing Teacher-Student Interaction in Reading Recovery Lessons*. National Reading Research Center Report No. 17. National Reading Research Project of the Universities of Georgia and Maryland.

Index

Matching Books to Readers
Using Leveled Books in Guided Reading, K-3

Matching Books to Readers compiles more than seven thousand caption books, natural language texts, series books, and children's literature for kindergarten through grade three—making it the most comprehensive, up-to-date leveled reading list ever. Books are organized by title and by level of difficulty; plus, there's lots of information on how you can use, acquire, and level books for yourself.

Word Matters
Teaching Phonics and Spelling
in the Reading/Writing Classroom

A companion volume to Guided Reading

Word Matters presents essential information on designing and implementing a high-quality, systematic literacy program to help children learn about letters, sounds, and words. The central goal is to teach children to become "word solvers": readers who can take words apart while reading for meaning, and writers who can construct words while writing to communicate.

Voices on Word Matters
Learning About Phonics and Spelling
in the Literacy Classroom

This follow-up to *Word Matters* is a rich extension of Fountas and Pinnell's instructional system for word study, featuring chapters by the field's most important scholars and practitioners. Letter and word learning are explored in a variety of reading, writing, and language contexts.

Help America Read
A Handbook for Volunteers

There has been an explosion of volunteerism in today's literacy programs and the need for a concise and practical handbook has never been greater. *Help America Read* fills this void, providing everything you want a literacy volunteer to know about tutoring young children.

Coordinator's Guide to Help America Read
A Handbook for Volunteers

This outstanding resource provides the best information available on building a high-quality literacy volunteer program along with practical suggestions on effective training. It will help make the literacy volunteer service a worthwhile experience for everyone involved—the children served as well as those who serve them.

For more information,
call 800-541-2086, fax 800-847-0938,
or write: Heinemann, Promotions Department,
361 Hanover Street, Portsmouth, NH 03801